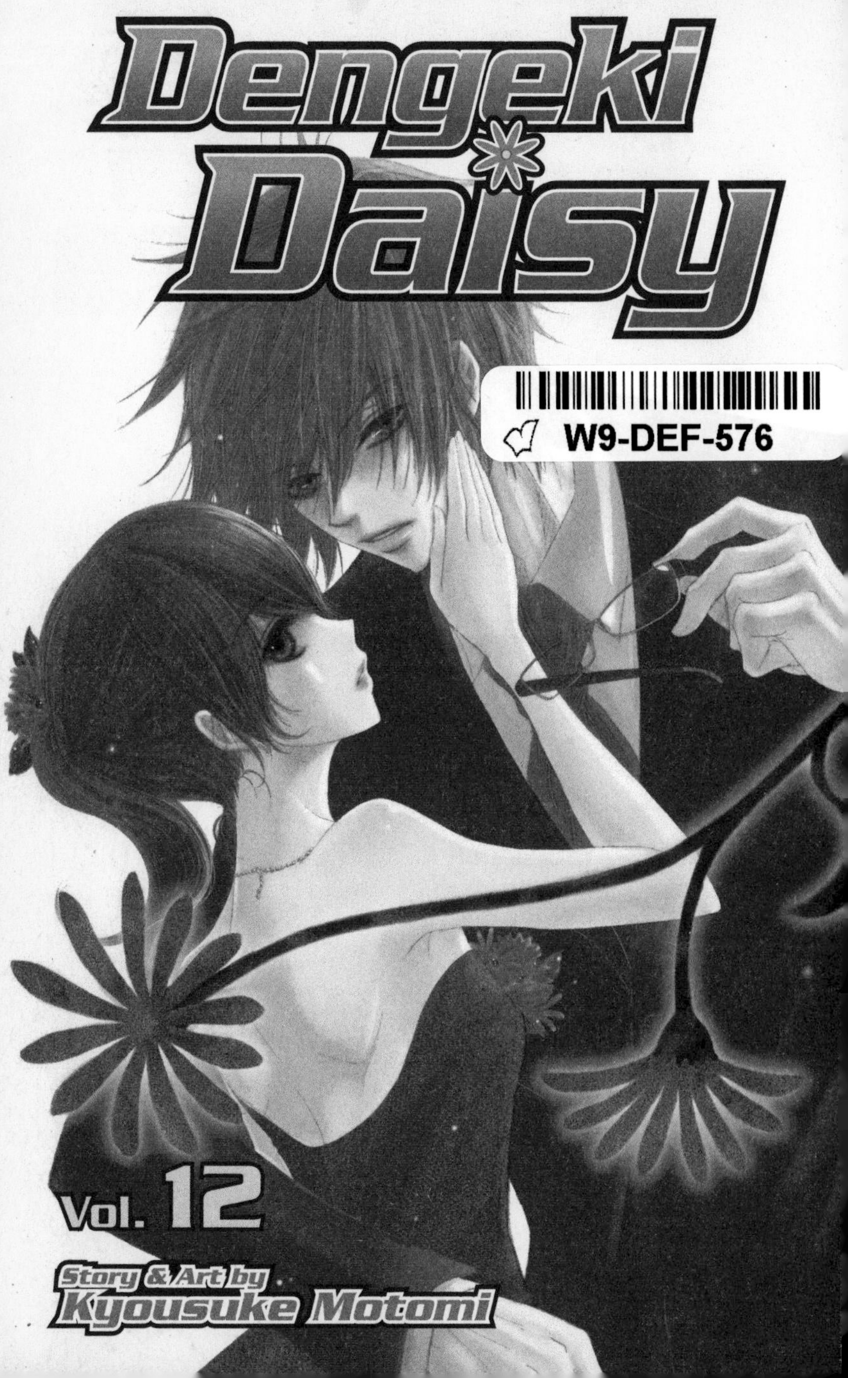
Dengeki Daisy
W9-DEF-576
Vol. 12
Story & Art by
Kyousuke Motomi

# Dengeki Daisy

## Volume 12 CONTENTS

DAISY

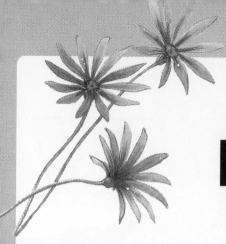

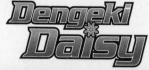

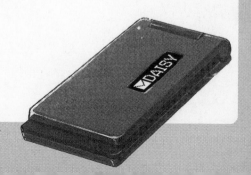

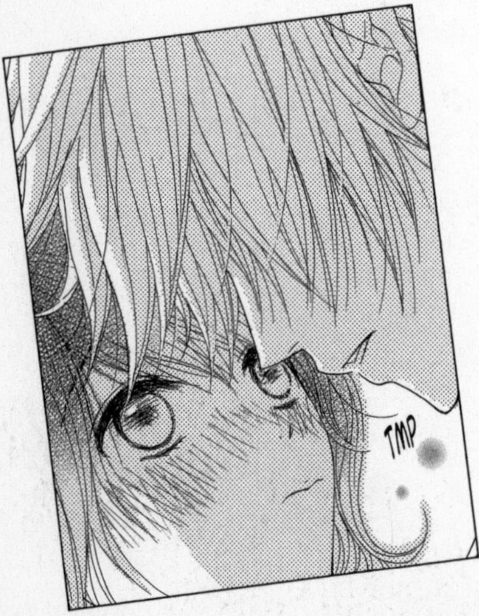
TMP

# Dengeki Daisy Vol. 12

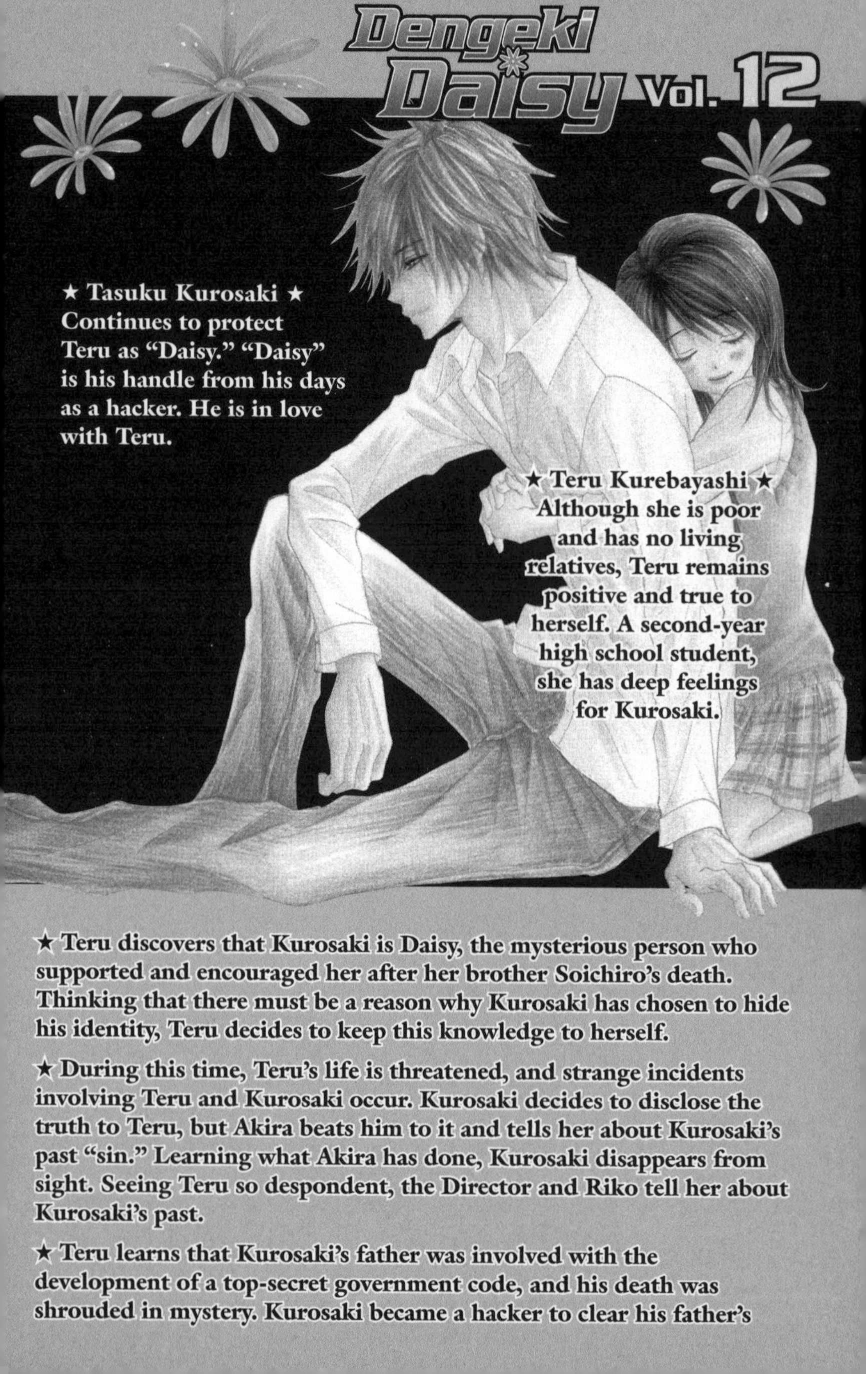
★ Tasuku Kurosaki ★
Continues to protect Teru as "Daisy." "Daisy" is his handle from his days as a hacker. He is in love with Teru.
★ Teru Kurebayashi ★
Although she is poor and has no living relatives, Teru remains positive and true to herself. A second-year high school student, she has deep feelings for Kurosaki.

★ Teru discovers that Kurosaki is Daisy, the mysterious person who supported and encouraged her after her brother Soichiro's death. Thinking that there must be a reason why Kurosaki has chosen to hide his identity, Teru decides to keep this knowledge to herself.

★ During this time, Teru's life is threatened, and strange incidents involving Teru and Kurosaki occur. Kurosaki decides to disclose the truth to Teru, but Akira beats him to it and tells her about Kurosaki's past "sin." Learning what Akira has done, Kurosaki disappears from sight. Seeing Teru so despondent, the Director and Riko tell her about Kurosaki's past.

★ Teru learns that Kurosaki's father was involved with the development of a top-secret government code, and his death was shrouded in mystery. Kurosaki became a hacker to clear his father's

# CHARACTERS...

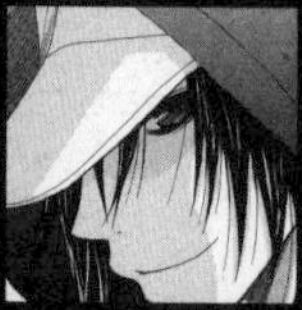

★ Akira ★
Chiharu Mori's partner-in-crime. He continues to stalk Teru and Kurosaki.

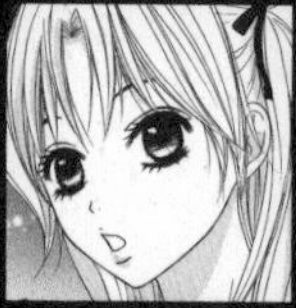

★ Rena Ichinose ★
Teru's friend. Certainly not the docile type, but she tends to value her friends.

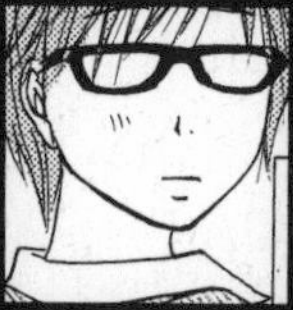

★ Kiyoshi Hasegawa ★
Teru's friend since grade school and Kurosaki's number two servant.

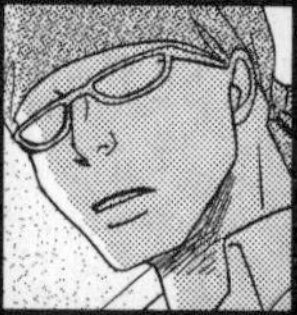

★ Boss (Masuda) ★
Currently runs the snack shop "Flower Garden" but used to work with Soichiro.

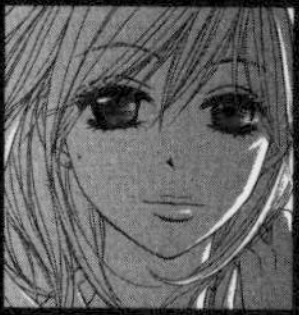

★ Chiharu Mori ★
She used to work at Teru's school. Teaming up with Akira, she continues to target Teru and Kurosaki.

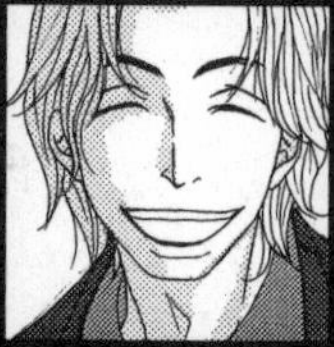

★ Kazuki Morizono ★
Rena's fiancé. He plans to sell the new version of the "Jack Frost" code virus.

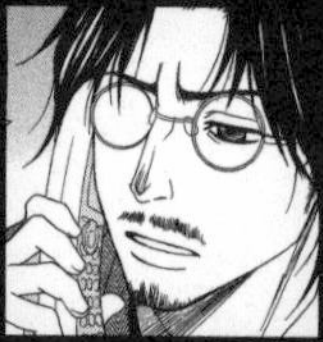

★ Director (Kazumasa Ando) ★
He used to work with Soichiro and is currently the director of Teru's school.

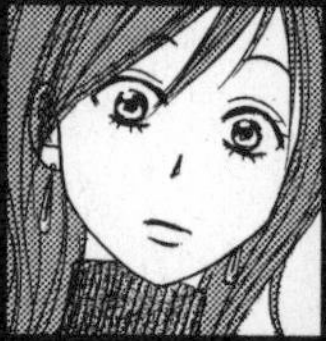

★ Riko Onizuka ★
She was Soichiro's girlfriend and is now a counselor at Teru's school.

# STORY...

name and created the code virus known as "Jack Frost." In order to save Kurosaki from being charged with a "Jack Frost"-related murder, Soichiro worked nonstop to decipher the code and died in the process. Teru accepts this newfound knowledge about Kurosaki. She thanks him for all that he has done for her and asks him to stay by her side.

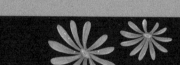

★ One day, Rena discovers that her fiancé Morizono is trying to use a new version of the "Jack Frost" virus for foul purposes. Morizono takes Rena to a hotel abroad and keeps her confined. After receiving Rena's plea for help, Teru and friends sneak into the couple's engagement party in order to rescue Rena and crush Morizono's plans.

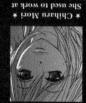

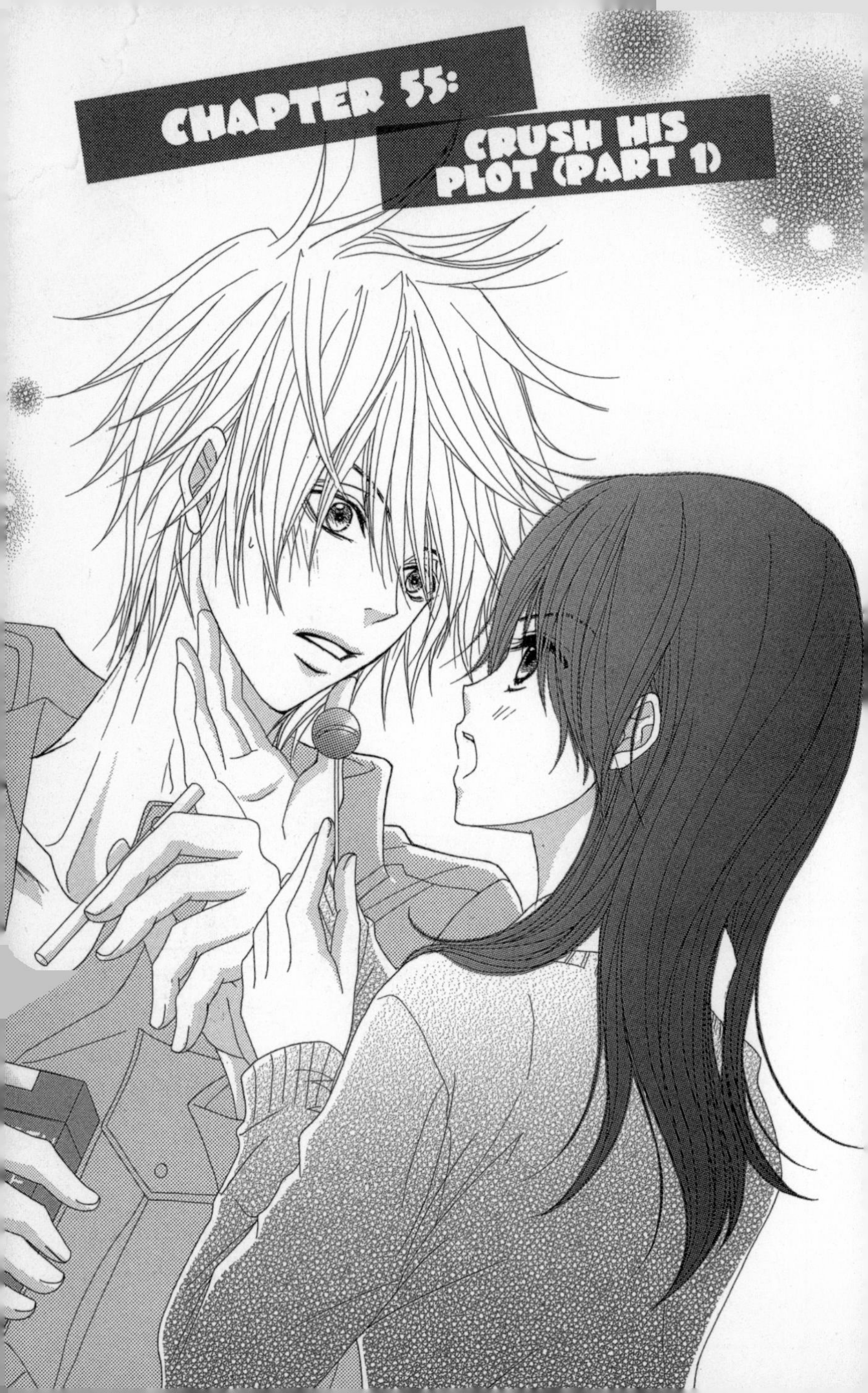
CHAPTER 55:
CRUSH HIS PLOT (PART 1)

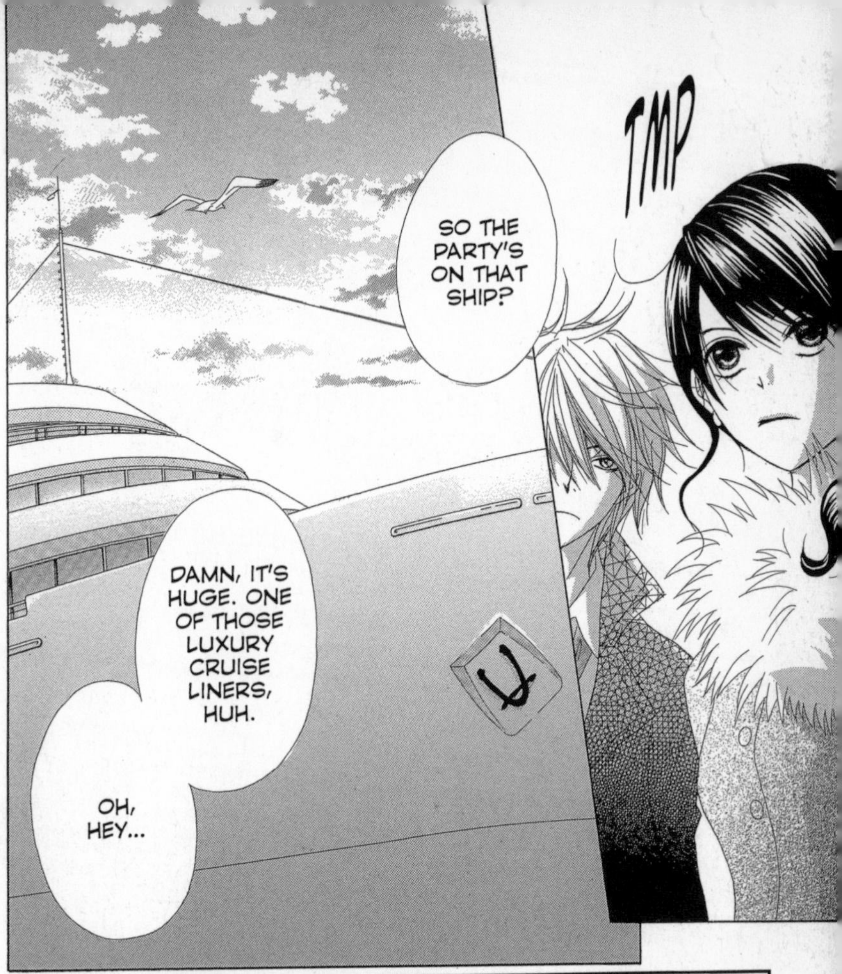
TMP
SO THE PARTY'S ON THAT SHIP?
DAMN, IT'S HUGE. ONE OF THOSE LUXURY CRUISE LINERS, HUH.
OH, HEY...

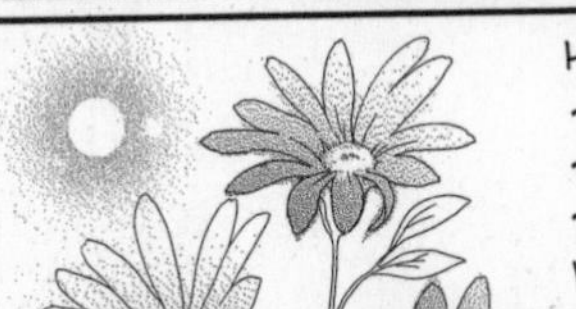
It's spring, and my daisies are blooming one after the other.

HELLO, EVERYONE!! IT'S KYOUSUKE MOTOMI.
THIS IS VOLUME 12 OF *DENGEKI DAISY*!! THANK YOU!
TWELVE VOLUMES MEANS...IF YOU READ ONE VOLUME A MONTH, ***IT'D TAKE A YEAR TO READ IT ALL!!!***

WELL... NOT THAT THAT MEANS ANYTHING. JUST READ IT AT YOUR OWN PACE.

AND IF YOU ENJOY IT, I'D BE VERY HAPPY.

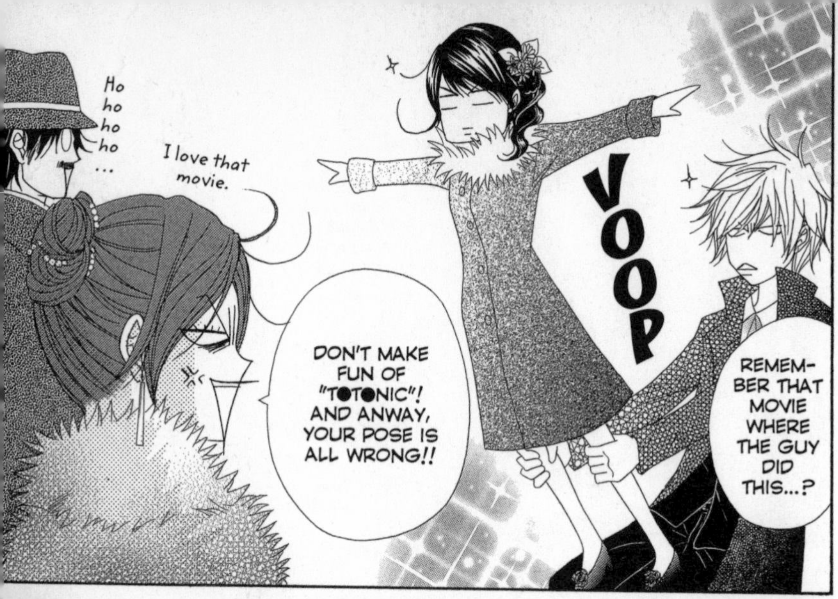
REMEMBER THAT MOVIE WHERE THE GUY DID THIS...?
VOOP
DON'T MAKE FUN OF "T●T●NIC"! AND ANWAY, YOUR POSE IS ALL WRONG!!
I love that movie.
Ho ho ho ho ...

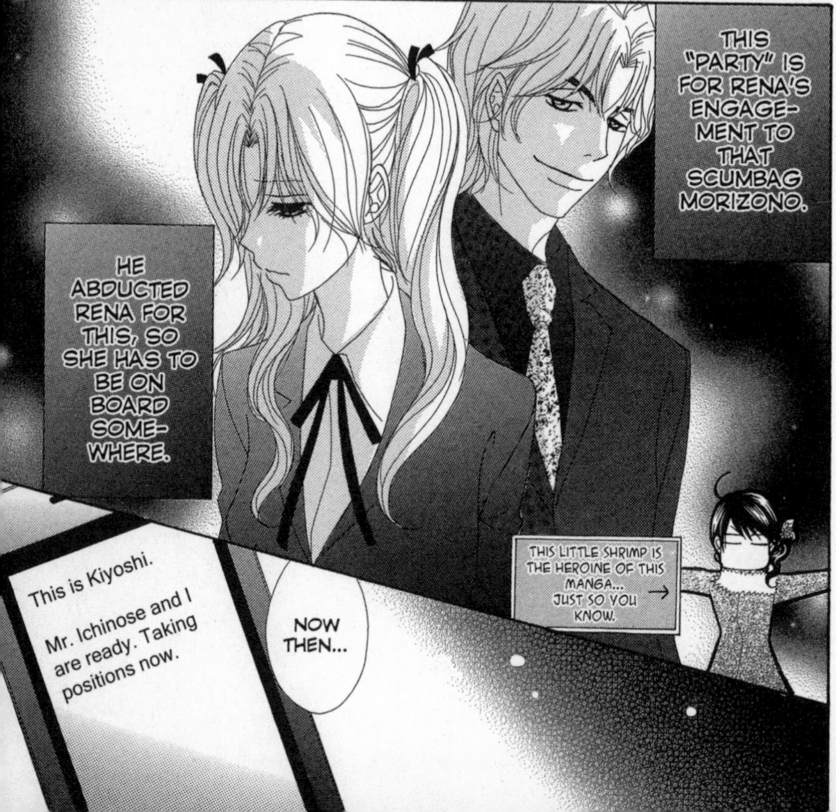
THIS "PARTY" IS FOR RENA'S ENGAGEMENT TO THAT SCUMBAG MORIZONO.
HE ABDUCTED RENA FOR THIS, SO SHE HAS TO BE ON BOARD SOMEWHERE.
THIS LITTLE SHRIMP IS THE HEROINE OF THIS MANGA... JUST SO YOU KNOW.
NOW THEN...
This is Kiyoshi.
Mr. Ichinose and I are ready. Taking positions now.

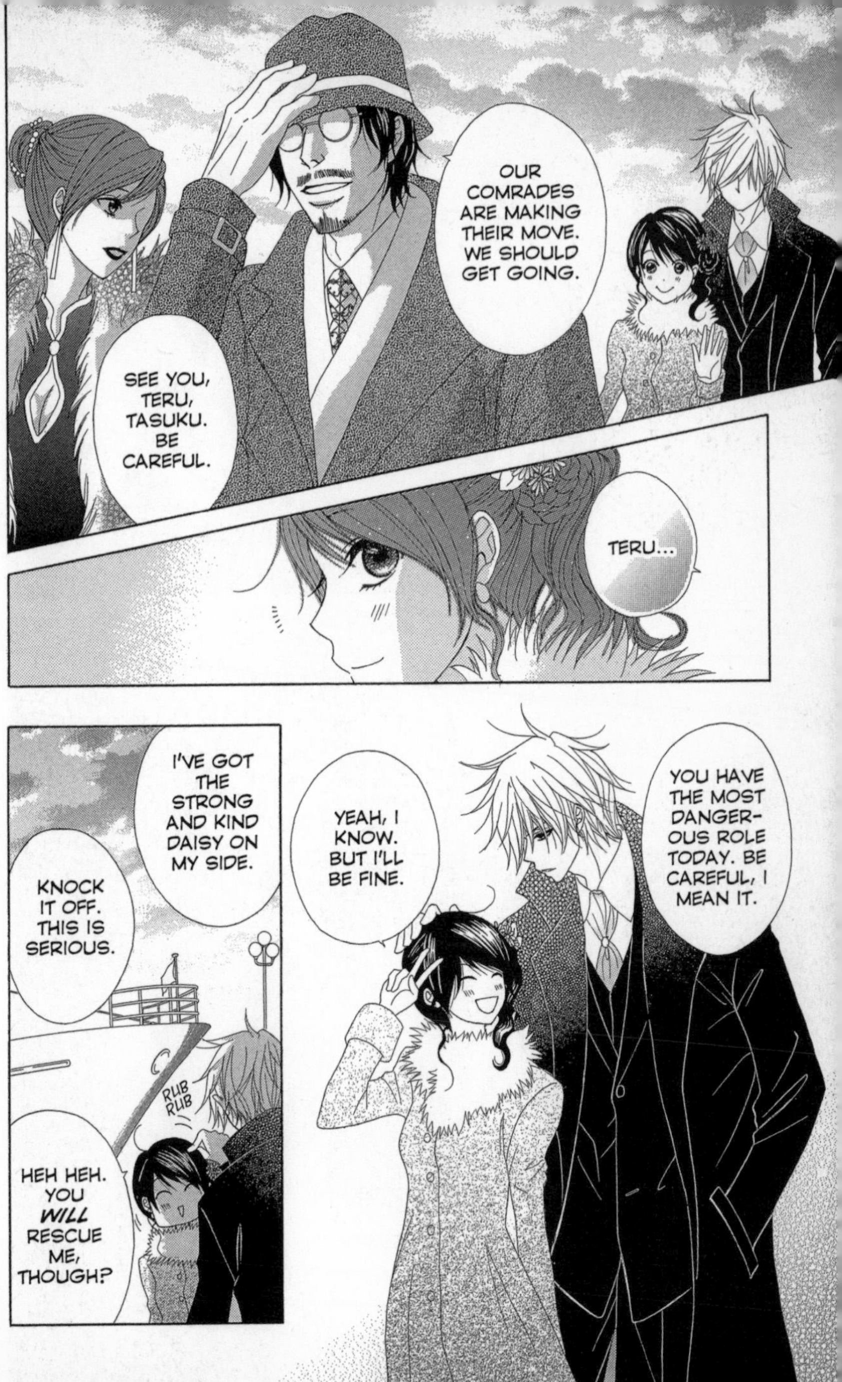
OUR COMRADES ARE MAKING THEIR MOVE. WE SHOULD GET GOING.
SEE YOU, TERU, TASUKU. BE CAREFUL.
TERU...
YOU HAVE THE MOST DANGER-OUS ROLE TODAY. BE CAREFUL, I MEAN IT.
YEAH, I KNOW. BUT I'LL BE FINE.
I'VE GOT THE STRONG AND KIND DAISY ON MY SIDE.
KNOCK IT OFF. THIS IS SERIOUS.
RUB RUB
HEH HEH. YOU *WILL* RESCUE ME, THOUGH?

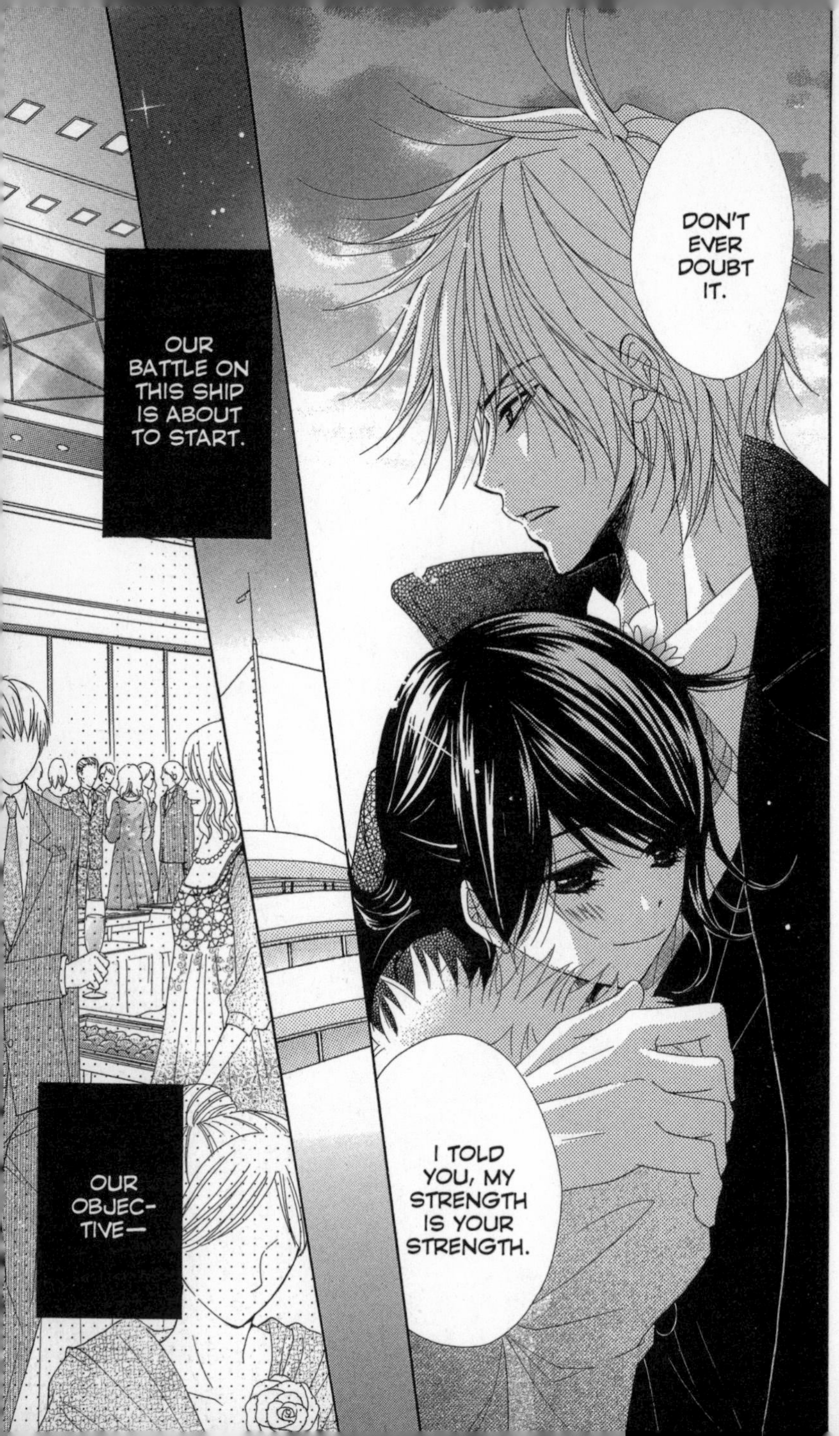
DON'T EVER DOUBT IT.
I TOLD YOU, MY STRENGTH IS YOUR STRENGTH.
OUR BATTLE ON THIS SHIP IS ABOUT TO START.
OUR OBJEC-TIVE—

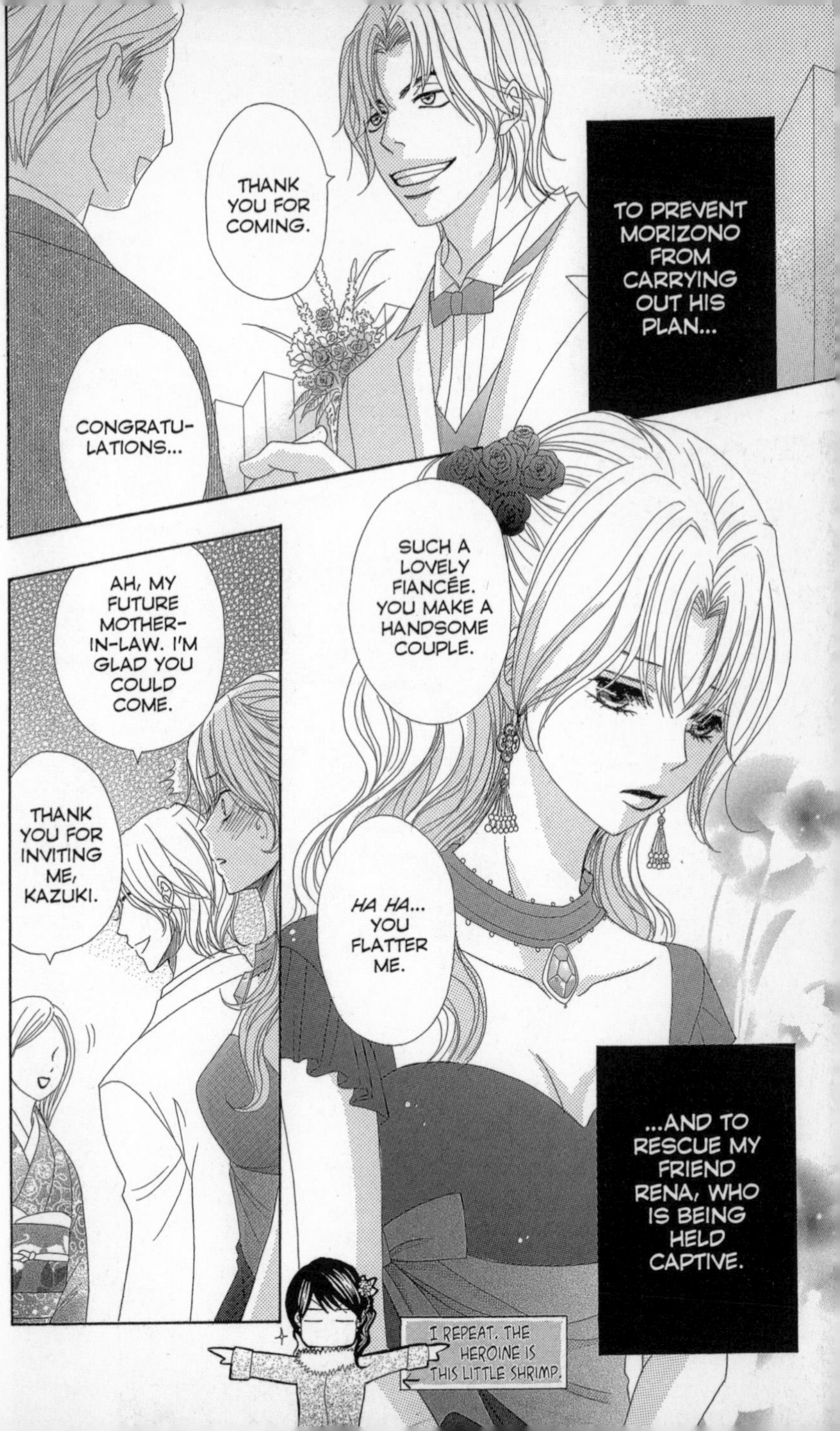
TO PREVENT MORIZONO FROM CARRYING OUT HIS PLAN...
THANK YOU FOR COMING.
CONGRATULATIONS...
SUCH A LOVELY FIANCÉE. YOU MAKE A HANDSOME COUPLE.
HA HA... YOU FLATTER ME.
AH, MY FUTURE MOTHER-IN-LAW. I'M GLAD YOU COULD COME.
THANK YOU FOR INVITING ME, KAZUKI.
...AND TO RESCUE MY FRIEND RENA, WHO IS BEING HELD CAPTIVE.
I REPEAT. THE HEROINE IS THIS LITTLE SHRIMP.

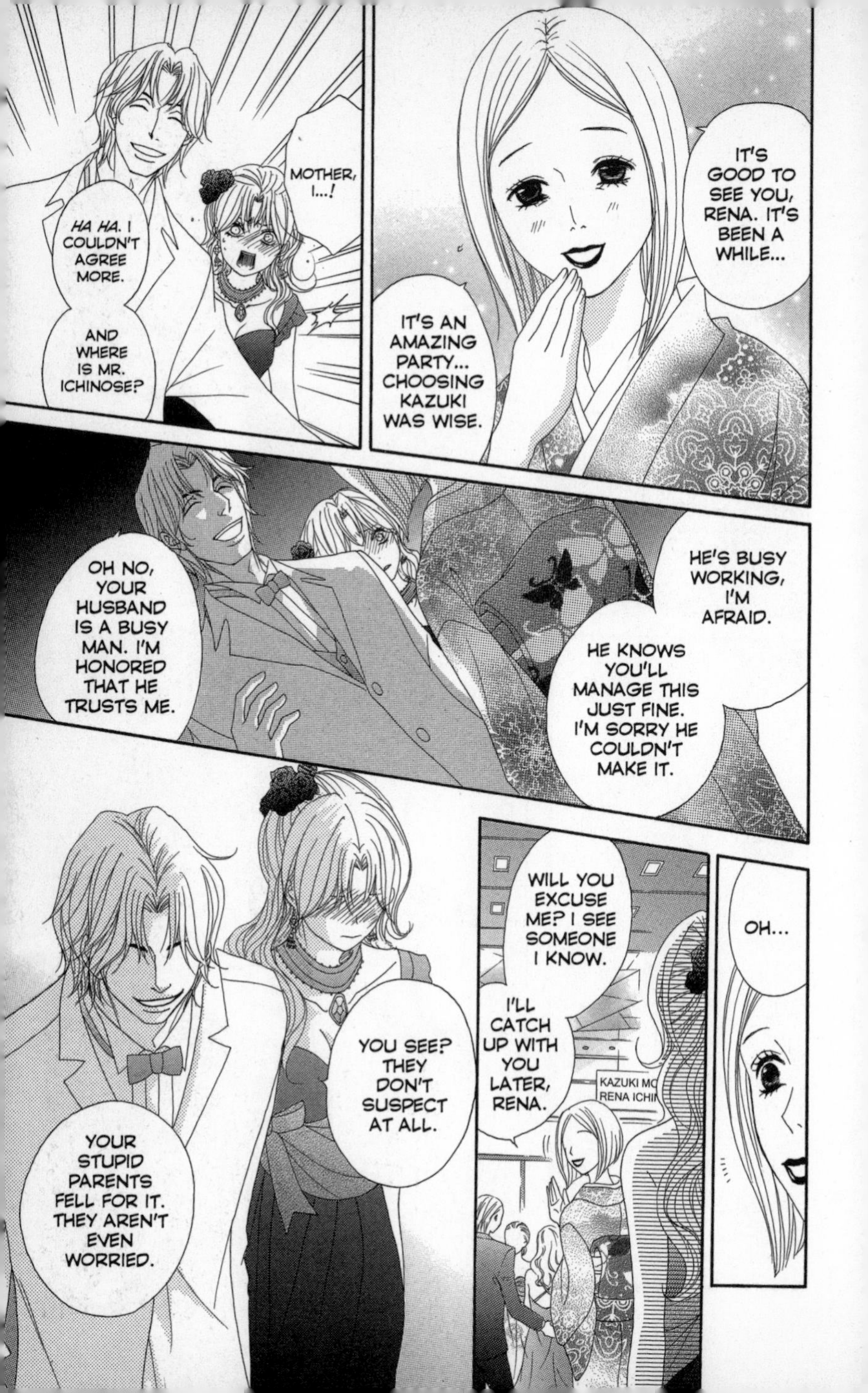
IT'S GOOD TO SEE YOU, RENA. IT'S BEEN A WHILE...
IT'S AN AMAZING PARTY... CHOOSING KAZUKI WAS WISE.
MOTHER, I...!
HA HA. I COULDN'T AGREE MORE.
AND WHERE IS MR. ICHINOSE?
HE'S BUSY WORKING, I'M AFRAID.
HE KNOWS YOU'LL MANAGE THIS JUST FINE. I'M SORRY HE COULDN'T MAKE IT.
OH NO, YOUR HUSBAND IS A BUSY MAN. I'M HONORED THAT HE TRUSTS ME.
OH...
WILL YOU EXCUSE ME? I SEE SOMEONE I KNOW.
I'LL CATCH UP WITH YOU LATER, RENA.
KAZUKI MO
RENA ICHIN
YOU SEE? THEY DON'T SUSPECT AT ALL.
YOUR STUPID PARENTS FELL FOR IT. THEY AREN'T EVEN WORRIED.

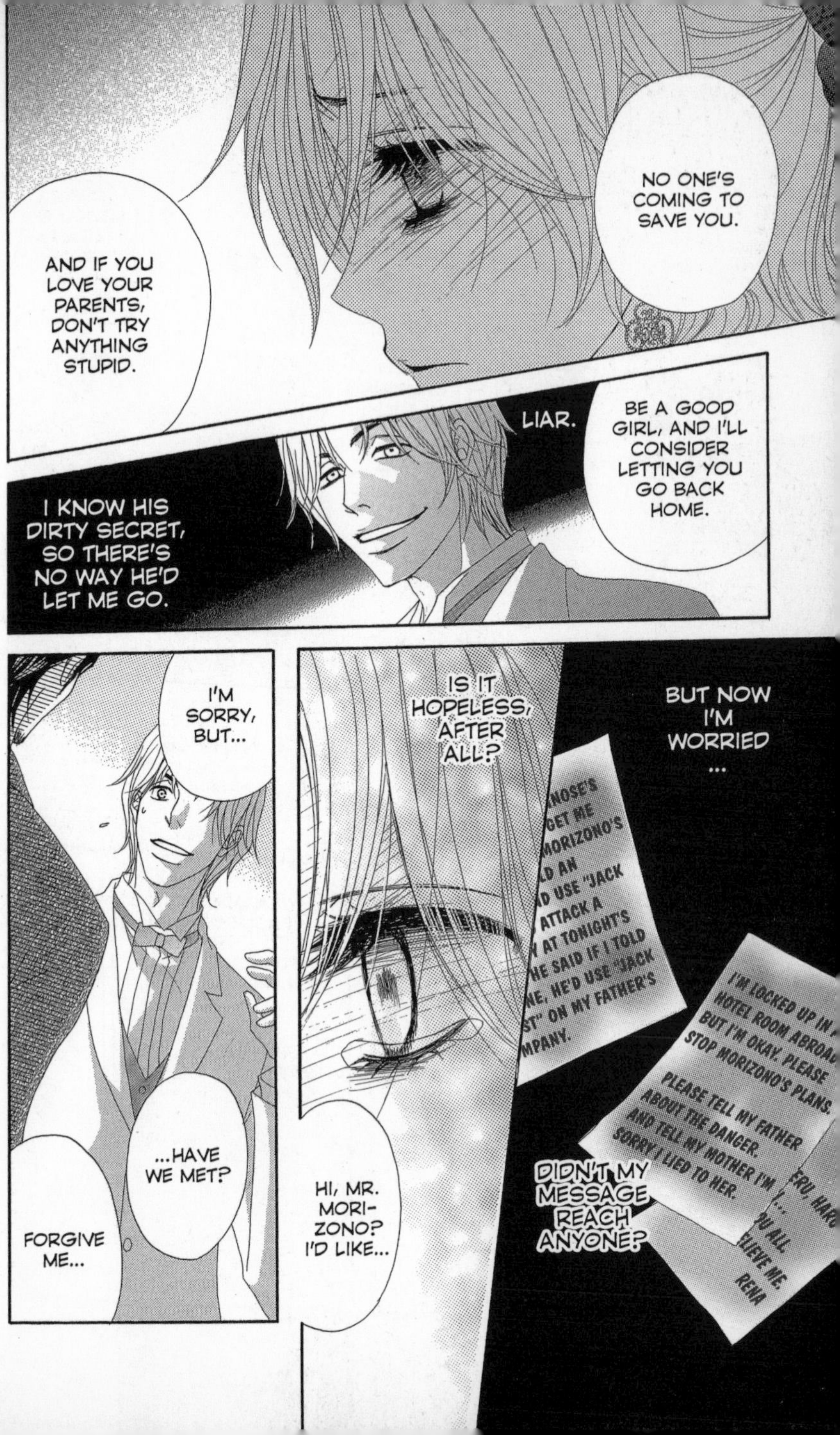
NO ONE'S COMING TO SAVE YOU.
AND IF YOU LOVE YOUR PARENTS, DON'T TRY ANYTHING STUPID.
BE A GOOD GIRL, AND I'LL CONSIDER LETTING YOU GO BACK HOME.
LIAR.
I KNOW HIS DIRTY SECRET, SO THERE'S NO WAY HE'D LET ME GO.
BUT NOW I'M WORRIED ...
IS IT HOPELESS, AFTER ALL?
I'M LOCKED UP IN
BUT I'M OKAY. PLEASE
STOP MORIZONO'S PLANS.
PLEASE TELL MY FATHER
ABOUT THE DANGER.
AND TELL MY MOTHER I'M
SORRY I LIED TO HER.
RENA
DIDN'T MY MESSAGE REACH ANYONE?
HI, MR. MORI-ZONO? I'D LIKE...
I'M SORRY, BUT...
...HAVE WE MET?
FORGIVE ME...

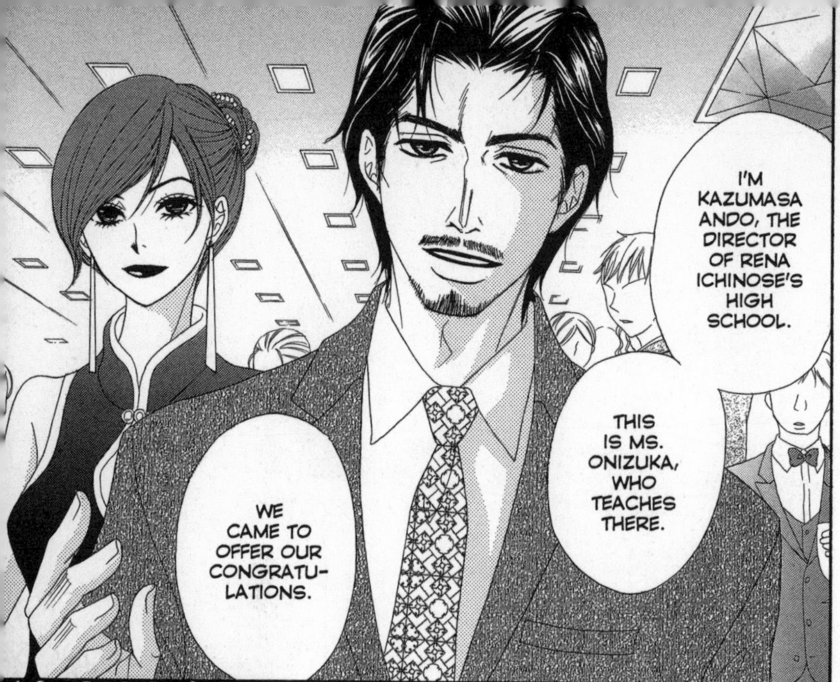
I'M KAZUMASA ANDO, THE DIRECTOR OF RENA ICHINOSE'S HIGH SCHOOL.
THIS IS MS. ONIZUKA, WHO TEACHES THERE.
WE CAME TO OFFER OUR CONGRATULATIONS.
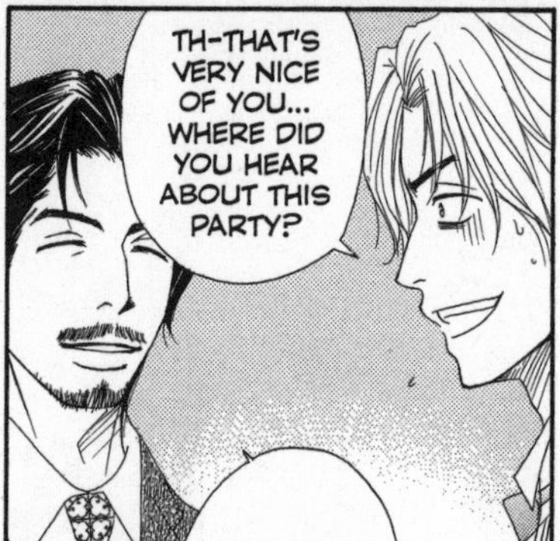
TH-THAT'S VERY NICE OF YOU... WHERE DID YOU HEAR ABOUT THIS PARTY?
SEVERAL PEOPLE INSISTED WE COME.
WE DIDN'T GET AN INVITATION, BUT THAT'S NOT A PROBLEM, IS IT?
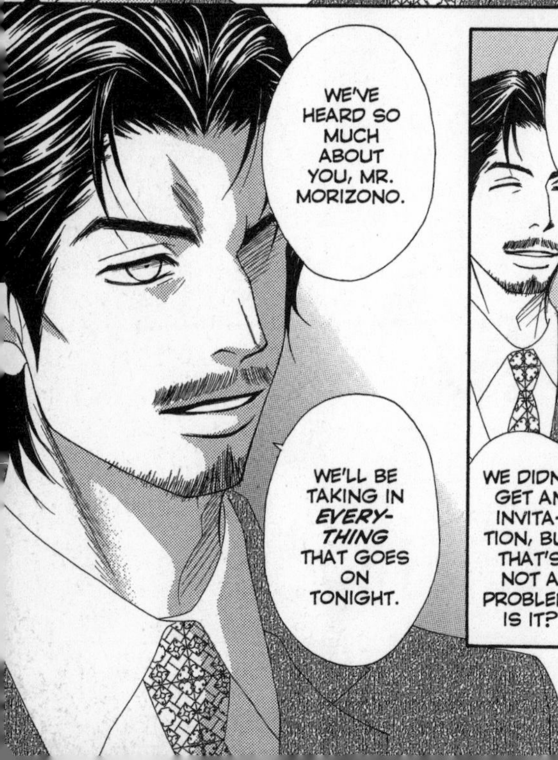
WE'VE HEARD SO MUCH ABOUT YOU, MR. MORIZONO.
WE'LL BE TAKING IN *EVERYTHING* THAT GOES ON TONIGHT.

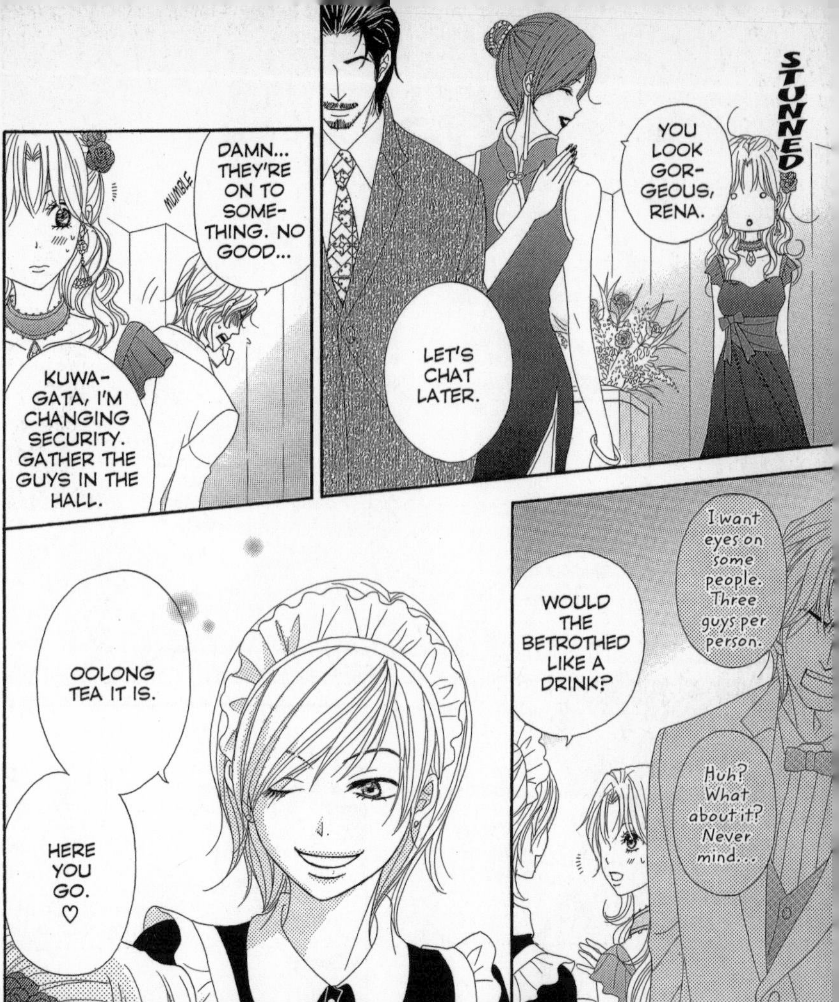
STUNNED
YOU LOOK GORGEOUS, RENA.
LET'S CHAT LATER.
DAMN... THEY'RE ON TO SOMETHING. NO GOOD...
MUMBLE
KUWAGATA, I'M CHANGING SECURITY. GATHER THE GUYS IN THE HALL.
I want eyes on some people. Three guys per person.
WOULD THE BETROTHED LIKE A DRINK?
Huh? What about it? Never mind...
...!
OH, YES. OOLONG TEA, PLEASE...
OOLONG TEA IT IS.
HERE YOU GO. ♡

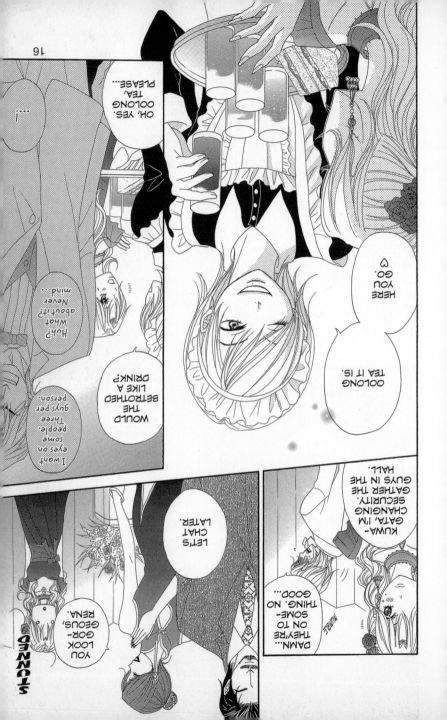

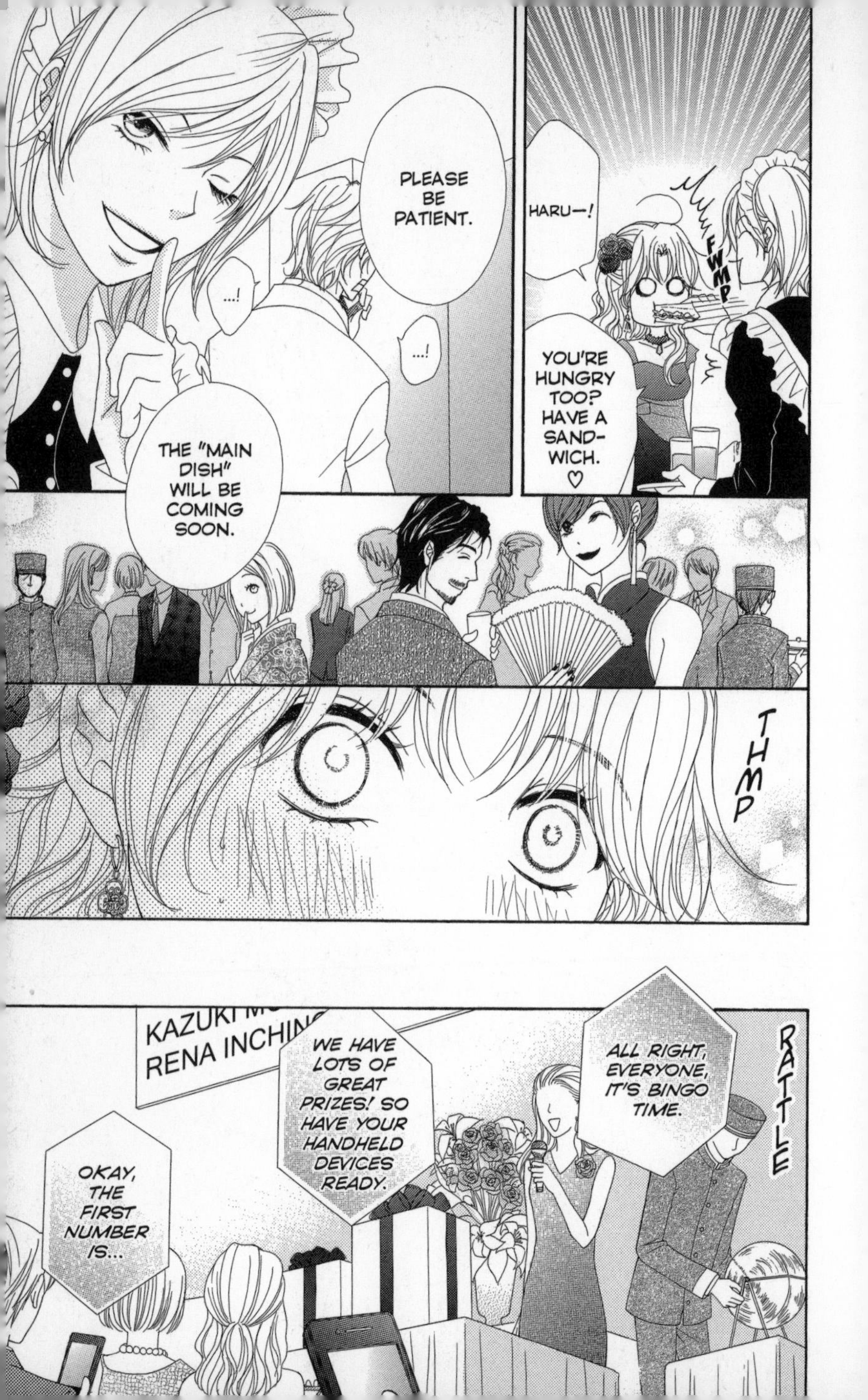
HARU—!
FWMP
YOU'RE HUNGRY TOO? HAVE A SANDWICH. ♡
PLEASE BE PATIENT.
...!
...!
THE "MAIN DISH" WILL BE COMING SOON.
THMP
RATTLE
ALL RIGHT, EVERYONE, IT'S BINGO TIME.
KAZUKI M
RENA INCHIN
WE HAVE LOTS OF GREAT PRIZES! SO HAVE YOUR HANDHELD DEVICES READY.
OKAY, THE FIRST NUMBER IS...

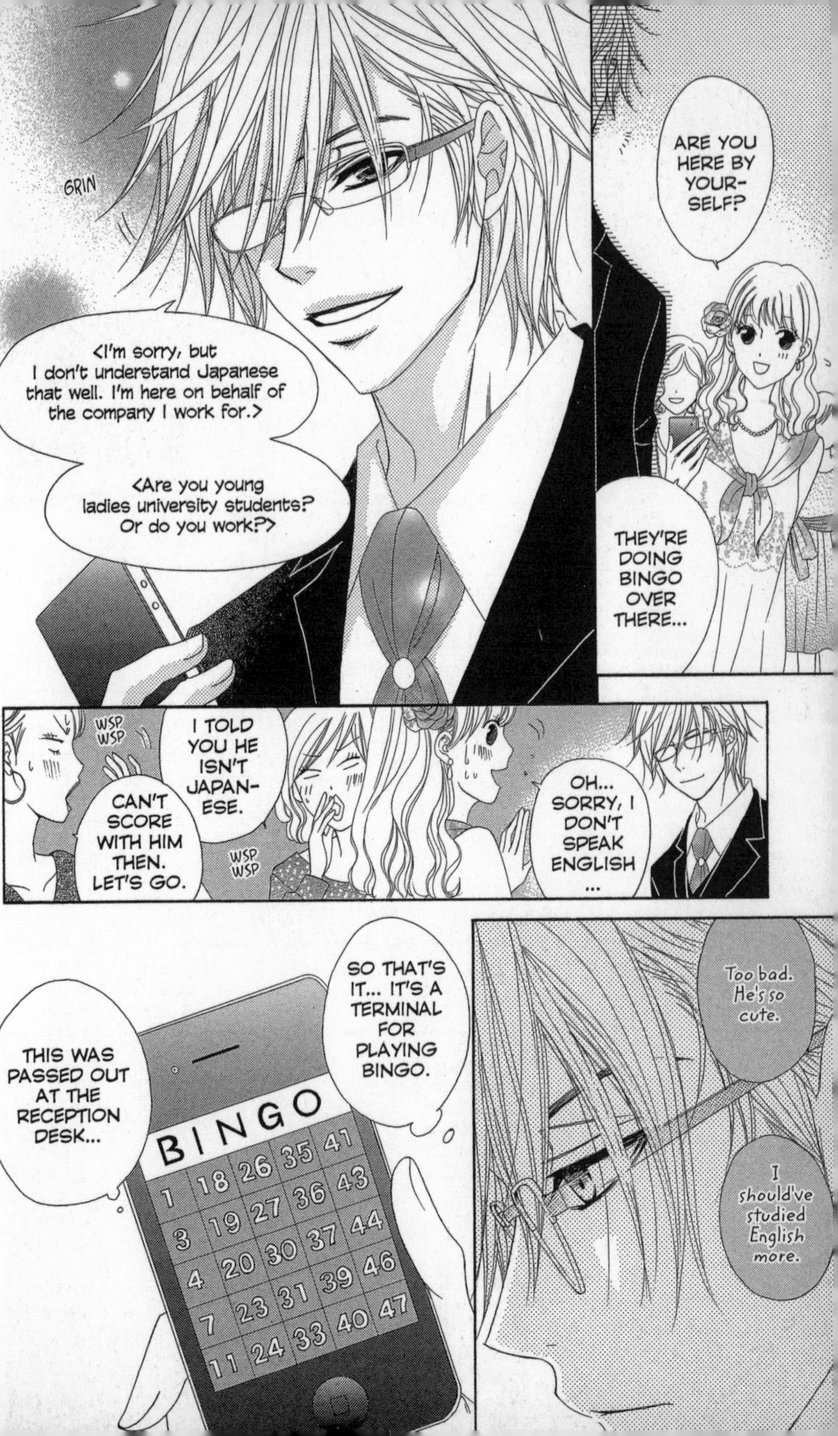
ARE YOU HERE BY YOUR-SELF?
THEY'RE DOING BINGO OVER THERE...
GRIN
<I'm sorry, but I don't understand Japanese that well. I'm here on behalf of the company I work for.>
<Are you young ladies university students? Or do you work?>
OH... SORRY, I DON'T SPEAK ENGLISH ...
WSP WSP
I TOLD YOU HE ISN'T JAPAN-ESE.
CAN'T SCORE WITH HIM THEN. LET'S GO.
WSP WSP
Too bad. He's so cute.
I should've studied English more.
SO THAT'S IT... IT'S A TERMINAL FOR PLAYING BINGO.
THIS WAS PASSED OUT AT THE RECEPTION DESK...
BINGO
1 18 26 35 41
3 19 27 36 43
4 20 30 37 44
7 23 31 39 46
11 24 33 40 47

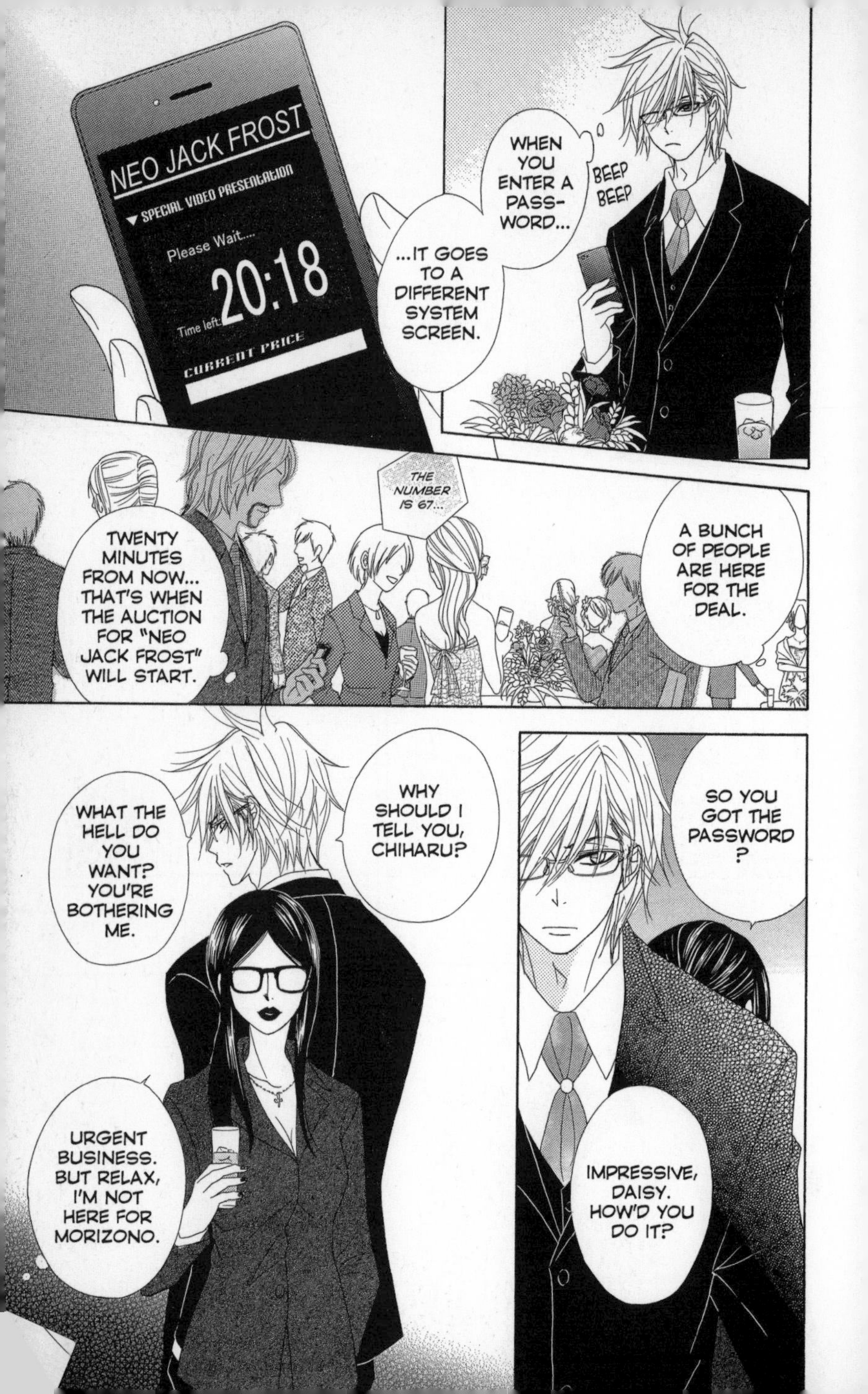
WHEN YOU ENTER A PASS-WORD...
BEEP BEEP
...IT GOES TO A DIFFERENT SYSTEM SCREEN.
NEO JACK FROST
SPECIAL VIDEO PRESENTATION
Please Wait....
Time left: 20:18
CURRENT PRICE
A BUNCH OF PEOPLE ARE HERE FOR THE DEAL.
THE NUMBER IS 67...
TWENTY MINUTES FROM NOW... THAT'S WHEN THE AUCTION FOR "NEO JACK FROST" WILL START.
SO YOU GOT THE PASSWORD ?
IMPRESSIVE, DAISY. HOW'D YOU DO IT?
WHY SHOULD I TELL YOU, CHIHARU?
WHAT THE HELL DO YOU WANT? YOU'RE BOTHERING ME.
URGENT BUSINESS. BUT RELAX, I'M NOT HERE FOR MORIZONO.

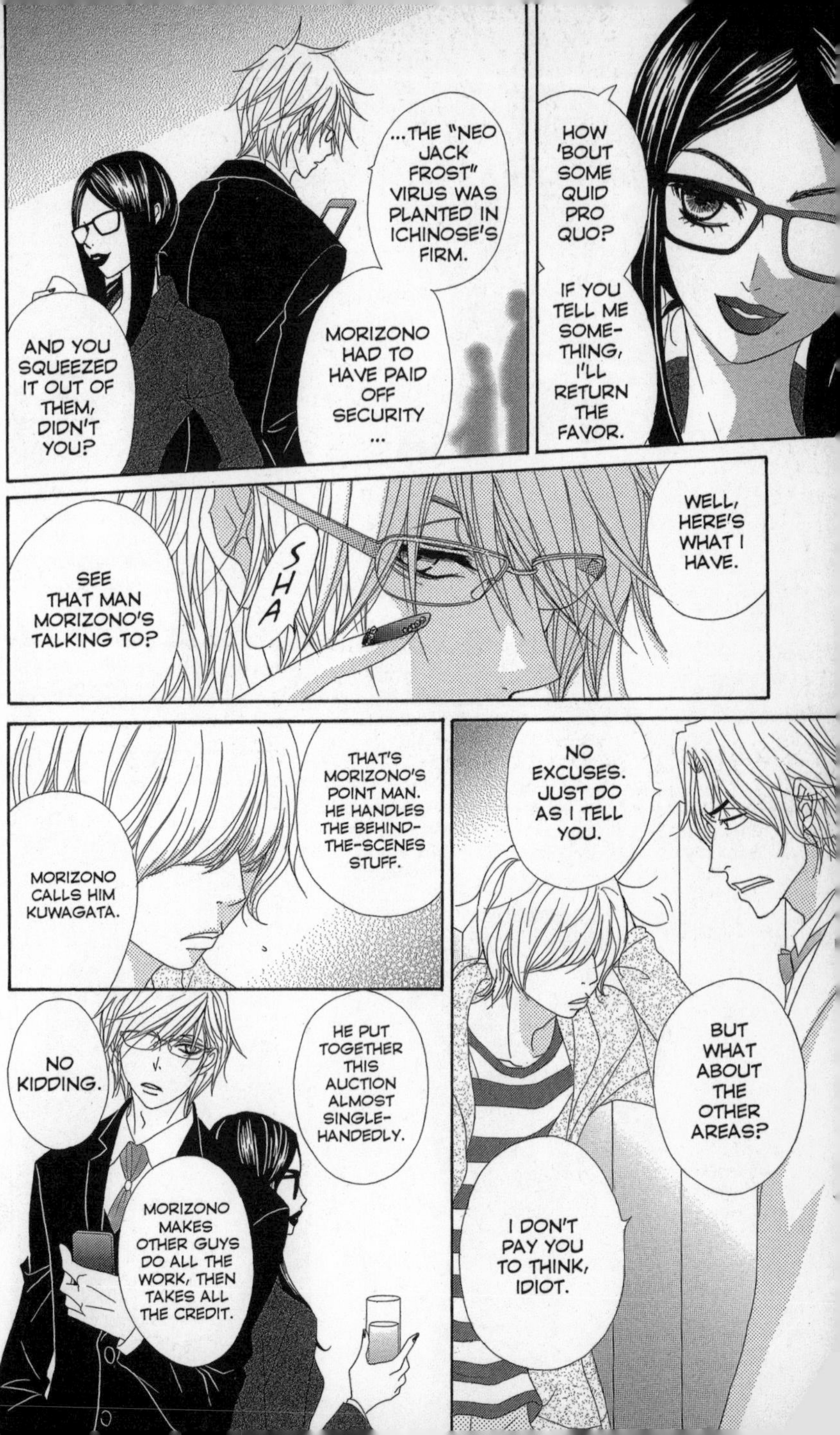
HOW 'BOUT SOME QUID PRO QUO?
IF YOU TELL ME SOME-THING, I'LL RETURN THE FAVOR.
...THE "NEO JACK FROST" VIRUS WAS PLANTED IN ICHINOSE'S FIRM.
MORIZONO HAD TO HAVE PAID OFF SECURITY ...
AND YOU SQUEEZED IT OUT OF THEM, DIDN'T YOU?
WELL, HERE'S WHAT I HAVE.
SHA
SEE THAT MAN MORIZONO'S TALKING TO?
NO EXCUSES. JUST DO AS I TELL YOU.
BUT WHAT ABOUT THE OTHER AREAS?
I DON'T PAY YOU TO THINK, IDIOT.
THAT'S MORIZONO'S POINT MAN. HE HANDLES THE BEHIND-THE-SCENES STUFF.
MORIZONO CALLS HIM KUWAGATA.
NO KIDDING.
HE PUT TOGETHER THIS AUCTION ALMOST SINGLE-HANDEDLY.
MORIZONO MAKES OTHER GUYS DO ALL THE WORK, THEN TAKES ALL THE CREDIT.

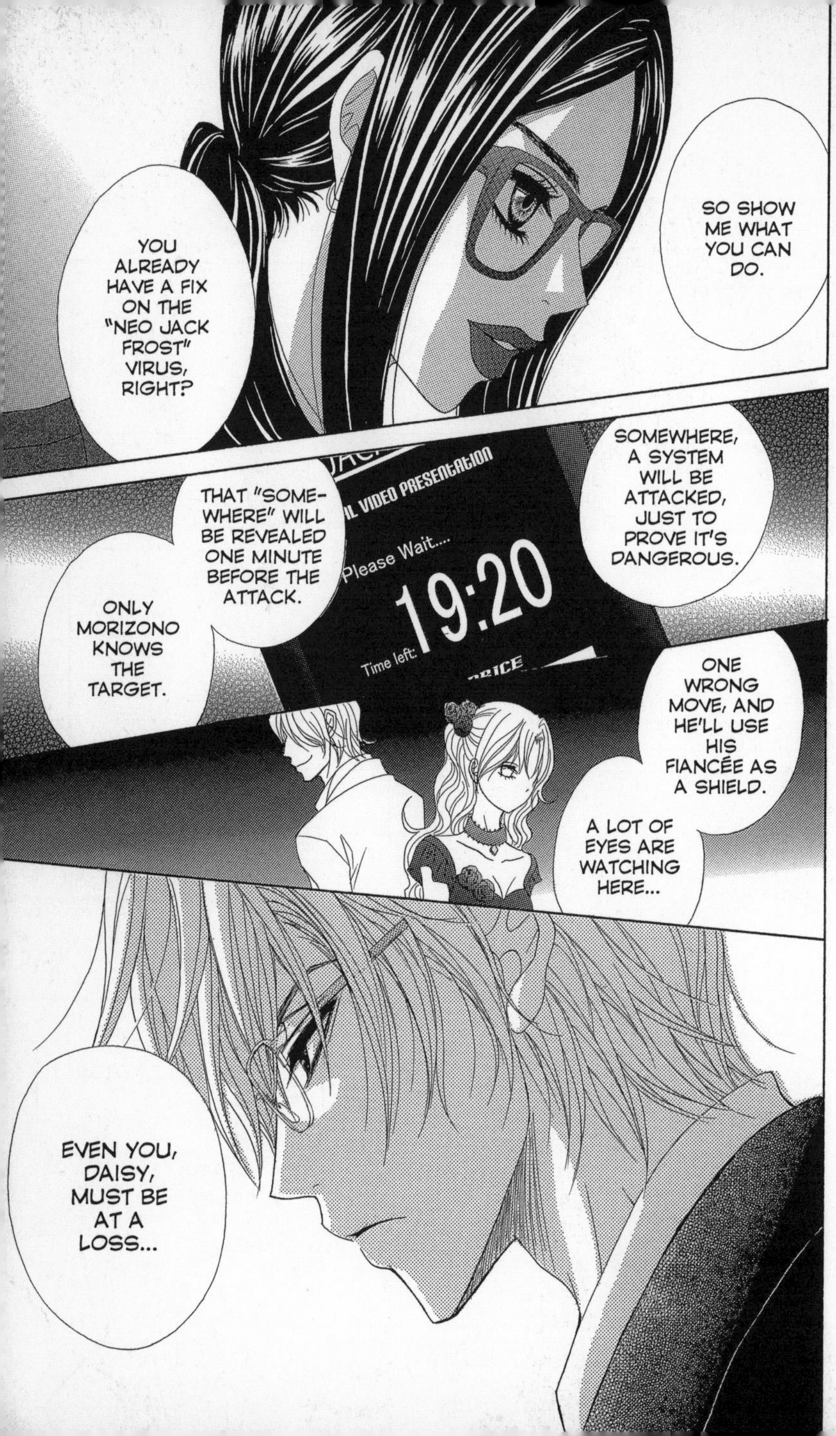
SO SHOW ME WHAT YOU CAN DO.
YOU ALREADY HAVE A FIX ON THE "NEO JACK FROST" VIRUS, RIGHT?
SOMEWHERE, A SYSTEM WILL BE ATTACKED, JUST TO PROVE IT'S DANGEROUS.
IL VIDEO PRESENTATION
Please Wait....
Time left: 19:20
THAT "SOMEWHERE" WILL BE REVEALED ONE MINUTE BEFORE THE ATTACK.
ONLY MORIZONO KNOWS THE TARGET.
ONE WRONG MOVE, AND HE'LL USE HIS FIANCÉE AS A SHIELD.
A LOT OF EYES ARE WATCHING HERE...
EVEN YOU, DAISY, MUST BE AT A LOSS...

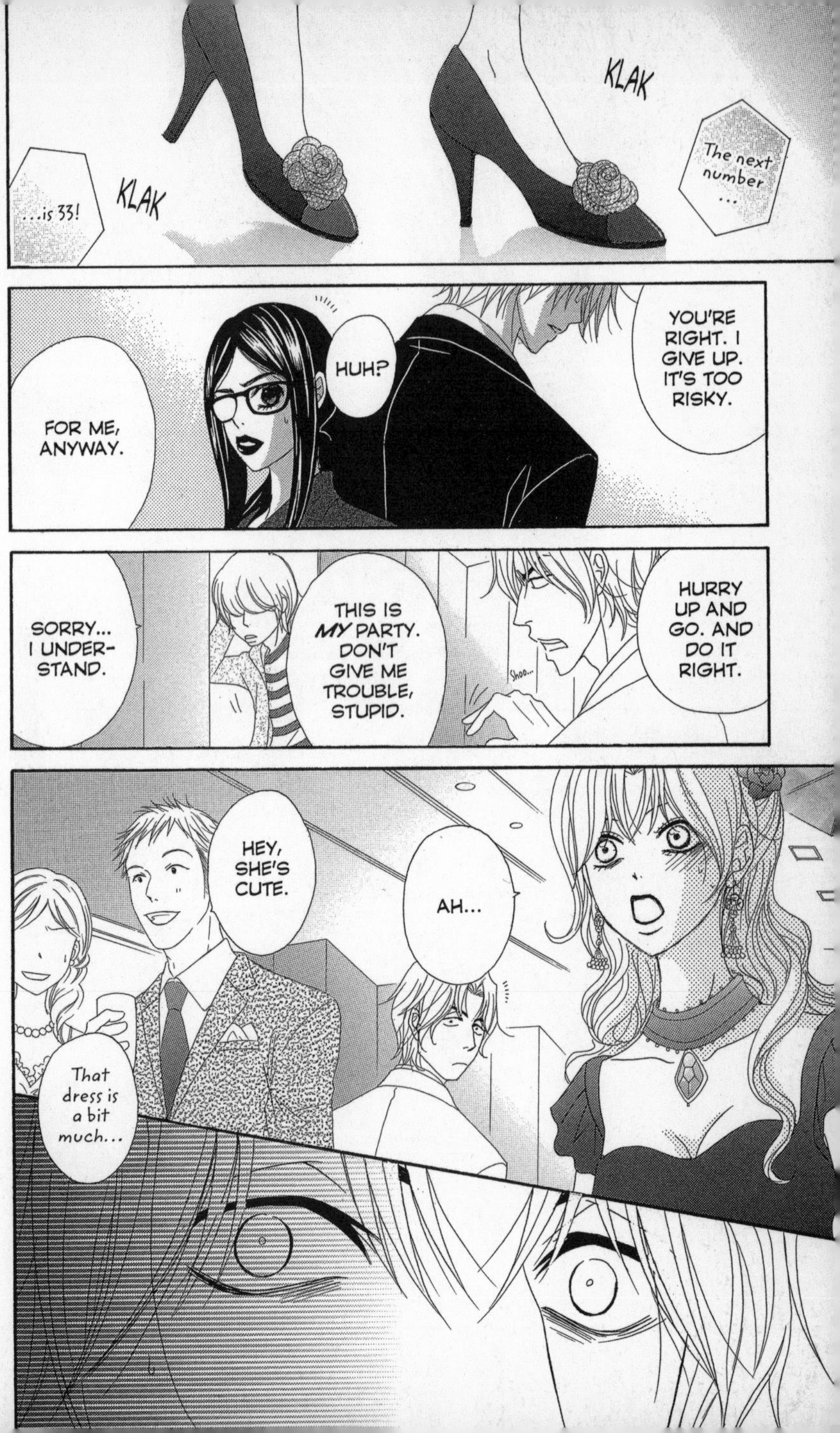
KLAK
The next number ...
KLAK
...is 33!
YOU'RE RIGHT. I GIVE UP. IT'S TOO RISKY.
HUH?
FOR ME, ANYWAY.
HURRY UP AND GO. AND DO IT RIGHT.
Shoo...
THIS IS MY PARTY. DON'T GIVE ME TROUBLE, STUPID.
SORRY... I UNDERSTAND.
AH...
HEY, SHE'S CUTE.
That dress is a bit much...

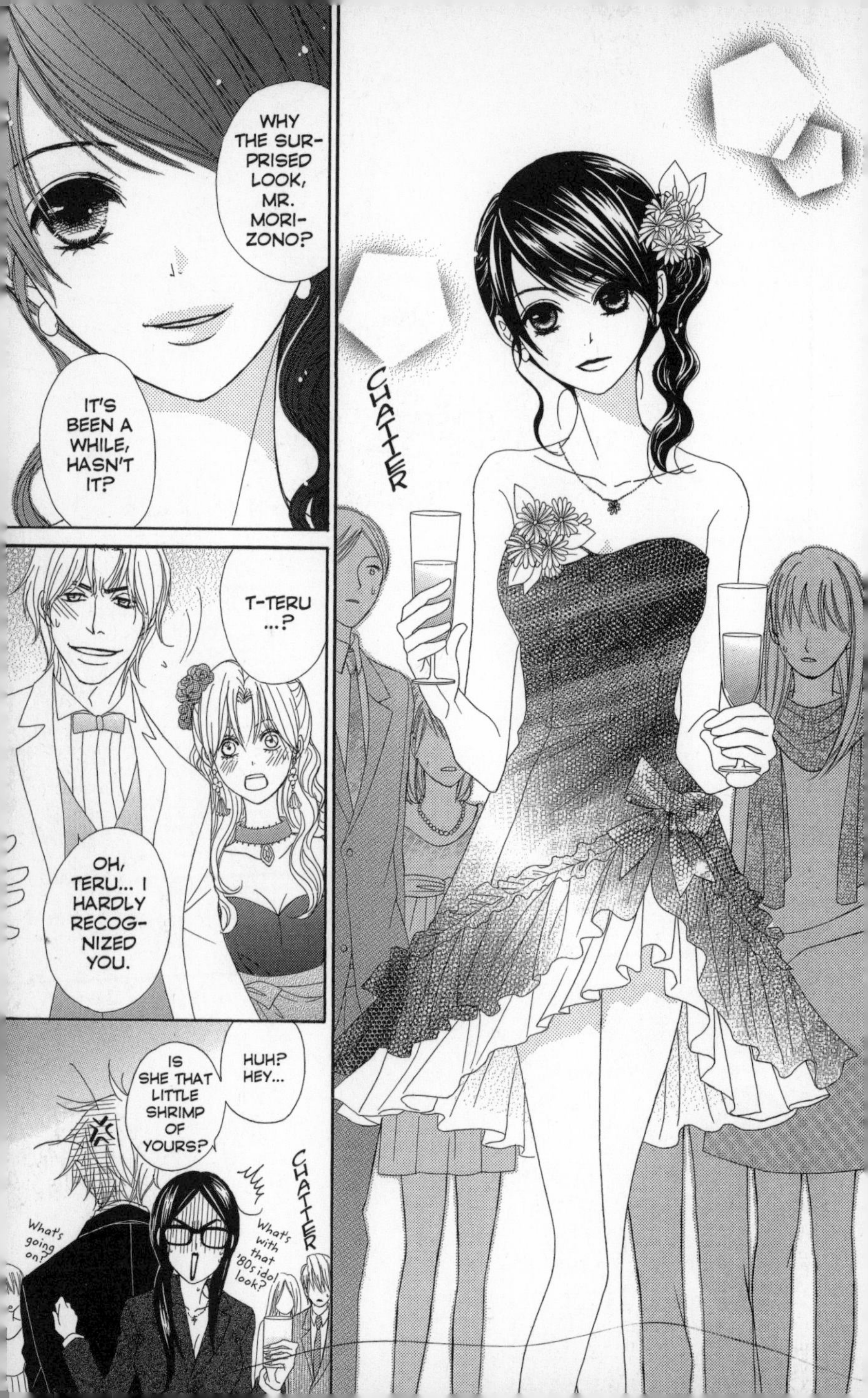
CHATTER
WHY THE SUR-PRISED LOOK, MR. MORI-ZONO?
IT'S BEEN A WHILE, HASN'T IT?
T-TERU ...?
OH, TERU... I HARDLY RECOG-NIZED YOU.
HUH? HEY...
IS SHE THAT LITTLE SHRIMP OF YOURS?
CHATTER
What's with that '80s idol look?
What's going on?

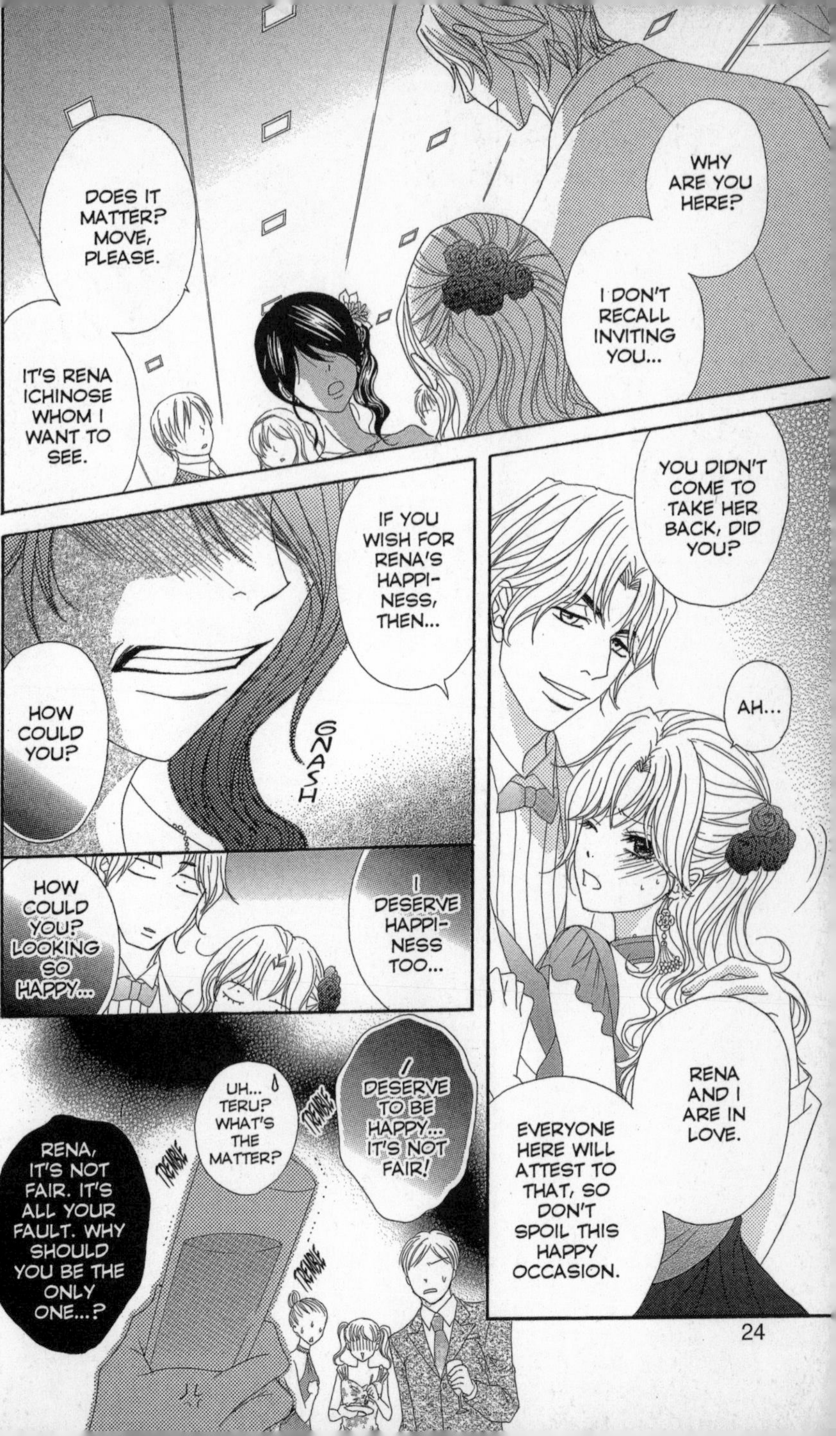
WHY ARE YOU HERE?
I DON'T RECALL INVITING YOU...
DOES IT MATTER? MOVE, PLEASE.
IT'S RENA ICHINOSE WHOM I WANT TO SEE.
YOU DIDN'T COME TO TAKE HER BACK, DID YOU?
AH...
RENA AND I ARE IN LOVE.
EVERYONE HERE WILL ATTEST TO THAT, SO DON'T SPOIL THIS HAPPY OCCASION.
IF YOU WISH FOR RENA'S HAPPINESS, THEN...
GNASH
HOW COULD YOU?
I DESERVE HAPPINESS TOO...
HOW COULD YOU? LOOKING SO HAPPY...
I DESERVE TO BE HAPPY... IT'S NOT FAIR!
TREMBLE
UH... TERU? WHAT'S THE MATTER?
TREMBLE
RENA, IT'S NOT FAIR. IT'S ALL YOUR FAULT. WHY SHOULD YOU BE THE ONLY ONE...?
TREMBLE

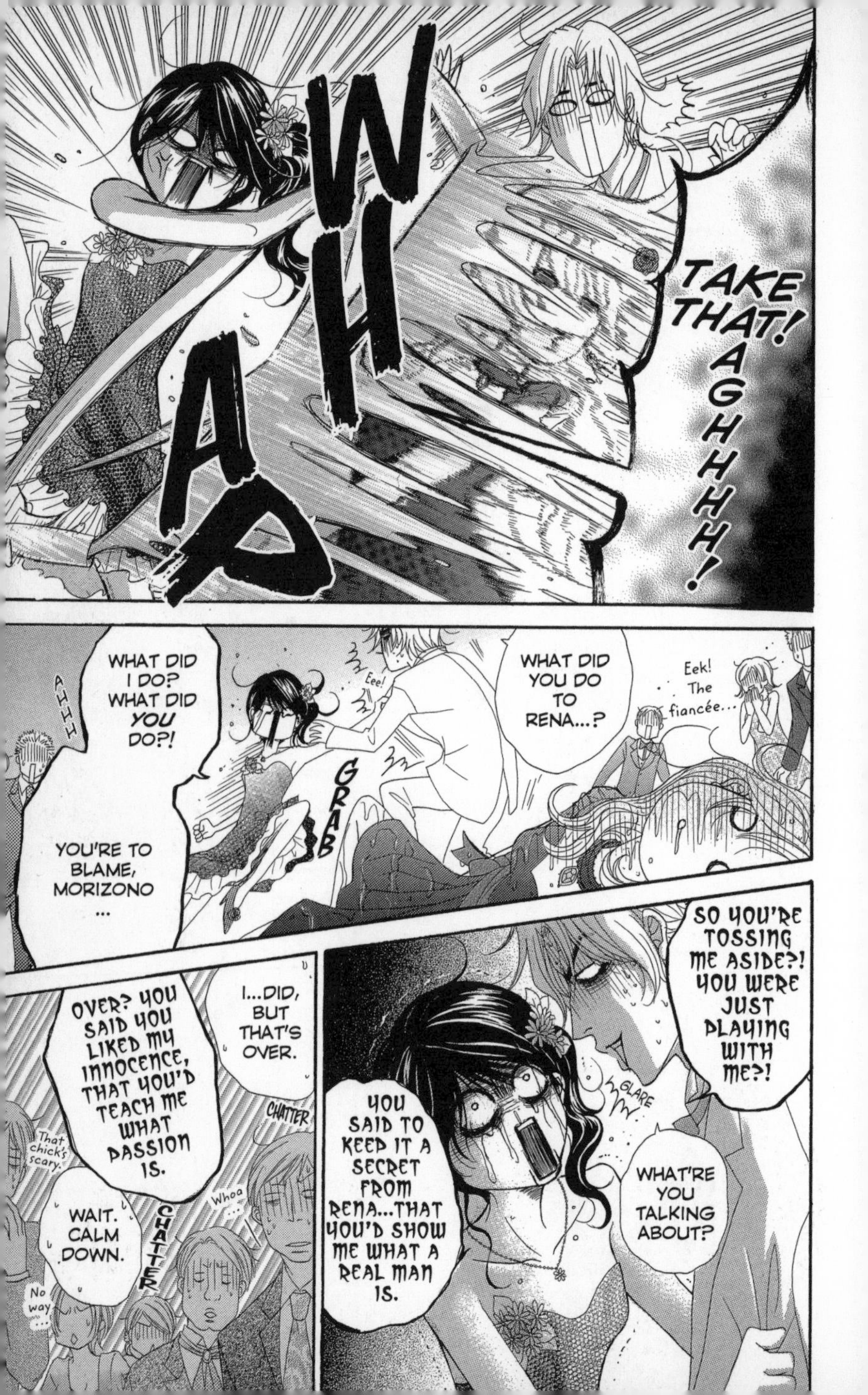
WHAM
TAKE THAT!
AGHHHHH!
Eek! The fiancée...
WHAT DID YOU DO TO RENA...?
Eee!
GRAB
WHAT DID I DO? WHAT DID YOU DO?!
AHHH
YOU'RE TO BLAME, MORIZONO...
SO YOU'RE TOSSING ME ASIDE?! YOU WERE JUST PLAYING WITH ME?!
GLARE
WHAT'RE YOU TALKING ABOUT?
YOU SAID TO KEEP IT A SECRET FROM RENA...THAT YOU'D SHOW ME WHAT A REAL MAN IS.
I...DID, BUT THAT'S OVER.
OVER? YOU SAID YOU LIKED MY INNOCENCE, THAT YOU'D TEACH ME WHAT PASSION IS.
CHATTER
That chick's scary.
Whoa...
WAIT. CALM DOWN.
CHATTER
No way...

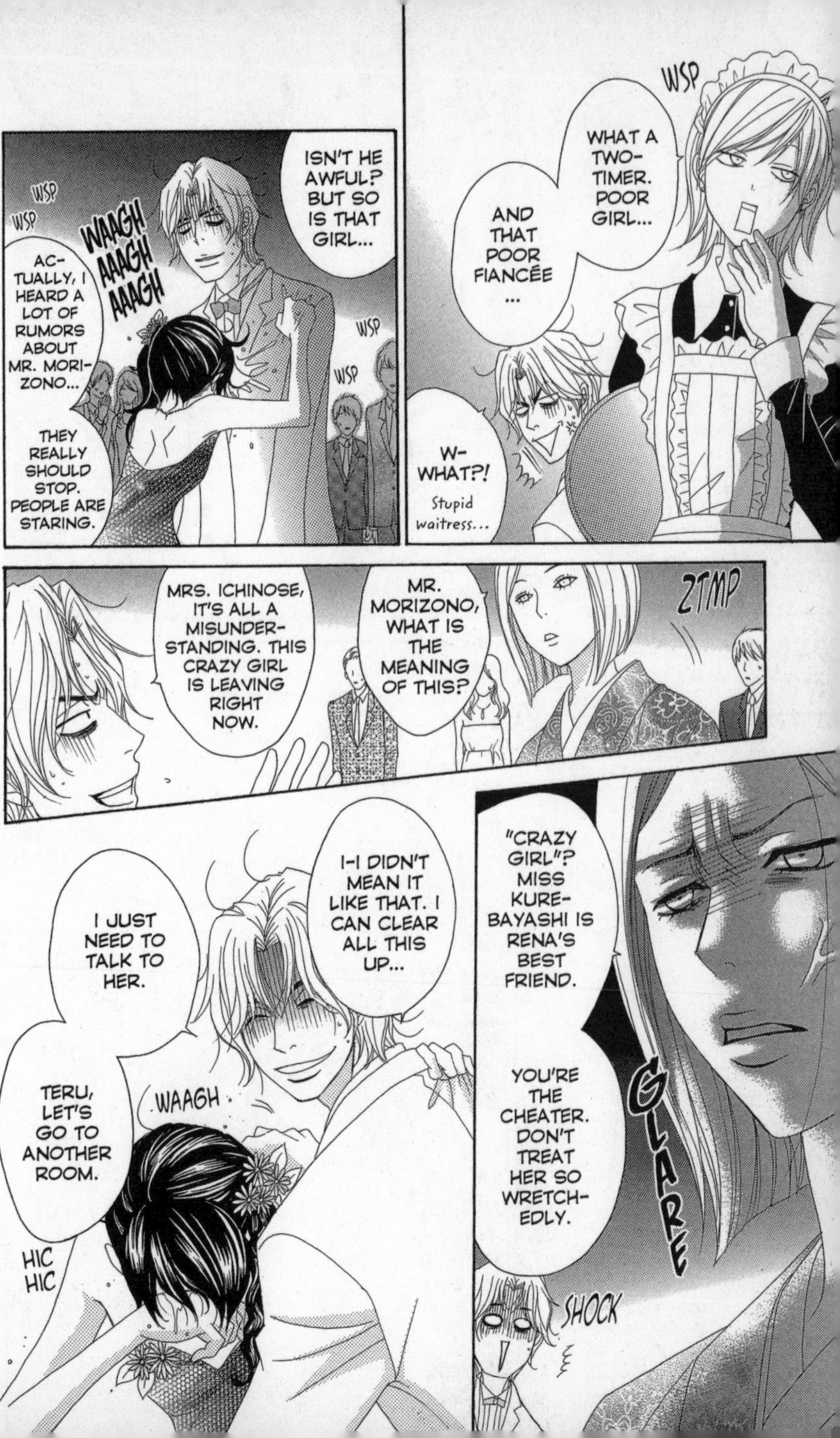
WSP
WHAT A TWO-TIMER. POOR GIRL...
AND THAT POOR FIANCÉE ...
W-WHAT?!
Stupid waitress...
ISN'T HE AWFUL? BUT SO IS THAT GIRL...
WSP
WSP
WAAGH AAAGH AAAGH
AC-TUALLY, I HEARD A LOT OF RUMORS ABOUT MR. MORI-ZONO...
WSP
WSP
THEY REALLY SHOULD STOP. PEOPLE ARE STARING.
ZTMP
MR. MORIZONO, WHAT IS THE MEANING OF THIS?
MRS. ICHINOSE, IT'S ALL A MISUNDER-STANDING. THIS CRAZY GIRL IS LEAVING RIGHT NOW.
"CRAZY GIRL"? MISS KURE-BAYASHI IS RENA'S BEST FRIEND.
YOU'RE THE CHEATER. DON'T TREAT HER SO WRETCH-EDLY.
GLARE
SHOCK
I-I DIDN'T MEAN IT LIKE THAT. I CAN CLEAR ALL THIS UP...
I JUST NEED TO TALK TO HER.
WAAGH
TERU, LET'S GO TO ANOTHER ROOM.
HIC HIC

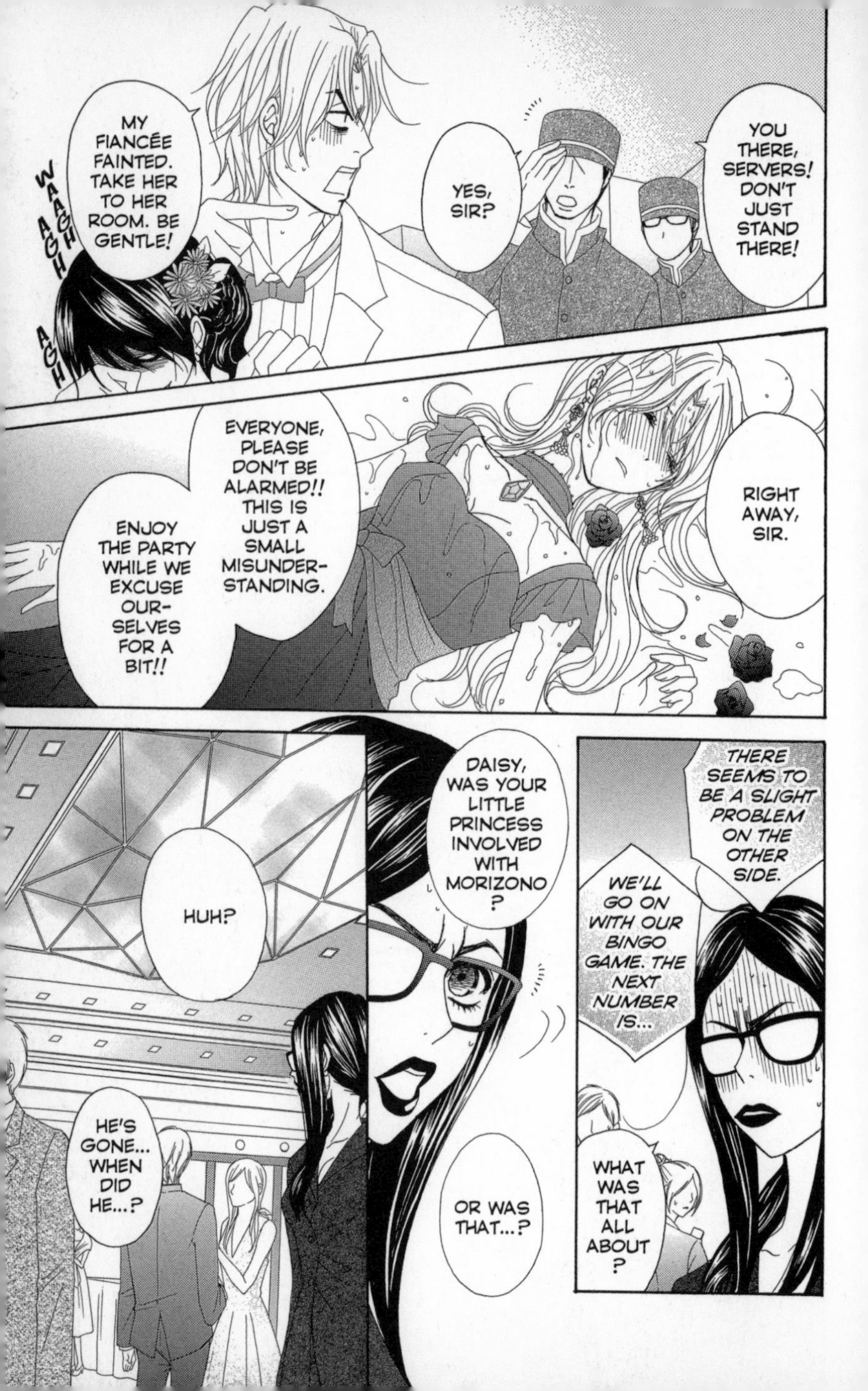
YOU THERE, SERVERS! DON'T JUST STAND THERE!
YES, SIR?
MY FIANCÉE FAINTED. TAKE HER TO HER ROOM. BE GENTLE!
WAAAGH
AGH
AGH
RIGHT AWAY, SIR.
EVERYONE, PLEASE DON'T BE ALARMED!! THIS IS JUST A SMALL MISUNDER-STANDING.
ENJOY THE PARTY WHILE WE EXCUSE OUR-SELVES FOR A BIT!!
THERE SEEMS TO BE A SLIGHT PROBLEM ON THE OTHER SIDE.
WE'LL GO ON WITH OUR BINGO GAME. THE NEXT NUMBER IS...
WHAT WAS THAT ALL ABOUT ?
DAISY, WAS YOUR LITTLE PRINCESS INVOLVED WITH MORIZONO ?
OR WAS THAT...?
HUH?
HE'S GONE... WHEN DID HE...?

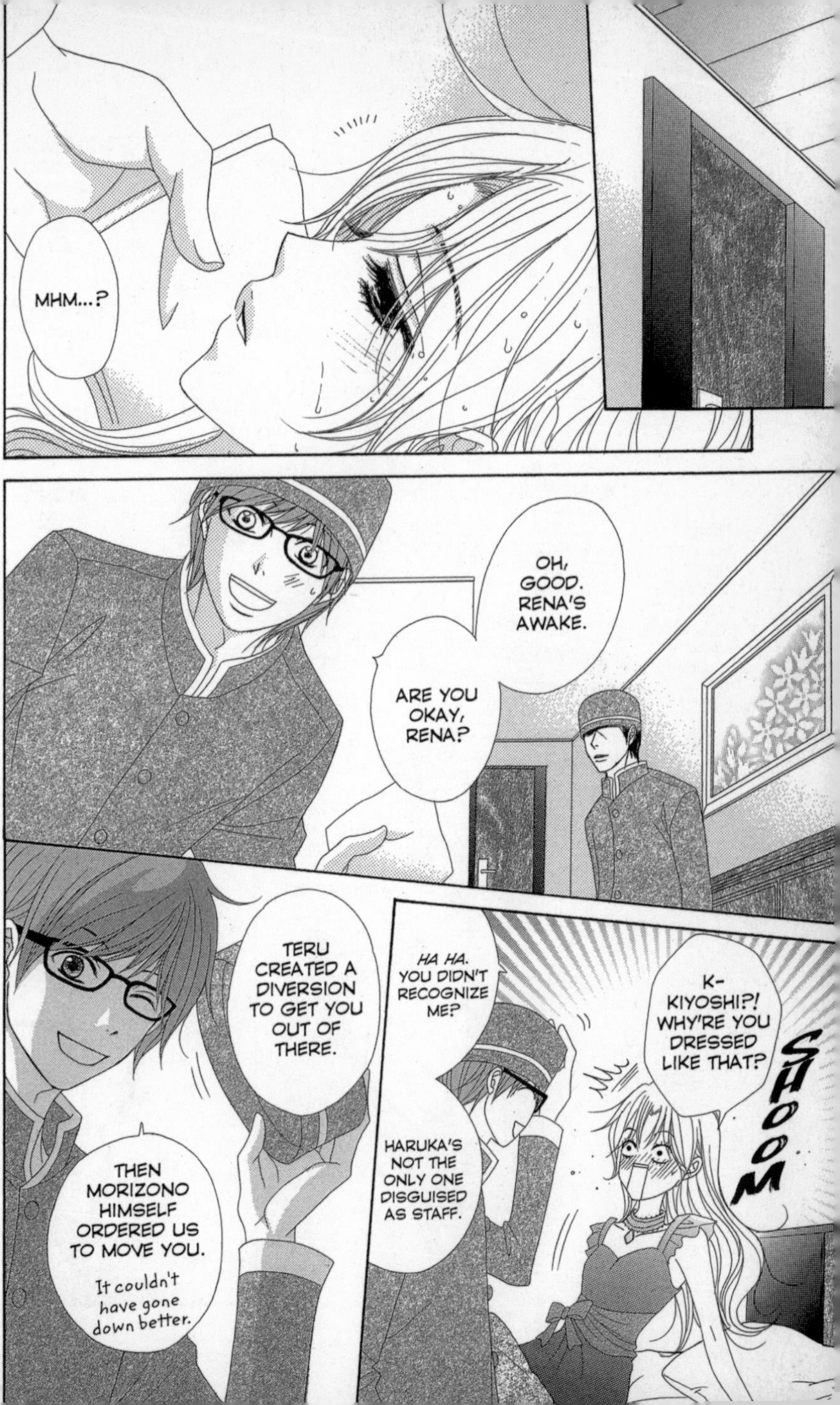
MHM...?
OH, GOOD. RENA'S AWAKE.
ARE YOU OKAY, RENA?
K-KIYOSHI?! WHY'RE YOU DRESSED LIKE THAT?
SHOOM
HA HA. YOU DIDN'T RECOGNIZE ME?
HARUKA'S NOT THE ONLY ONE DISGUISED AS STAFF.
TERU CREATED A DIVERSION TO GET YOU OUT OF THERE.
THEN MORIZONO HIMSELF ORDERED US TO MOVE YOU.
It couldn't have gone down better.

THANKS TO YOU, MY COMPANY IS SAFE. WE TOOK CARE OF THE VIRUS.

BUT YOU STUCK IT OUT, AND I COULDN'T BE PROUDER OF YOU.

I'M SORRY YOU HAD SUCH A ROUGH TIME.

TERU AND HER FRIENDS TOLD ME EVERY-THING.

FATHER...!

THAT WAS SMART OF YOU.

TERU FIGURED THERE WAS A HIDDEN MESSAGE.

KEEP IT DOWN, YOU TWO.

MORIZO-NO'S MEN COULD BE AROUND.

THERE'S NO SIGN OF THEM NOW...

THE OTHERS MUST BE KEEPING THEM BUSY.

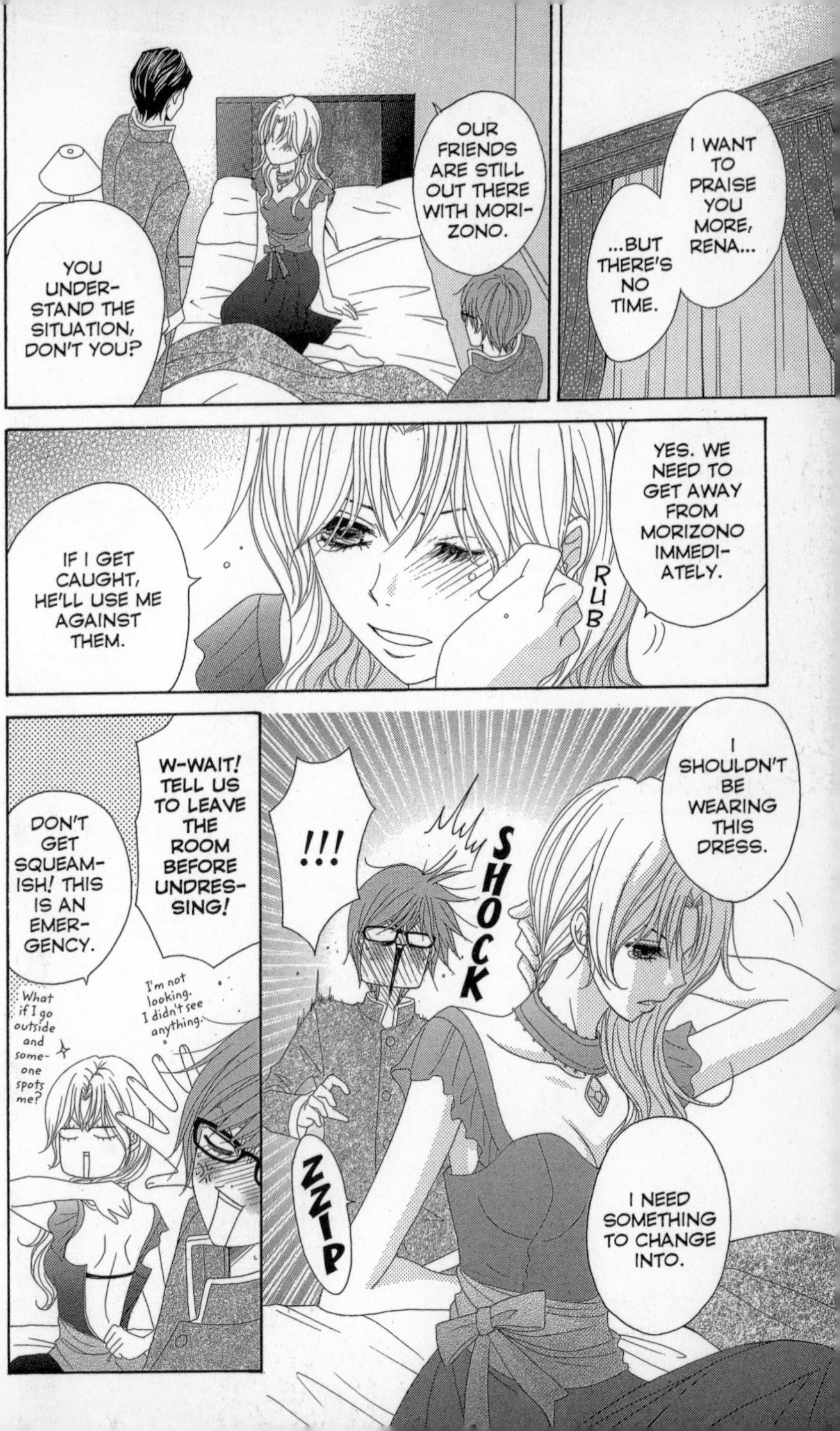
I WANT TO PRAISE YOU MORE, RENA...
...BUT THERE'S NO TIME.
OUR FRIENDS ARE STILL OUT THERE WITH MORIZONO.
YOU UNDERSTAND THE SITUATION, DON'T YOU?
YES. WE NEED TO GET AWAY FROM MORIZONO IMMEDIATELY.
RUB
IF I GET CAUGHT, HE'LL USE ME AGAINST THEM.
I SHOULDN'T BE WEARING THIS DRESS.
SHOCK
!!!
I NEED SOMETHING TO CHANGE INTO.
ZZIP
W-WAIT! TELL US TO LEAVE THE ROOM BEFORE UNDRESSING!
DON'T GET SQUEAMISH! THIS IS AN EMERGENCY.
I'm not looking. I didn't see anything.
What if I go outside and someone spots me?

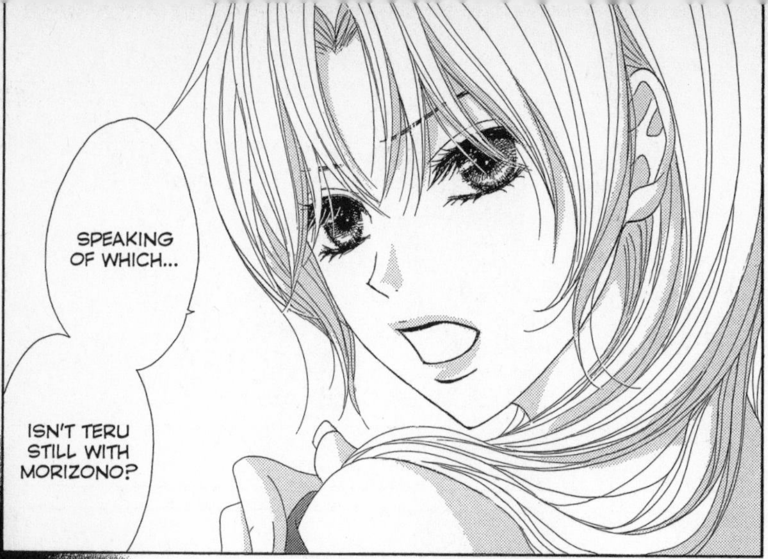
SPEAKING OF WHICH...
ISN'T TERU STILL WITH MORIZONO?
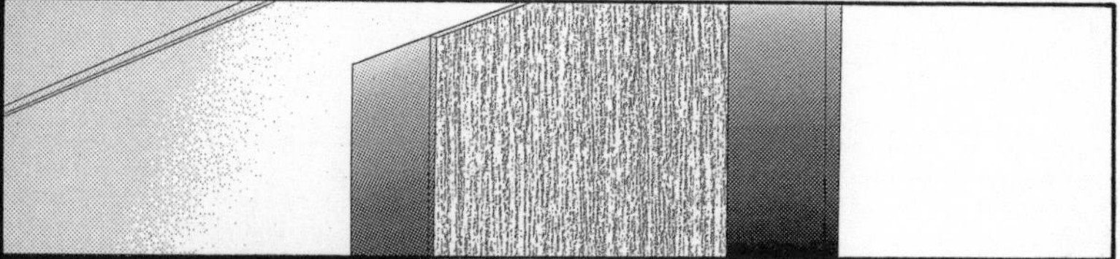
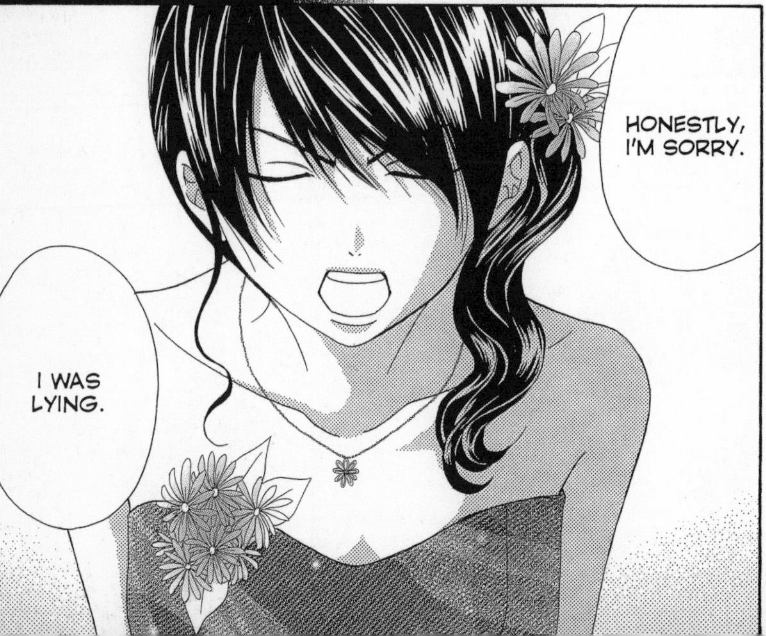
HONESTLY, I'M SORRY.
I WAS LYING.

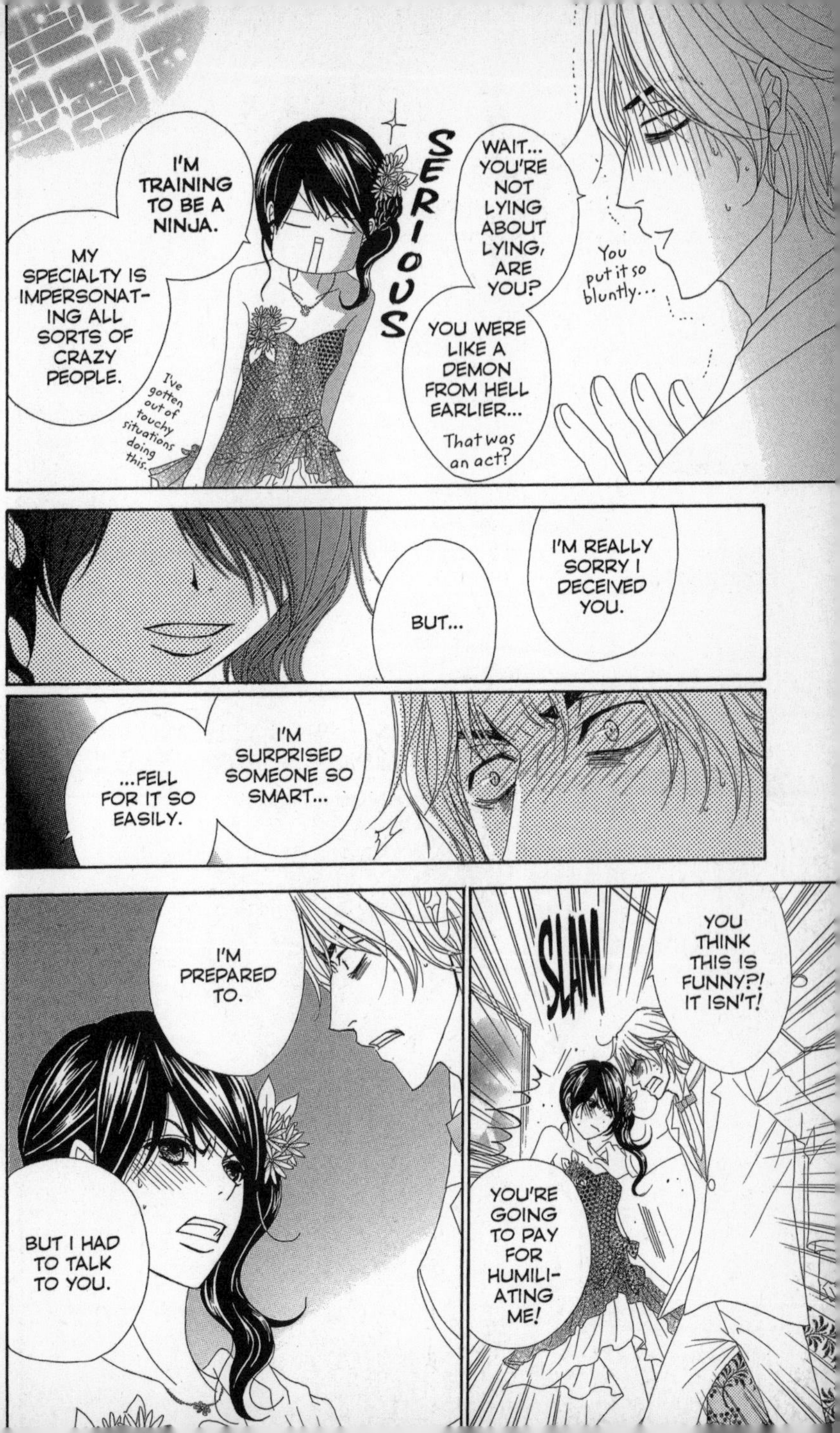
WAIT... YOU'RE NOT LYING ABOUT LYING, ARE YOU?
You put it so bluntly...
YOU WERE LIKE A DEMON FROM HELL EARLIER...
That was an act?
SERIOUS
I'M TRAINING TO BE A NINJA.
MY SPECIALTY IS IMPERSONATING ALL SORTS OF CRAZY PEOPLE.
I've gotten out of touchy situations doing this.
I'M REALLY SORRY I DECEIVED YOU.
BUT...
I'M SURPRISED SOMEONE SO SMART...
...FELL FOR IT SO EASILY.
YOU THINK THIS IS FUNNY?! IT ISN'T!
SLAM
YOU'RE GOING TO PAY FOR HUMILIATING ME!
I'M PREPARED TO.
BUT I HAD TO TALK TO YOU.

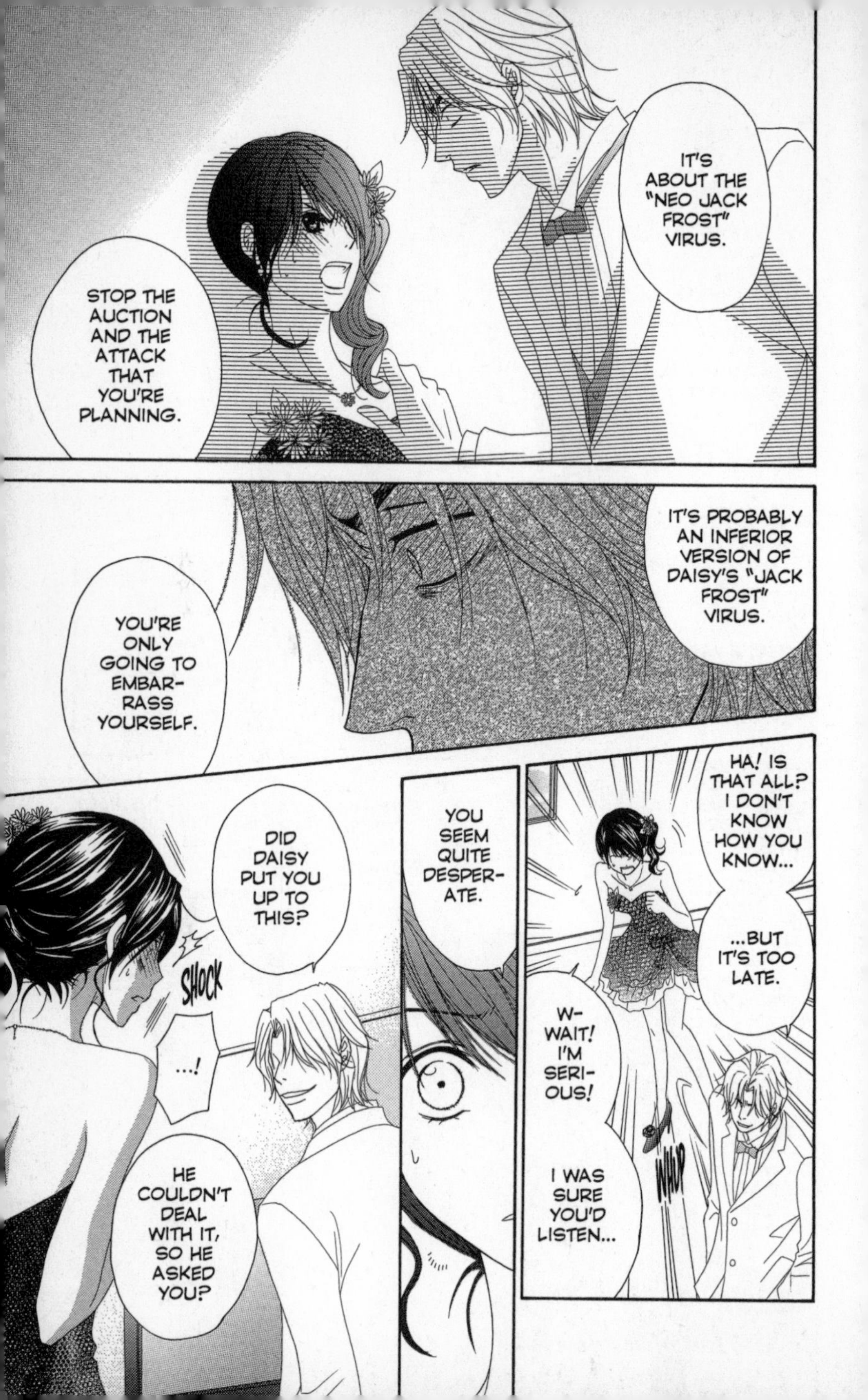
IT'S ABOUT THE "NEO JACK FROST" VIRUS.
STOP THE AUCTION AND THE ATTACK THAT YOU'RE PLANNING.
IT'S PROBABLY AN INFERIOR VERSION OF DAISY'S "JACK FROST" VIRUS.
YOU'RE ONLY GOING TO EMBARRASS YOURSELF.
HA! IS THAT ALL? I DON'T KNOW HOW YOU KNOW...
...BUT IT'S TOO LATE.
W-WAIT! I'M SERIOUS!
WHUP
I WAS SURE YOU'D LISTEN...
YOU SEEM QUITE DESPERATE.
DID DAISY PUT YOU UP TO THIS?
SHOCK
...!
HE COULDN'T DEAL WITH IT, SO HE ASKED YOU?

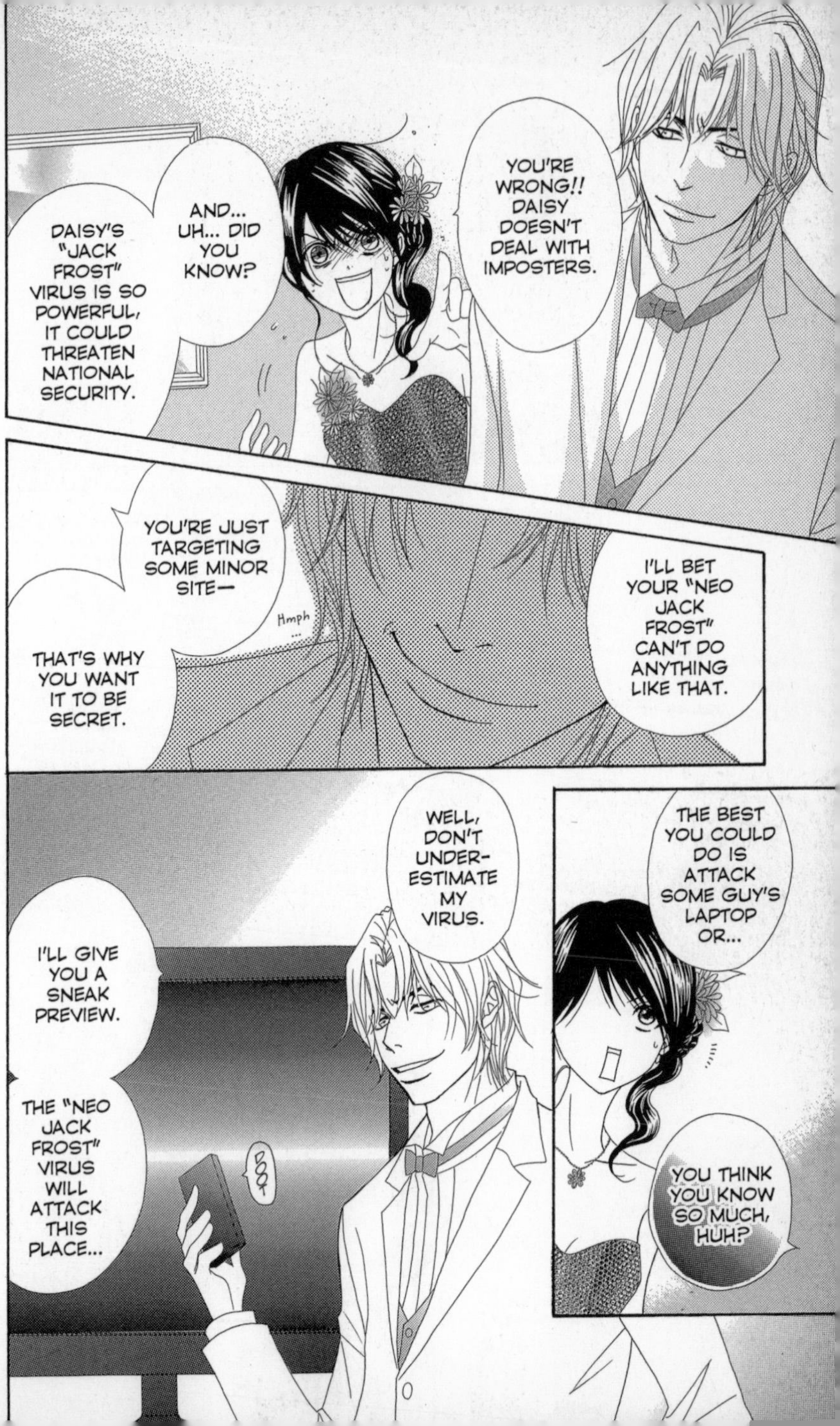
YOU'RE WRONG!! DAISY DOESN'T DEAL WITH IMPOSTERS.
AND... UH... DID YOU KNOW?
DAISY'S "JACK FROST" VIRUS IS SO POWERFUL, IT COULD THREATEN NATIONAL SECURITY.
I'LL BET YOUR "NEO JACK FROST" CAN'T DO ANYTHING LIKE THAT.
Hmph...
YOU'RE JUST TARGETING SOME MINOR SITE—
THAT'S WHY YOU WANT IT TO BE SECRET.
THE BEST YOU COULD DO IS ATTACK SOME GUY'S LAPTOP OR...
YOU THINK YOU KNOW SO MUCH, HUH?
WELL, DON'T UNDER-ESTIMATE MY VIRUS.
I'LL GIVE YOU A SNEAK PREVIEW.
THE "NEO JACK FROST" VIRUS WILL ATTACK THIS PLACE...
DOOT

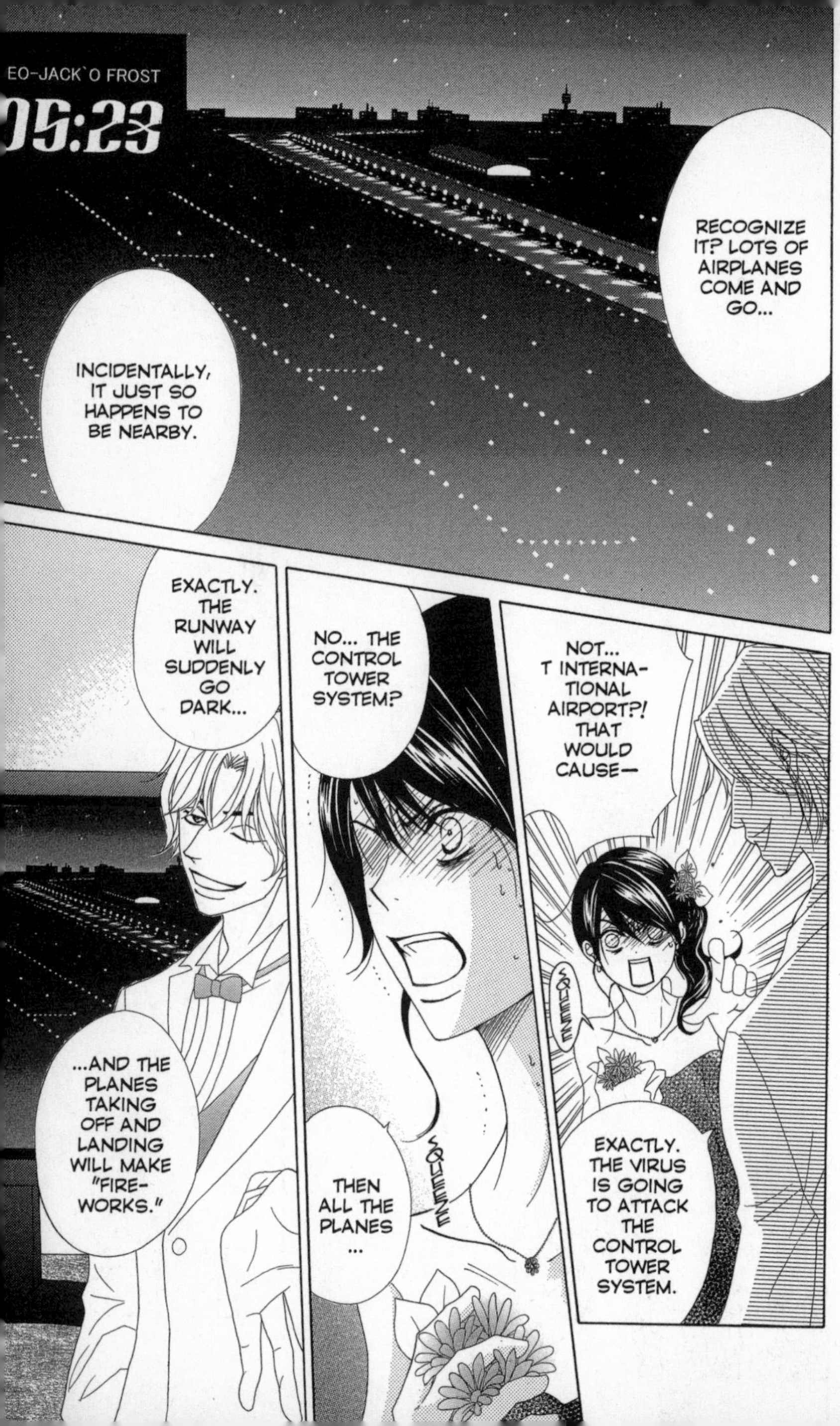
EO-JACK`O FROST
05:23
RECOGNIZE IT? LOTS OF AIRPLANES COME AND GO...
INCIDENTALLY, IT JUST SO HAPPENS TO BE NEARBY.
NOT... T INTERNA-TIONAL AIRPORT?! THAT WOULD CAUSE—
SQUEEZE
EXACTLY. THE VIRUS IS GOING TO ATTACK THE CONTROL TOWER SYSTEM.
NO... THE CONTROL TOWER SYSTEM?
SQUEEZE
THEN ALL THE PLANES ...
EXACTLY. THE RUNWAY WILL SUDDENLY GO DARK...
...AND THE PLANES TAKING OFF AND LANDING WILL MAKE "FIRE-WORKS."

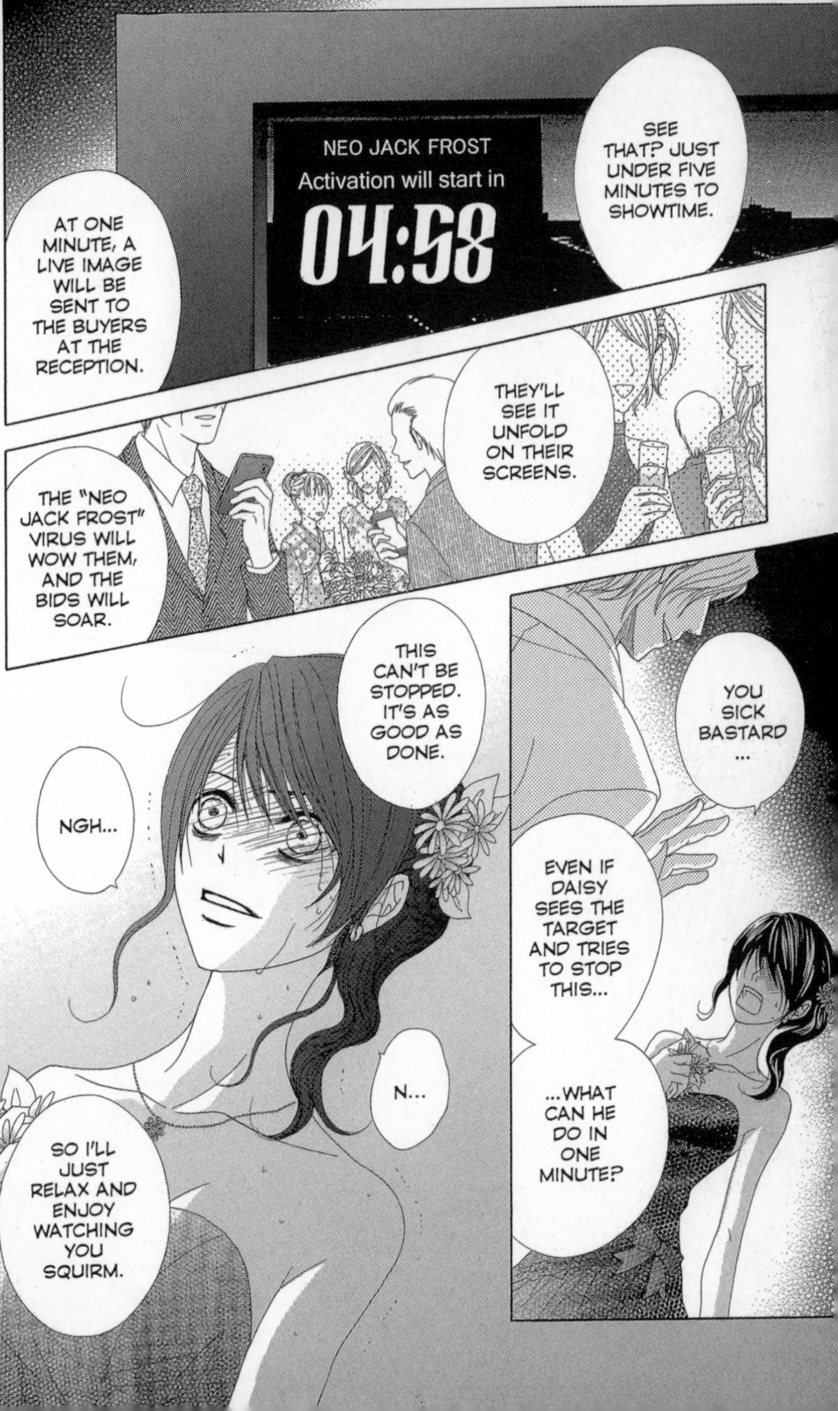
SEE THAT? JUST UNDER FIVE MINUTES TO SHOWTIME.
NEO JACK FROST
Activation will start in
04:58
AT ONE MINUTE, A LIVE IMAGE WILL BE SENT TO THE BUYERS AT THE RECEPTION.
THEY'LL SEE IT UNFOLD ON THEIR SCREENS.
THE "NEO JACK FROST" VIRUS WILL WOW THEM, AND THE BIDS WILL SOAR.
YOU SICK BASTARD ...
EVEN IF DAISY SEES THE TARGET AND TRIES TO STOP THIS...
...WHAT CAN HE DO IN ONE MINUTE?
THIS CAN'T BE STOPPED. IT'S AS GOOD AS DONE.
NGH...
N...
SO I'LL JUST RELAX AND ENJOY WATCHING YOU SQUIRM.

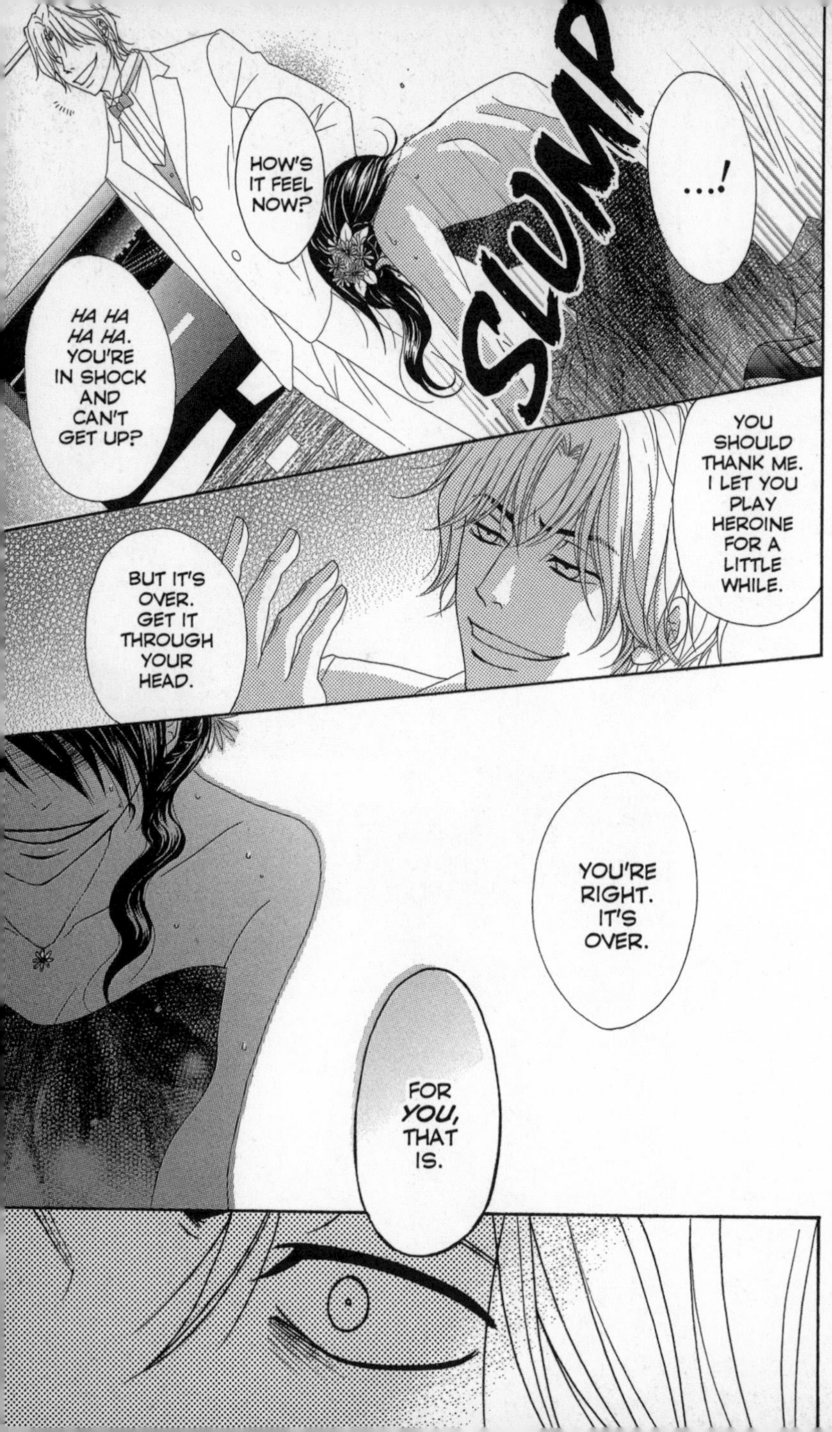
...!
SLUMP
HOW'S IT FEEL NOW?
HA HA HA HA. YOU'RE IN SHOCK AND CAN'T GET UP?
YOU SHOULD THANK ME. I LET YOU PLAY HEROINE FOR A LITTLE WHILE.
BUT IT'S OVER. GET IT THROUGH YOUR HEAD.
YOU'RE RIGHT. IT'S OVER.
FOR *YOU*, THAT IS.

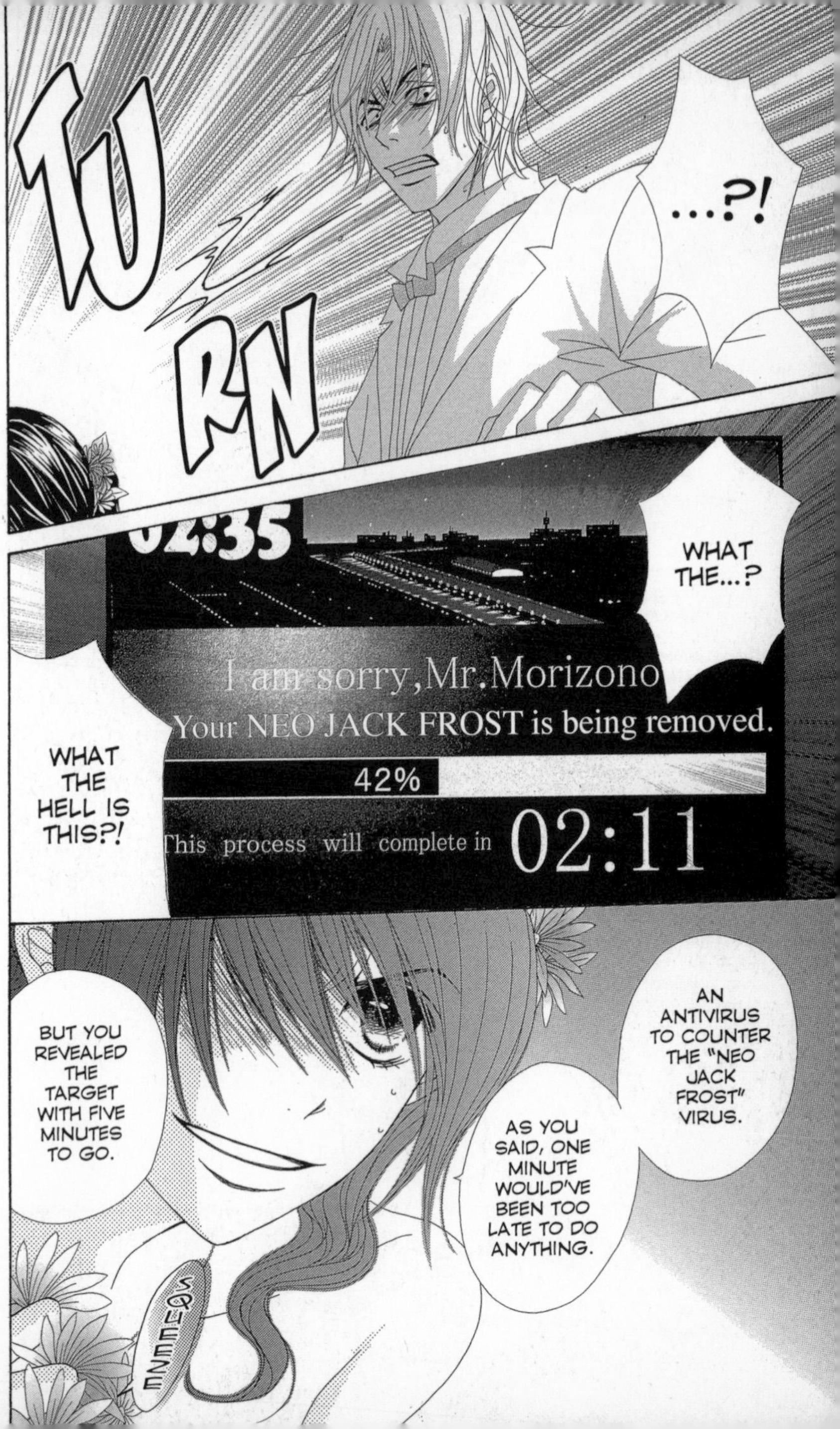
...?!
TURN
WHAT THE...?
02:35
I am sorry,Mr.Morizono
Your NEO JACK FROST is being removed.
42%
This process will complete in 02:11
WHAT THE HELL IS THIS?!
AN ANTIVIRUS TO COUNTER THE "NEO JACK FROST" VIRUS.
AS YOU SAID, ONE MINUTE WOULD'VE BEEN TOO LATE TO DO ANYTHING.
BUT YOU REVEALED THE TARGET WITH FIVE MINUTES TO GO.
SQUEEEZE

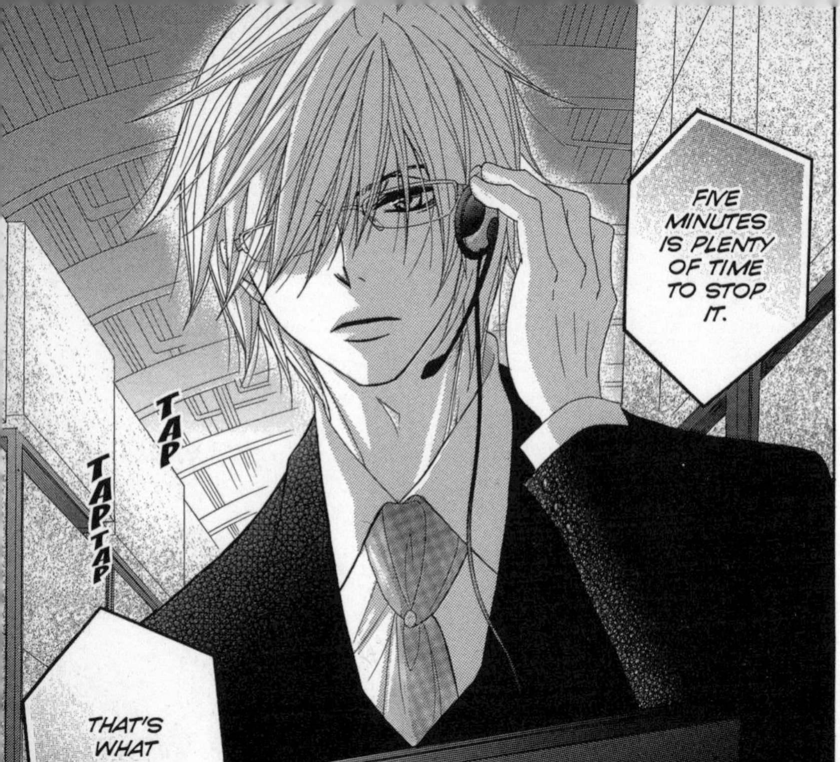
FIVE MINUTES IS PLENTY OF TIME TO STOP IT.
TAP
TAPTAP
THAT'S WHAT DAISY SAID.
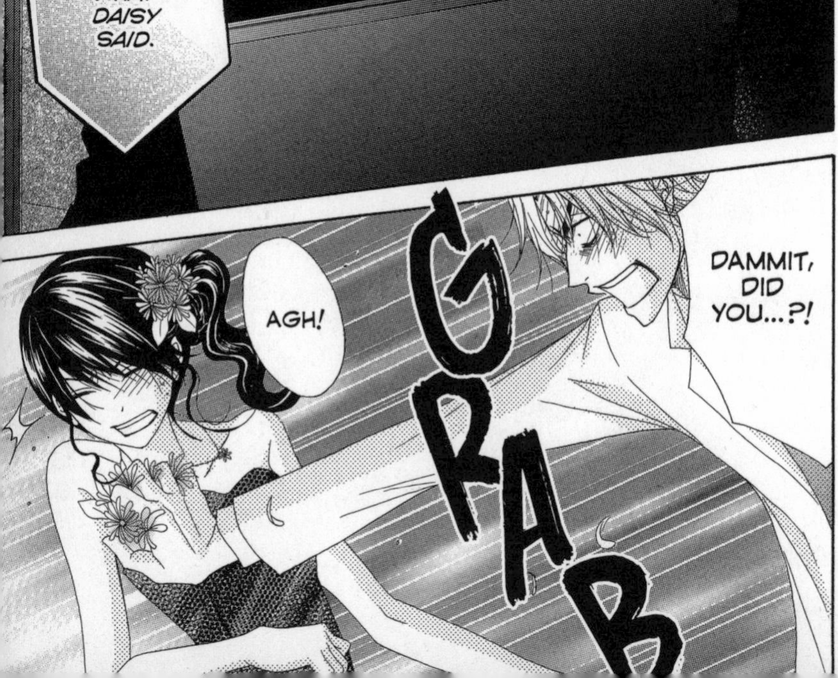
DAMMIT, DID YOU...?!
GRAB
AGH!

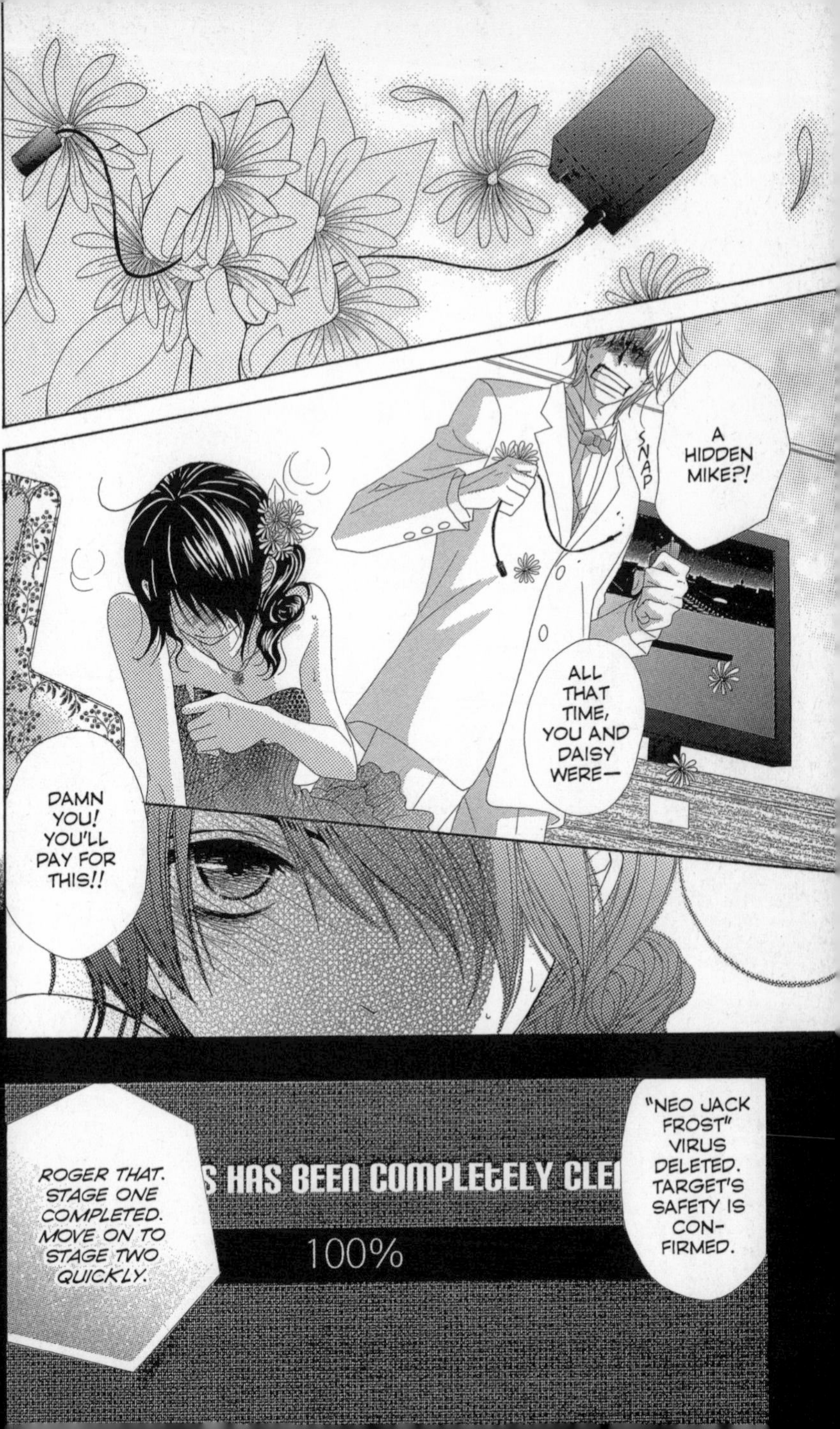
SNAP
A HIDDEN MIKE?!
ALL THAT TIME, YOU AND DAISY WERE—
DAMN YOU! YOU'LL PAY FOR THIS!!
"NEO JACK FROST" VIRUS DELETED. TARGET'S SAFETY IS CON-FIRMED.
S HAS BEEN COMPLETELY CLE
100%
ROGER THAT. STAGE ONE COMPLETED. MOVE ON TO STAGE TWO QUICKLY.

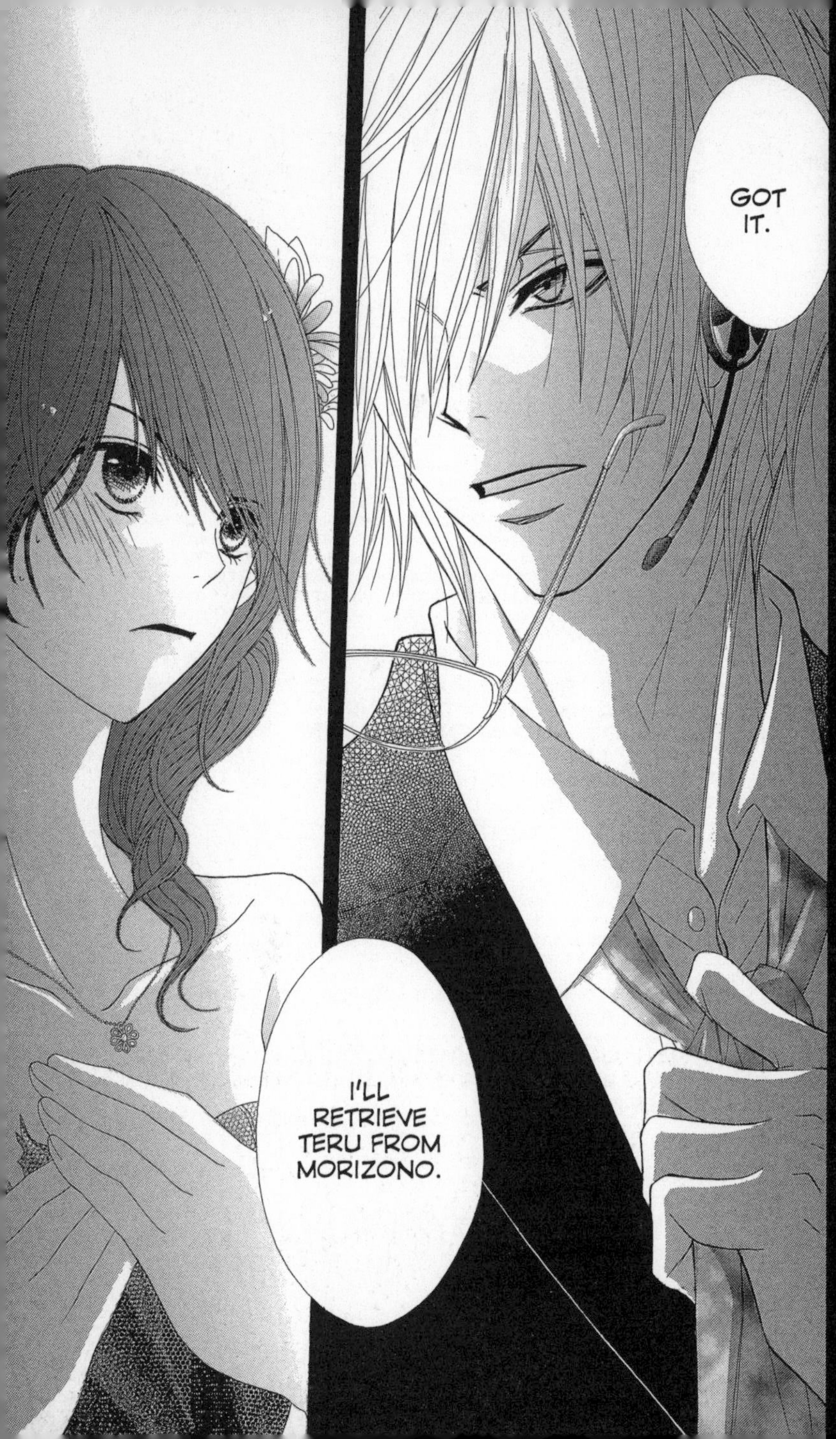
GOT IT.
I'LL RETRIEVE TERU FROM MORIZONO.

DENGEKI DAISY
QUESTION CORNER

(RELOCATED)→ **BALDLY ASK!!!** ①

ONCE AGAIN, THERE WASN'T ENOUGH SPACE, SO HERE GOES WITH A "RELOCATED" EDITION. ALSO, MY MOM AND YOUNGER SISTER (A MOTHER OF TWO) SAID, "HANDWRITING LOOKS LIKE YOU'RE TRYING HARDER, EVEN IF YOUR PENMANSHIP IS BAD," SO I'VE WRITTEN PART OF THIS BY HAND.

---

**IN VOLUME 1, WHEN THEY WERE LOOKING FOR AN APARTMENT FOR TERU, KUROSAKI SAID, "I'LL PAY THE DIFFERENCE." DOES KUROSAKI HAVE A LOT OF SAVINGS?**

(Y.O, MIYAGI PREFECTURE)

A. MANY PEOPLE HAVE BEEN WONDERING ABOUT KUROSAKI'S EARNINGS FROM WAY BACK. IN ADDITION TO HIS DUTIES AS A SCHOOL CUSTODIAN, HE OFTEN STAYS UP LATE WORKING ON THE DATA SYSTEM. I THINK HE HAS A MODEST AMOUNT OF INCOME, EVEN IF IT DOESN'T MAKE HIM RICH. IN ADDITION, THE RENT FOR HIS APARTMENT IS CHEAP, THANKS TO ANDY'S CONNECTIONS. PLUS, HE GOT HIS BELOVED JEEP CHEROKEE USED—FOR A SONG, IN FACT, SINCE BOSS WAS THE PREVIOUS OWNER. DURING THE TIME KUROSAKI WORKED IN THE PRIVATE SECTOR, HE SAVED UP A BIT, THANKS TO THE PERSISTENT ADMONITIONS OF THE STRICT ELDERS AROUND HIM. HIS MAIN COMPUTER IS ONE HE BUILT HIMSELF, AND HE ALWAYS WEARS THE SAME CLOTHES. HE LIVES A RATHER FRUGAL LIFE WITHOUT EXCESS. ABOUT THE ONLY THING THAT'S EXTREME ABOUT HIM IS HIS BLOND HAIR.

---

**IN VOLUME 9 WHERE TERU AND KUROSAKI ARE REUNITED, WAS IT ROUGHLY IN THE EVENING WHEN TERU AND THE OTHERS WERE TALKING ON THE ROOF, AND WHEN KIYOSHI AND RENA WERE LEAVING SCHOOL? LATER, IT IS "EARLY MORNING" WHEN TERU AND KUROSAKI ARE REUNITED. I DON'T UNDERSTAND THE TIMELINE. PLEASE FILL ME IN.**

(OLDER GUY WEARING A WIG, NAGANO PREFECTURE)

A. IT WAS DIFFICULT TO UNDERSTAND, WASN'T IT? I'M SORRY.
KIYOSHI HAVING TEA WITH RENA, TERU ON THE PHONE WITH AKIRA, AND KUROSAKI MEETING/LEAVING BOSS ALL HAPPENED AT ABOUT THE SAME TIME—IN THE EVENING. AFTER THAT, TERU AND THE OTHERS SPENT THE REST OF THAT NIGHT HEADING OVER TO THE DESIGNATED PLACE ON THE BEACH WHERE THEY WERE GOING TO LURE KUROSAKI. KUROSAKI READ TERU'S MESSAGE, THEN SPENT THAT ENTIRE NIGHT MOVING TO THE SPECIFIED LOCATION ON THE BEACH. AND THAT'S WHERE THEY MET.
SO, KUROSAKI AND TERU'S REUNION TOOK PLACE AT A FAR-AWAY LOCATION THAT TOOK THE BOTH OF THEM HALF A DAY TO GET THERE.

---

**WHAT'S THE NAME OF TERU'S FRIEND—NOT RENA, HARUKA, OR HELMET—THE ONE WHO PULLS HER BANGS UP AND TIES HER HAIR IN A SINGLE PONYTAIL?**

(GOVEJOULE ITO AND OTHERS, AICHI PREFECTURE)

A. THIS IS ANOTHER QUESTION I'VE BEEN ASKED A LOT SINCE WAY BACK. SIMPLY PUT, I NEVER HAD THE CHANCE TO HAVE HER NAME SPOKEN. I'M REALLY SORRY.

← MEI
(MEI TSUKAMOTO)
AMONG THE SILLY GROUP OF GIRLFRIENDS, SHE HAS BIG BOOBS. (BUT RENA'S ARE BIGGER.) SHE'S VERY INTO TRENDS, AND IS A CLOSET YAOI FAN.

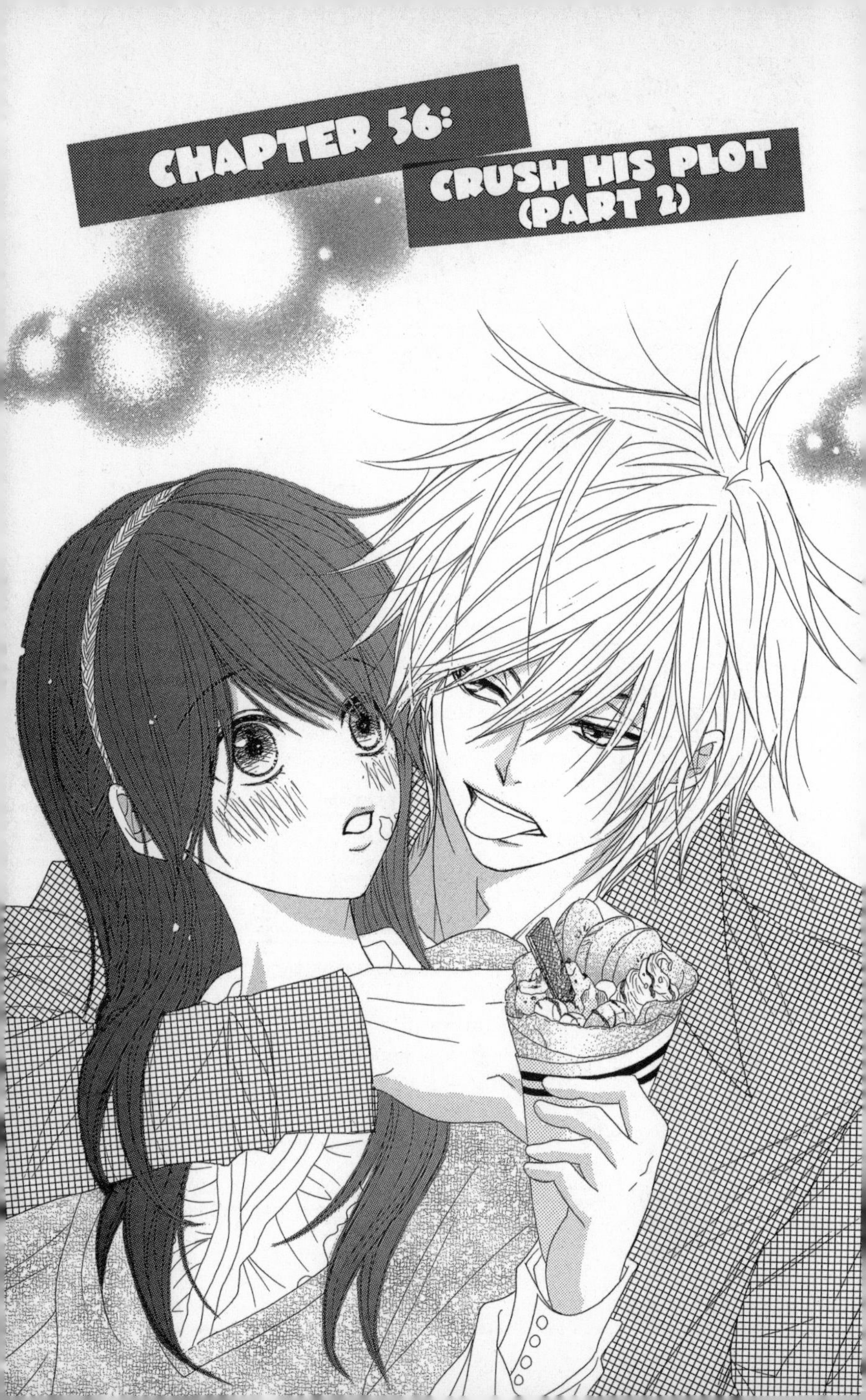
CHAPTER 56:
CRUSH HIS PLOT
(PART 2)

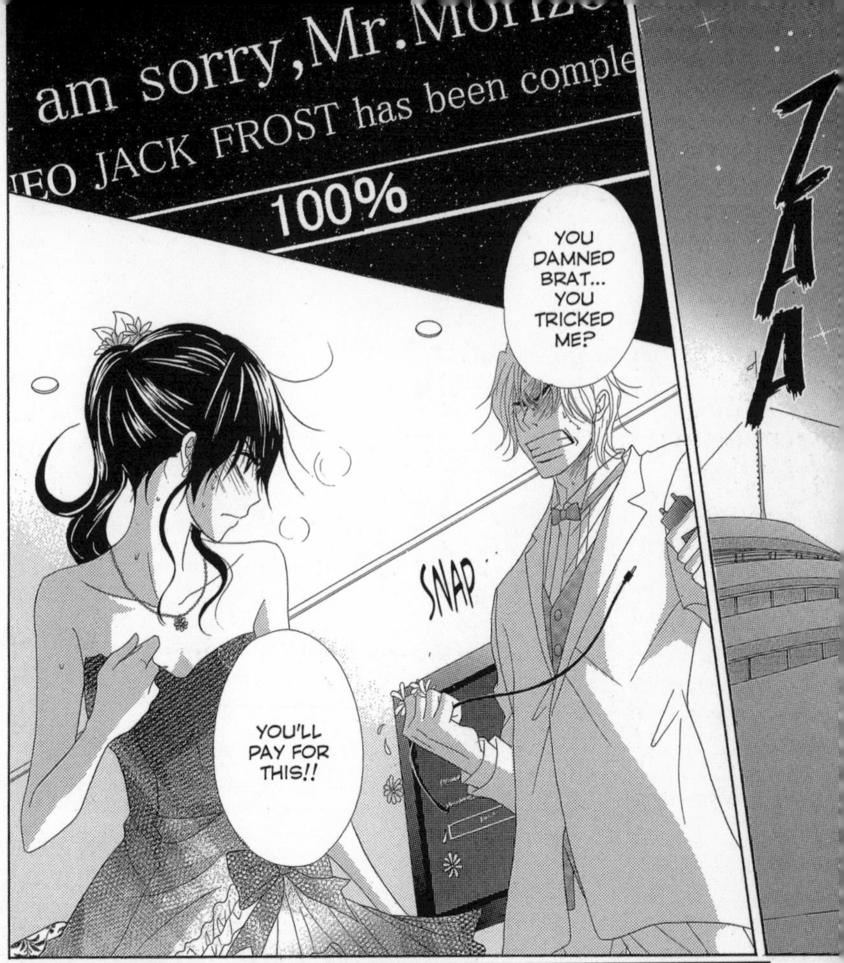
am sorry, Mr.
JACK FROST has been
100%
ZAA
YOU DAMNED BRAT... YOU TRICKED ME?
SNAP
YOU'LL PAY FOR THIS!!

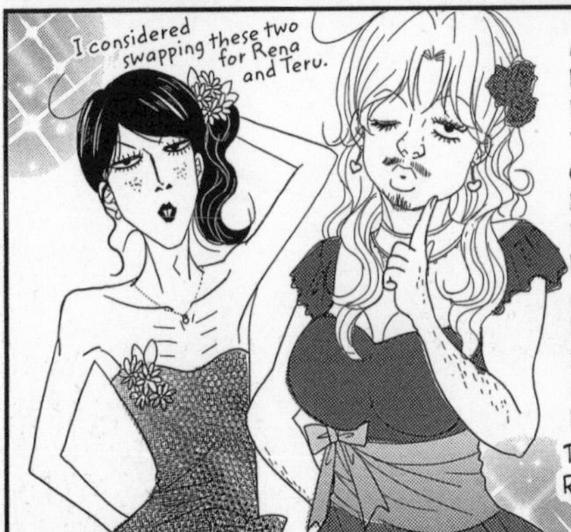
I considered swapping these two for Rena and Teru.

MY INITIAL CONCEPT FOR THE PARTY-CRASHING VOLUME WAS TO HAVE ALL OF THE SILLY MEMBERS OF THE CLASS STORM THE PARTY AND CREATE CHAOS.
BUT THAT WOULD HAVE BEEN QUITE IMPOSSIBLE GIVEN THE NUMBER OF PAGES I HAD TO WORK WITH AND THE NUMBER OF PEOPLE WHO WOULD HAVE TO APPEAR, SO I HAD THEM STAY BACK. (TRUTH IS, IF I MADE THEM ALL APPEAR, I'D BE OVERWORKED AND DEAD.)
THEY HAVEN'T APPEARED MUCH RECENTLY, WHICH MAKES ME A BIT SAD.

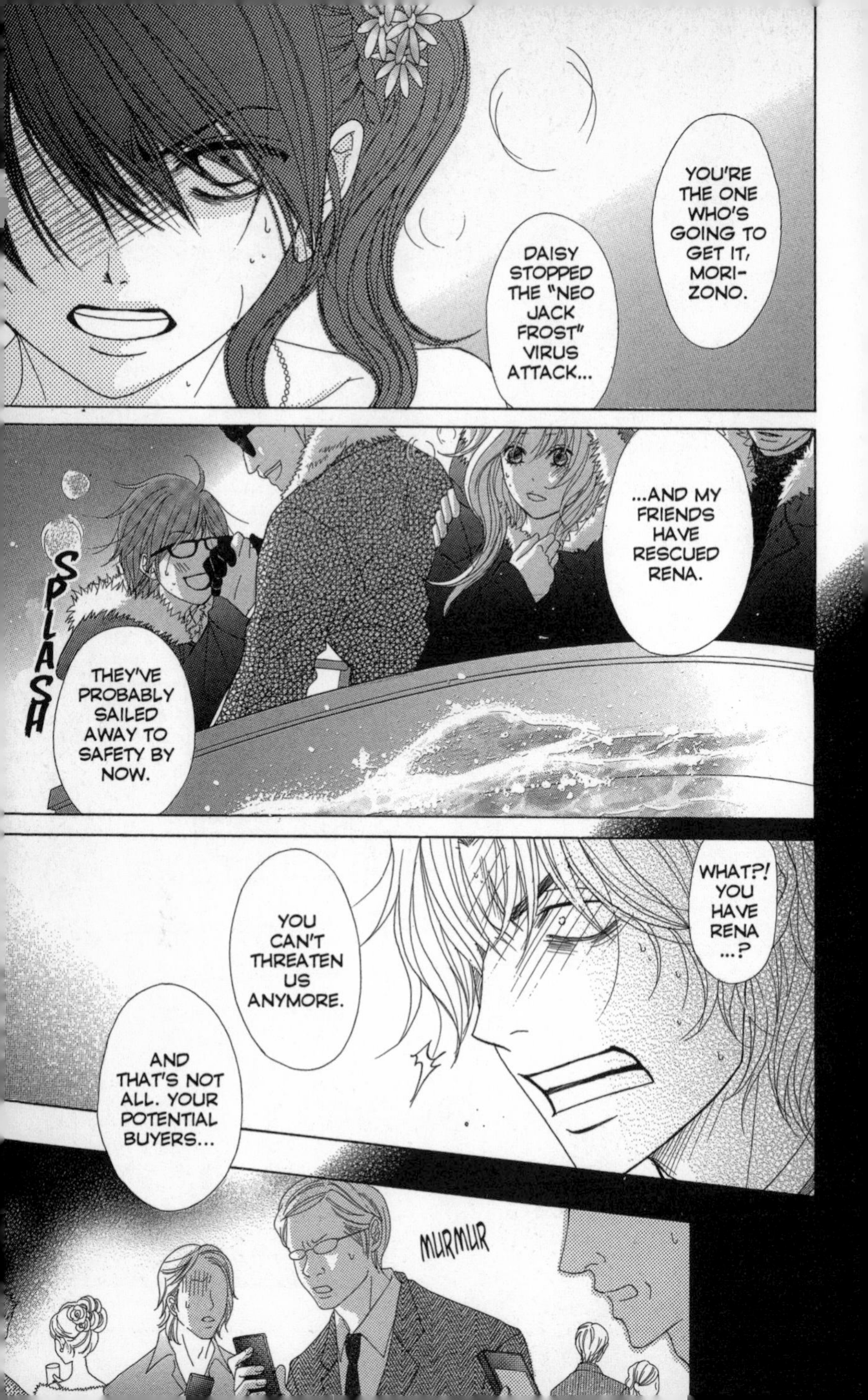
YOU'RE THE ONE WHO'S GOING TO GET IT, MORI-ZONO.
DAISY STOPPED THE "NEO JACK FROST" VIRUS ATTACK...
...AND MY FRIENDS HAVE RESCUED RENA.
SPLASH
THEY'VE PROBABLY SAILED AWAY TO SAFETY BY NOW.
WHAT?! YOU HAVE RENA ...?
YOU CAN'T THREATEN US ANYMORE.
AND THAT'S NOT ALL. YOUR POTENTIAL BUYERS...
MURMUR

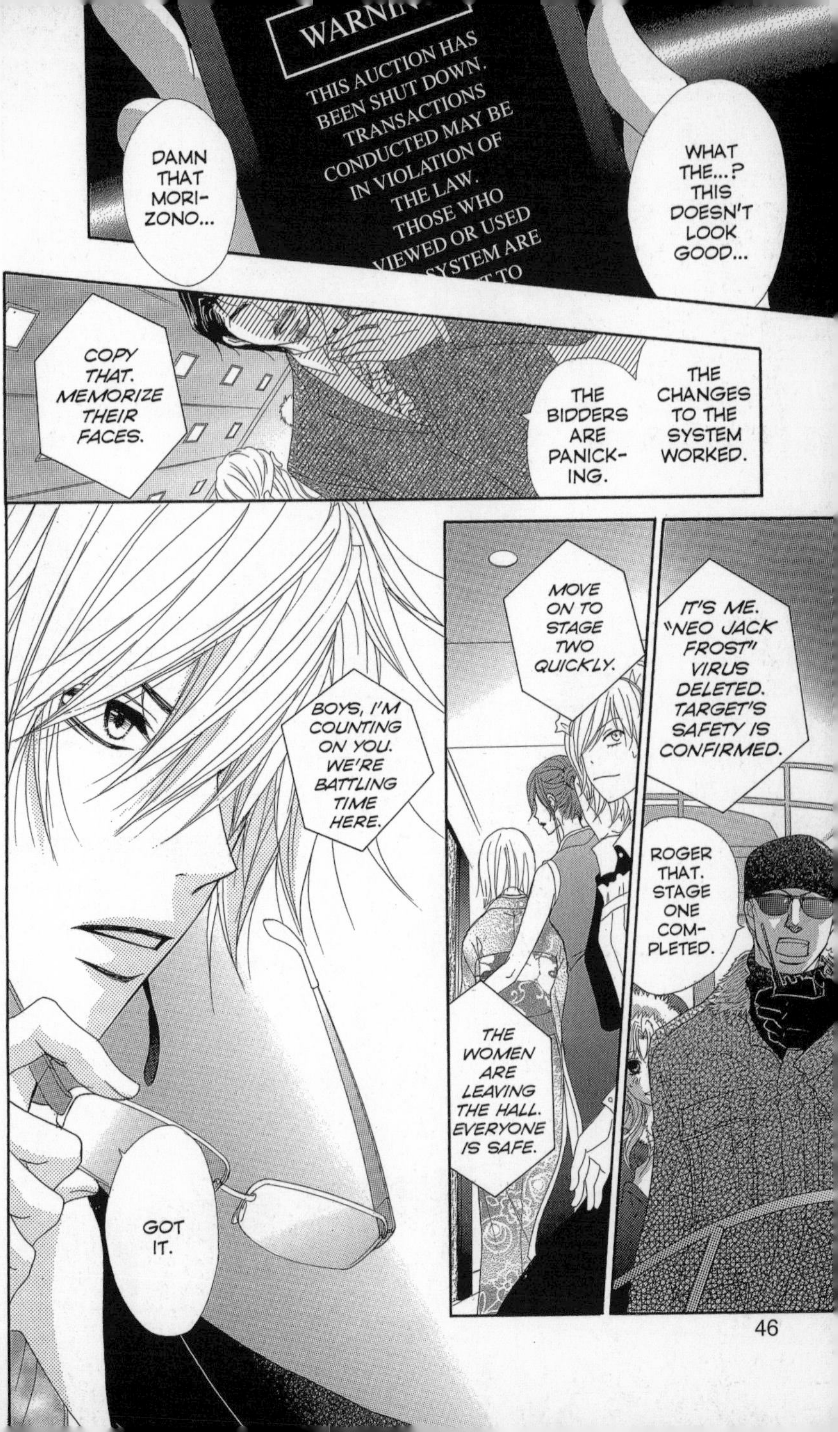
WARNING
THIS AUCTION HAS BEEN SHUT DOWN. TRANSACTIONS CONDUCTED MAY BE IN VIOLATION OF THE LAW. THOSE WHO VIEWED OR USED SYSTEM ARE
WHAT THE...? THIS DOESN'T LOOK GOOD...
DAMN THAT MORI-ZONO...
THE CHANGES TO THE SYSTEM WORKED.
THE BIDDERS ARE PANICK-ING.
COPY THAT. MEMORIZE THEIR FACES.
IT'S ME. "NEO JACK FROST" VIRUS DELETED. TARGET'S SAFETY IS CONFIRMED.
ROGER THAT. STAGE ONE COM-PLETED.
MOVE ON TO STAGE TWO QUICKLY.
THE WOMEN ARE LEAVING THE HALL. EVERYONE IS SAFE.
BOYS, I'M COUNTING ON YOU. WE'RE BATTLING TIME HERE.
GOT IT.

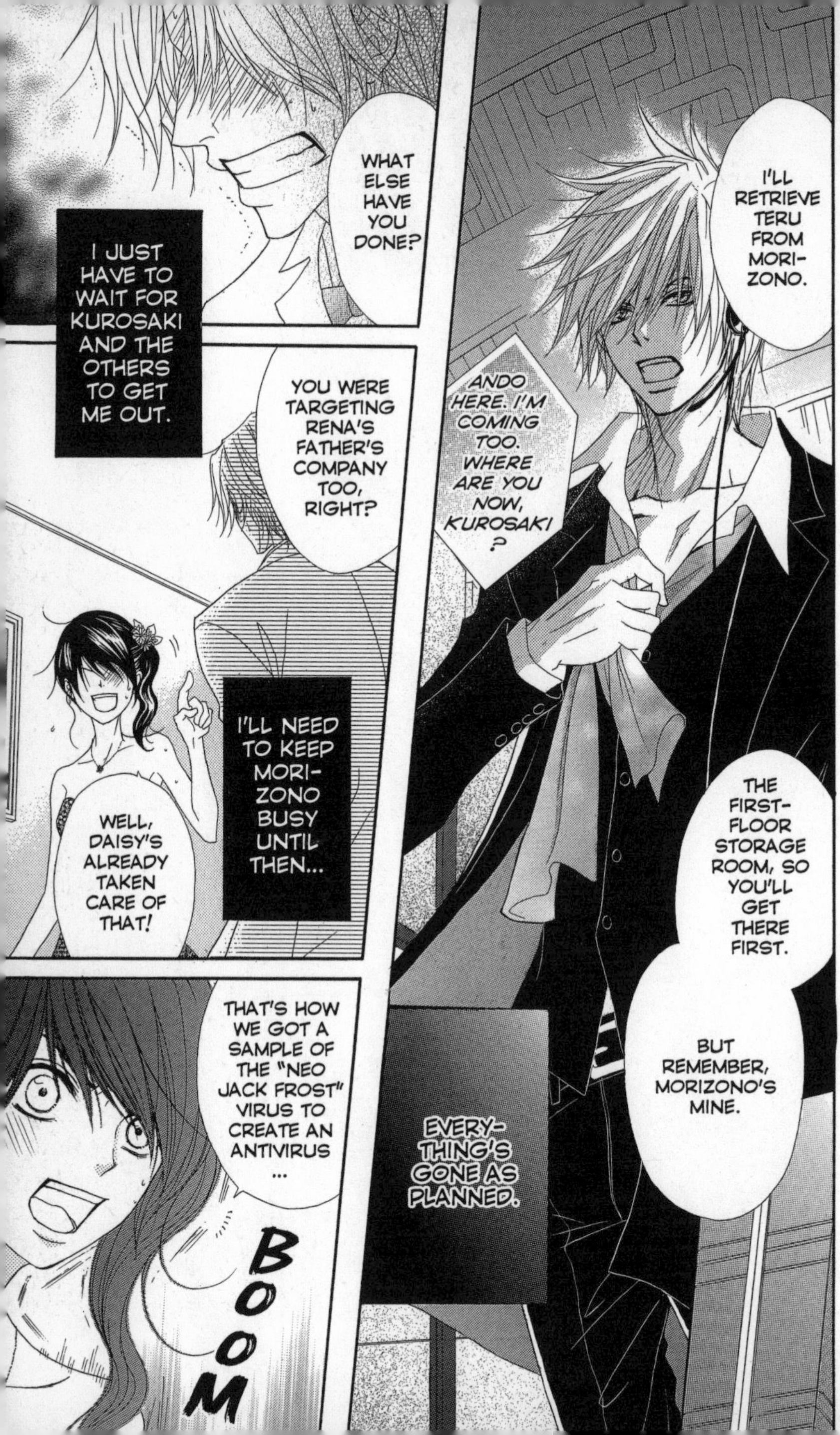
I'LL RETRIEVE TERU FROM MORI-ZONO.
ANDO HERE. I'M COMING TOO. WHERE ARE YOU NOW, KUROSAKI?
THE FIRST-FLOOR STORAGE ROOM, SO YOU'LL GET THERE FIRST.
BUT REMEMBER, MORIZONO'S MINE.
EVERY-THING'S GONE AS PLANNED.
WHAT ELSE HAVE YOU DONE?
I JUST HAVE TO WAIT FOR KUROSAKI AND THE OTHERS TO GET ME OUT.
YOU WERE TARGETING RENA'S FATHER'S COMPANY TOO, RIGHT?
I'LL NEED TO KEEP MORI-ZONO BUSY UNTIL THEN...
WELL, DAISY'S ALREADY TAKEN CARE OF THAT!
THAT'S HOW WE GOT A SAMPLE OF THE "NEO JACK FROST" VIRUS TO CREATE AN ANTIVIRUS ...
BOOOM

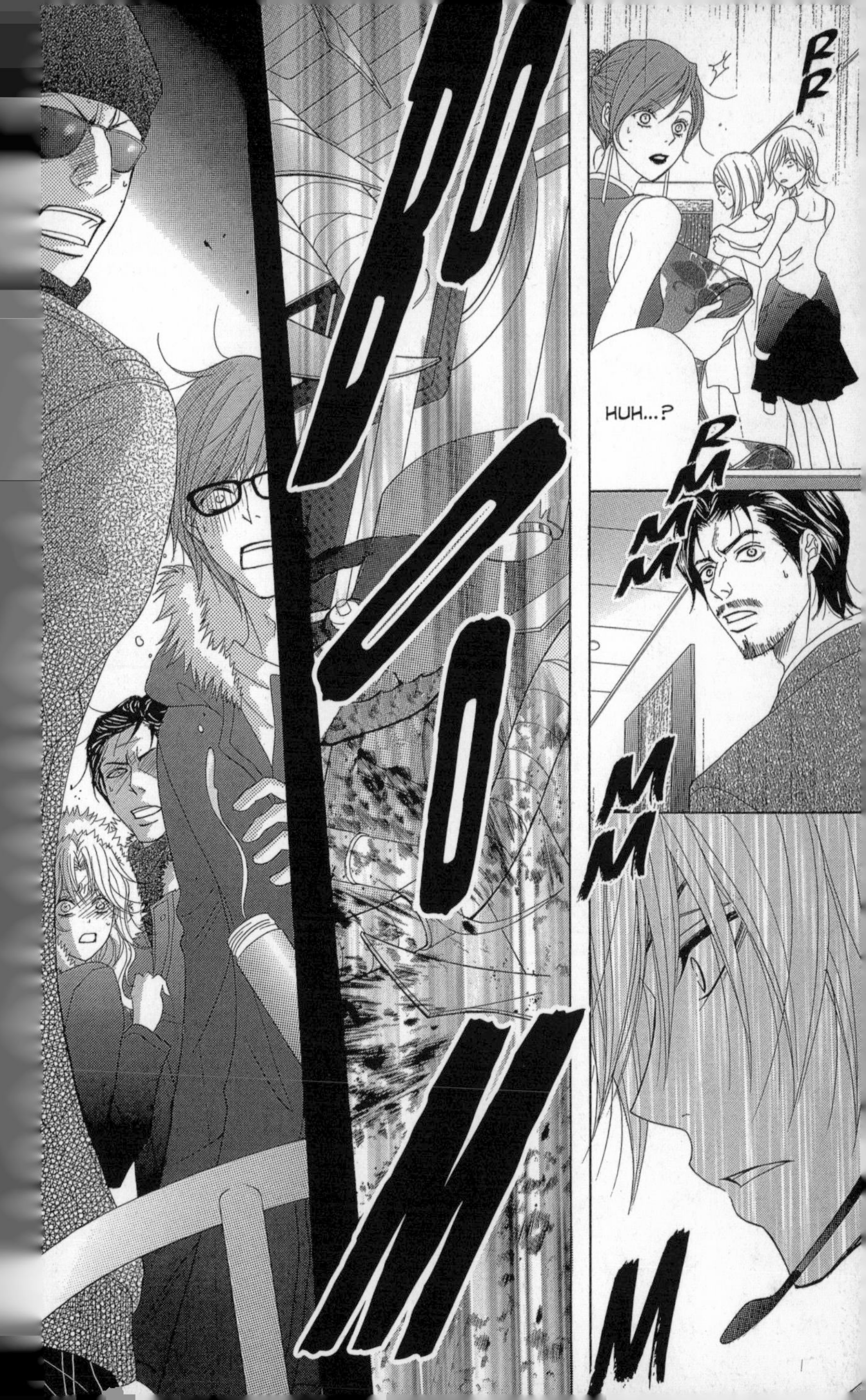
RR
HUH...?
RUMMMMMMM
DOOOM

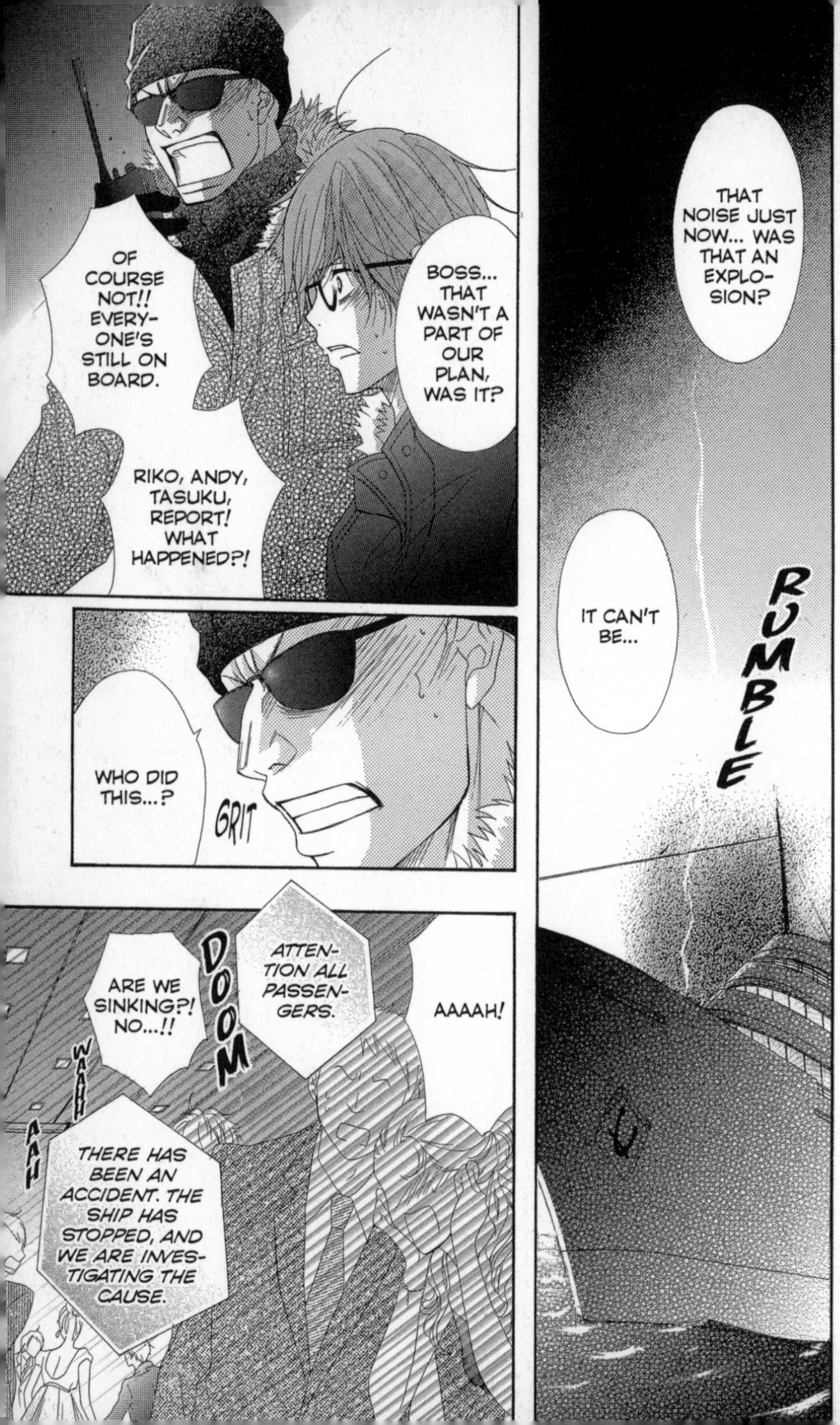
THAT NOISE JUST NOW... WAS THAT AN EXPLOSION?
IT CAN'T BE...
RUMBLE
BOSS... THAT WASN'T A PART OF OUR PLAN, WAS IT?
OF COURSE NOT!! EVERYONE'S STILL ON BOARD.
RIKO, ANDY, TASUKU, REPORT! WHAT HAPPENED?!
WHO DID THIS...?
GRIT
AAAAH!
ATTENTION ALL PASSENGERS.
DOOM
ARE WE SINKING?! NO...!!
WAAHH
AAH
THERE HAS BEEN AN ACCIDENT. THE SHIP HAS STOPPED, AND WE ARE INVESTIGATING THE CAUSE.

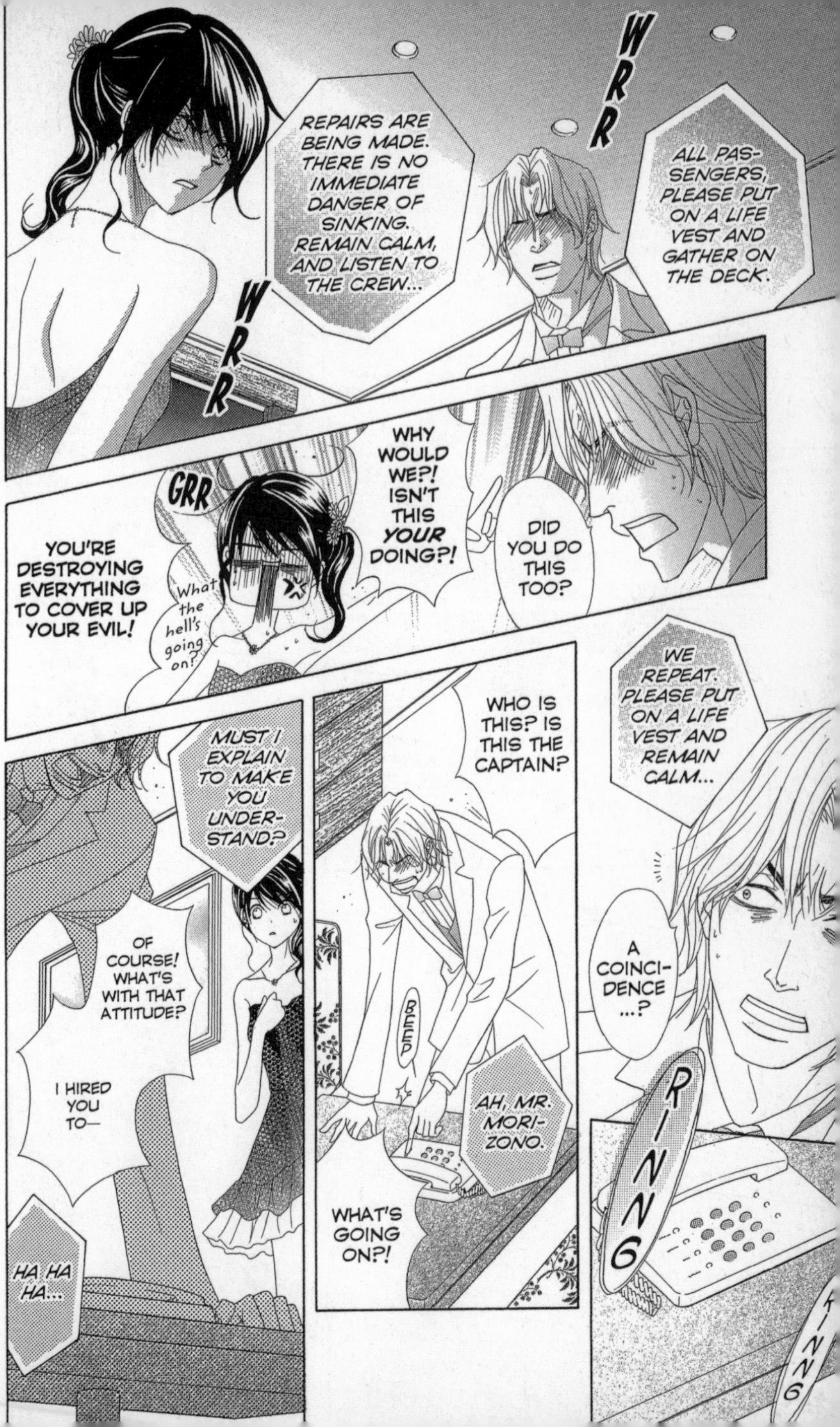
ALL PAS-SENGERS, PLEASE PUT ON A LIFE VEST AND GATHER ON THE DECK.
WRR
REPAIRS ARE BEING MADE. THERE IS NO IMMEDIATE DANGER OF SINKING. REMAIN CALM, AND LISTEN TO THE CREW...
WRR
DID YOU DO THIS TOO?
WHY WOULD WE?! ISN'T THIS YOUR DOING?!
GRR
What the hell's going on?
YOU'RE DESTROYING EVERYTHING TO COVER UP YOUR EVIL!
WE REPEAT. PLEASE PUT ON A LIFE VEST AND REMAIN CALM...
A COINCI-DENCE ...?
RINNG
RINNG
WHO IS THIS? IS THIS THE CAPTAIN?
BEEP
AH, MR. MORI-ZONO.
WHAT'S GOING ON?!
MUST I EXPLAIN TO MAKE YOU UNDER-STAND?
OF COURSE! WHAT'S WITH THAT ATTITUDE?
I HIRED YOU TO—
HA HA HA...

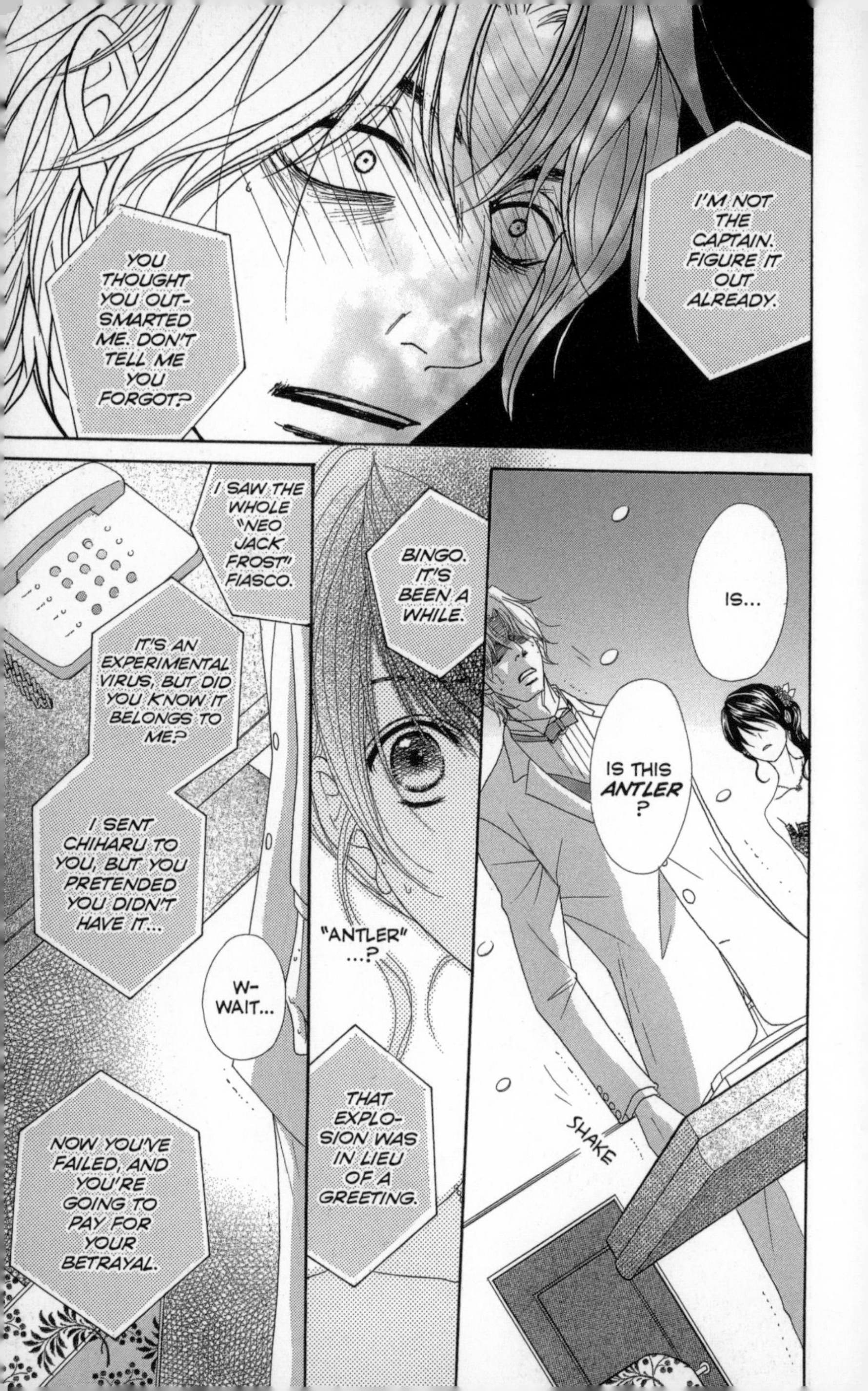
I'M NOT THE CAPTAIN. FIGURE IT OUT ALREADY.
YOU THOUGHT YOU OUT-SMARTED ME. DON'T TELL ME YOU FORGOT?
IS...
IS THIS ANTLER ?
SHAKE
BINGO. IT'S BEEN A WHILE.
"ANTLER" ...?
THAT EXPLO-SION WAS IN LIEU OF A GREETING.
I SAW THE WHOLE "NEO JACK FROST" FIASCO.
IT'S AN EXPERIMENTAL VIRUS, BUT DID YOU KNOW IT BELONGS TO ME?
I SENT CHIHARU TO YOU, BUT YOU PRETENDED YOU DIDN'T HAVE IT...
W-WAIT...
NOW YOU'VE FAILED, AND YOU'RE GOING TO PAY FOR YOUR BETRAYAL.

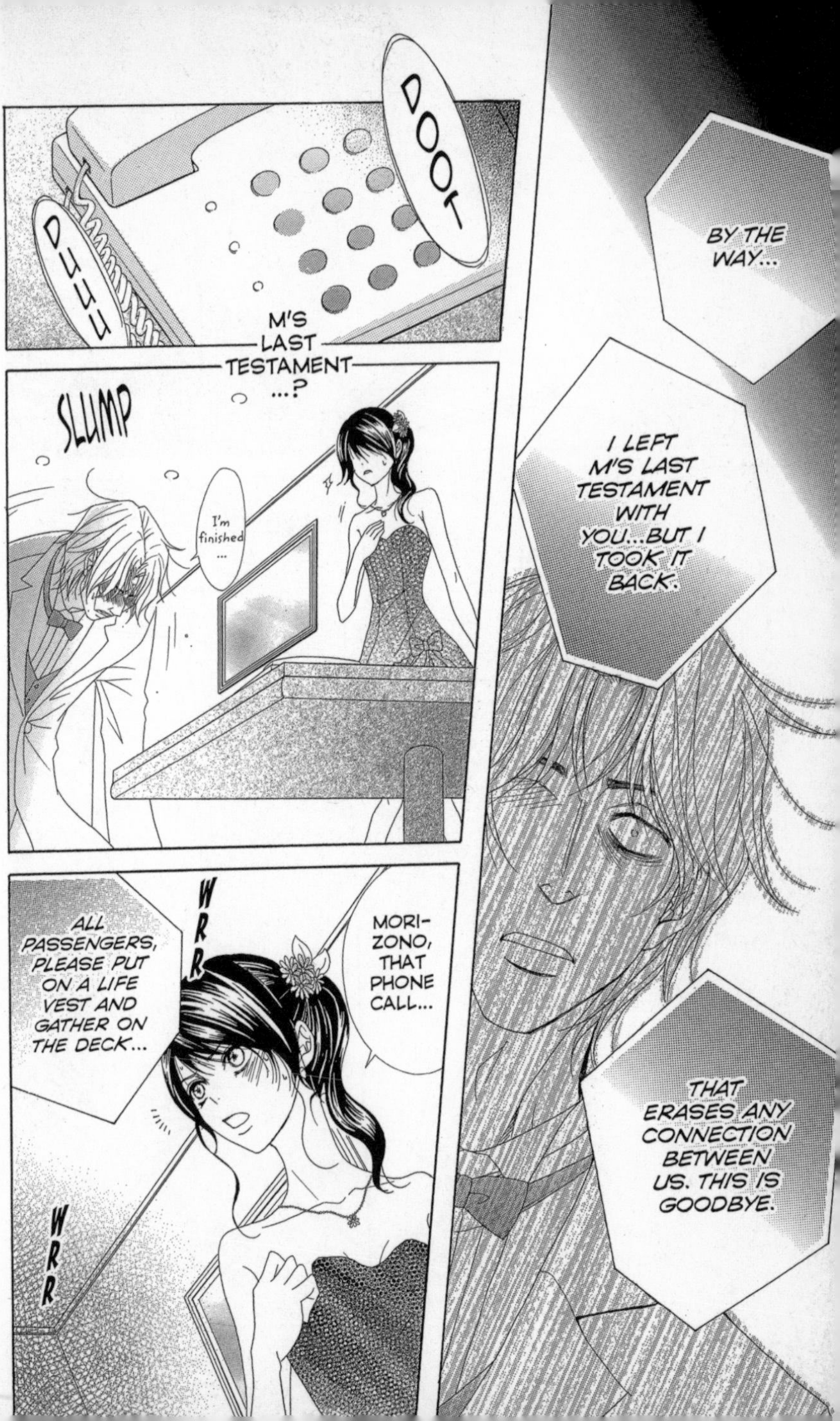
BY THE WAY...
I LEFT M'S LAST TESTAMENT WITH YOU...BUT I TOOK IT BACK.
THAT ERASES ANY CONNECTION BETWEEN US. THIS IS GOODBYE.
DOOT
Duuu
M'S LAST TESTAMENT ...?
SLUMP
I'm finished ...
MORI-ZONO, THAT PHONE CALL...
WRR
ALL PASSENGERS, PLEASE PUT ON A LIFE VEST AND GATHER ON THE DECK...
WRR

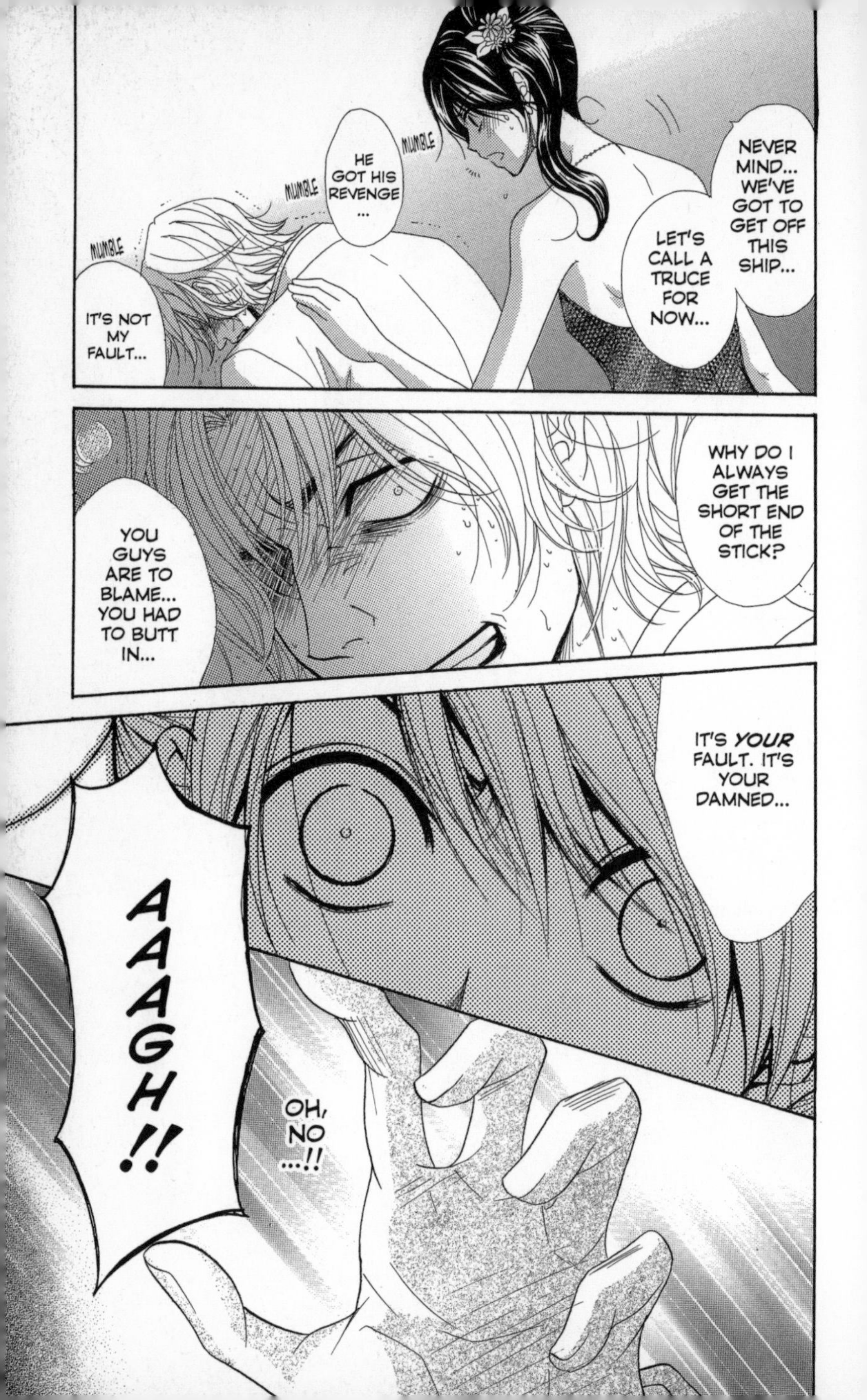
NEVER MIND... WE'VE GOT TO GET OFF THIS SHIP...
LET'S CALL A TRUCE FOR NOW...
MUMBLE
HE GOT HIS REVENGE ...
MUMBLE
MUMBLE
IT'S NOT MY FAULT...
WHY DO I ALWAYS GET THE SHORT END OF THE STICK?
YOU GUYS ARE TO BLAME... YOU HAD TO BUTT IN...
IT'S *YOUR* FAULT. IT'S YOUR DAMNED...
OH, NO ...!!
AAAGH!!

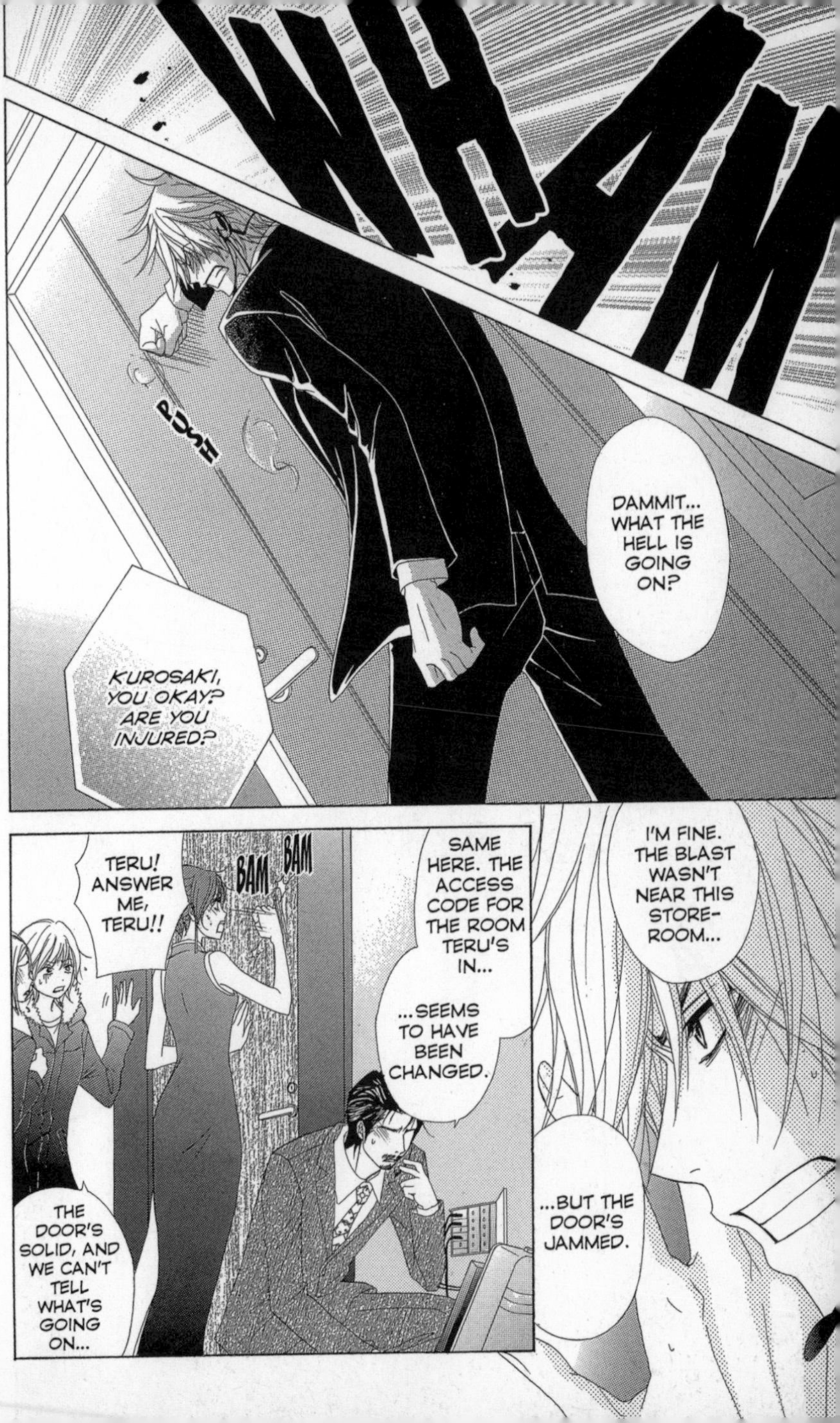
WHAM
PUSH
DAMMIT... WHAT THE HELL IS GOING ON?
KUROSAKI, YOU OKAY? ARE YOU INJURED?
I'M FINE. THE BLAST WASN'T NEAR THIS STORE-ROOM...
...BUT THE DOOR'S JAMMED.
SAME HERE. THE ACCESS CODE FOR THE ROOM TERU'S IN...
...SEEMS TO HAVE BEEN CHANGED.
BAM
BAM
TERU! ANSWER ME, TERU!!
THE DOOR'S SOLID, AND WE CAN'T TELL WHAT'S GOING ON...

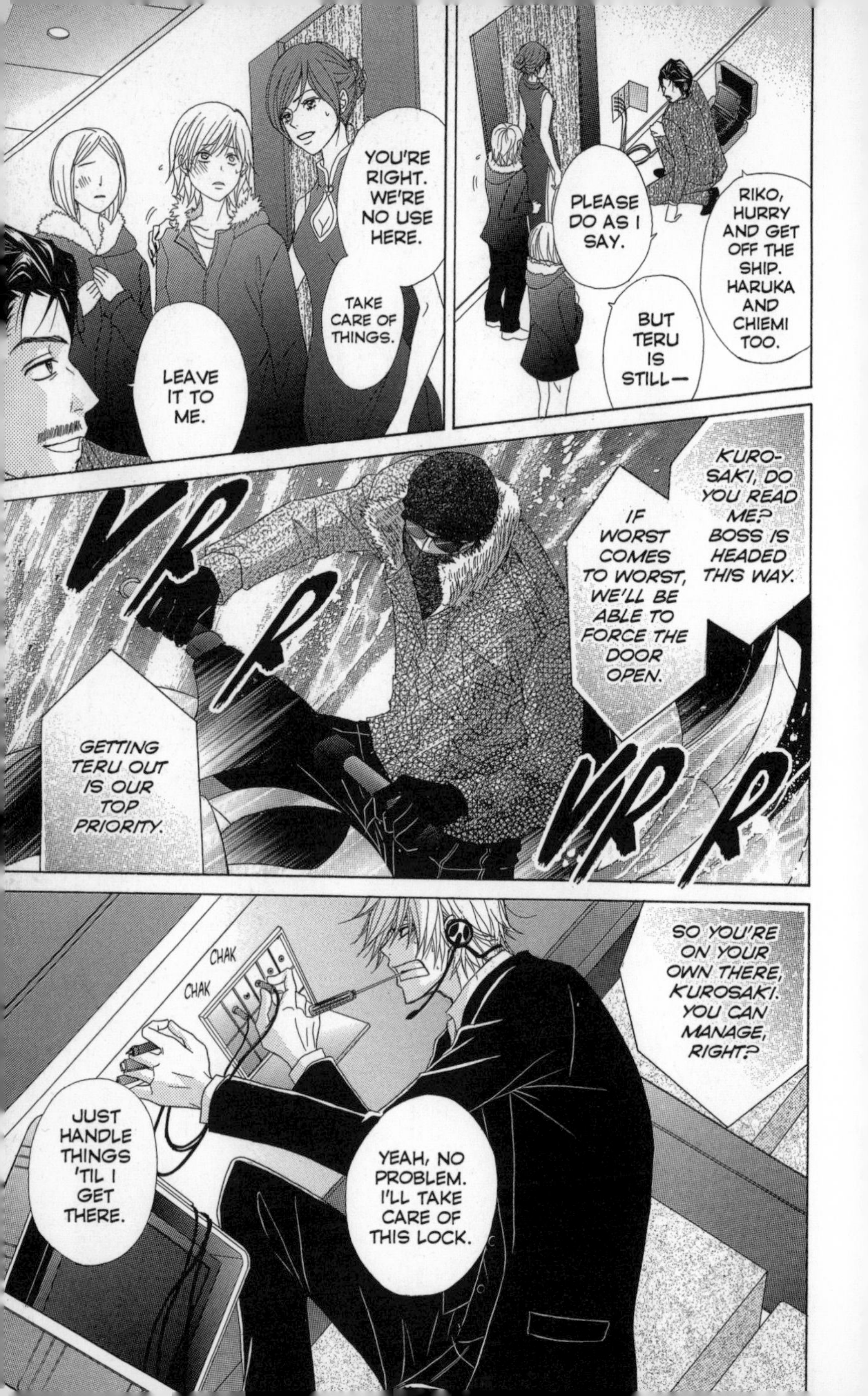
RIKO, HURRY AND GET OFF THE SHIP. HARUKA AND CHIEMI TOO.
PLEASE DO AS I SAY.
BUT TERU IS STILL—
YOU'RE RIGHT. WE'RE NO USE HERE.
TAKE CARE OF THINGS.
LEAVE IT TO ME.
KURO-SAKI, DO YOU READ ME? BOSS IS HEADED THIS WAY.
IF WORST COMES TO WORST, WE'LL BE ABLE TO FORCE THE DOOR OPEN.
VRRR
GETTING TERU OUT IS OUR TOP PRIORITY.
VRRR
SO YOU'RE ON YOUR OWN THERE, KUROSAKI. YOU CAN MANAGE, RIGHT?
CHAK
CHAK
YEAH, NO PROBLEM. I'LL TAKE CARE OF THIS LOCK.
JUST HANDLE THINGS 'TIL I GET THERE.

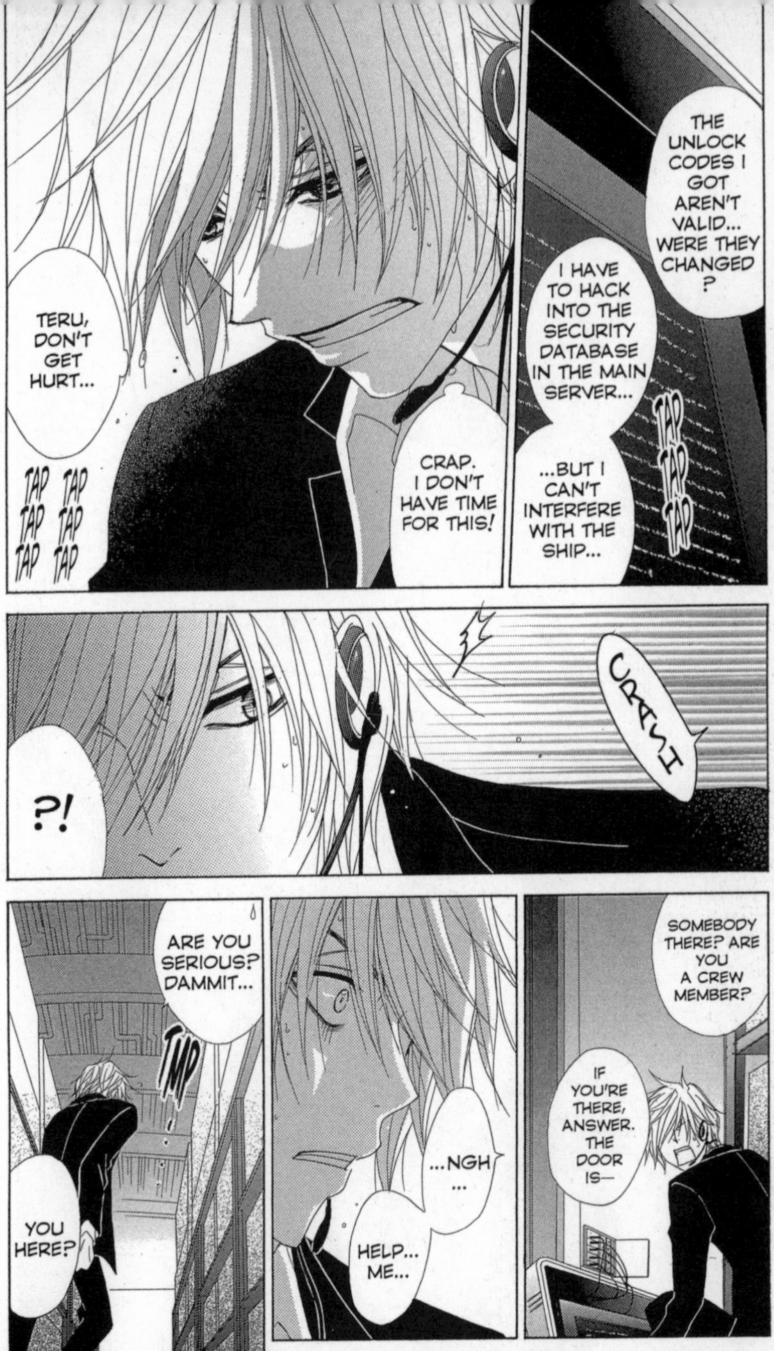
THE UNLOCK CODES I GOT AREN'T VALID... WERE THEY CHANGED?
I HAVE TO HACK INTO THE SECURITY DATABASE IN THE MAIN SERVER...
TAP TAP TAP
...BUT I CAN'T INTERFERE WITH THE SHIP...
CRAP. I DON'T HAVE TIME FOR THIS!
TERU, DON'T GET HURT...
TAP TAP TAP TAP TAP TAP
CRASH
?!
SOMEBODY THERE? ARE YOU A CREW MEMBER?
IF YOU'RE THERE, ANSWER. THE DOOR IS—
...NGH...
HELP... ME...
ARE YOU SERIOUS? DAMMIT...
TMP
YOU HERE?

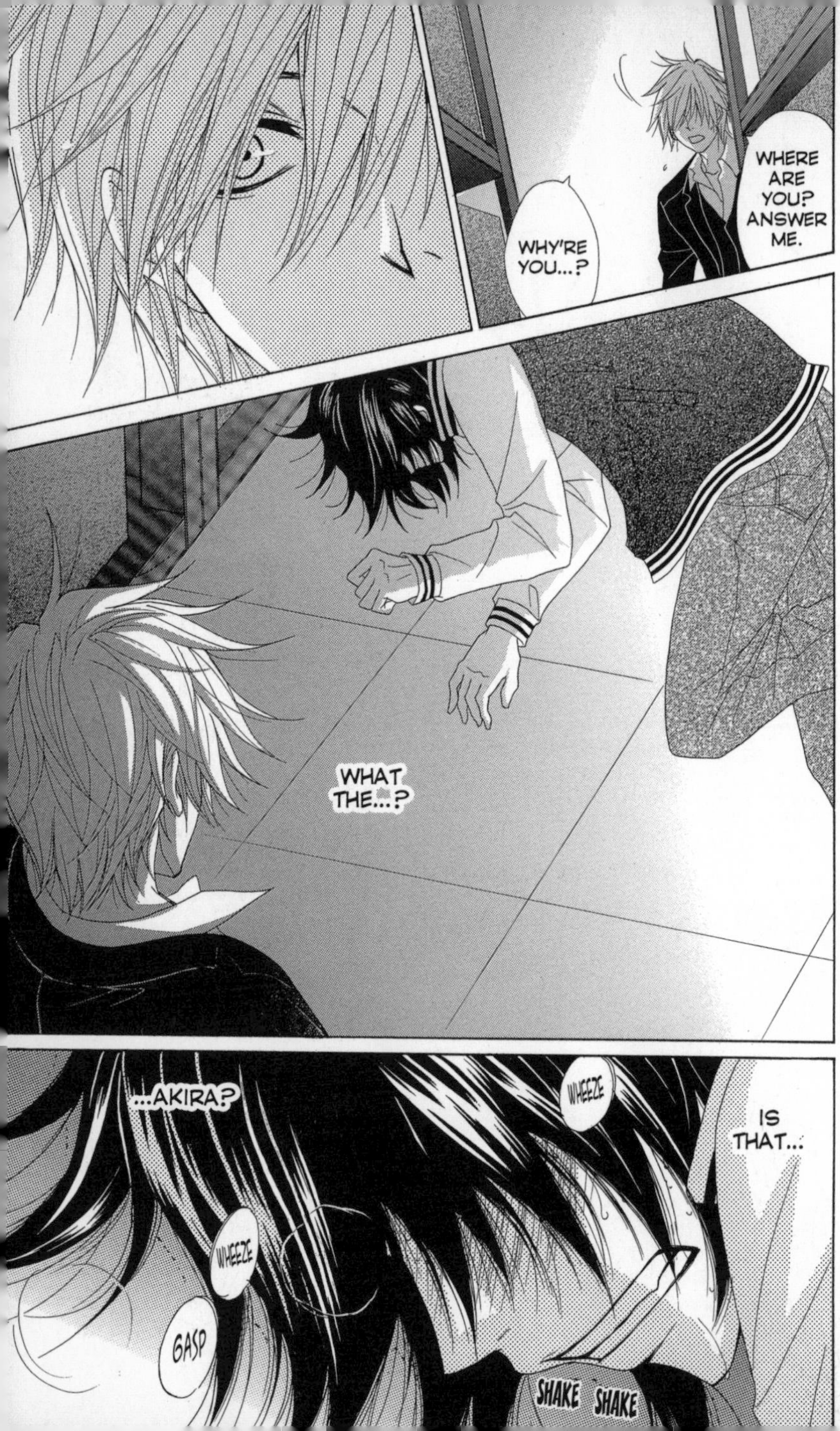
WHERE ARE YOU? ANSWER ME.
WHY'RE YOU...?
WHAT THE...?
IS THAT...
WHEEZE
...AKIRA?
WHEEZE
GASP
SHAKE SHAKE

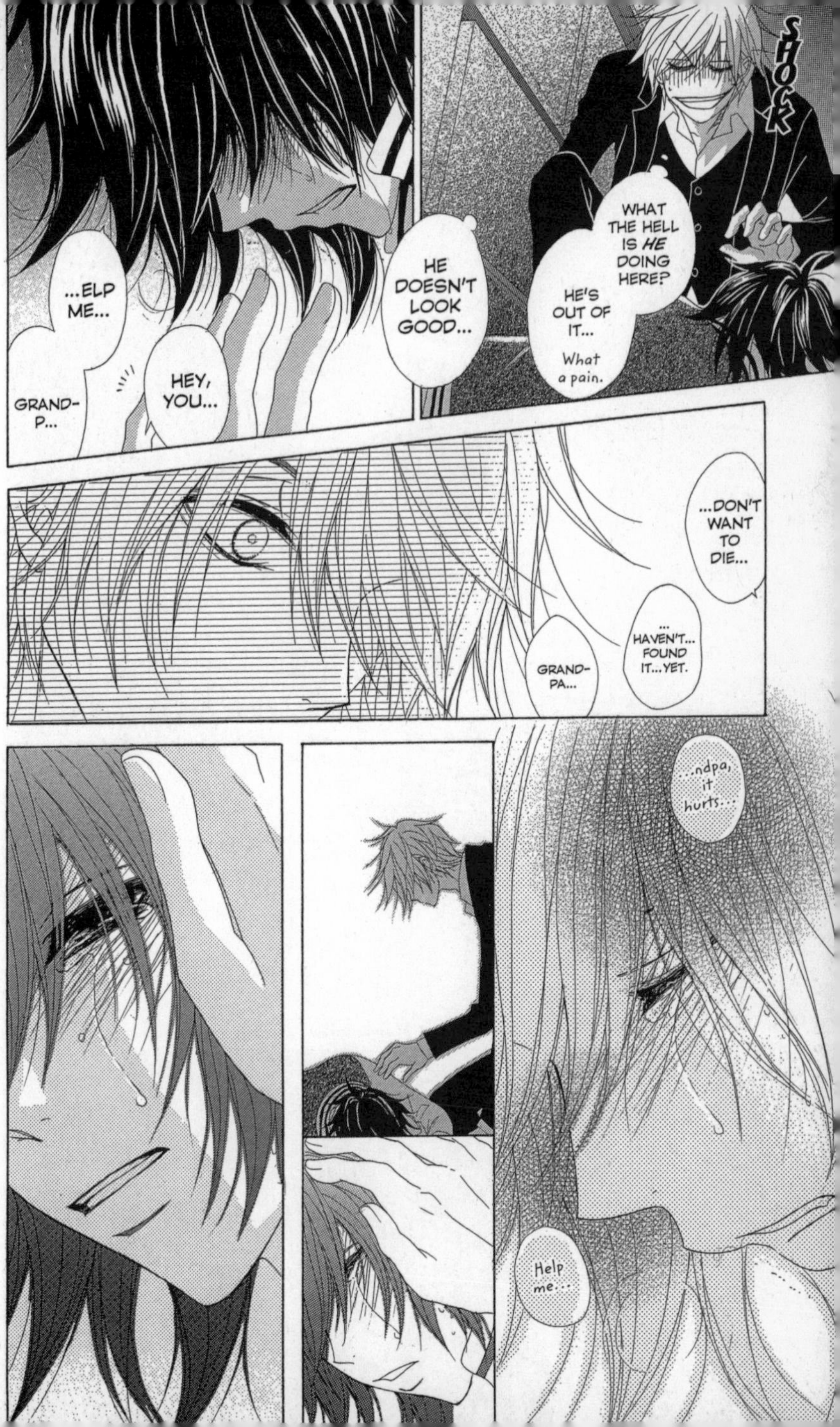
SHOCK
WHAT THE HELL IS HE DOING HERE?
HE'S OUT OF IT...
What a pain.
HE DOESN'T LOOK GOOD...
...ELP ME...
HEY, YOU...
GRAND-P...
...DON'T WANT TO DIE...
... HAVEN'T... FOUND IT...YET.
GRAND-PA...
...ndpa, it hurts...
Help me...

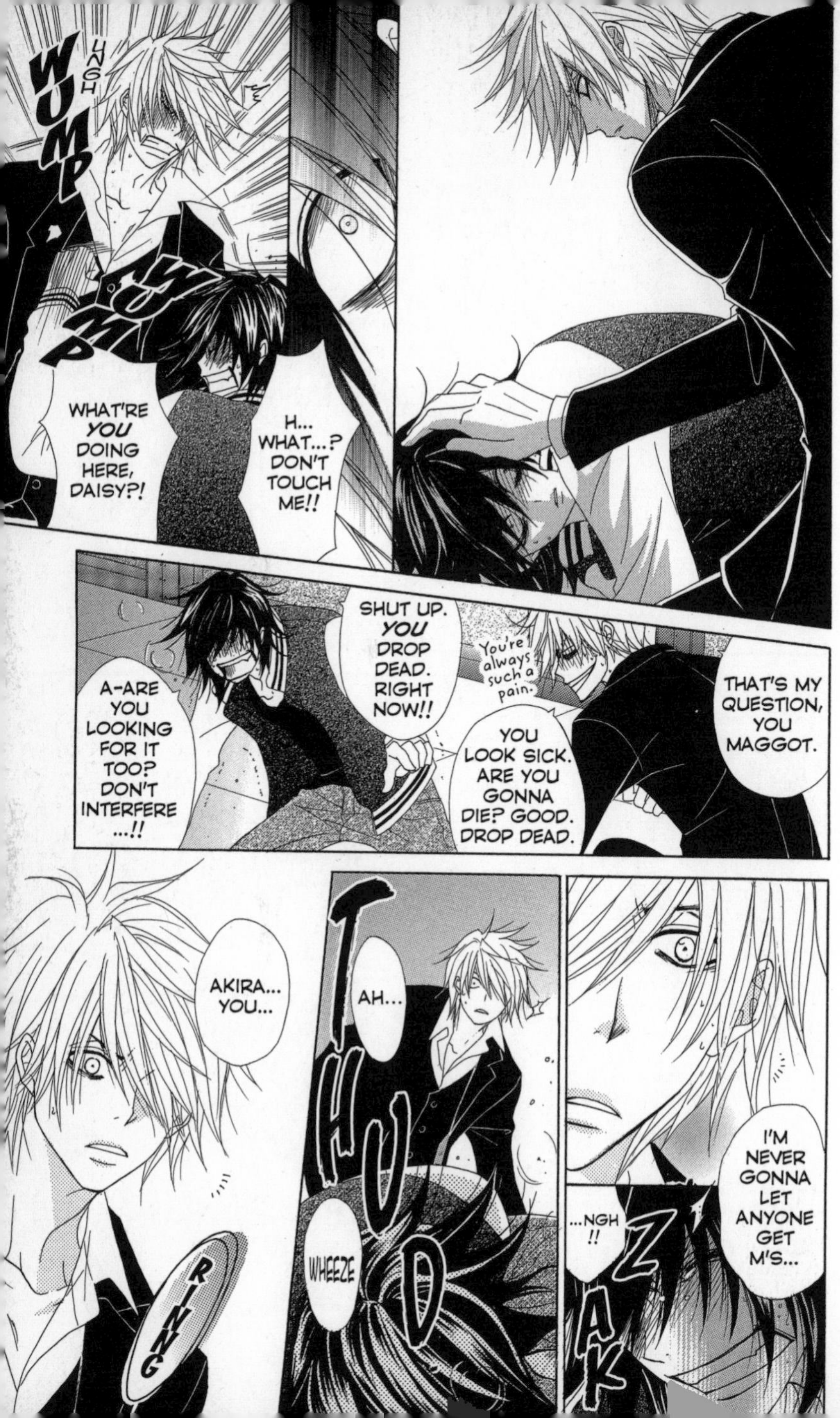
H... WHAT...? DON'T TOUCH ME!!
WUMP
UNGH
WUMP
WHAT'RE *YOU* DOING HERE, DAISY?!
THAT'S MY QUESTION, YOU MAGGOT.
You're always such a pain.
YOU LOOK SICK. ARE YOU GONNA DIE? GOOD. DROP DEAD.
SHUT UP. *YOU* DROP DEAD. RIGHT NOW!!
A-ARE YOU LOOKING FOR IT TOO? DON'T INTERFERE ...!!
I'M NEVER GONNA LET ANYONE GET M'S...
...NGH !!
ZAK
AH...
THUD
WHEEZE
AKIRA... YOU...
RINNG

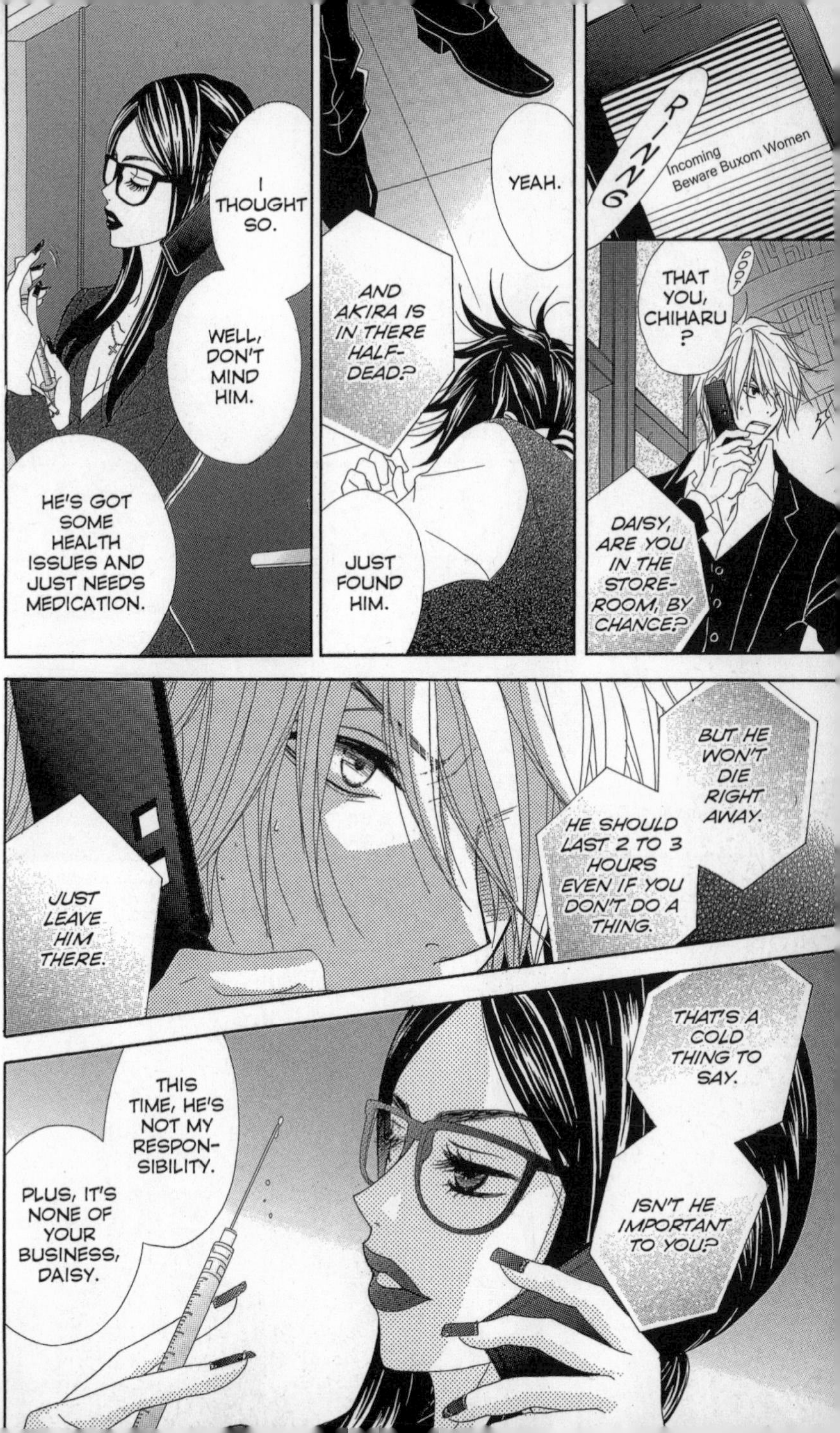
Incoming
Beware Buxom Women
RINNG
DOOT
THAT YOU, CHIHARU?
DAISY, ARE YOU IN THE STORE-ROOM, BY CHANCE?
YEAH.
AND AKIRA IS IN THERE HALF-DEAD?
JUST FOUND HIM.
I THOUGHT SO.
WELL, DON'T MIND HIM.
HE'S GOT SOME HEALTH ISSUES AND JUST NEEDS MEDICATION.
BUT HE WON'T DIE RIGHT AWAY.
HE SHOULD LAST 2 TO 3 HOURS EVEN IF YOU DON'T DO A THING.
JUST LEAVE HIM THERE.
THAT'S A COLD THING TO SAY.
ISN'T HE IMPORTANT TO YOU?
THIS TIME, HE'S NOT MY RESPON-SIBILITY.
PLUS, IT'S NONE OF YOUR BUSINESS, DAISY.

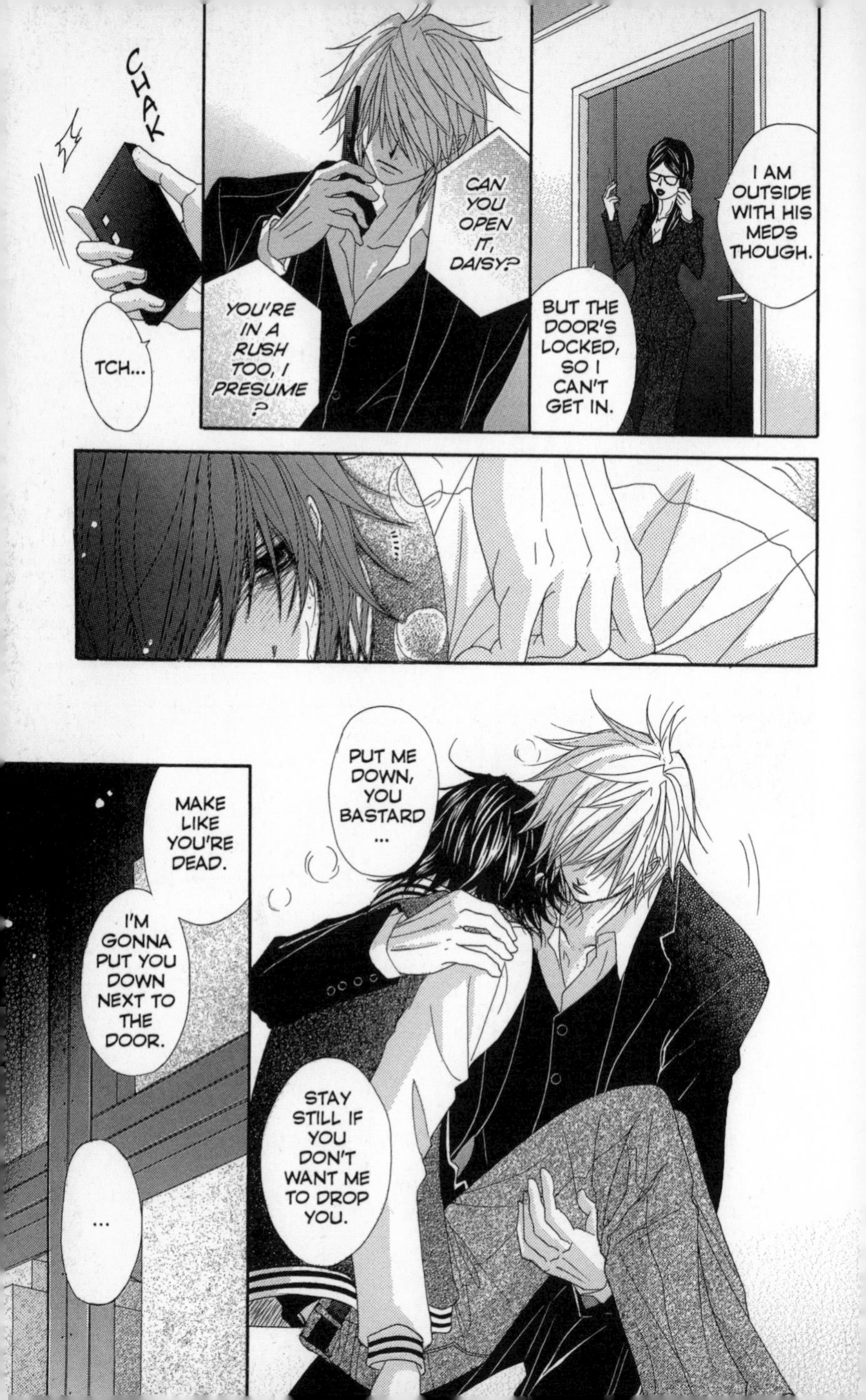
I AM OUTSIDE WITH HIS MEDS THOUGH.
BUT THE DOOR'S LOCKED, SO I CAN'T GET IN.
CAN YOU OPEN IT, DAISY?
YOU'RE IN A RUSH TOO, I PRESUME?
CHAK
TCH...
PUT ME DOWN, YOU BASTARD...
MAKE LIKE YOU'RE DEAD.
I'M GONNA PUT YOU DOWN NEXT TO THE DOOR.
STAY STILL IF YOU DON'T WANT ME TO DROP YOU.
...

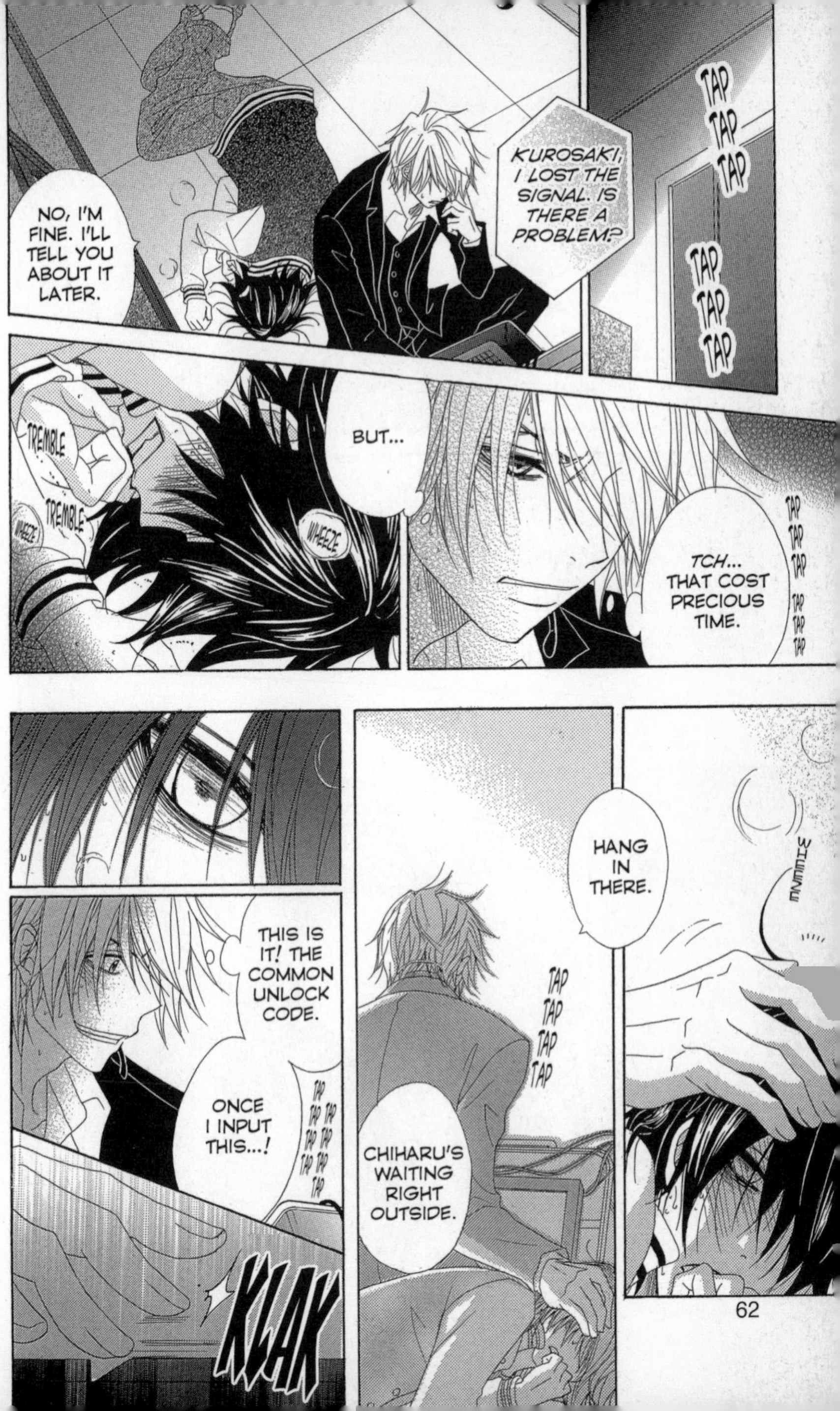
TAP TAP TAP
KUROSAKI, I LOST THE SIGNAL. IS THERE A PROBLEM?
TAP TAP TAP
NO, I'M FINE. I'LL TELL YOU ABOUT IT LATER.
TAP TAP TAP
TCH... THAT COST PRECIOUS TIME.
TAP TAP TAP
BUT...
WHEEZE
TREMBLE
TREMBLE
WHEEZE
WHEEZE
HANG IN THERE.
TAP TAP TAP TAP TAP
CHIHARU'S WAITING RIGHT OUTSIDE.
THIS IS IT! THE COMMON UNLOCK CODE.
ONCE I INPUT THIS...!
TAP TAP TAP TAP TAP TAP TAP TAP TAP
KLAK

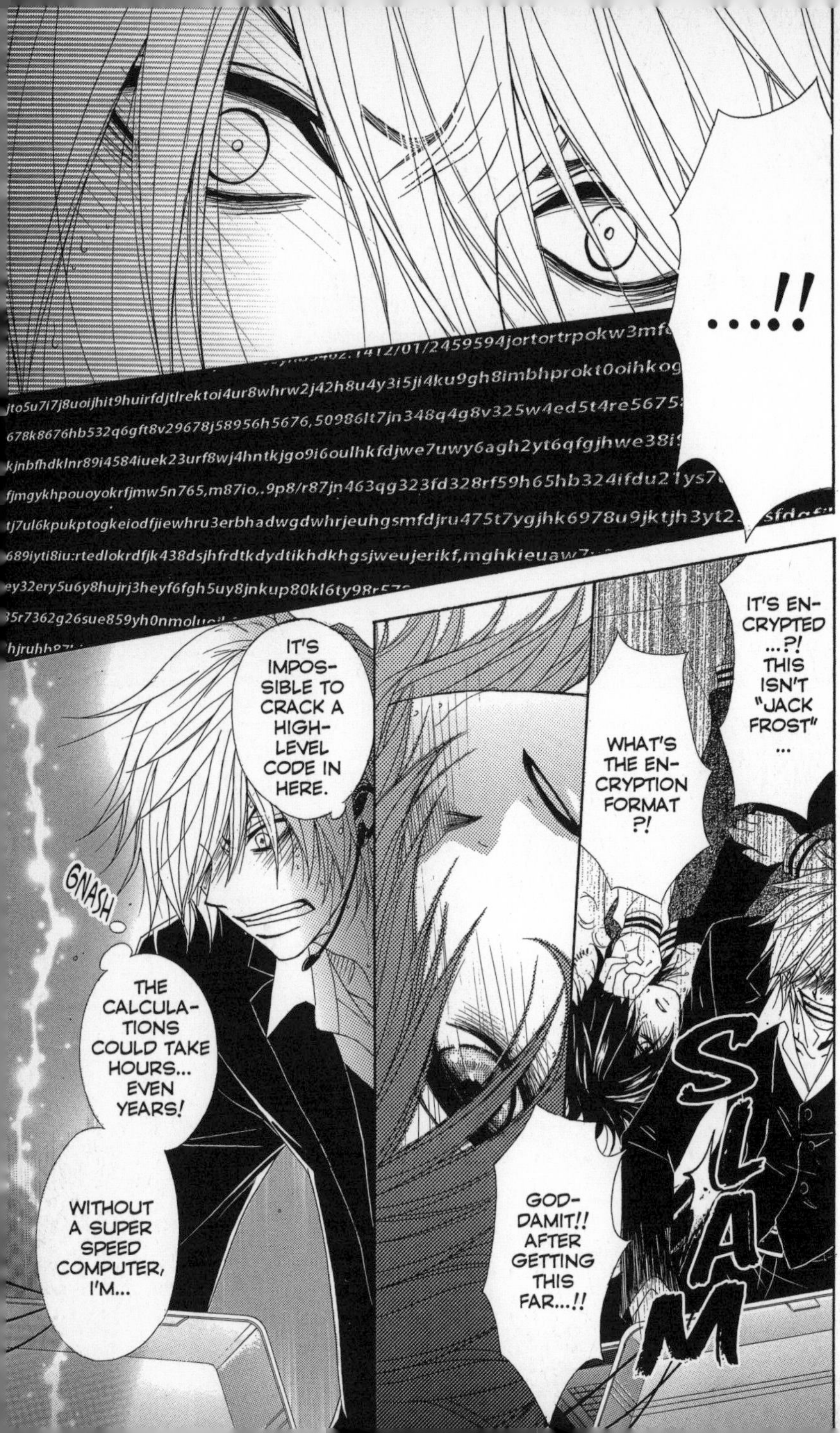
...!!
IT'S EN-CRYPTED ...?! THIS ISN'T "JACK FROST" ...
WHAT'S THE EN-CRYPTION FORMAT ?!
GOD-DAMIT!! AFTER GETTING THIS FAR...!!
SLAM
IT'S IMPOS-SIBLE TO CRACK A HIGH-LEVEL CODE IN HERE.
GNASH
THE CALCULA-TIONS COULD TAKE HOURS... EVEN YEARS!
WITHOUT A SUPER SPEED COMPUTER, I'M...

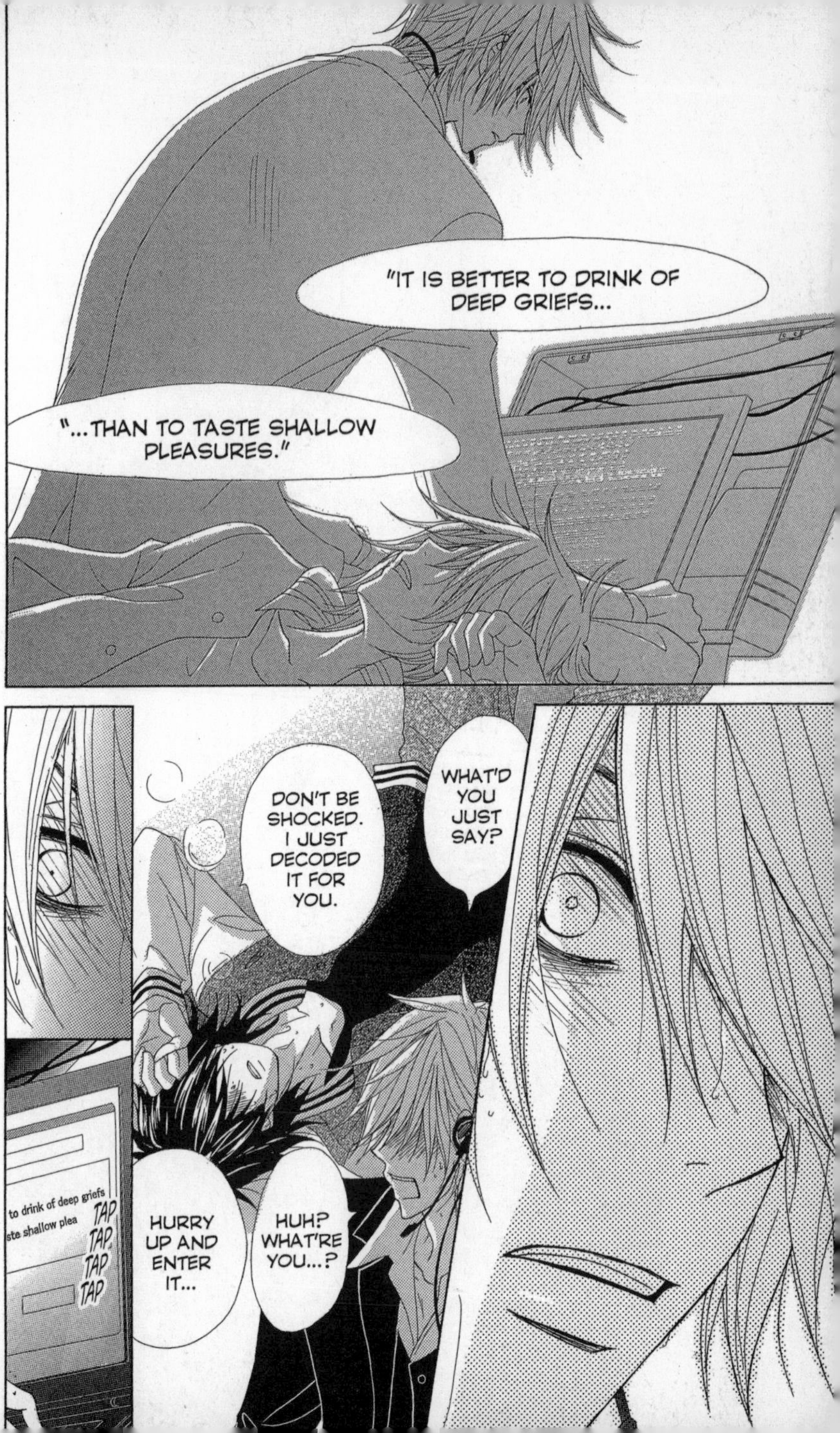
"IT IS BETTER TO DRINK OF DEEP GRIEFS...
"...THAN TO TASTE SHALLOW PLEASURES."
WHAT'D YOU JUST SAY?
DON'T BE SHOCKED. I JUST DECODED IT FOR YOU.
HUH? WHAT'RE YOU...?
HURRY UP AND ENTER IT...
to drink of deep griefs
ste shallow plea
TAP TAP TAP TAP

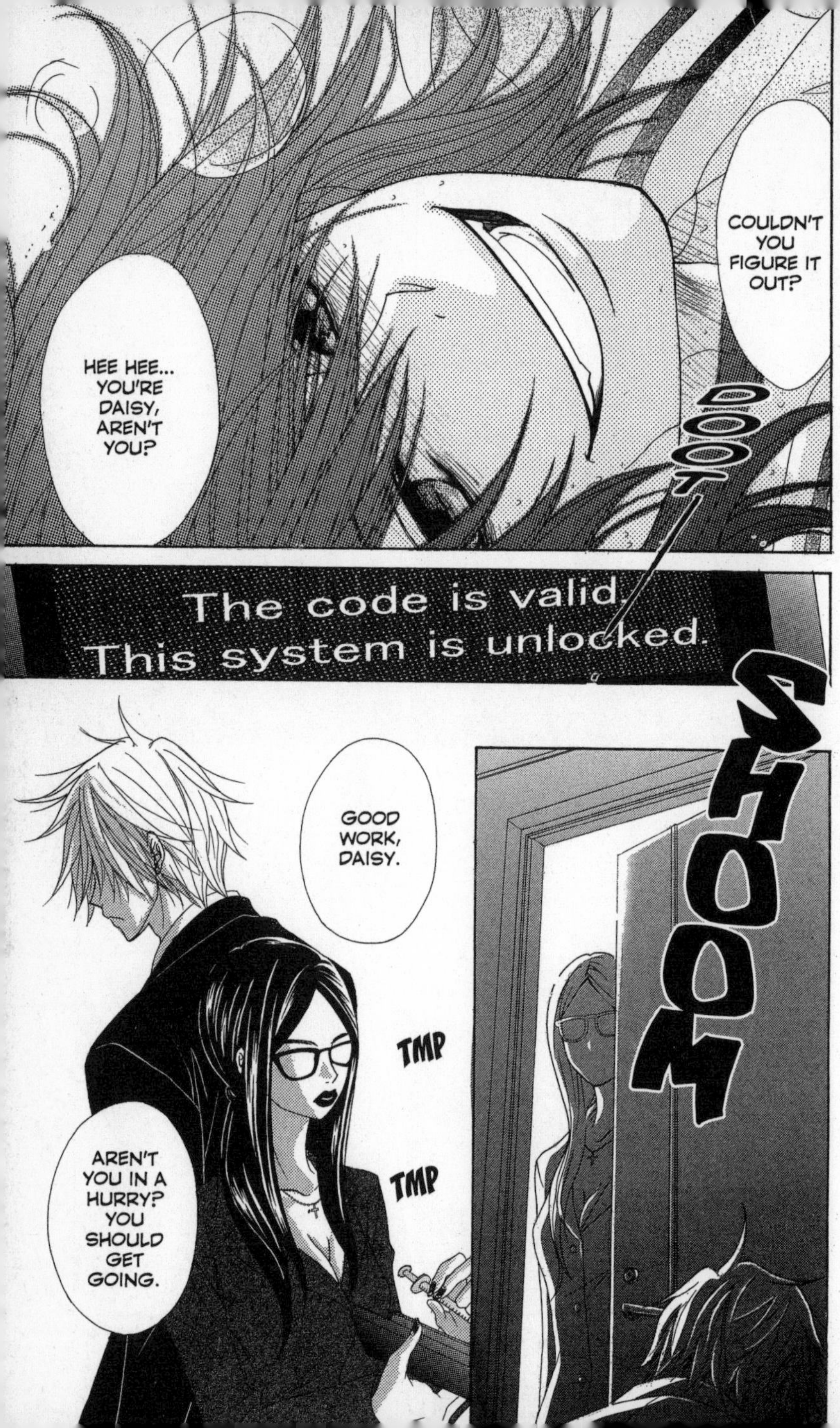
COULDN'T YOU FIGURE IT OUT?
DOOT
HEE HEE... YOU'RE DAISY, AREN'T YOU?
The code is valid.
This system is unlocked.
SHOOM
GOOD WORK, DAISY.
TMP
TMP
AREN'T YOU IN A HURRY? YOU SHOULD GET GOING.

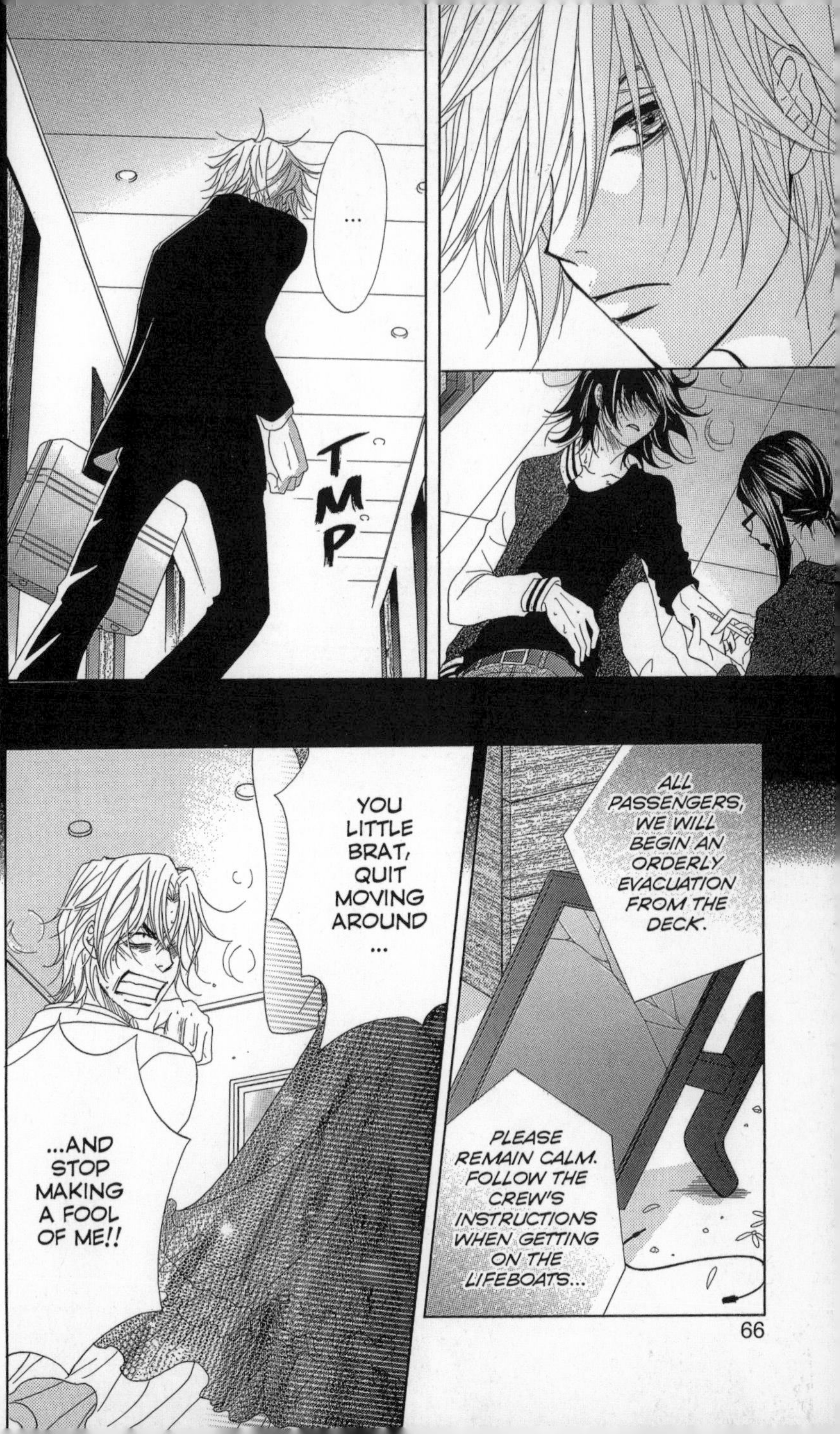
...
TMP
ALL PASSENGERS, WE WILL BEGIN AN ORDERLY EVACUATION FROM THE DECK.
PLEASE REMAIN CALM. FOLLOW THE CREW'S INSTRUCTIONS WHEN GETTING ON THE LIFEBOATS...
YOU LITTLE BRAT, QUIT MOVING AROUND ...
...AND STOP MAKING A FOOL OF ME!!

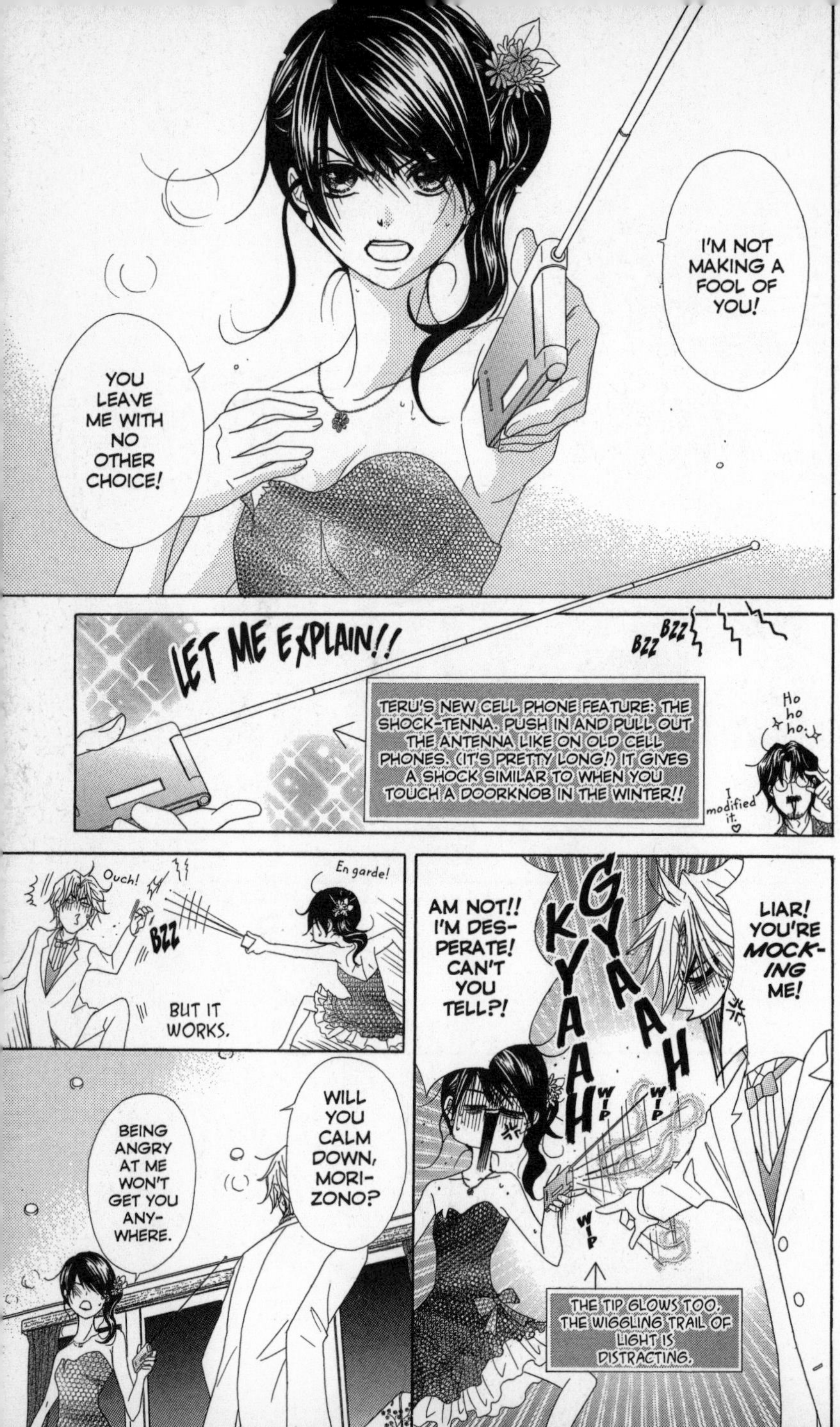
I'M NOT MAKING A FOOL OF YOU!
YOU LEAVE ME WITH NO OTHER CHOICE!
BZZ BZZ
LET ME EXPLAIN!!
TERU'S NEW CELL PHONE FEATURE: THE SHOCK-TENNA. PUSH IN AND PULL OUT THE ANTENNA LIKE ON OLD CELL PHONES. (IT'S PRETTY LONG!) IT GIVES A SHOCK SIMILAR TO WHEN YOU TOUCH A DOORKNOB IN THE WINTER!!
Ho ho ho.
I modified it.
LIAR! YOU'RE MOCKING ME!
GYAAAH
KYAAAH
AM NOT!! I'M DESPERATE! CAN'T YOU TELL?!
WIP WIP WIP
THE TIP GLOWS TOO. THE WIGGLING TRAIL OF LIGHT IS DISTRACTING.
En garde!
BZZ
Ouch!
BUT IT WORKS.
WILL YOU CALM DOWN, MORIZONO?
BEING ANGRY AT ME WON'T GET YOU ANYWHERE.

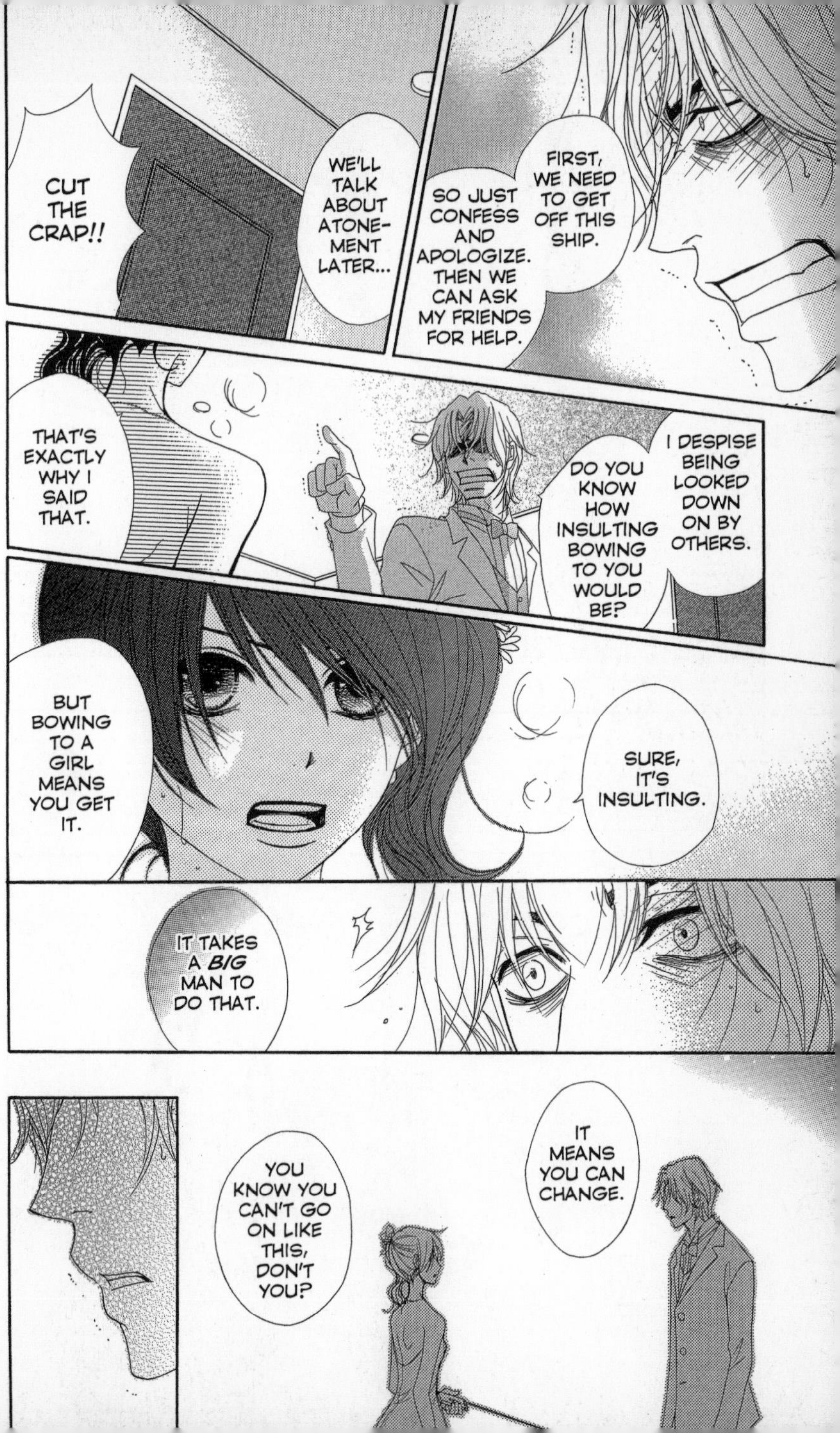
FIRST, WE NEED TO GET OFF THIS SHIP.
SO JUST CONFESS AND APOLOGIZE. THEN WE CAN ASK MY FRIENDS FOR HELP.
WE'LL TALK ABOUT ATONE-MENT LATER...
CUT THE CRAP!!
I DESPISE BEING LOOKED DOWN ON BY OTHERS.
DO YOU KNOW HOW INSULTING BOWING TO YOU WOULD BE?
THAT'S EXACTLY WHY I SAID THAT.
SURE, IT'S INSULTING.
BUT BOWING TO A GIRL MEANS YOU GET IT.
IT TAKES A *BIG* MAN TO DO THAT.
IT MEANS YOU CAN CHANGE.
YOU KNOW YOU CAN'T GO ON LIKE THIS, DON'T YOU?

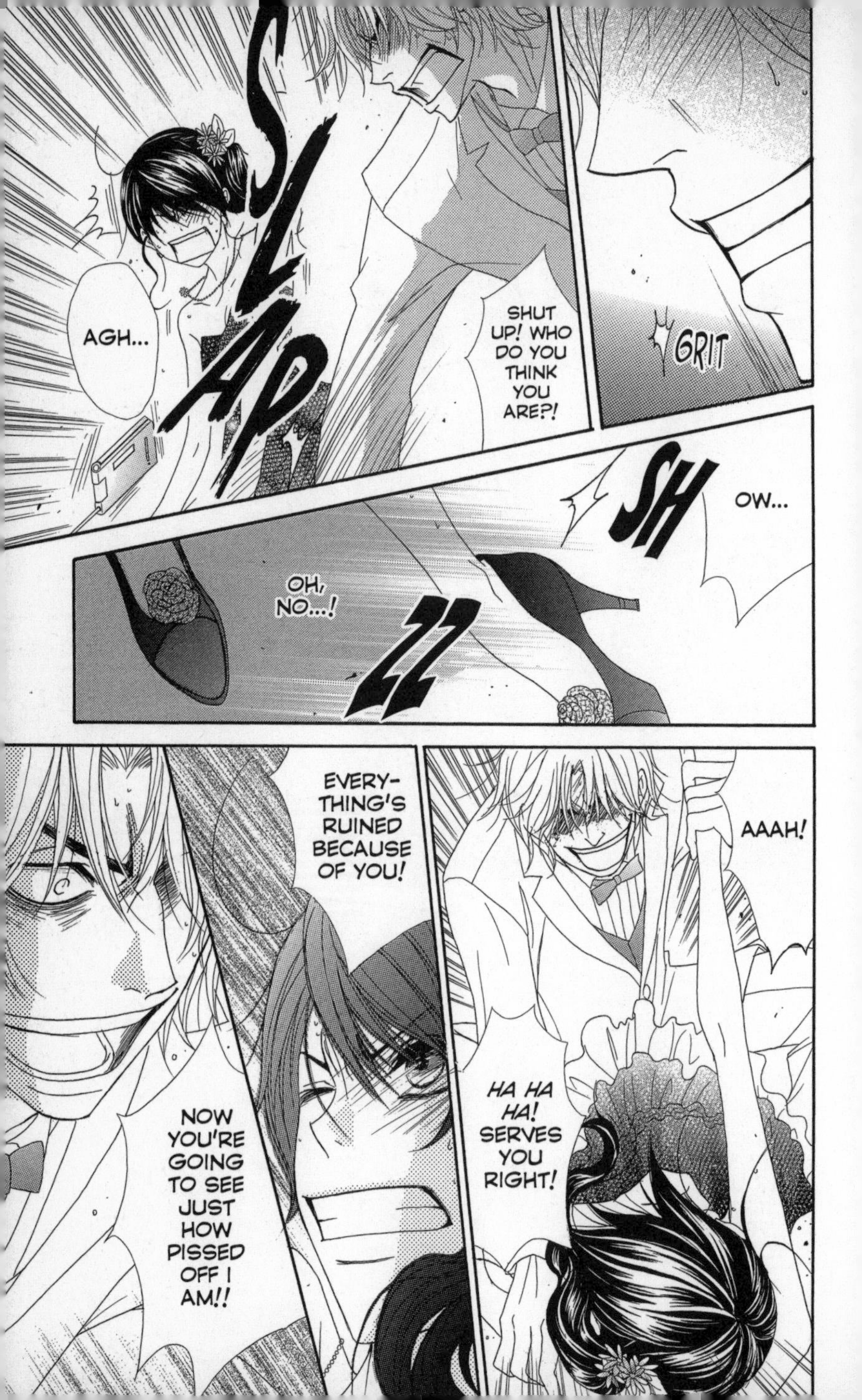
GRIT
SHUT UP! WHO DO YOU THINK YOU ARE?!
SLAP
AGH...
OW...
SH
ZZ
OH, NO...!
AAAH!
HA HA HA! SERVES YOU RIGHT!
EVERY-THING'S RUINED BECAUSE OF YOU!
NOW YOU'RE GOING TO SEE JUST HOW PISSED OFF I AM!!

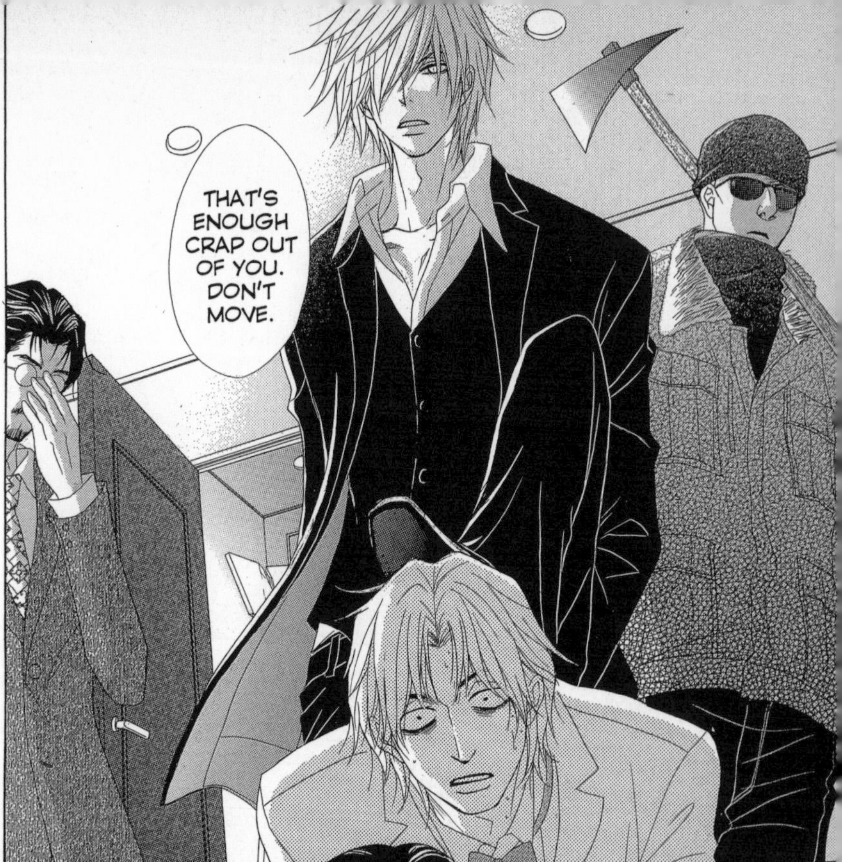
THAT'S ENOUGH CRAP OUT OF YOU. DON'T MOVE.

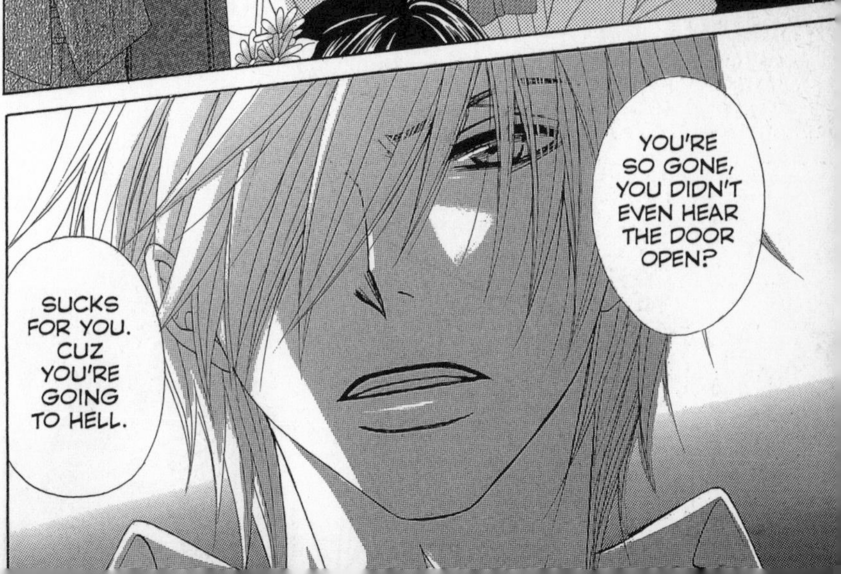
YOU'RE SO GONE, YOU DIDN'T EVEN HEAR THE DOOR OPEN?
SUCKS FOR YOU. CUZ YOU'RE GOING TO HELL.

JUST ONE KICK? YOU SHOULD'VE MADE IT MORE SLOW AND PAINFUL.

NAH, BETTER TO SHUT HIM UP BEFORE HE MADE A BIGGER ASS OF HIMSELF.

Sorry.

...

OKAY, WE'RE DONE HERE! LET'S GO.

PAT

WHAM

WH

THIS WOMAN SEDUCED ME.

I'M NOT THE BAD GUY. I WAS TRICKED.

W-WAIT, THIS IS ALL A MISTAKE.

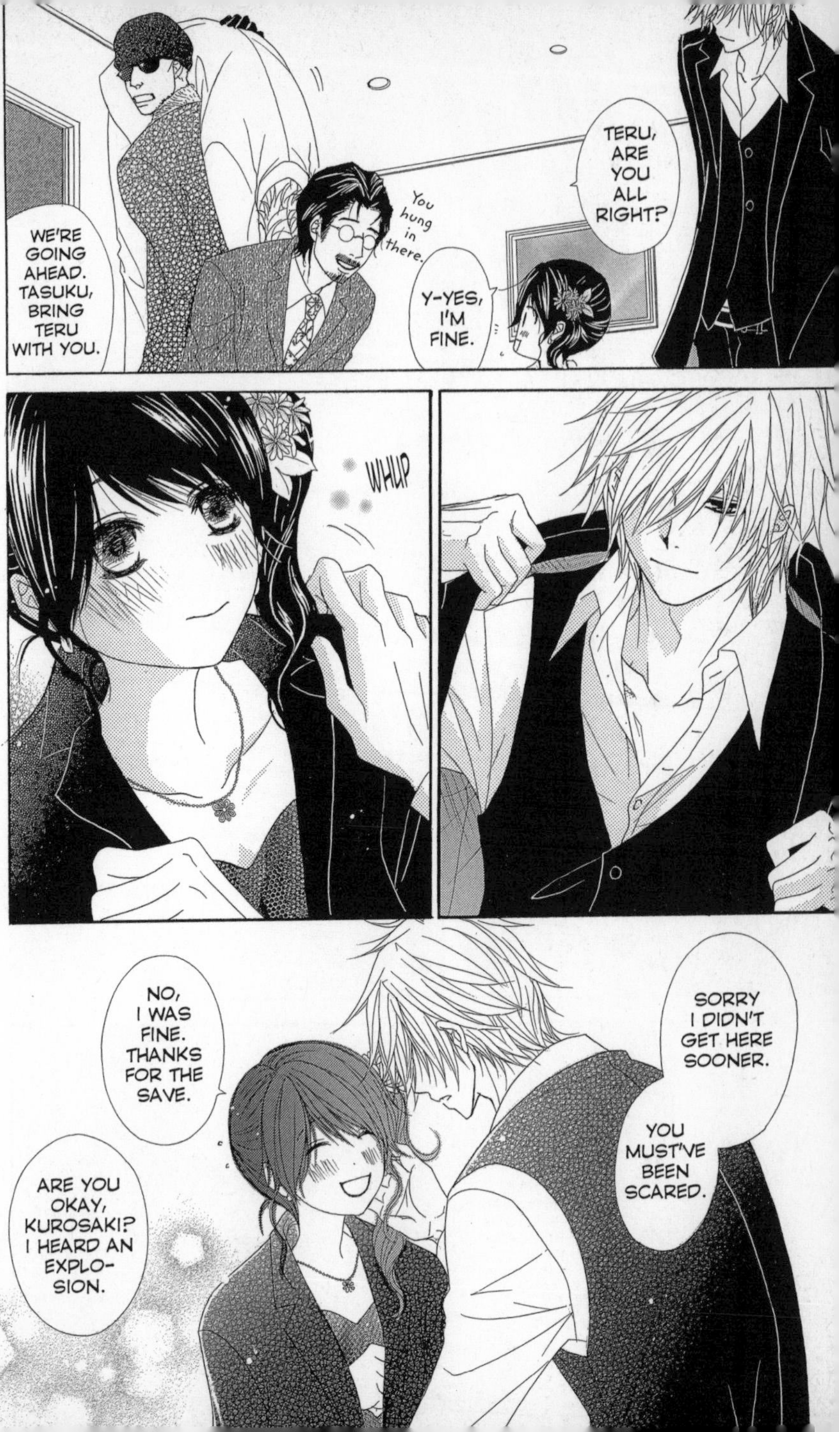
TERU, ARE YOU ALL RIGHT?
Y-YES, I'M FINE.
You hung in there.
WE'RE GOING AHEAD. TASUKU, BRING TERU WITH YOU.
WHUP
SORRY I DIDN'T GET HERE SOONER.
YOU MUST'VE BEEN SCARED.
NO, I WAS FINE. THANKS FOR THE SAVE.
ARE YOU OKAY, KUROSAKI? I HEARD AN EXPLOSION.

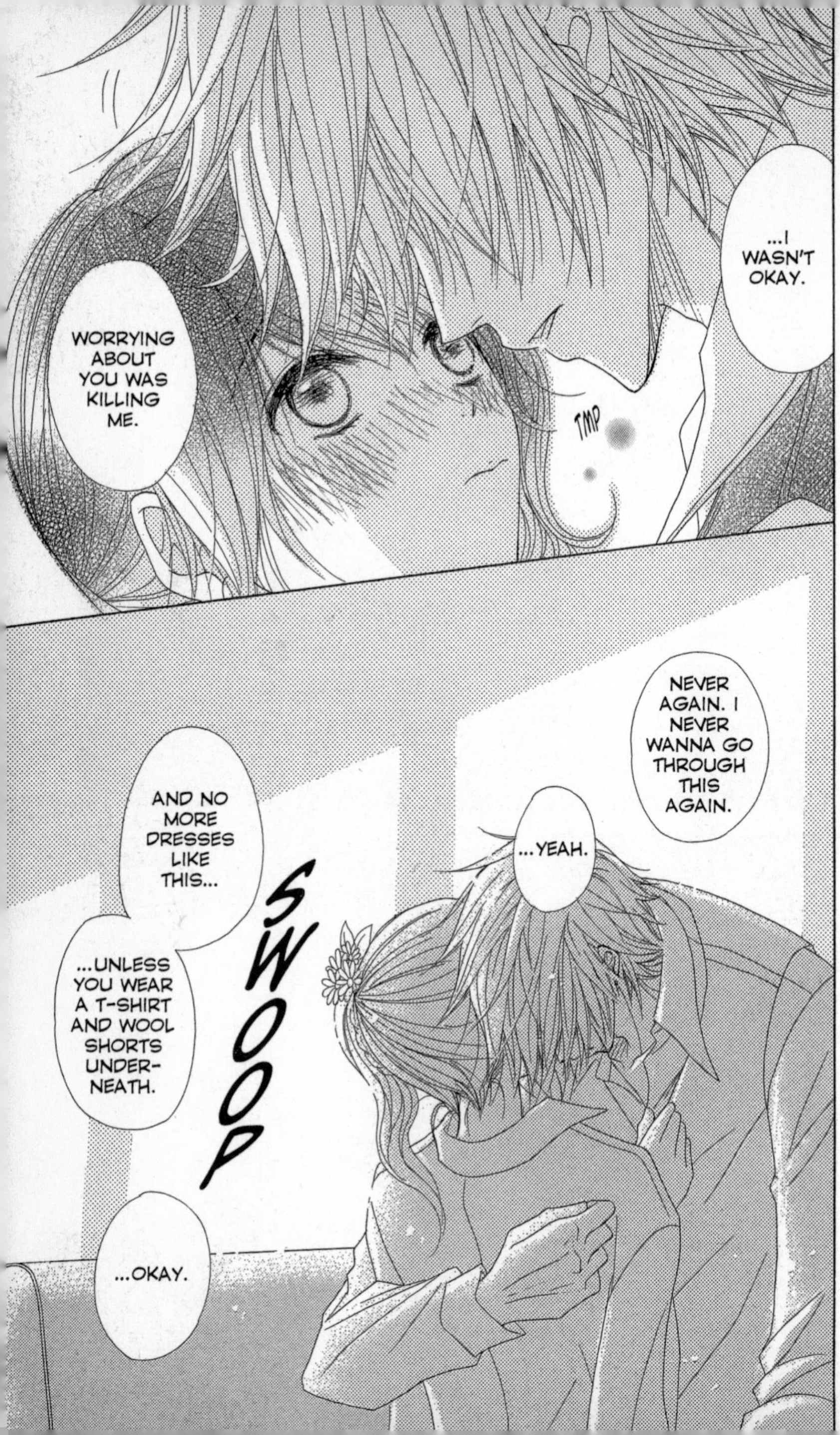
...I WASN'T OKAY.
TMP
WORRYING ABOUT YOU WAS KILLING ME.
NEVER AGAIN. I NEVER WANNA GO THROUGH THIS AGAIN.
...YEAH.
AND NO MORE DRESSES LIKE THIS...
...UNLESS YOU WEAR A T-SHIRT AND WOOL SHORTS UNDER-NEATH.
SWOOP
...OKAY.

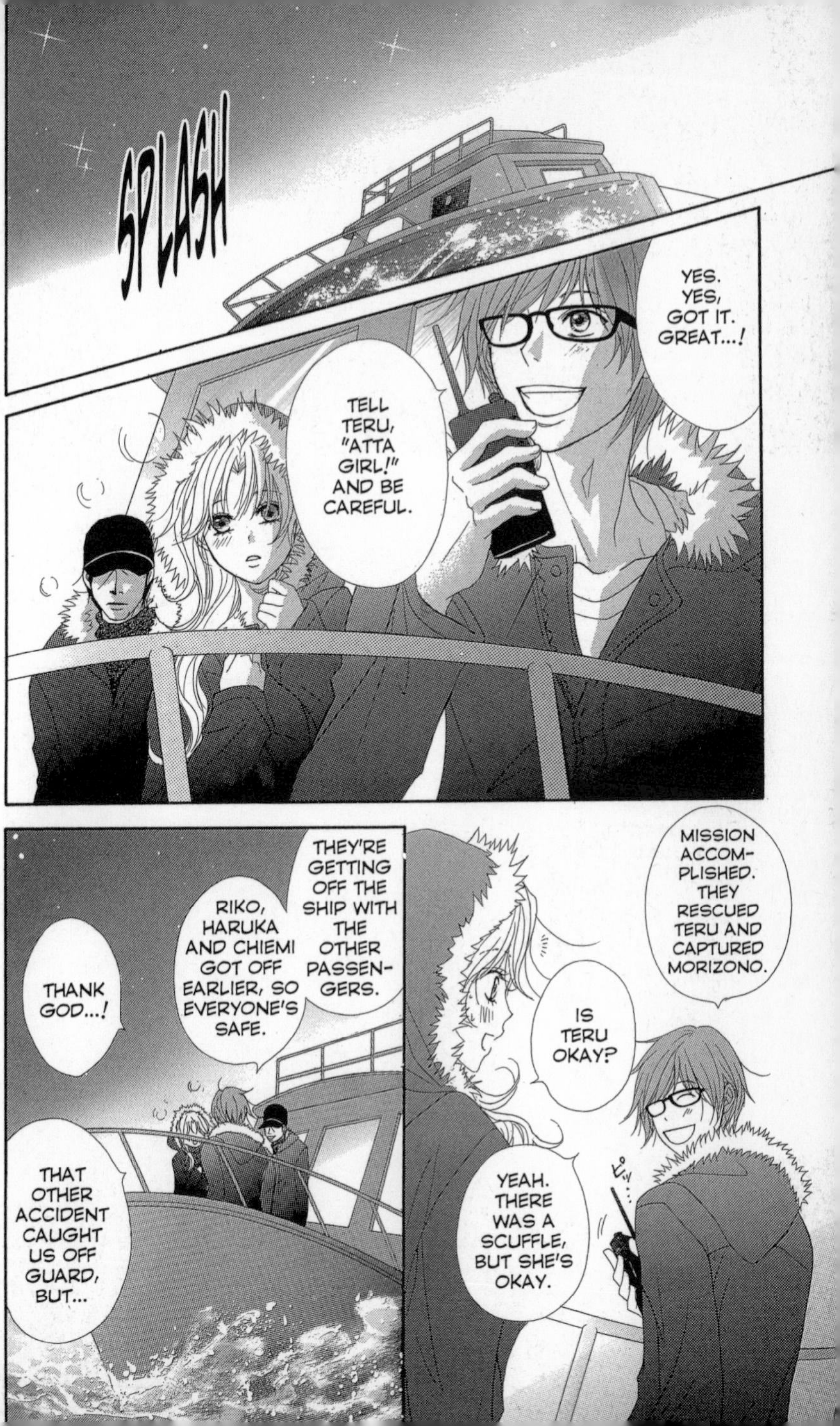
SPLASH
YES. YES, GOT IT. GREAT...!
TELL TERU, "ATTA GIRL!" AND BE CAREFUL.
MISSION ACCOM-PLISHED. THEY RESCUED TERU AND CAPTURED MORIZONO.
IS TERU OKAY?
YEAH. THERE WAS A SCUFFLE, BUT SHE'S OKAY.
THEY'RE GETTING OFF THE SHIP WITH THE OTHER PASSEN-GERS.
RIKO, HARUKA AND CHIEMI GOT OFF EARLIER, SO EVERYONE'S SAFE.
THANK GOD...!
THAT OTHER ACCIDENT CAUGHT US OFF GUARD, BUT...

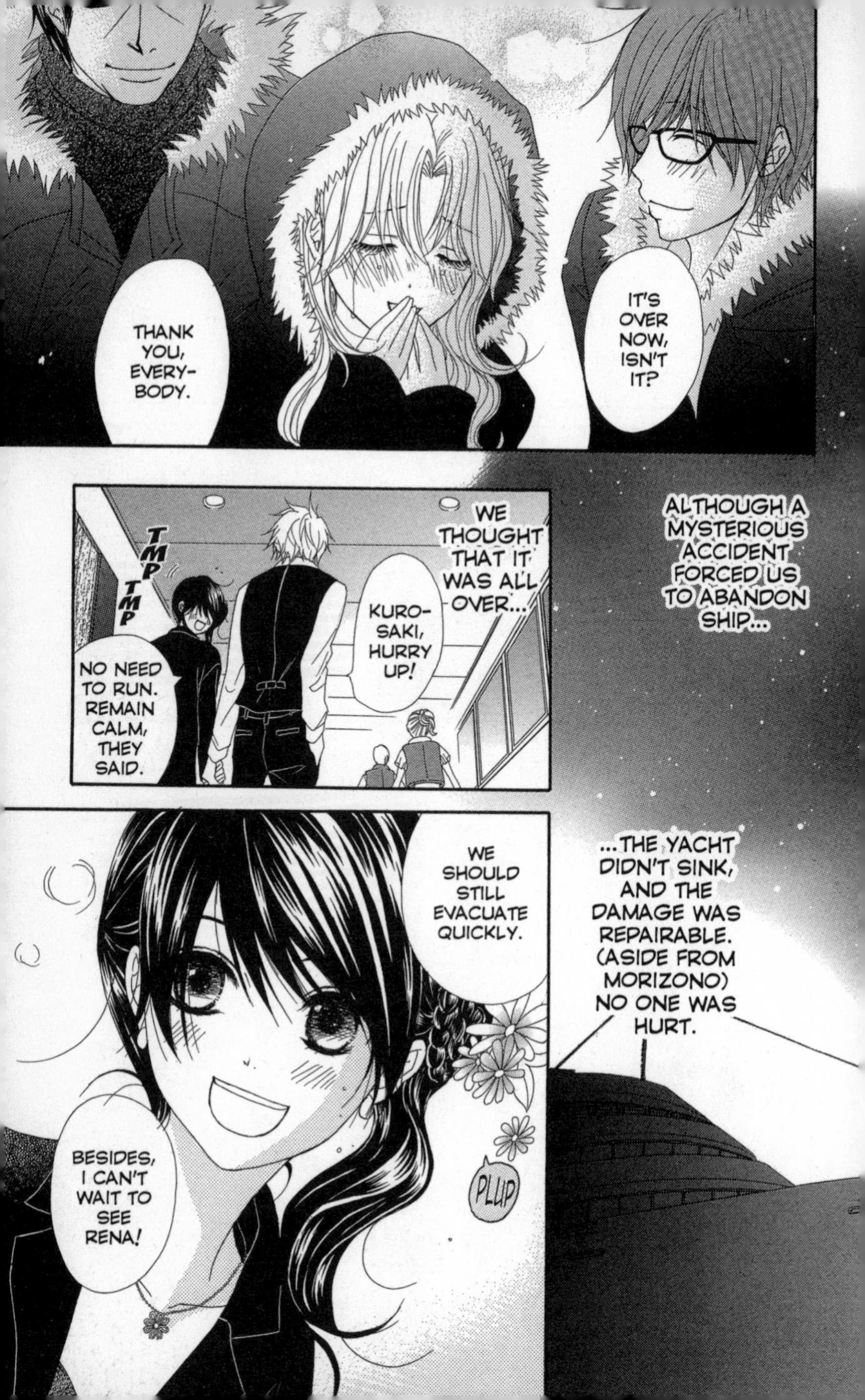
IT'S OVER NOW, ISN'T IT?
THANK YOU, EVERYBODY.
ALTHOUGH A MYSTERIOUS ACCIDENT FORCED US TO ABANDON SHIP...
WE THOUGHT THAT IT WAS ALL OVER...
KURO-SAKI, HURRY UP!
TMP TMP
NO NEED TO RUN. REMAIN CALM, THEY SAID.
...THE YACHT DIDN'T SINK, AND THE DAMAGE WAS REPAIRABLE. (ASIDE FROM MORIZONO) NO ONE WAS HURT.
WE SHOULD STILL EVACUATE QUICKLY.
PLUP
BESIDES, I CAN'T WAIT TO SEE RENA!

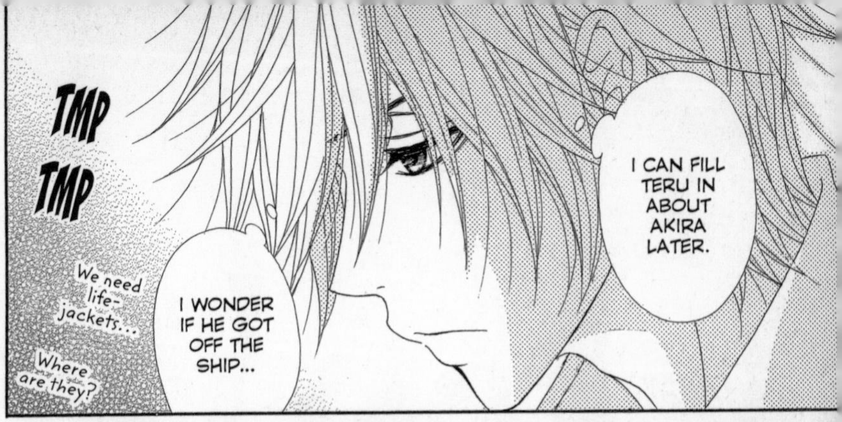
I CAN FILL TERU IN ABOUT AKIRA LATER.
I WONDER IF HE GOT OFF THE SHIP...
TMP TMP
We need life-jackets...
Where are they?

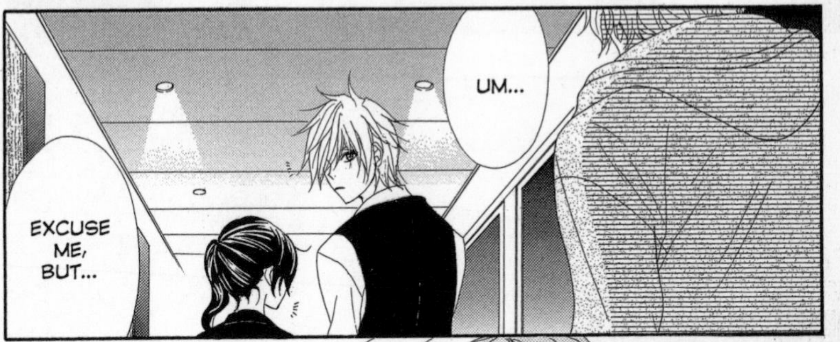
UM...
EXCUSE ME, BUT...

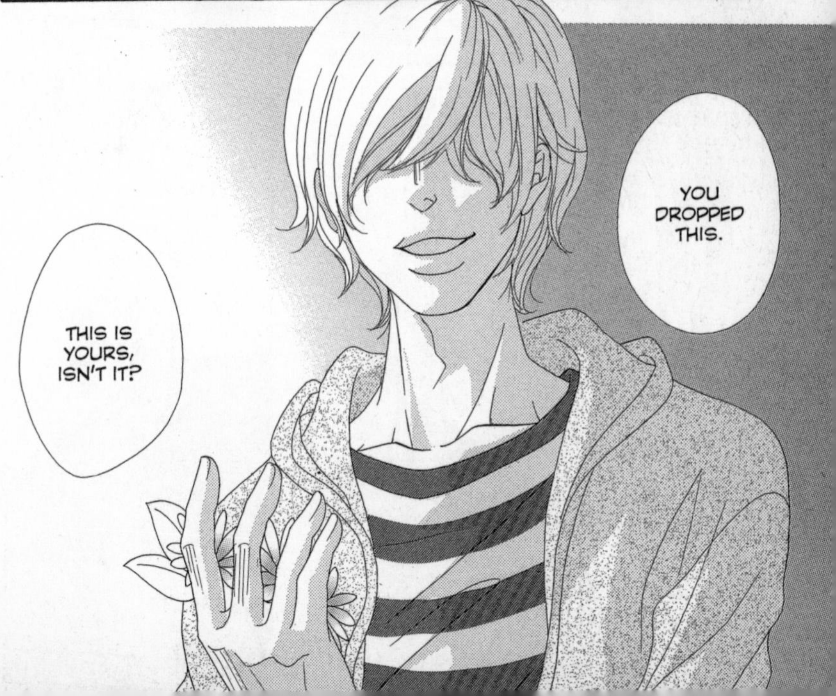
YOU DROPPED THIS.
THIS IS YOURS, ISN'T IT?

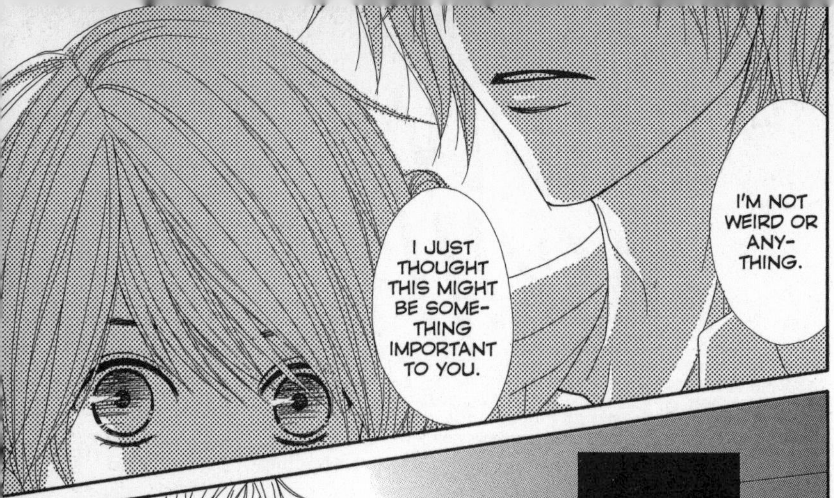
I'M NOT WEIRD OR ANY-THING.
I JUST THOUGHT THIS MIGHT BE SOME-THING IMPORTANT TO YOU.
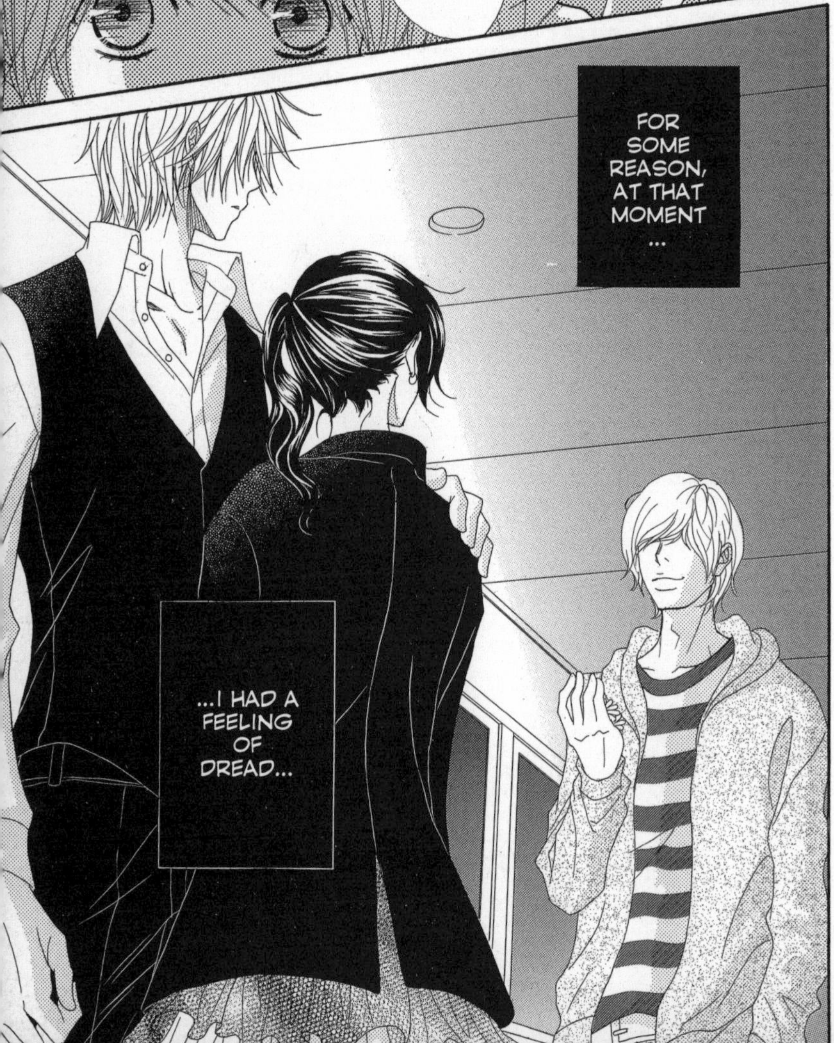
FOR SOME REASON, AT THAT MOMENT...
...I HAD A FEELING OF DREAD...

DENGEKI DAISY QUESTION CORNER

RELOCATED

# BALDLY ASK!!! ②

HOW ABOUT I MAKE SOME TEA?

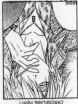

VOLUME 2 (WEIRD CAMOUFLAGE PRINT)

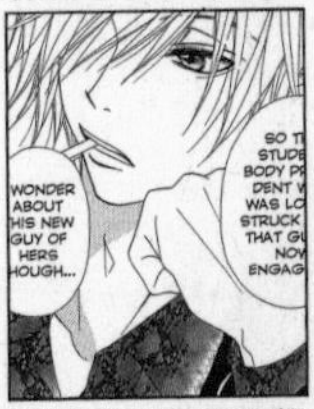

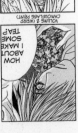

VOLUME 8 (LEOPARD PRINT)

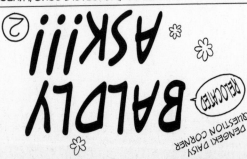

VOLUME 10 (SNAKE PRINT)

IN VOLUME 8, CHAPTER 36, "MEMORABLE SONG," KUROSAKI IS WEARING A T-SHIRT UNDER HIS JACKET IN THE DAYTIME, RIGHT? BUT THAT NIGHT WHEN HE'S MEETING MATOBA, HE'S WEARING A LEOPARD-PRINT SHIRT. DID HE CHANGE SHIRTS JUST FOR THAT MEETING? DOES KUROSAKI LIKE LEOPARD-PRINT SHIRTS?

(CHIHIRO, HOKKAIDO PREFECTURE)

KUROSAKI WEARS SORT OF GANGSTER-LIKE CLOTHING AROUND VOLUME 2, BUT HE'S BEEN WEARING RATHER PLAIN-LOOKING SHIRTS RECENTLY. WAS THAT INTENDED TO GO ALONG WITH HOW KUROSAKI'S HAIR IS SUPPOSED TO BE SIMPLE IN THE FUTURE?

(BLUE SEVEN)

A. THE LEOPARD PRINT IN VOLUME 8 WAS PART OF AN ACT TO SCARE THE OTHER PARTY. KUROSAKI'S POOR TASTE IN SHIRTS, THOUGH, IS A REFLECTION OF THE AUTHOR'S LACK OF FASHION SENSE.
I DON'T THINK YOU'RE RIGHT, THOUGH. KUROSAKI STILL WEARS ODD SHIRTS EVEN NOW. MY EDITOR LAUGHED AT THE PYTHON-PRINT SHIRT IN VOLUME 10, CHAPTERS 48-49.
OH, AND BLUE SEVEN, KUROSAKI SAYS HE WANTS TO SEE YOU UP ON THE ROOF AFTER SCHOOL.

WHENEVER TERU TRIES TO EXPOSE HER BELLYBUTTON, KUROSAKI COVERS IT UP. IS IT BECAUSE HE'S EMBARRASSED TO SEE IT? WOULD HE BE OKAY IF SHE WAS WEARING A BIKINI?

(N.F., WAKAYAMA PREFECTURE) (C/M, HOKKAIDO PREFECTURE)

A. SEEING TERU'S BELLYBUTTON INCREASES KUROSAKI'S NERVOUSNESS, BLOOD PRESSURE, AND A LOT OF OTHER THINGS, SO HE STOPS HER IN ORDER TO CONTROL HIMSELF. (HALF OF IT, THOUGH, IS BECAUSE HE REALLY DOES WORRY ABOUT TERU GETTING COLD.) IN THIS STORY, KUROSAKI HASN'T SEEN TERU IN A BIKINI YET. I DO, HOWEVER, GET A LOT OF REQUESTS TO DRAW TERU IN A BIKINI FOR COLOR *BETSUCOMI* COVERS AND CALENDARS. (I'M DOING A COLOR DRAWING RIGHT NOW EVEN AS I WRITE THIS.) FOR NOW, PLEASE JUST THINK OF IT AS POOR KUROSAKI'S IMAGINATION.

THE OTHER DAY, A FRIEND ASKED ME FOR A GENERAL IDEA OF WHAT *DENGEKI DAISY* IS LIKE. I EXPLAINED, "IT'S A STORY OF A PUNY SECOND-YEAR HIGH SCHOOL STUDENT WITH A-CUP BOOBS AND A GANGSTER-LIKE BALDING PERV SCHOOL CUSTODIAN WITH A LOLITA COMPLEX."
MY FRIEND BEGAN TO WONDER ABOUT ME. "IS THAT MANGA OKAY?" WAS THE REPLY. HOW SHOULD I HAVE EXPLAINED IT, THEN? (THAT FRIEND IS NOW SUPER INTO *DAISY*.)

(POTATO, TOKYO)

A. YOU'RE CORRECT, SO I SEE NO PROBLEM (FOR SURE). THANK YOU FOR INTRODUCING *DAISY* TO YOUR FRIEND. IF I WERE TO ADD SOMETHING, IT'D BE THAT THIS MANGA IS A "LOVE COMEDY." (THAT'S WHAT MY EDITOR CALLED IT.) AND THAT'S EVEN WITH ALL THE COMPLICATED STUFF ABOUT CODES AND AN EXPLOSION ON A LUXURY YACHT. IT'S A LOVE COMEDY.

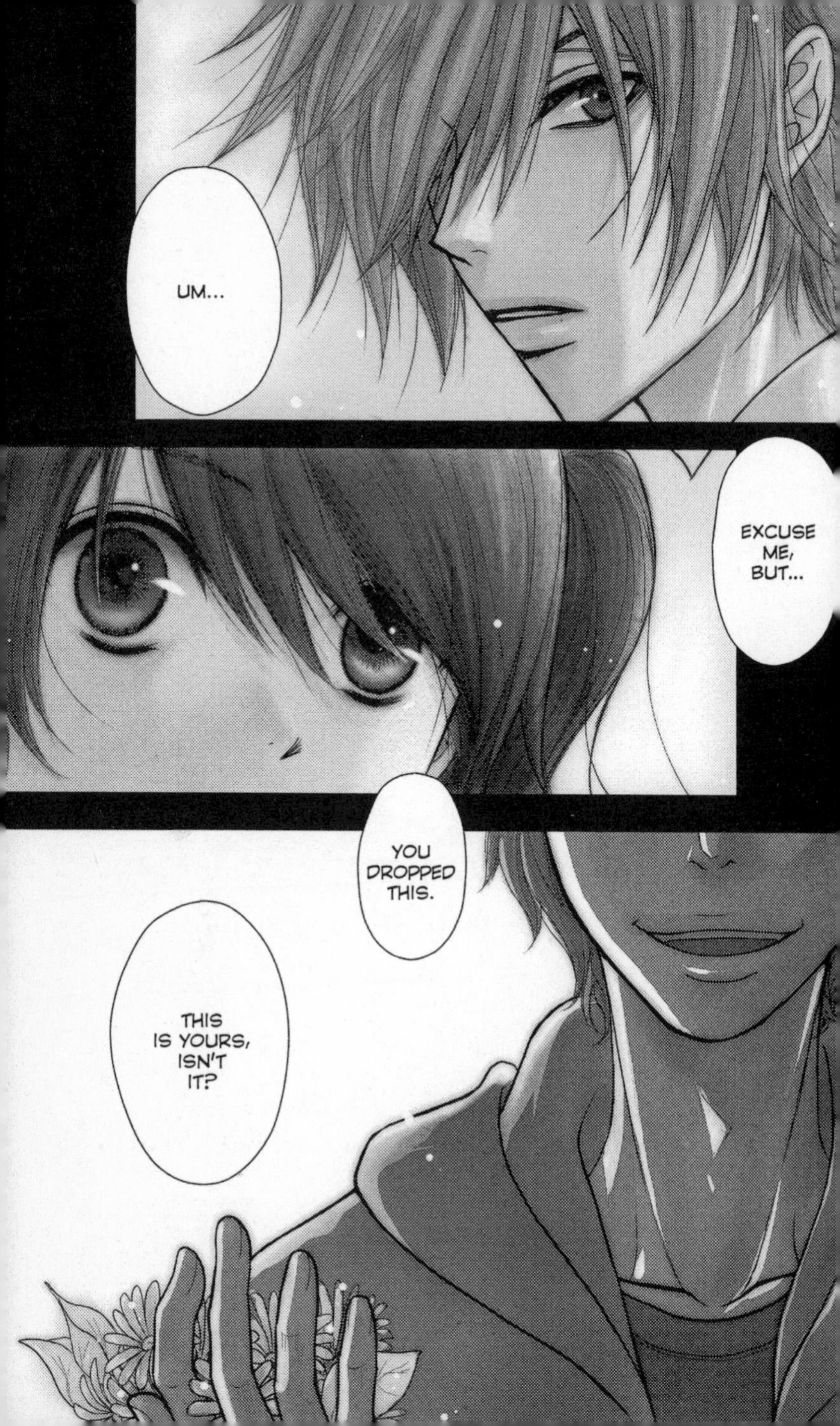
UM...
EXCUSE ME, BUT...
YOU DROPPED THIS.
THIS IS YOURS, ISN'T IT?

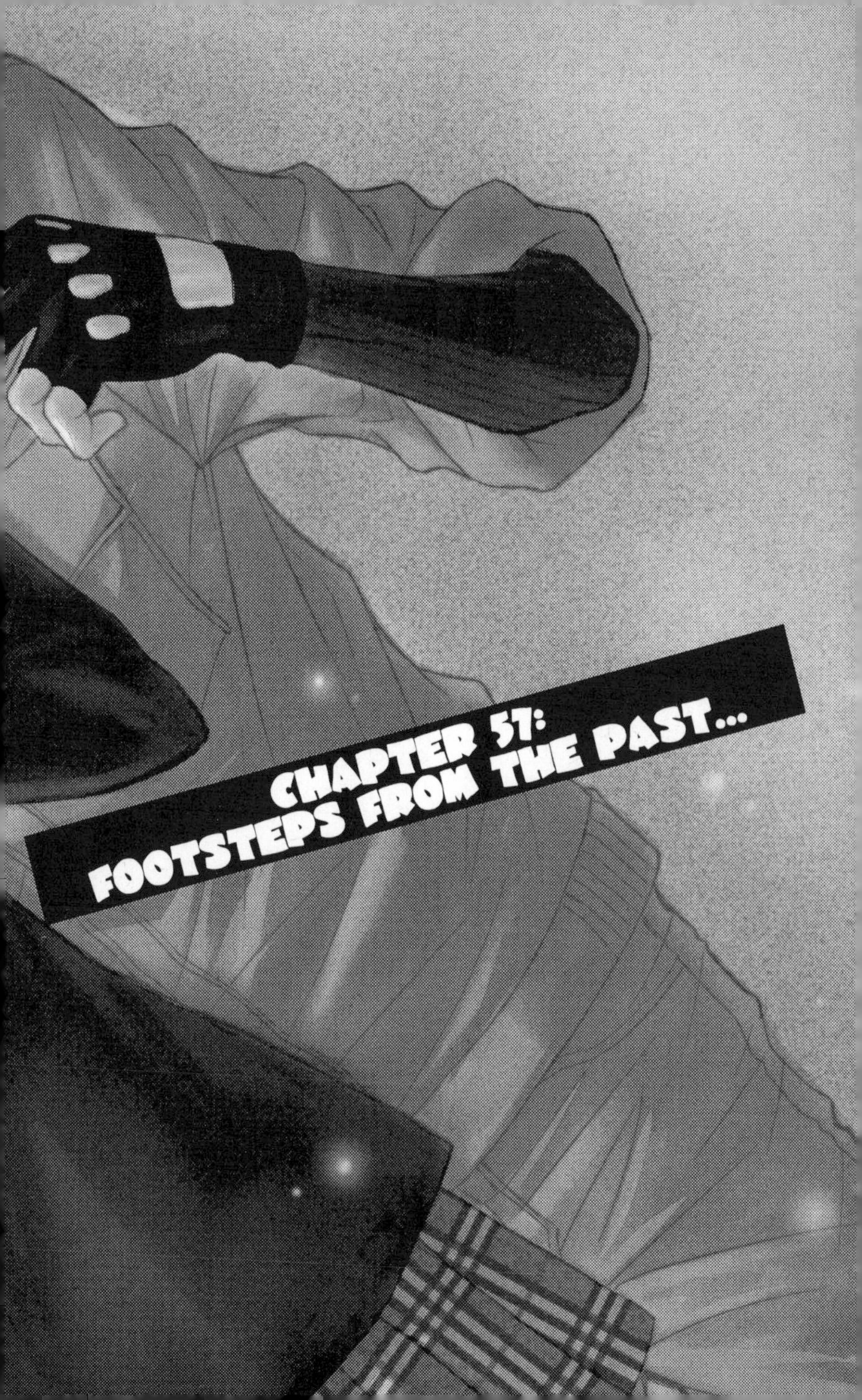
CHAPTER 57:
FOOTSTEPS FROM THE PAST...

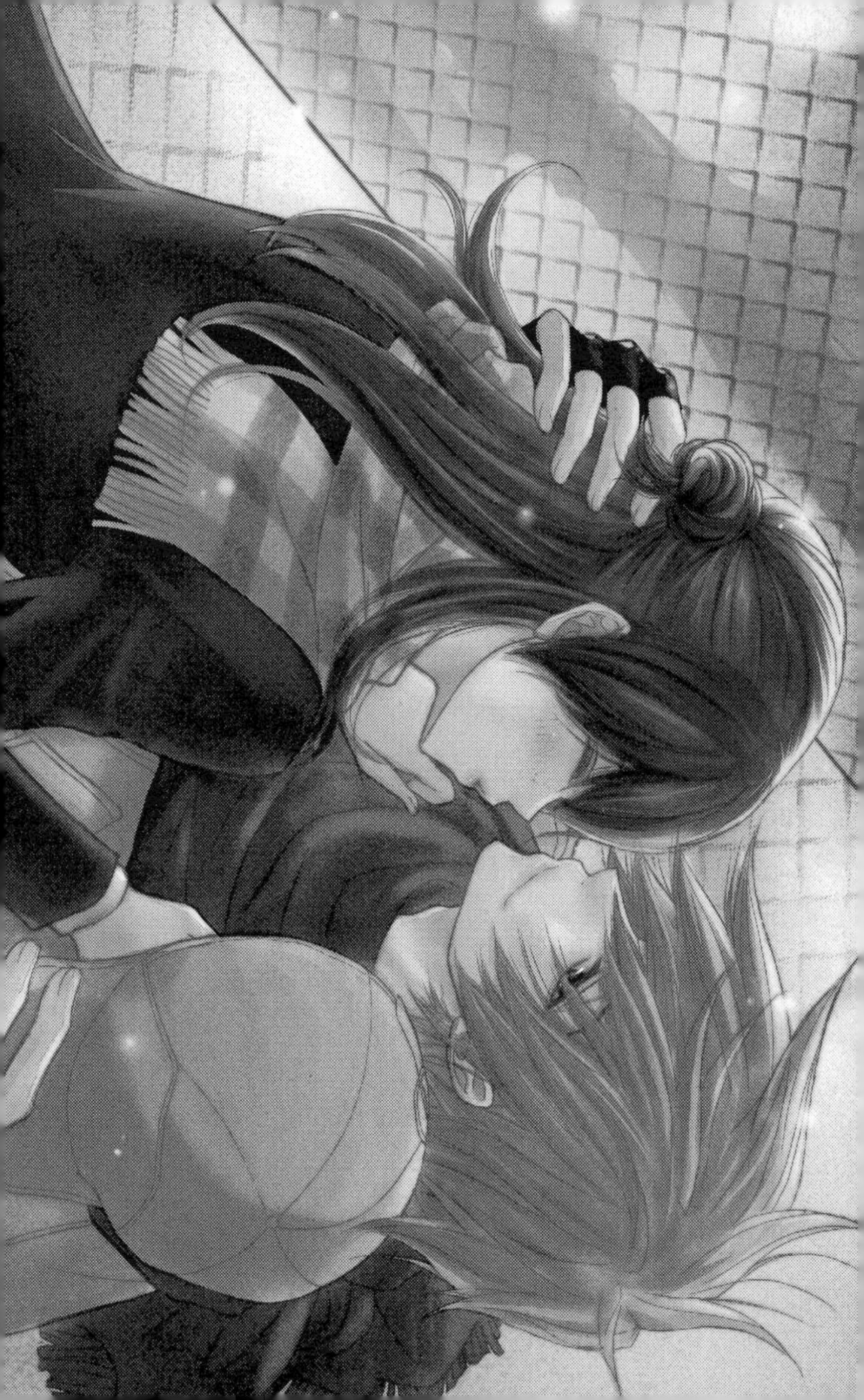

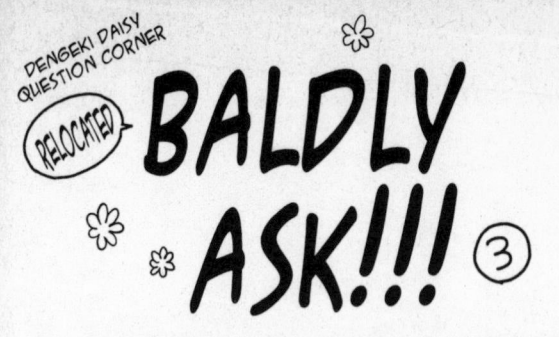

DENGEKI DAISY
QUESTION CORNER

RELOCATED

# BALDLY ASK!!! ③

IN DENGEKI DAISY VOLUME 3, CHAPTER 10, THERE'S A VERY IMPORTANT SCENE WHERE KUROSAKI HUGS TERU. MAYBE I HAVE A STRANGE WAY OF THINKING, BUT I CAN'T HELP BUT THINK THAT THIS MARK ON KUROSAKI'S NECK LOOKS LIKE A PI● ELEKIBAN [TYPE OF MAGNETIC BANDAGE]. ←

(FAWN, NARA PREFECTURE)

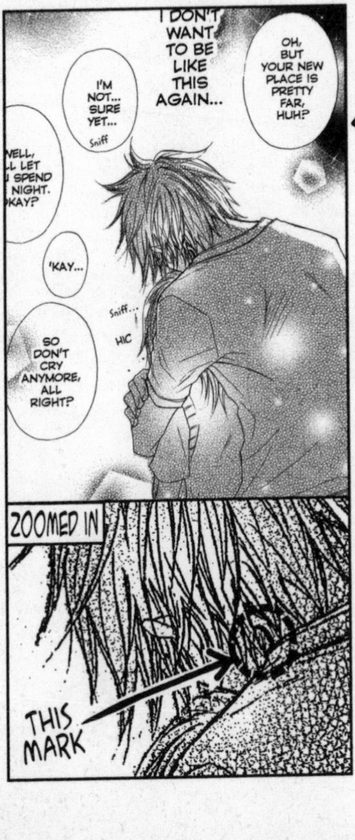


A.

YOU MEAN THIS SCENE, RIGHT?

OH YEAH, HE REALLY IS WEARING AN ELEKIBAN.
~~NO, WAIT. THAT'S SHADING SO THAT HIS NECK DOESN'T APPEAR SO THICK...~~

YUP, HE'S WEARING ONE, ALL RIGHT. HE REALLY IS. MAYBE IT'S BECAUSE HE GOT A CRICK IN HIS NECK FROM THE TIME HE WAS SLEEPING EVERY NIGHT ON HIS SOFA.

I'M REALLY SORRY ABOUT THAT. HAD I NOTICED IT, I WOULD'VE DEFINITELY MADE HIM PEEL IT OFF. THANK YOU, FAWN, FOR POINTING THAT OUT. FROM NOW ON, I'LL DO BETTER SO THAT I DON'T LET THESE BACKGROUND THINGS SHOW. I'M REALLY SORRY I'M NOT A VERY GOOD ARTIST.

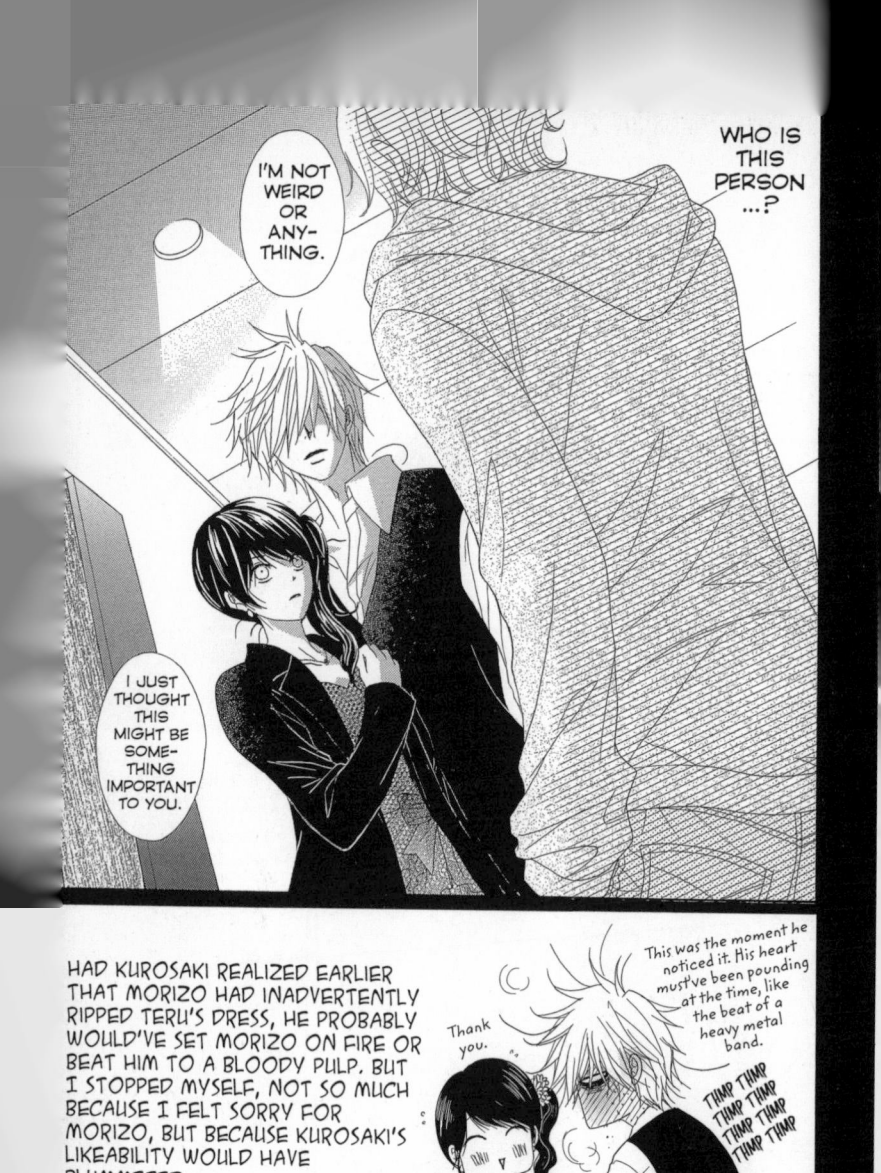

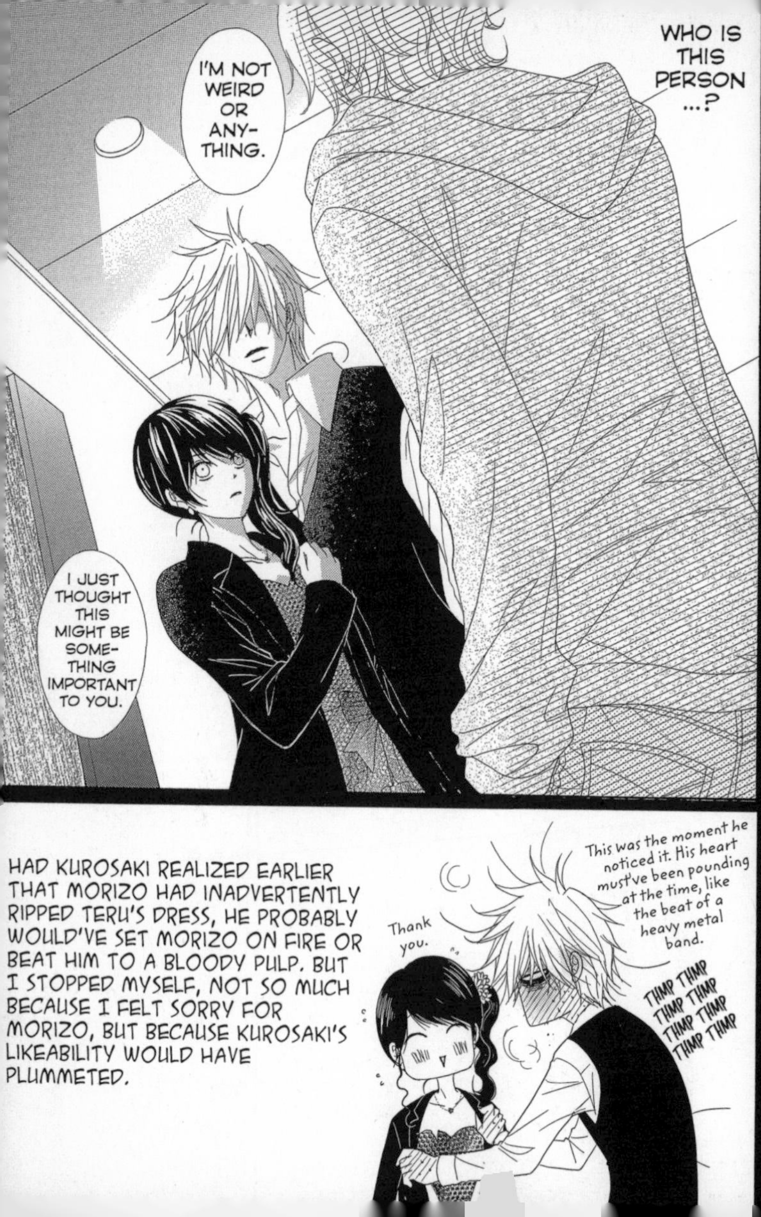
WHO IS THIS PERSON ...?
I'M NOT WEIRD OR ANY-THING.
I JUST THOUGHT THIS MIGHT BE SOME-THING IMPORTANT TO YOU.
This was the moment he noticed it. His heart must've been pounding at the time, like the beat of a heavy metal band.
THMP THMP THMP THMP THMP THMP THMP THMP
Thank you.
HAD KUROSAKI REALIZED EARLIER THAT MORIZO HAD INADVERTENTLY RIPPED TERU'S DRESS, HE PROBABLY WOULD'VE SET MORIZO ON FIRE OR BEAT HIM TO A BLOODY PULP. BUT I STOPPED MYSELF, NOT SO MUCH BECAUSE I FELT SORRY FOR MORIZO, BUT BECAUSE KUROSAKI'S LIKEABILITY WOULD HAVE PLUMMETED.

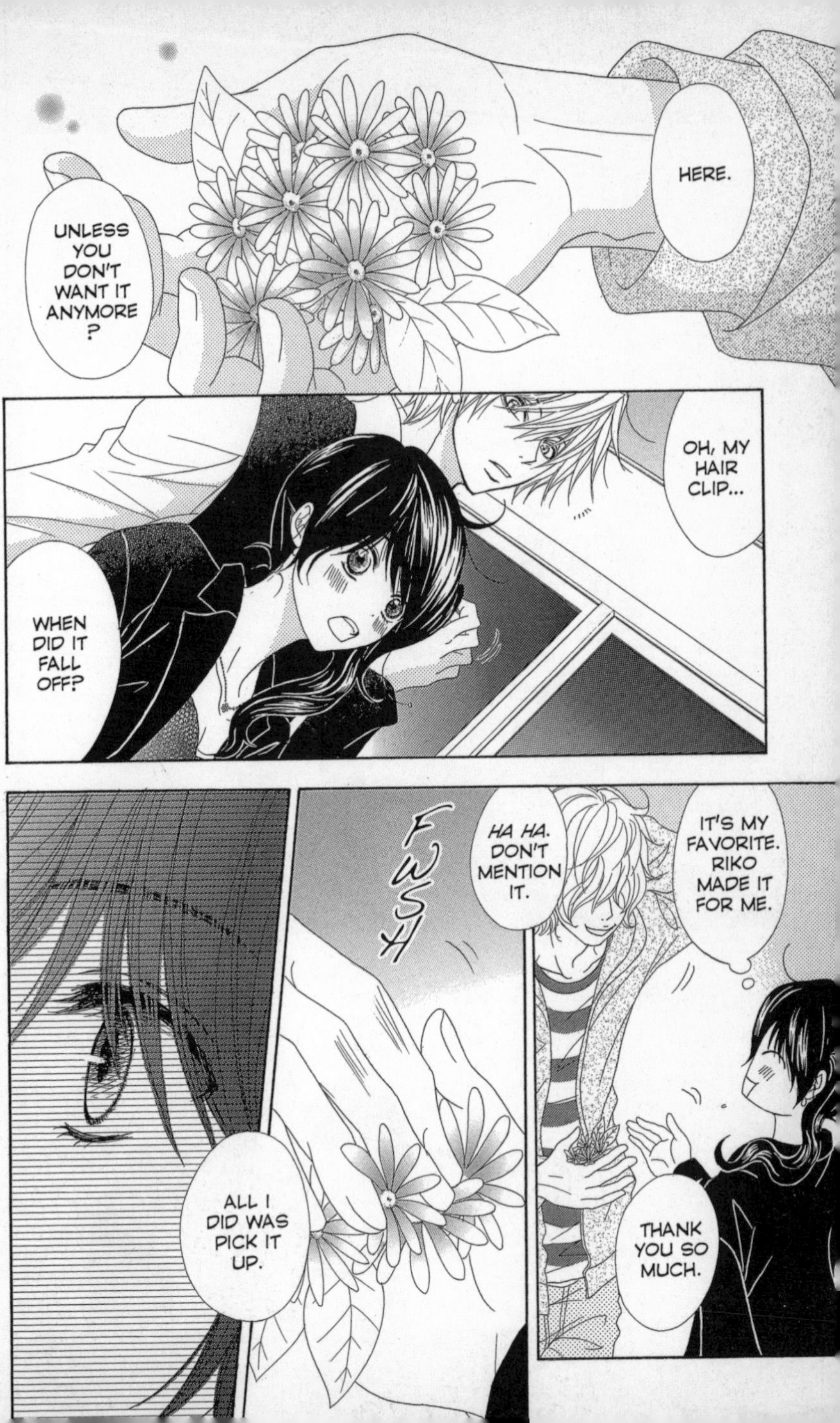
HERE.
UNLESS YOU DON'T WANT IT ANYMORE ?
OH, MY HAIR CLIP...
WHEN DID IT FALL OFF?
IT'S MY FAVORITE. RIKO MADE IT FOR ME.
THANK YOU SO MUCH.
HA HA. DON'T MENTION IT.
FWSH
ALL I DID WAS PICK IT UP.

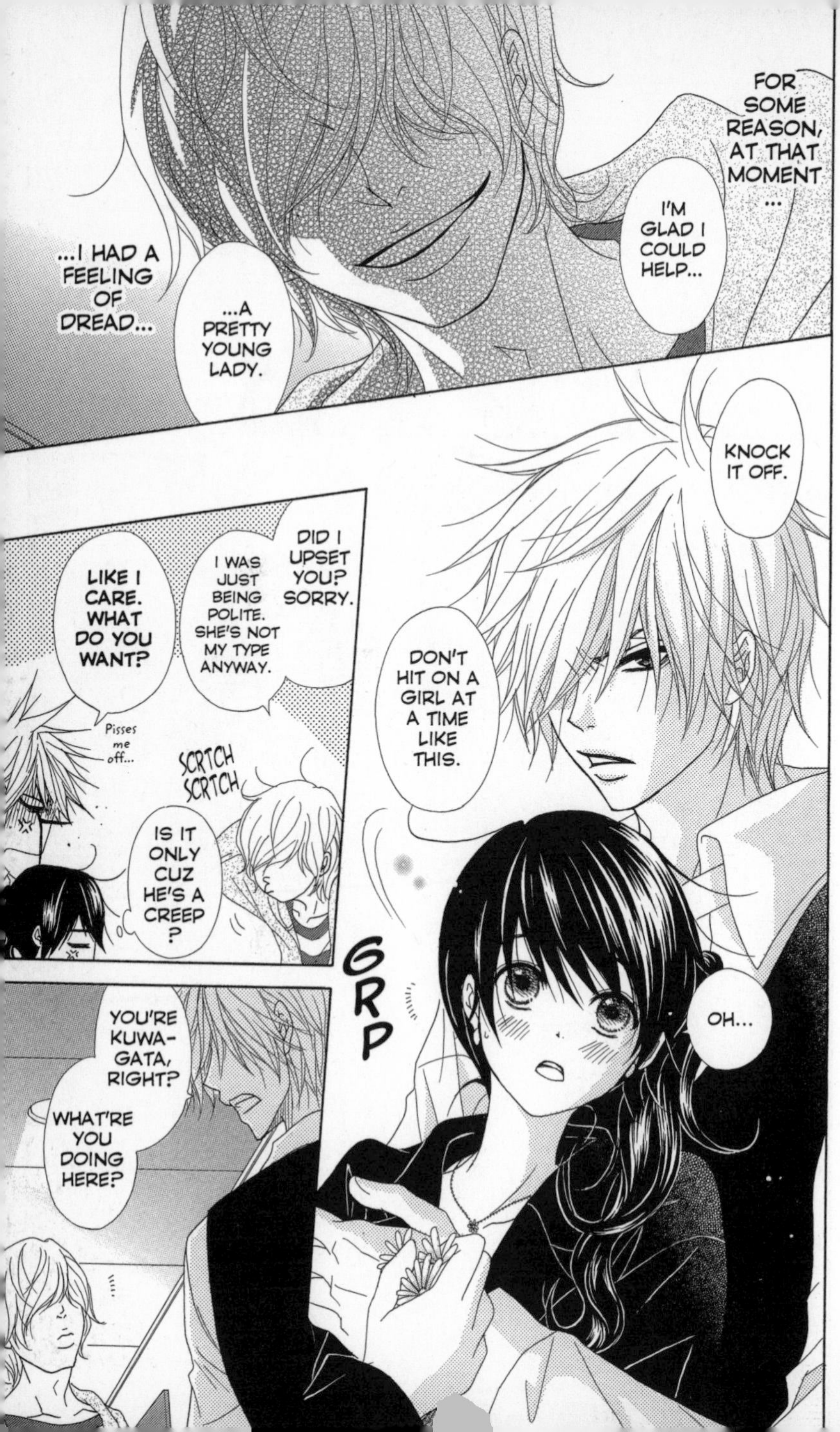
FOR SOME REASON, AT THAT MOMENT ...
I'M GLAD I COULD HELP...
...A PRETTY YOUNG LADY.
...I HAD A FEELING OF DREAD...
KNOCK IT OFF.
DON'T HIT ON A GIRL AT A TIME LIKE THIS.
DID I UPSET YOU? SORRY.
I WAS JUST BEING POLITE. SHE'S NOT MY TYPE ANYWAY.
LIKE I CARE. WHAT DO YOU WANT?
Pisses me off...
SCRTCH SCRTCH
IS IT ONLY CUZ HE'S A CREEP ?
GRP
OH...
YOU'RE KUWA-GATA, RIGHT?
WHAT'RE YOU DOING HERE?

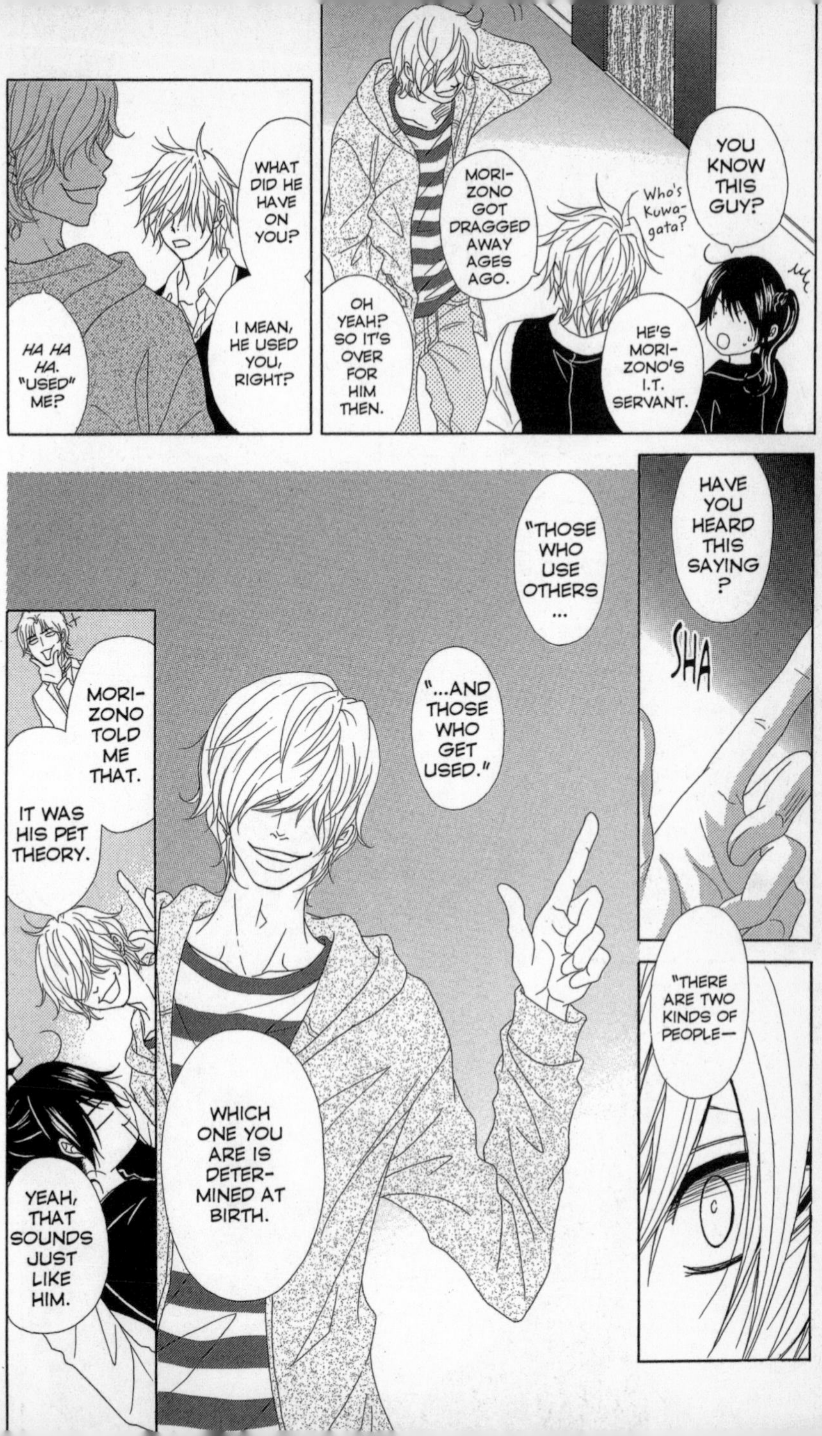
YOU KNOW THIS GUY?
Who's Kuwa-gata?
HE'S MORI-ZONO'S I.T. SERVANT.
MORI-ZONO GOT DRAGGED AWAY AGES AGO.
OH YEAH? SO IT'S OVER FOR HIM THEN.
WHAT DID HE HAVE ON YOU?
I MEAN, HE USED YOU, RIGHT?
HA HA HA. "USED" ME?
HAVE YOU HEARD THIS SAYING ?
SHA
"THERE ARE TWO KINDS OF PEOPLE—
"THOSE WHO USE OTHERS ...
"...AND THOSE WHO GET USED."
MORI-ZONO TOLD ME THAT.
IT WAS HIS PET THEORY.
WHICH ONE YOU ARE IS DETER-MINED AT BIRTH.
YEAH, THAT SOUNDS JUST LIKE HIM.

...KURO-SAKI?

...WHICH KIND ARE YOU...

DO YOU REMEM-BER...

OH, HEY...

MORI-ZONO WAS A PITIFUL GUY.

HE THOUGHT HE WAS THE ONE USING OTHERS.

SORRY FOR BOTHER-ING YOU.

HMM

HUH?

NEVER MIND.

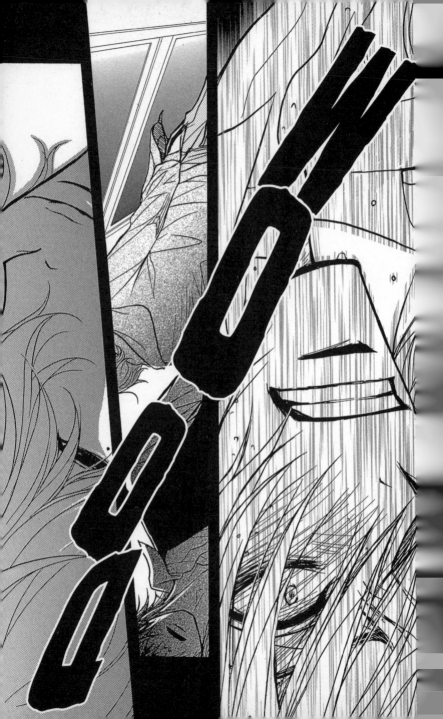

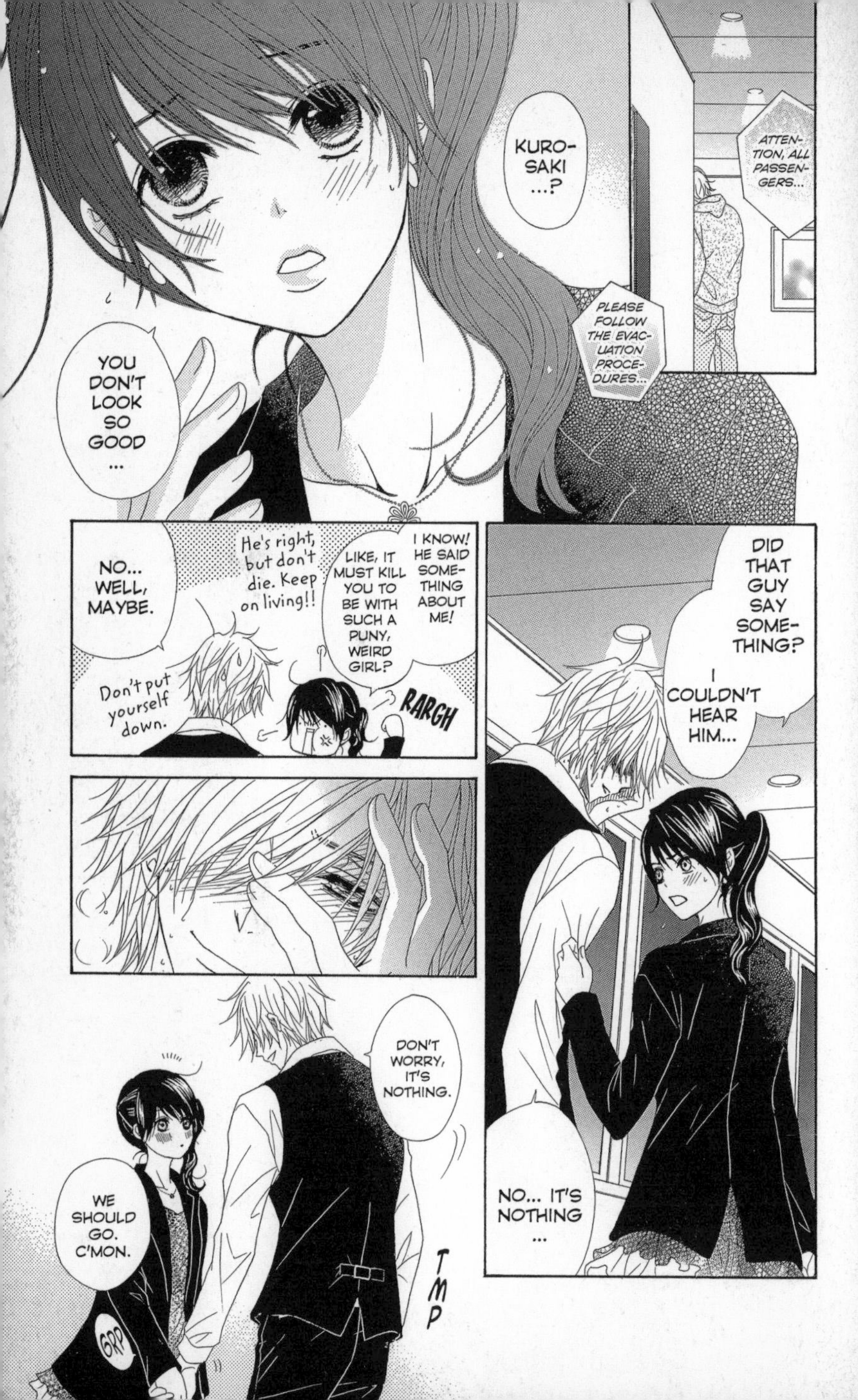
ATTENTION, ALL PASSENGERS...
PLEASE FOLLOW THE EVACUATION PROCEDURES...
KUROSAKI ...?
YOU DON'T LOOK SO GOOD ...
DID THAT GUY SAY SOMETHING?
I COULDN'T HEAR HIM...
NO... IT'S NOTHING ...
NO... WELL, MAYBE.
He's right, but don't die. Keep on living!!
Don't put yourself down.
I KNOW! HE SAID SOMETHING ABOUT ME!
LIKE, IT MUST KILL YOU TO BE WITH SUCH A PUNY, WEIRD GIRL?
RARGH
DON'T WORRY, IT'S NOTHING.
TMP
WE SHOULD GO. C'MON.
GRP

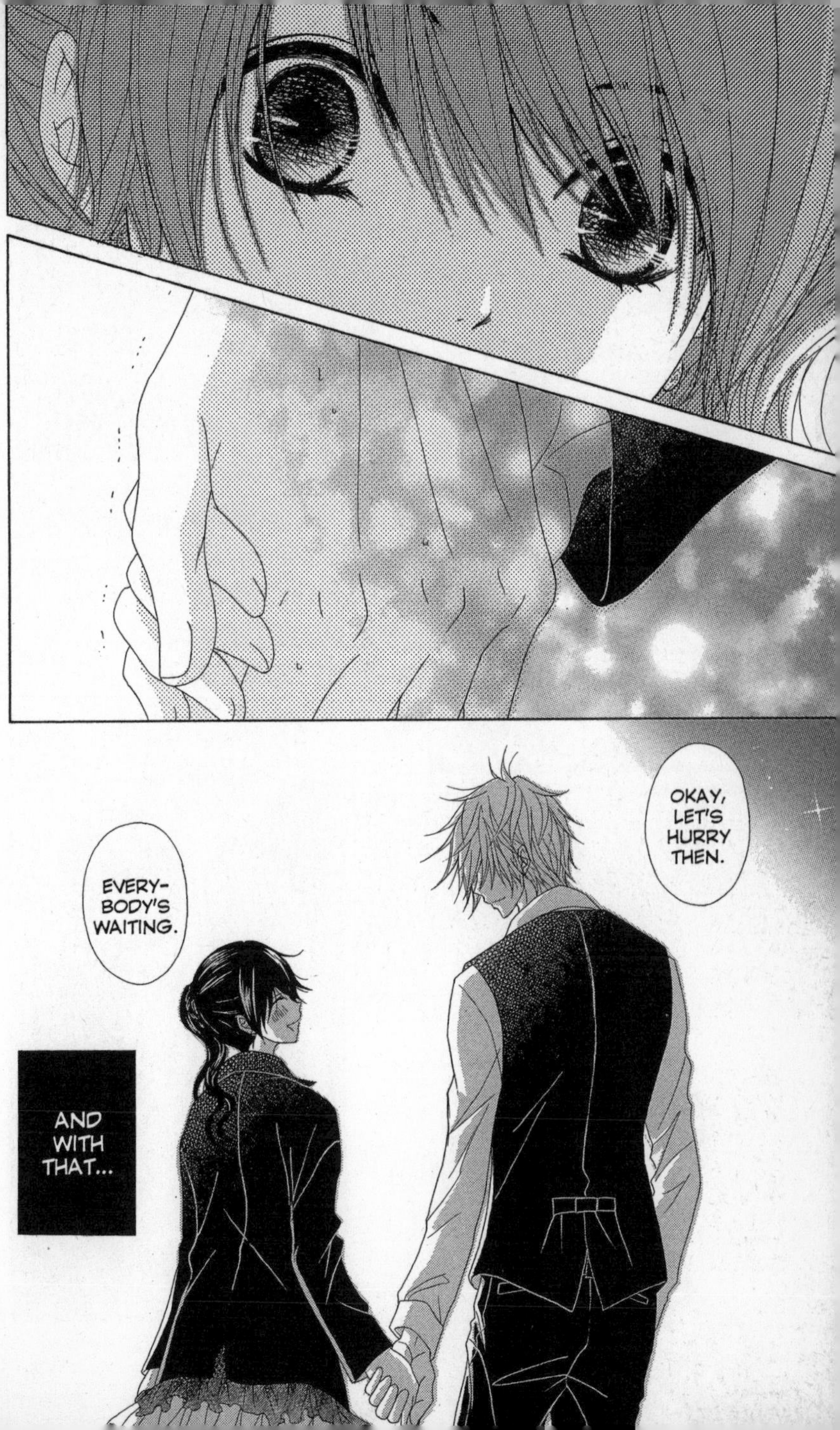
...
...
OKAY, LET'S HURRY THEN.
EVERY-BODY'S WAITING.
AND WITH THAT...

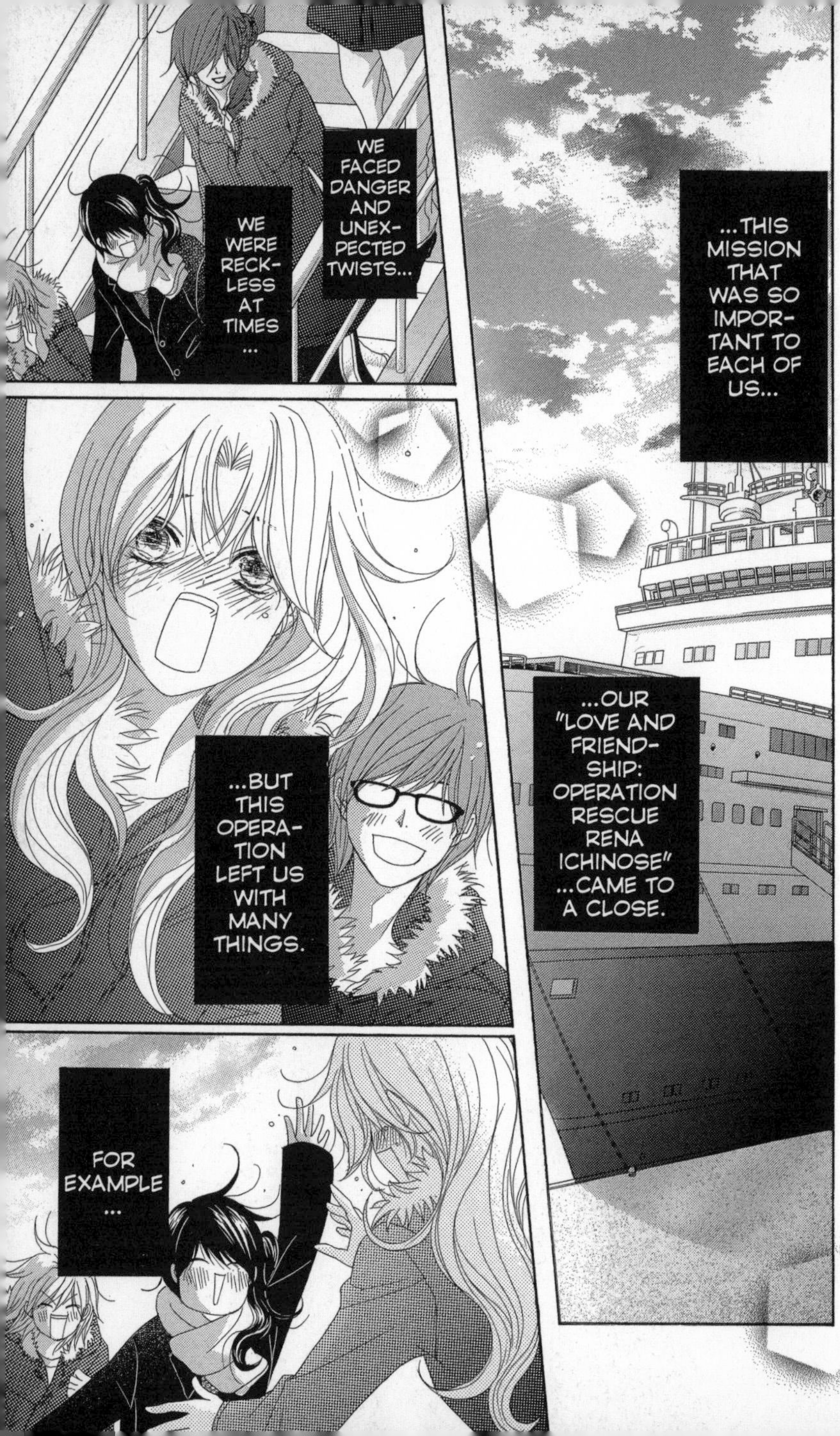
...THIS MISSION THAT WAS SO IMPORTANT TO EACH OF US...
...OUR "LOVE AND FRIENDSHIP: OPERATION RESCUE RENA ICHINOSE" ...CAME TO A CLOSE.
WE FACED DANGER AND UNEXPECTED TWISTS...
WE WERE RECKLESS AT TIMES...
...BUT THIS OPERATION LEFT US WITH MANY THINGS.
FOR EXAMPLE...

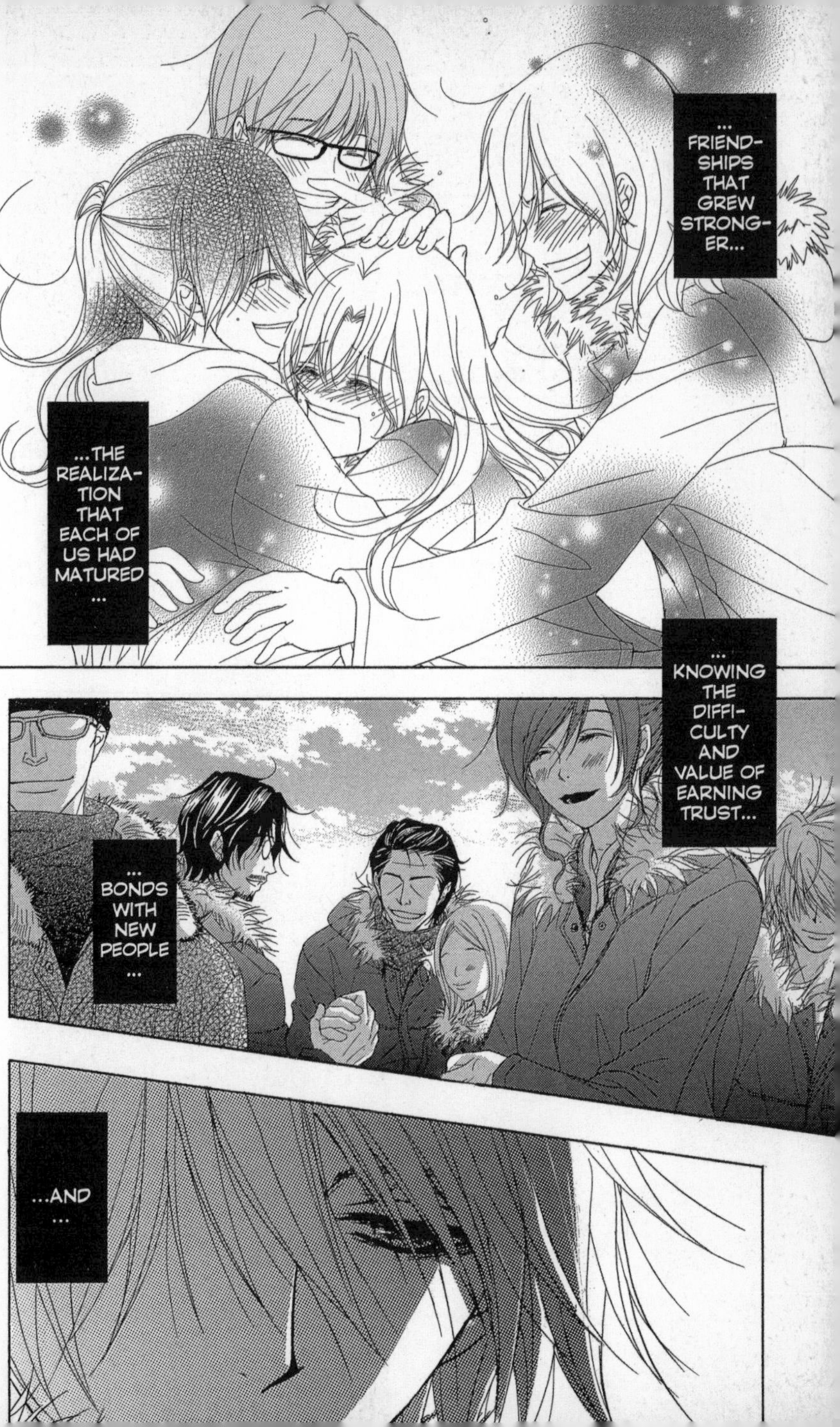
...FRIEND-SHIPS THAT GREW STRONG-ER...
...THE REALIZA-TION THAT EACH OF US HAD MATURED...
...KNOWING THE DIFFI-CULTY AND VALUE OF EARNING TRUST...
...BONDS WITH NEW PEOPLE...
...AND...

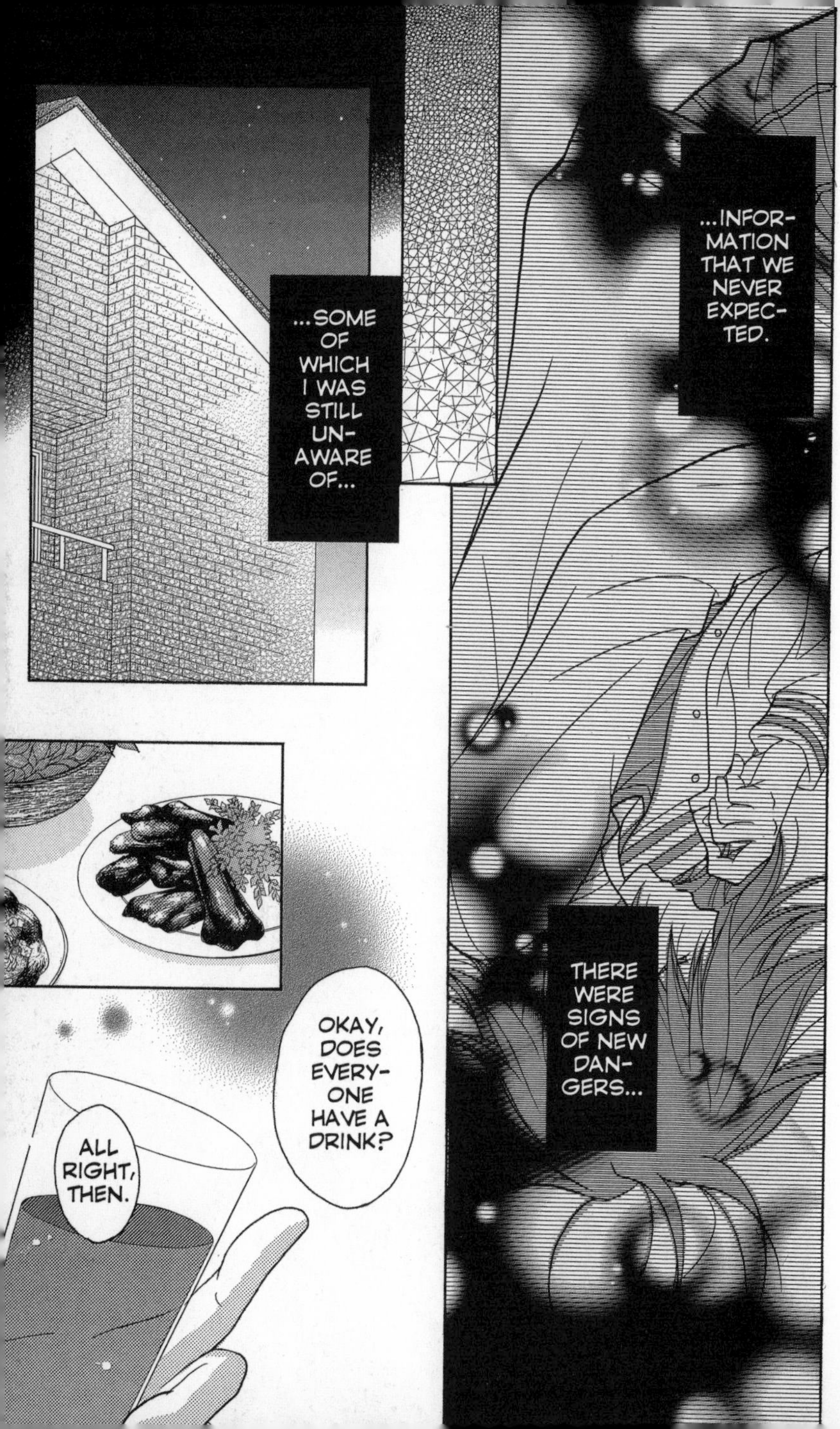
...INFORMATION THAT WE NEVER EXPECTED.
THERE WERE SIGNS OF NEW DANGERS...
...SOME OF WHICH I WAS STILL UNAWARE OF...
OKAY, DOES EVERYONE HAVE A DRINK?
ALL RIGHT, THEN.

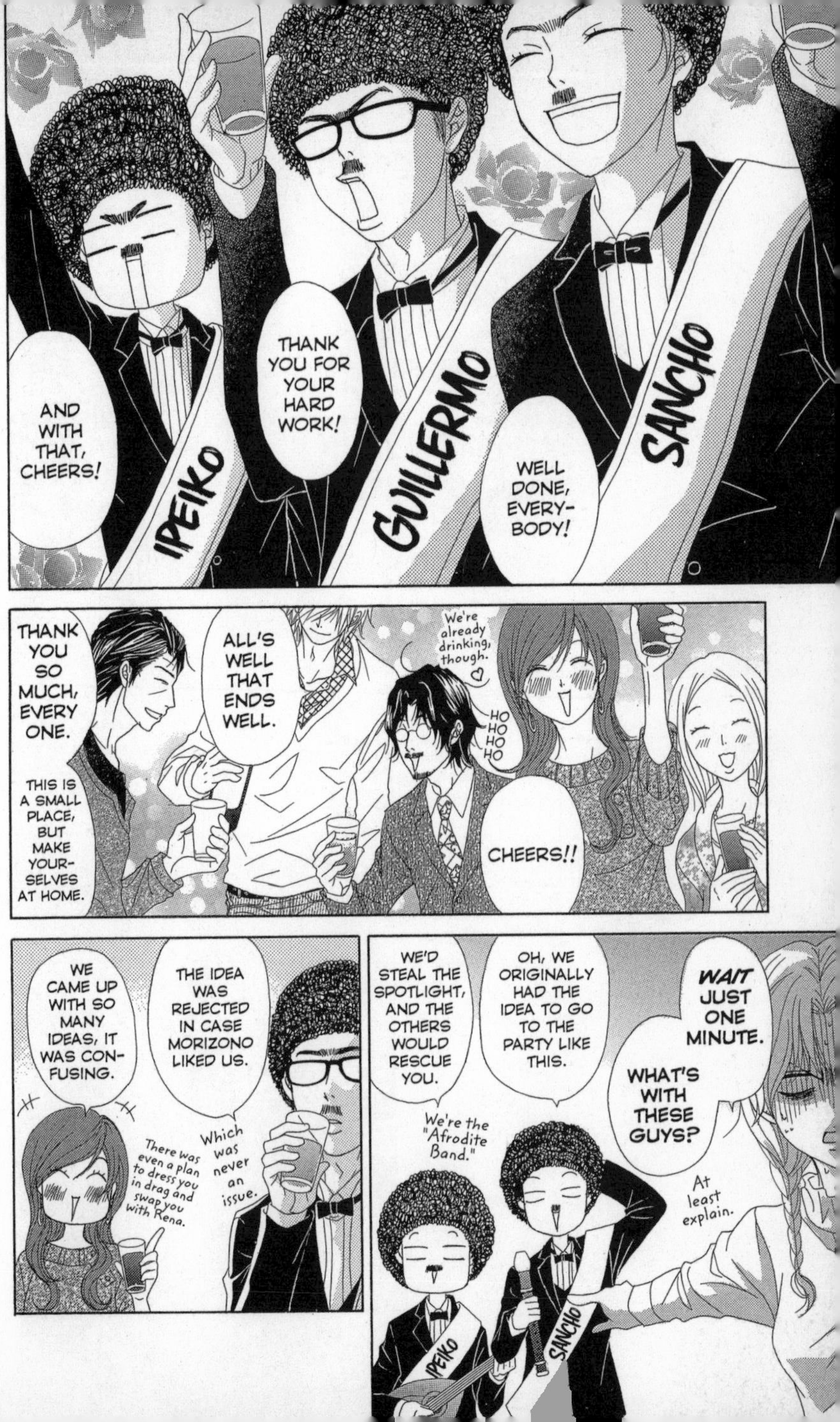
AND WITH THAT, CHEERS!
IPEIKO
THANK YOU FOR YOUR HARD WORK!
GUILLERMO
WELL DONE, EVERY-BODY!
SANCHO
THANK YOU SO MUCH, EVERY ONE.
THIS IS A SMALL PLACE, BUT MAKE YOUR-SELVES AT HOME.
ALL'S WELL THAT ENDS WELL.
We're already drinking, though.
HO HO HO HO
CHEERS!!
WAIT JUST ONE MINUTE.
WHAT'S WITH THESE GUYS?
At least explain.
OH, WE ORIGINALLY HAD THE IDEA TO GO TO THE PARTY LIKE THIS.
WE'D STEAL THE SPOTLIGHT, AND THE OTHERS WOULD RESCUE YOU.
We're the "Afrodite Band."
IPEIKO
SANCHO
THE IDEA WAS REJECTED IN CASE MORIZONO LIKED US.
Which was never an issue.
WE CAME UP WITH SO MANY IDEAS, IT WAS CON-FUSING.
There was even a plan to dress you in drag and swap you with Rena.

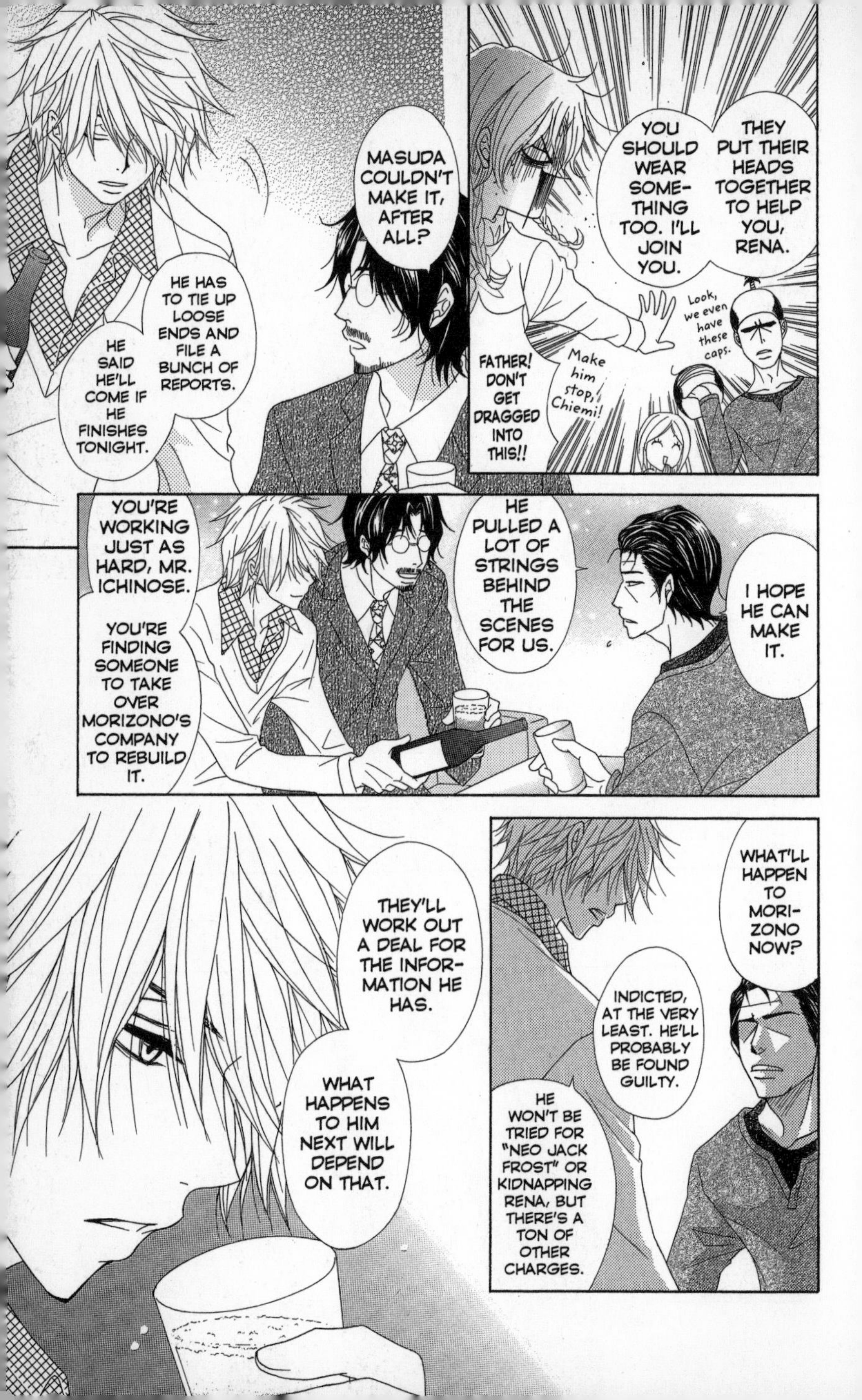
THEY PUT THEIR HEADS TOGETHER TO HELP YOU, RENA.
YOU SHOULD WEAR SOME-THING TOO. I'LL JOIN YOU.
Look, we even have these caps.
Make him stop, Chiemi!
FATHER! DON'T GET DRAGGED INTO THIS!!
MASUDA COULDN'T MAKE IT, AFTER ALL?
HE HAS TO TIE UP LOOSE ENDS AND FILE A BUNCH OF REPORTS.
HE SAID HE'LL COME IF HE FINISHES TONIGHT.
I HOPE HE CAN MAKE IT.
HE PULLED A LOT OF STRINGS BEHIND THE SCENES FOR US.
YOU'RE WORKING JUST AS HARD, MR. ICHINOSE.
YOU'RE FINDING SOMEONE TO TAKE OVER MORIZONO'S COMPANY TO REBUILD IT.
WHAT'LL HAPPEN TO MORI-ZONO NOW?
INDICTED, AT THE VERY LEAST. HE'LL PROBABLY BE FOUND GUILTY.
HE WON'T BE TRIED FOR "NEO JACK FROST" OR KIDNAPPING RENA, BUT THERE'S A TON OF OTHER CHARGES.
THEY'LL WORK OUT A DEAL FOR THE INFOR-MATION HE HAS.
WHAT HAPPENS TO HIM NEXT WILL DEPEND ON THAT.

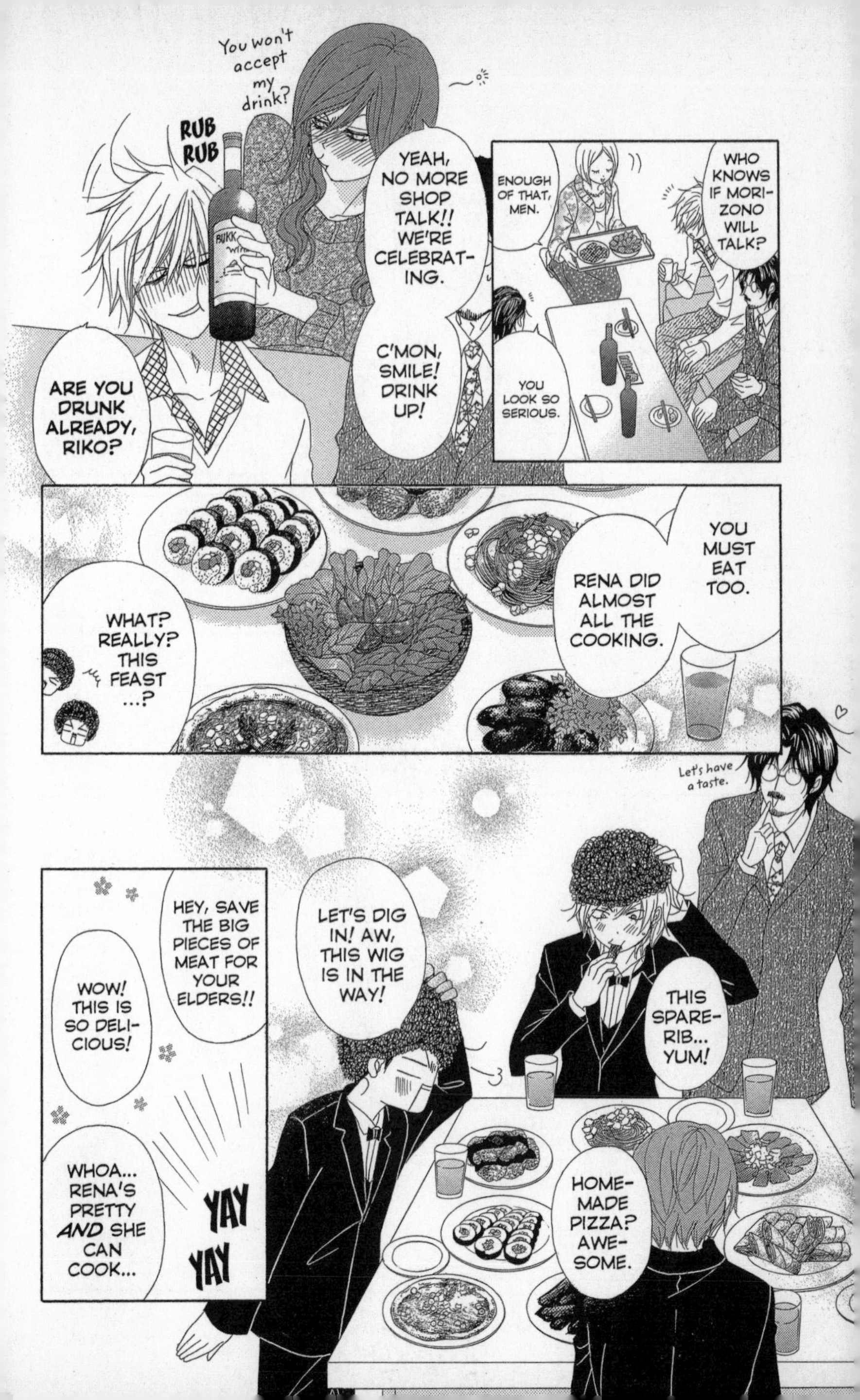
WHO KNOWS IF MORI-ZONO WILL TALK?
ENOUGH OF THAT, MEN.
YOU LOOK SO SERIOUS.
You won't accept my drink?
YEAH, NO MORE SHOP TALK!! WE'RE CELEBRAT-ING.
C'MON, SMILE! DRINK UP!
RUB RUB
ARE YOU DRUNK ALREADY, RIKO?
YOU MUST EAT TOO.
RENA DID ALMOST ALL THE COOKING.
WHAT? REALLY? THIS FEAST ...?
Let's have a taste.
THIS SPARE-RIB... YUM!
HOME-MADE PIZZA? AWE-SOME.
LET'S DIG IN! AW, THIS WIG IS IN THE WAY!
HEY, SAVE THE BIG PIECES OF MEAT FOR YOUR ELDERS!!
WOW! THIS IS SO DELI-CIOUS!
WHOA... RENA'S PRETTY AND SHE CAN COOK...
YAY
YAY

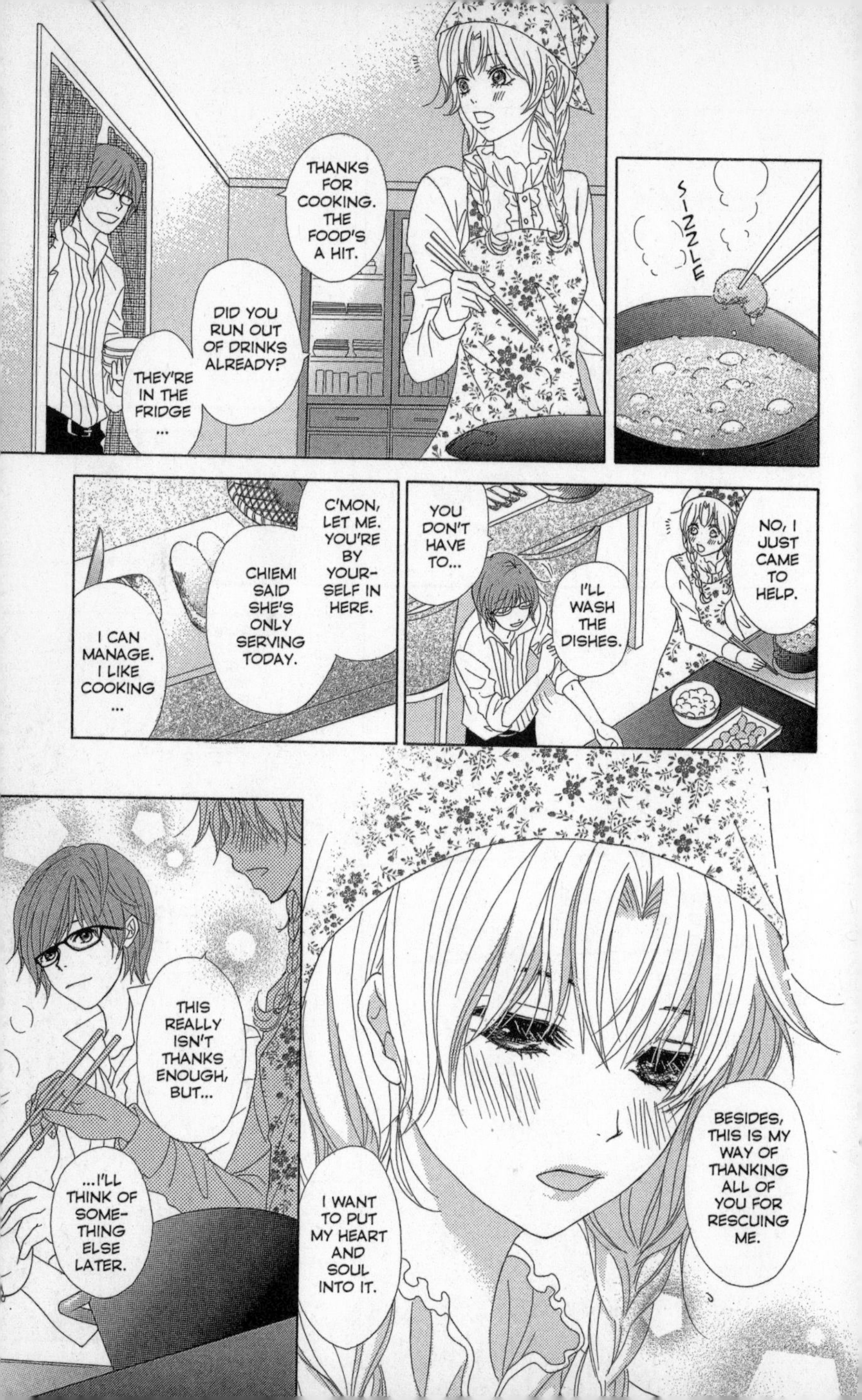
SIZZLE
THANKS FOR COOKING. THE FOOD'S A HIT.
DID YOU RUN OUT OF DRINKS ALREADY?
THEY'RE IN THE FRIDGE ...
NO, I JUST CAME TO HELP.
I'LL WASH THE DISHES.
YOU DON'T HAVE TO...
C'MON, LET ME. YOU'RE BY YOURSELF IN HERE.
CHIEMI SAID SHE'S ONLY SERVING TODAY.
I CAN MANAGE. I LIKE COOKING ...
BESIDES, THIS IS MY WAY OF THANKING ALL OF YOU FOR RESCUING ME.
I WANT TO PUT MY HEART AND SOUL INTO IT.
THIS REALLY ISN'T THANKS ENOUGH, BUT...
...I'LL THINK OF SOMETHING ELSE LATER.

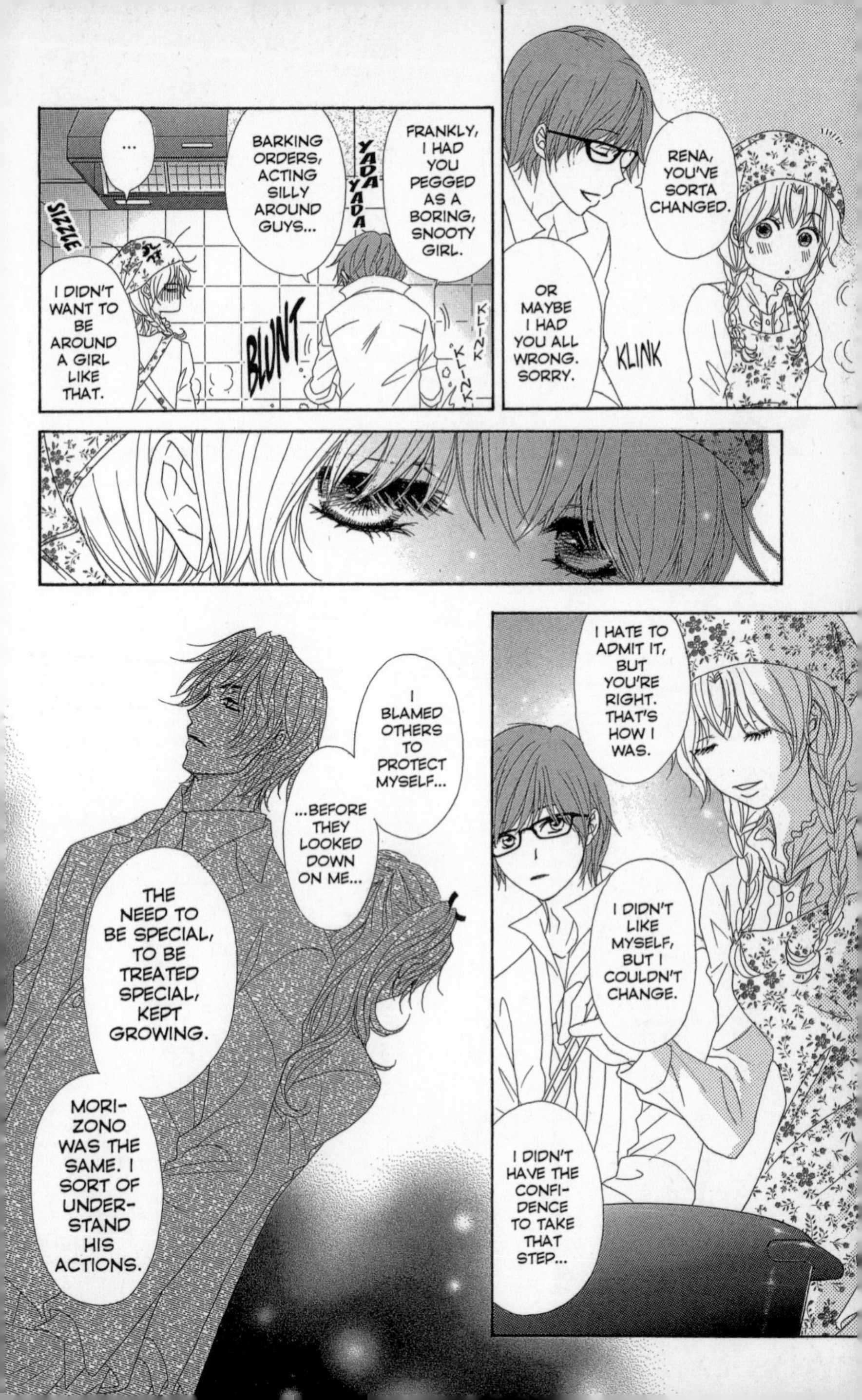
RENA, YOU'VE SORTA CHANGED.
OR MAYBE I HAD YOU ALL WRONG. SORRY.
KLINK
FRANKLY, I HAD YOU PEGGED AS A BORING, SNOOTY GIRL.
YADA YADA
BARKING ORDERS, ACTING SILLY AROUND GUYS...
...
KLINK KLINK
BLUNT
SIZZLE
I DIDN'T WANT TO BE AROUND A GIRL LIKE THAT.
I HATE TO ADMIT IT, BUT YOU'RE RIGHT. THAT'S HOW I WAS.
I DIDN'T LIKE MYSELF, BUT I COULDN'T CHANGE.
I DIDN'T HAVE THE CONFI-DENCE TO TAKE THAT STEP...
I BLAMED OTHERS TO PROTECT MYSELF...
...BEFORE THEY LOOKED DOWN ON ME...
THE NEED TO BE SPECIAL, TO BE TREATED SPECIAL, KEPT GROWING.
MORI-ZONO WAS THE SAME. I SORT OF UNDER-STAND HIS ACTIONS.

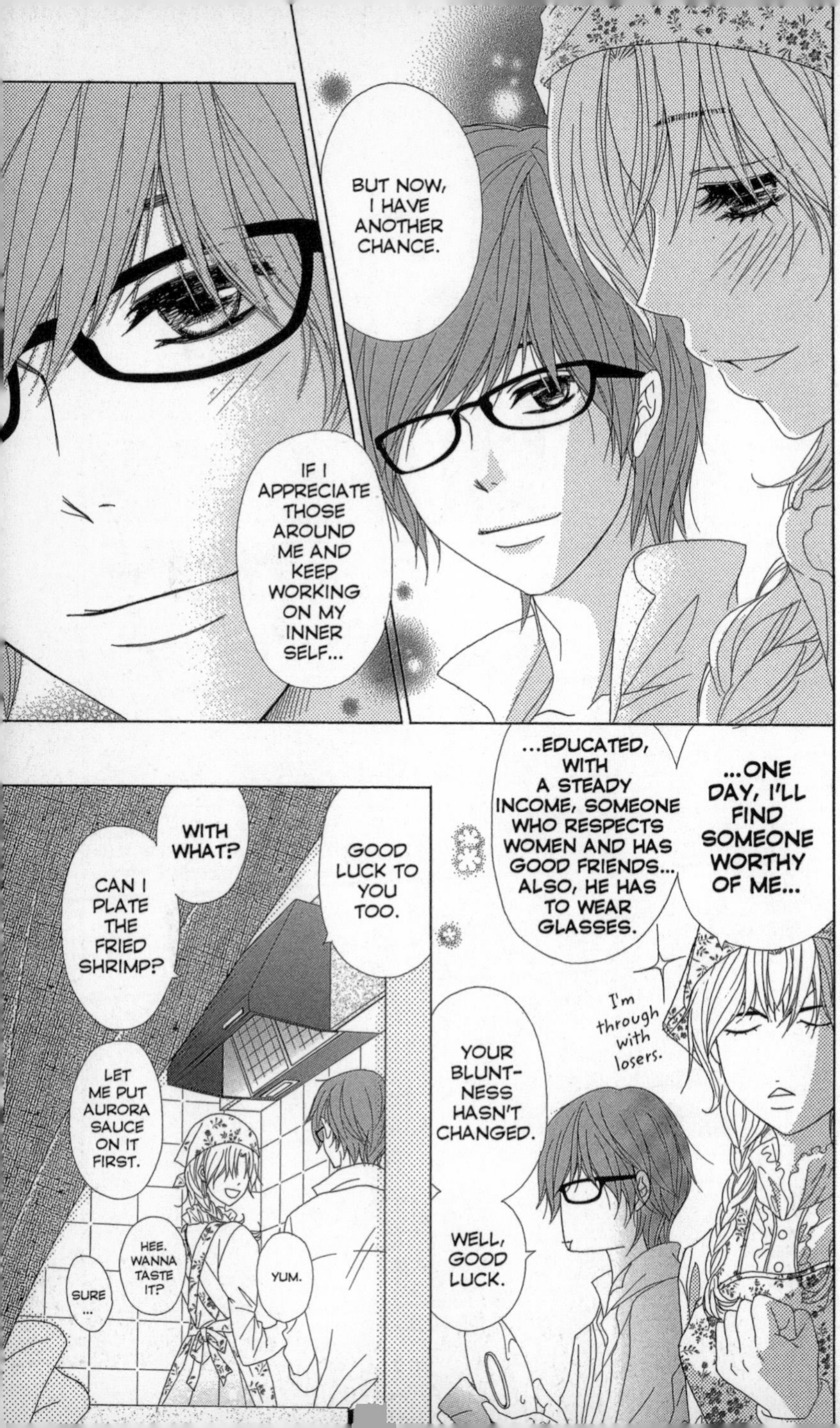
BUT NOW, I HAVE ANOTHER CHANCE.
IF I APPRECIATE THOSE AROUND ME AND KEEP WORKING ON MY INNER SELF...
...ONE DAY, I'LL FIND SOMEONE WORTHY OF ME...
...EDUCATED, WITH A STEADY INCOME, SOMEONE WHO RESPECTS WOMEN AND HAS GOOD FRIENDS... ALSO, HE HAS TO WEAR GLASSES.
I'm through with losers.
YOUR BLUNTNESS HASN'T CHANGED.
WELL, GOOD LUCK.
GOOD LUCK TO YOU TOO.
WITH WHAT?
CAN I PLATE THE FRIED SHRIMP?
LET ME PUT AURORA SAUCE ON IT FIRST.
YUM.
HEE. WANNA TASTE IT?
SURE...

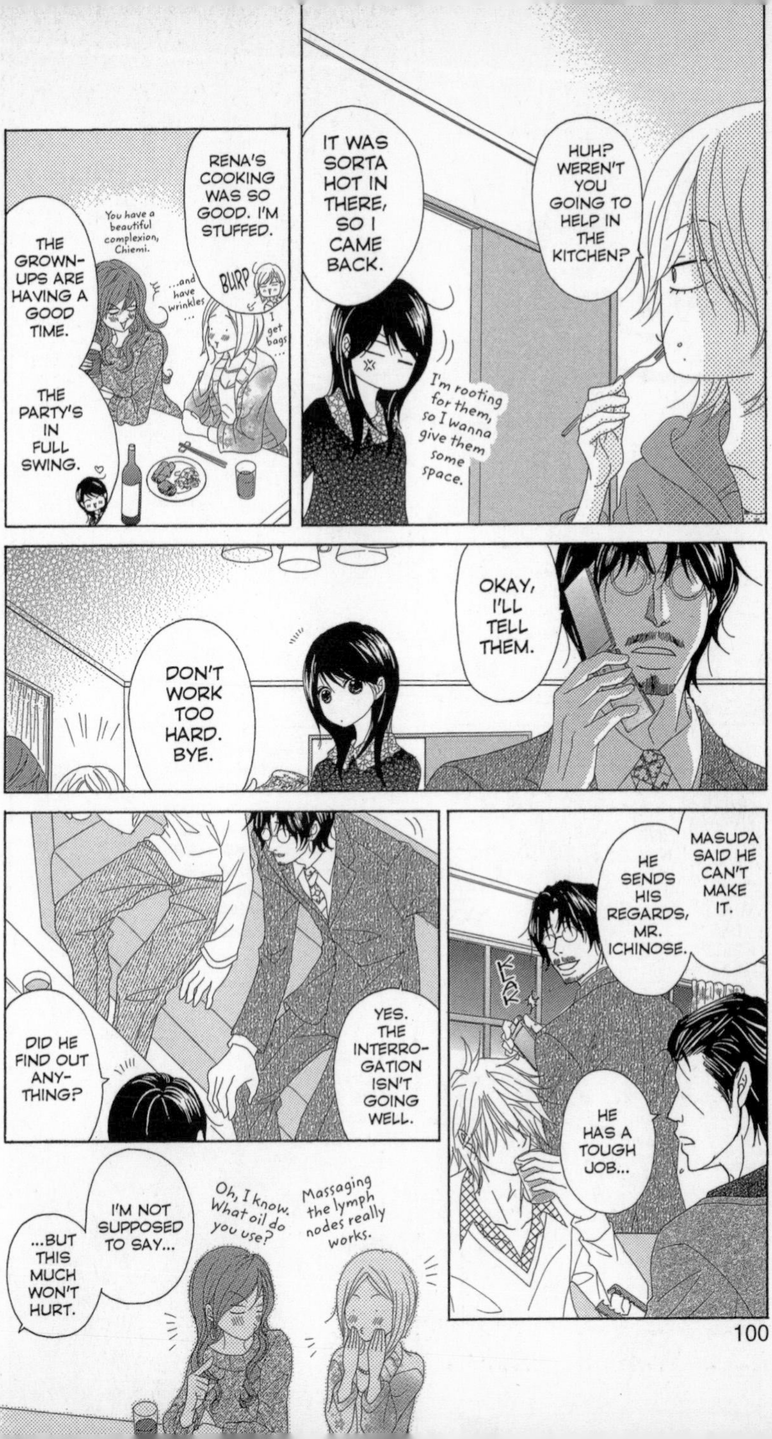
HUH? WEREN'T YOU GOING TO HELP IN THE KITCHEN?
IT WAS SORTA HOT IN THERE, SO I CAME BACK.
I'm rooting for them, so I wanna give them some space.
RENA'S COOKING WAS SO GOOD. I'M STUFFED.
BURP
I get bags...
...and have wrinkles...
You have a beautiful complexion, Chiemi.
THE GROWN-UPS ARE HAVING A GOOD TIME.
THE PARTY'S IN FULL SWING.
OKAY, I'LL TELL THEM.
DON'T WORK TOO HARD. BYE.
MASUDA SAID HE CAN'T MAKE IT.
HE SENDS HIS REGARDS, MR. ICHINOSE.
KLAK
HE HAS A TOUGH JOB...
YES. THE INTERROGATION ISN'T GOING WELL.
DID HE FIND OUT ANYTHING?
I'M NOT SUPPOSED TO SAY...
...BUT THIS MUCH WON'T HURT.
Massaging the lymph nodes really works.
Oh, I know. What oil do you use?

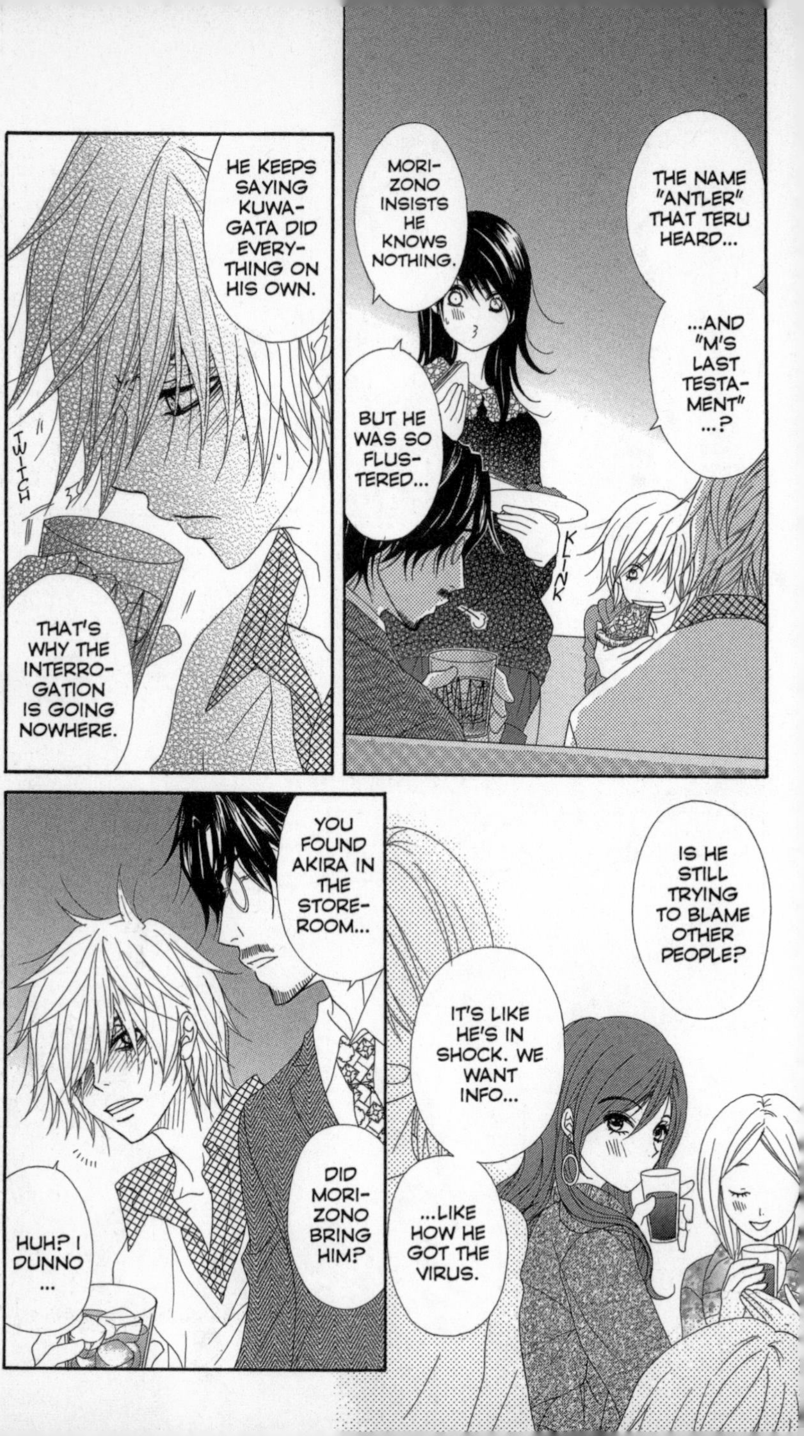
THE NAME "ANTLER" THAT TERU HEARD...
...AND "M'S LAST TESTAMENT" ...?
MORIZONO INSISTS HE KNOWS NOTHING.
BUT HE WAS SO FLUSTERED...
KLINK
HE KEEPS SAYING KUWAGATA DID EVERYTHING ON HIS OWN.
TWITCH
THAT'S WHY THE INTERROGATION IS GOING NOWHERE.
IS HE STILL TRYING TO BLAME OTHER PEOPLE?
IT'S LIKE HE'S IN SHOCK. WE WANT INFO...
...LIKE HOW HE GOT THE VIRUS.
YOU FOUND AKIRA IN THE STOREROOM...
DID MORIZONO BRING HIM?
HUH? I DUNNO ...

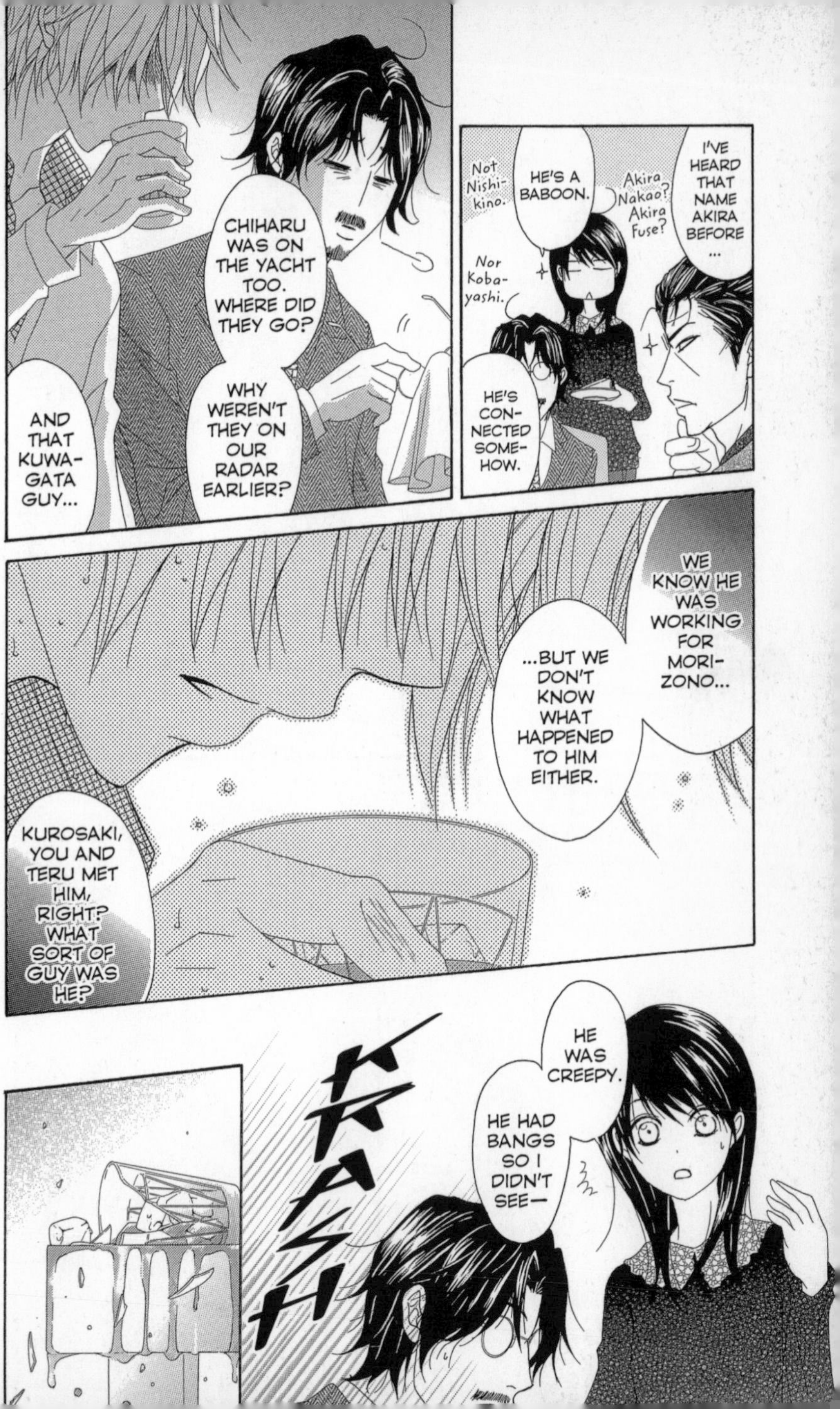
I'VE HEARD THAT NAME AKIRA BEFORE ...
Akira Nakao? Akira Fuse?
HE'S A BABOON.
Not Nishikino.
Nor Kobayashi.
HE'S CONNECTED SOMEHOW.
CHIHARU WAS ON THE YACHT TOO. WHERE DID THEY GO?
WHY WEREN'T THEY ON OUR RADAR EARLIER?
AND THAT KUWAGATA GUY...
WE KNOW HE WAS WORKING FOR MORIZONO...
...BUT WE DON'T KNOW WHAT HAPPENED TO HIM EITHER.
KUROSAKI, YOU AND TERU MET HIM, RIGHT? WHAT SORT OF GUY WAS HE?
HE WAS CREEPY.
HE HAD BANGS SO I DIDN'T SEE—
KRASH

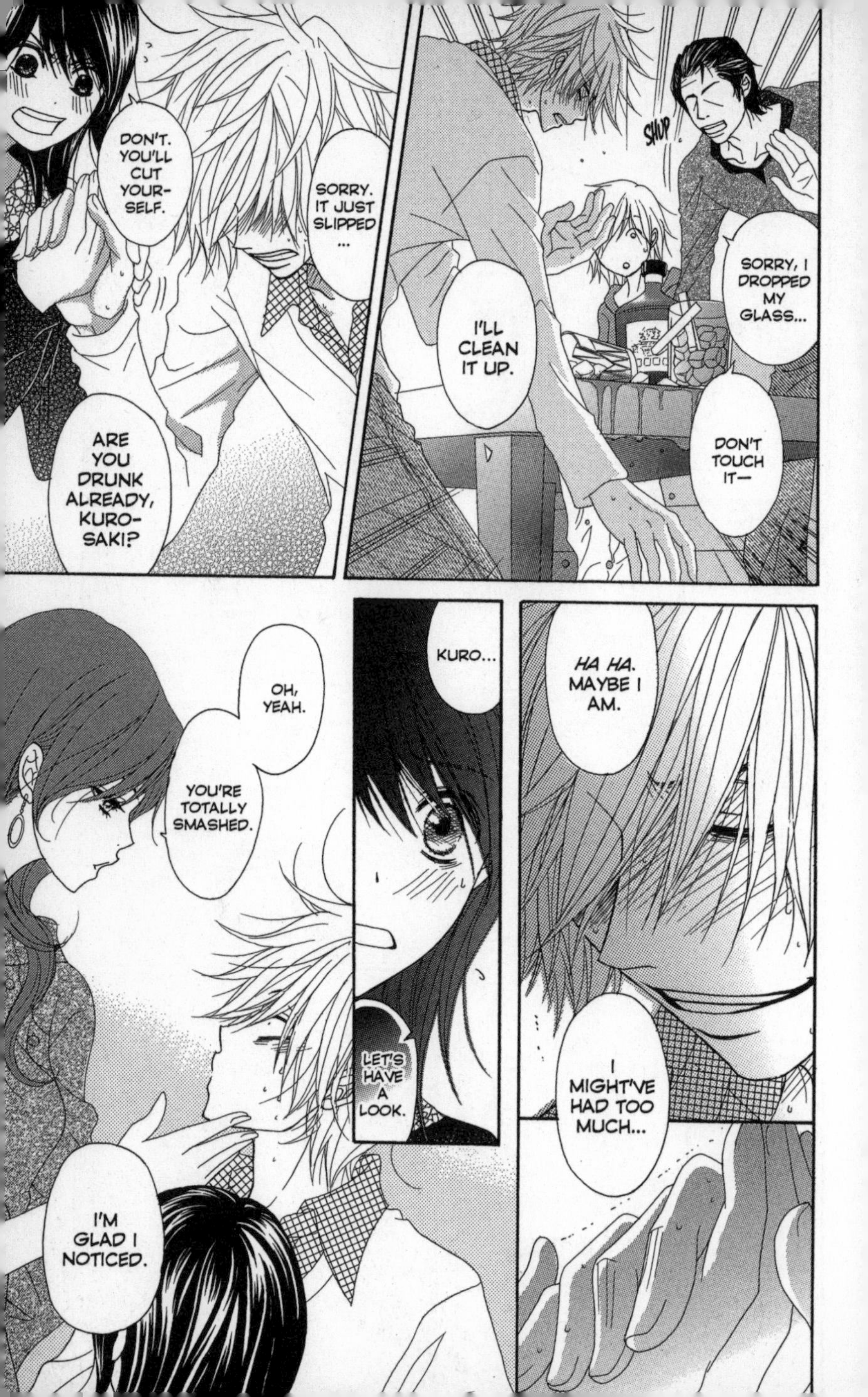
SHUP
SORRY, I DROPPED MY GLASS...
DON'T TOUCH IT—
I'LL CLEAN IT UP.
SORRY. IT JUST SLIPPED ...
DON'T. YOU'LL CUT YOUR-SELF.
ARE YOU DRUNK ALREADY, KURO-SAKI?
HA HA. MAYBE I AM.
I MIGHT'VE HAD TOO MUCH...
KURO...
LET'S HAVE A LOOK.
OH, YEAH.
YOU'RE TOTALLY SMASHED.
I'M GLAD I NOTICED.

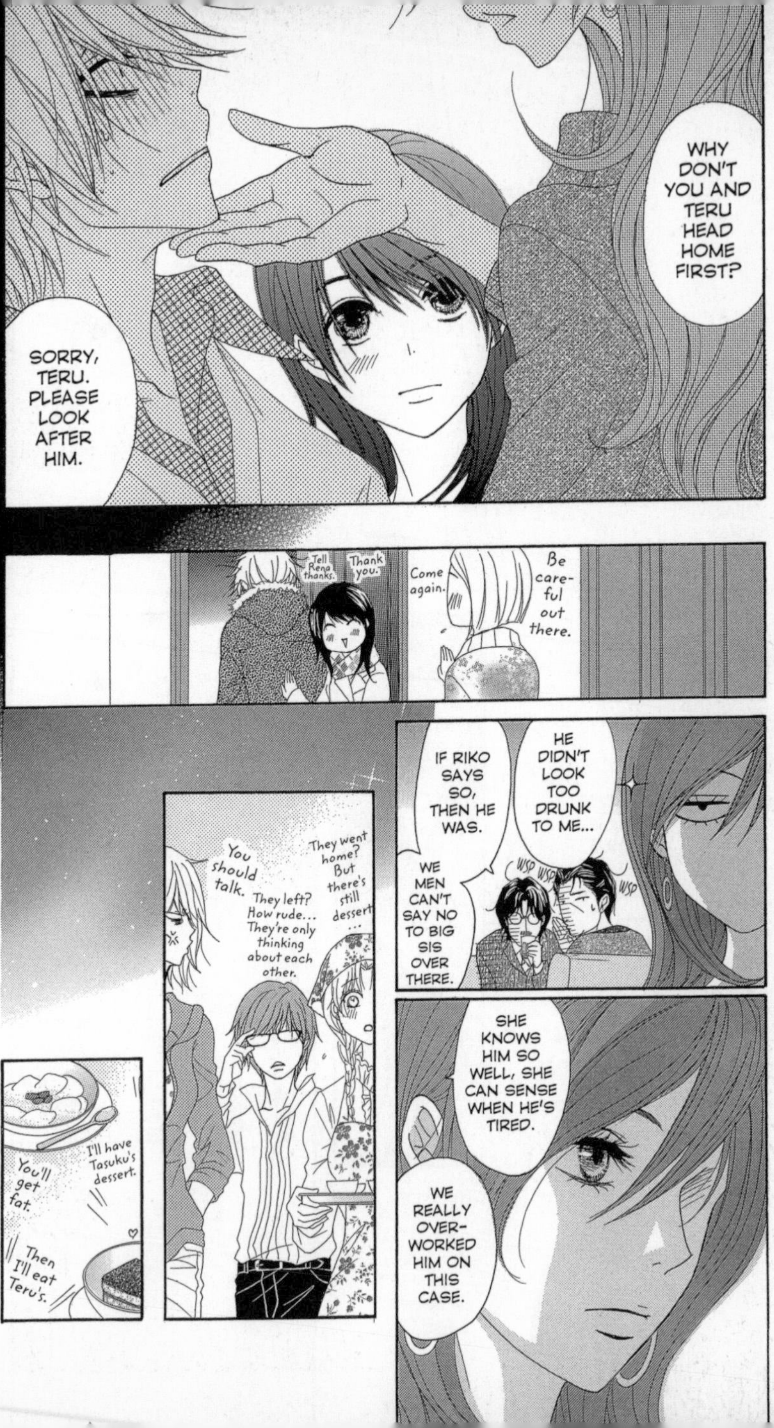
WHY DON'T YOU AND TERU HEAD HOME FIRST?
SORRY, TERU. PLEASE LOOK AFTER HIM.
Be careful out there.
Come again.
Thank you.
Tell Rena thanks.
HE DIDN'T LOOK TOO DRUNK TO ME...
IF RIKO SAYS SO, THEN HE WAS.
WE MEN CAN'T SAY NO TO BIG SIS OVER THERE.
WSP WSP WSP
SHE KNOWS HIM SO WELL, SHE CAN SENSE WHEN HE'S TIRED.
WE REALLY OVER-WORKED HIM ON THIS CASE.
They went home? But there's still dessert...
You should talk.
They left? How rude... They're only thinking about each other.
I'll have Tasuku's dessert.
You'll get fat.
Then I'll eat Teru's.

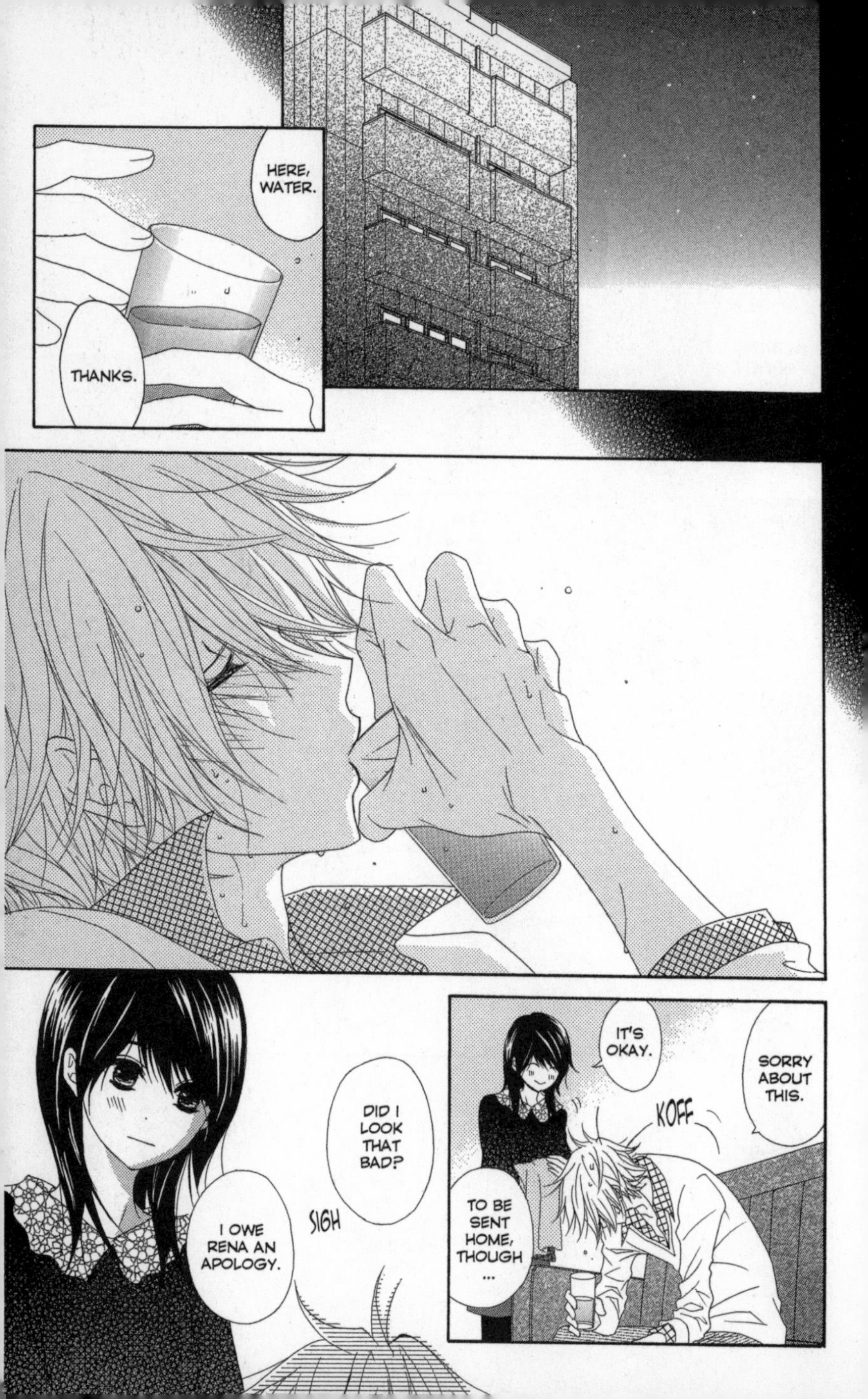
HERE, WATER.
THANKS.
SORRY ABOUT THIS.
KOFF
IT'S OKAY.
TO BE SENT HOME, THOUGH ...
DID I LOOK THAT BAD?
SIGH
I OWE RENA AN APOLOGY.

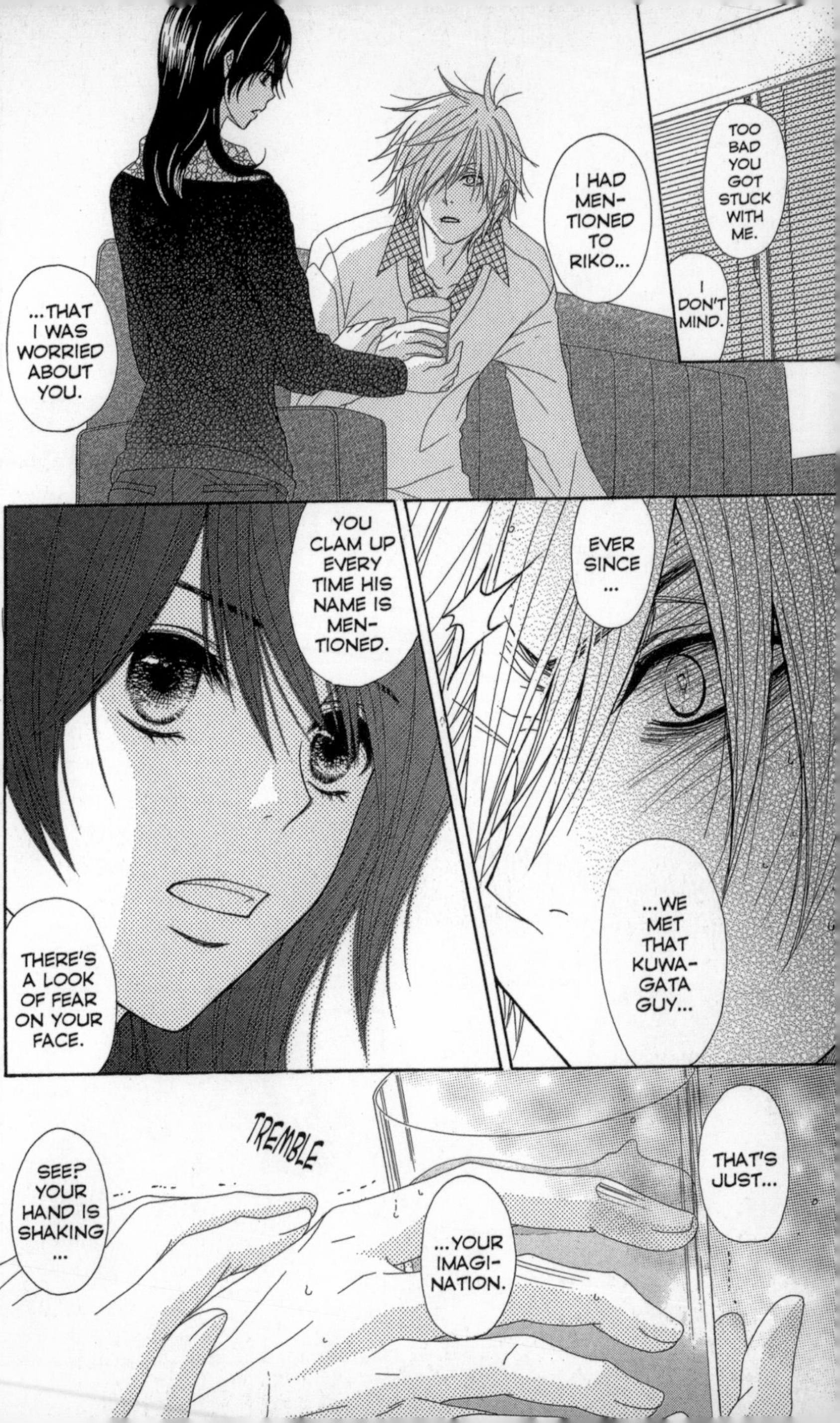
TOO BAD YOU GOT STUCK WITH ME.
I DON'T MIND.
I HAD MENTIONED TO RIKO...
...THAT I WAS WORRIED ABOUT YOU.
EVER SINCE ...
...WE MET THAT KUWAGATA GUY...
YOU CLAM UP EVERY TIME HIS NAME IS MENTIONED.
THERE'S A LOOK OF FEAR ON YOUR FACE.
THAT'S JUST...
...YOUR IMAGINATION.
TREMBLE
SEE? YOUR HAND IS SHAKING ...

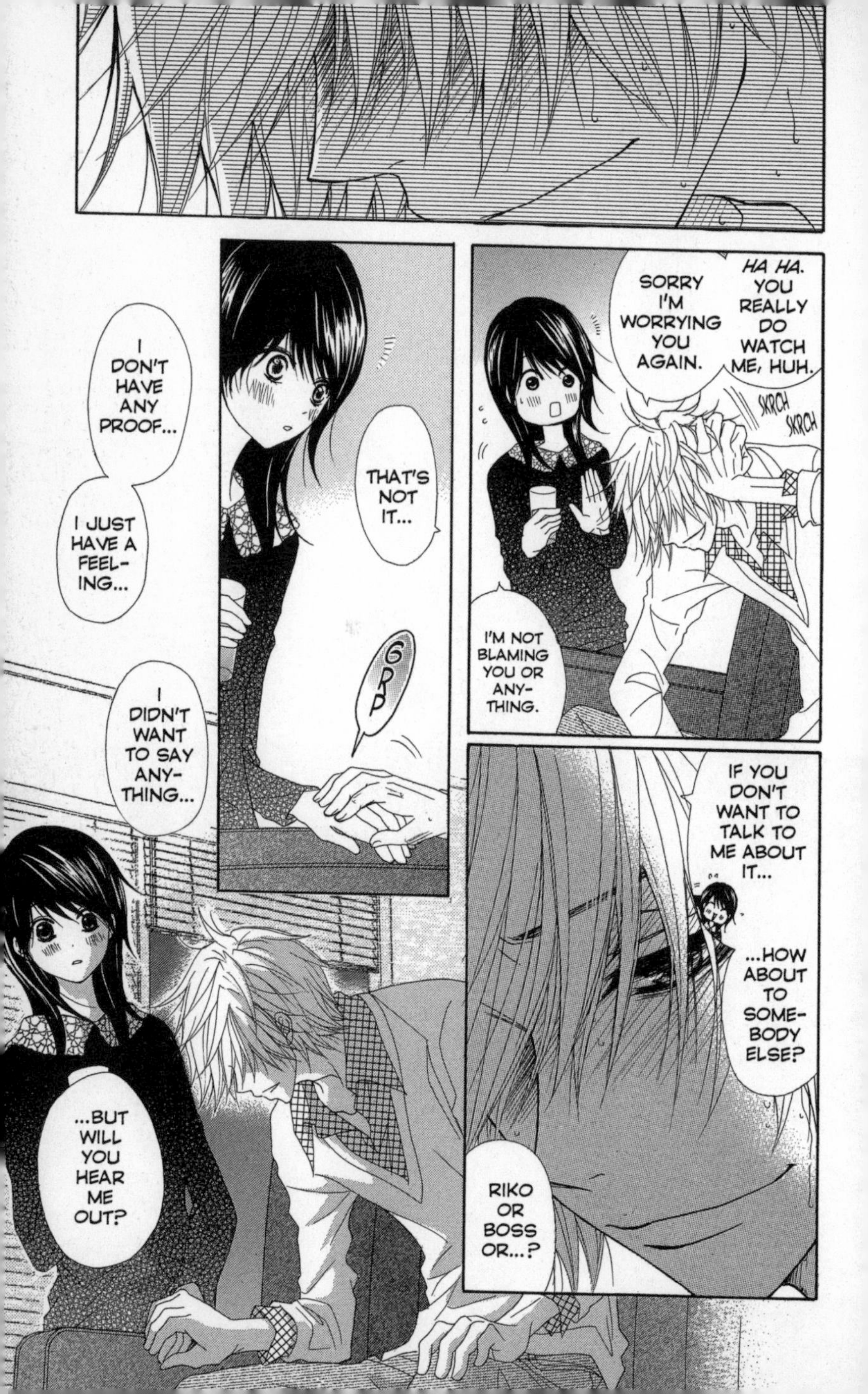
HA HA. YOU REALLY DO WATCH ME, HUH.
SORRY I'M WORRYING YOU AGAIN.
SKRCH SKRCH
I'M NOT BLAMING YOU OR ANY-THING.
IF YOU DON'T WANT TO TALK TO ME ABOUT IT...
...HOW ABOUT TO SOME-BODY ELSE?
RIKO OR BOSS OR...?
THAT'S NOT IT...
GRP
I DON'T HAVE ANY PROOF...
I JUST HAVE A FEEL-ING...
I DIDN'T WANT TO SAY ANY-THING...
...BUT WILL YOU HEAR ME OUT?

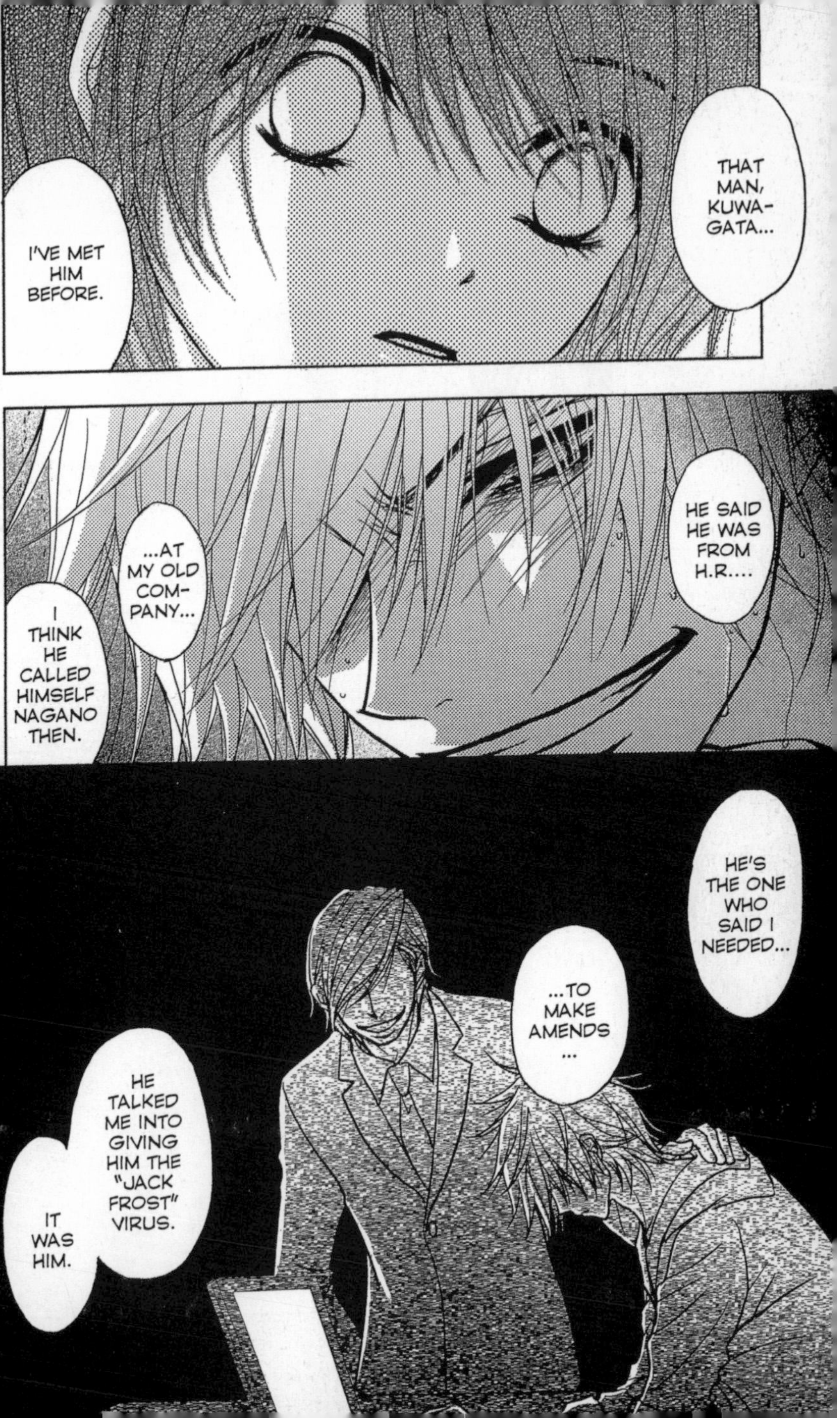
THAT MAN, KUWA-GATA...
I'VE MET HIM BEFORE.
HE SAID HE WAS FROM H.R....
...AT MY OLD COM-PANY...
I THINK HE CALLED HIMSELF NAGANO THEN.
HE'S THE ONE WHO SAID I NEEDED...
...TO MAKE AMENDS ...
HE TALKED ME INTO GIVING HIM THE "JACK FROST" VIRUS.
IT WAS HIM.

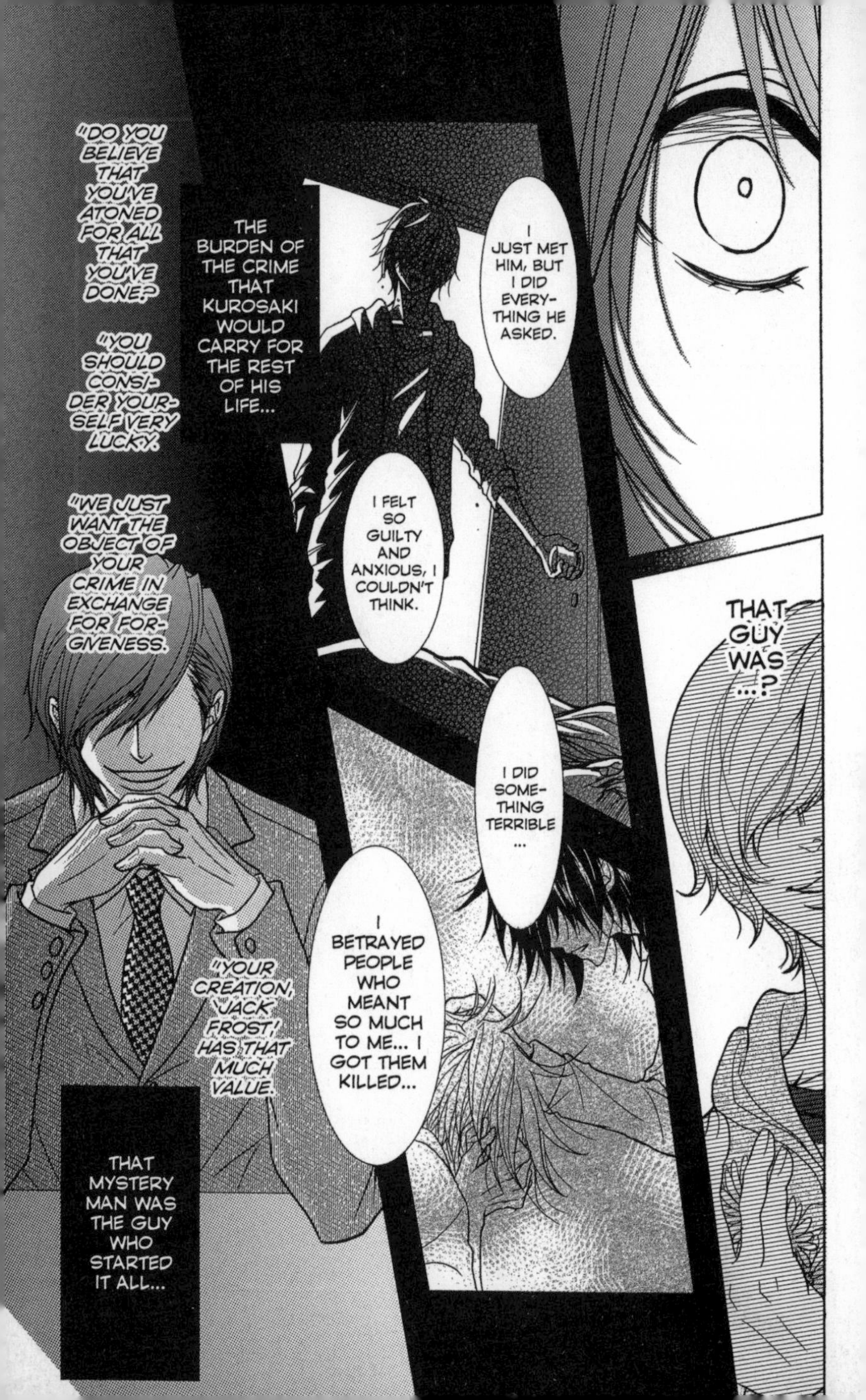
I JUST MET HIM, BUT I DID EVERYTHING HE ASKED.
I FELT SO GUILTY AND ANXIOUS, I COULDN'T THINK.
THE BURDEN OF THE CRIME THAT KUROSAKI WOULD CARRY FOR THE REST OF HIS LIFE...
"DO YOU BELIEVE THAT YOU'VE ATONED FOR ALL THAT YOU'VE DONE?
"YOU SHOULD CONSIDER YOURSELF VERY LUCKY.
"WE JUST WANT THE OBJECT OF YOUR CRIME IN EXCHANGE FOR FORGIVENESS.
THAT GUY WAS ...?
I DID SOMETHING TERRIBLE ...
I BETRAYED PEOPLE WHO MEANT SO MUCH TO ME... I GOT THEM KILLED...
"YOUR CREATION, 'JACK FROST,' HAS THAT MUCH VALUE.
THAT MYSTERY MAN WAS THE GUY WHO STARTED IT ALL...

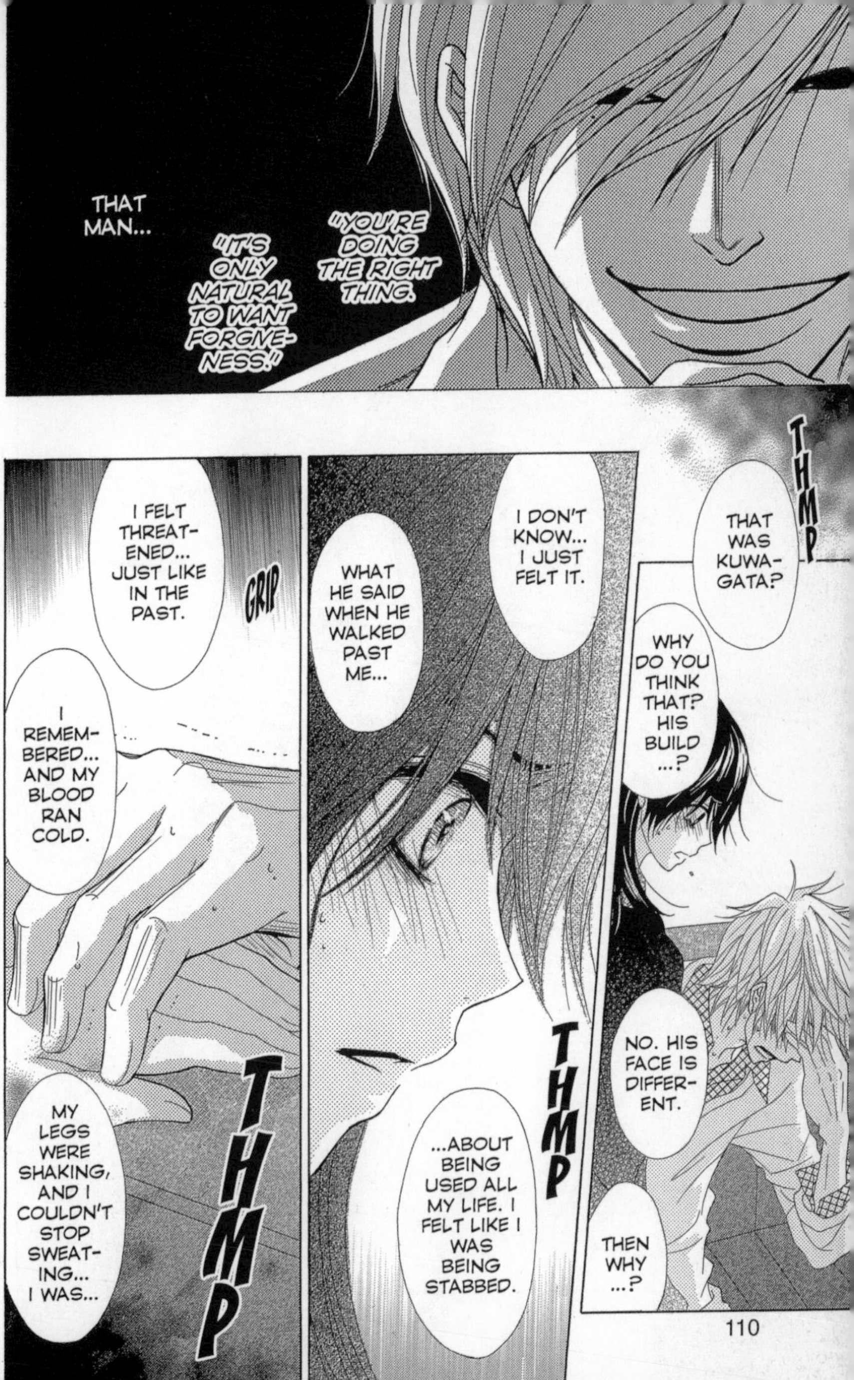
THAT MAN...
"YOU'RE DOING THE RIGHT THING.
"IT'S ONLY NATURAL TO WANT FORGIVENESS."
THMP
THAT WAS KUWAGATA?
WHY DO YOU THINK THAT? HIS BUILD ...?
NO. HIS FACE IS DIFFERENT.
THEN WHY ...?
I DON'T KNOW... I JUST FELT IT.
WHAT HE SAID WHEN HE WALKED PAST ME...
...ABOUT BEING USED ALL MY LIFE. I FELT LIKE I WAS BEING STABBED.
THMP
I FELT THREATENED... JUST LIKE IN THE PAST.
GRIP
I REMEMBERED... AND MY BLOOD RAN COLD.
MY LEGS WERE SHAKING, AND I COULDN'T STOP SWEATING... I WAS...
THMP

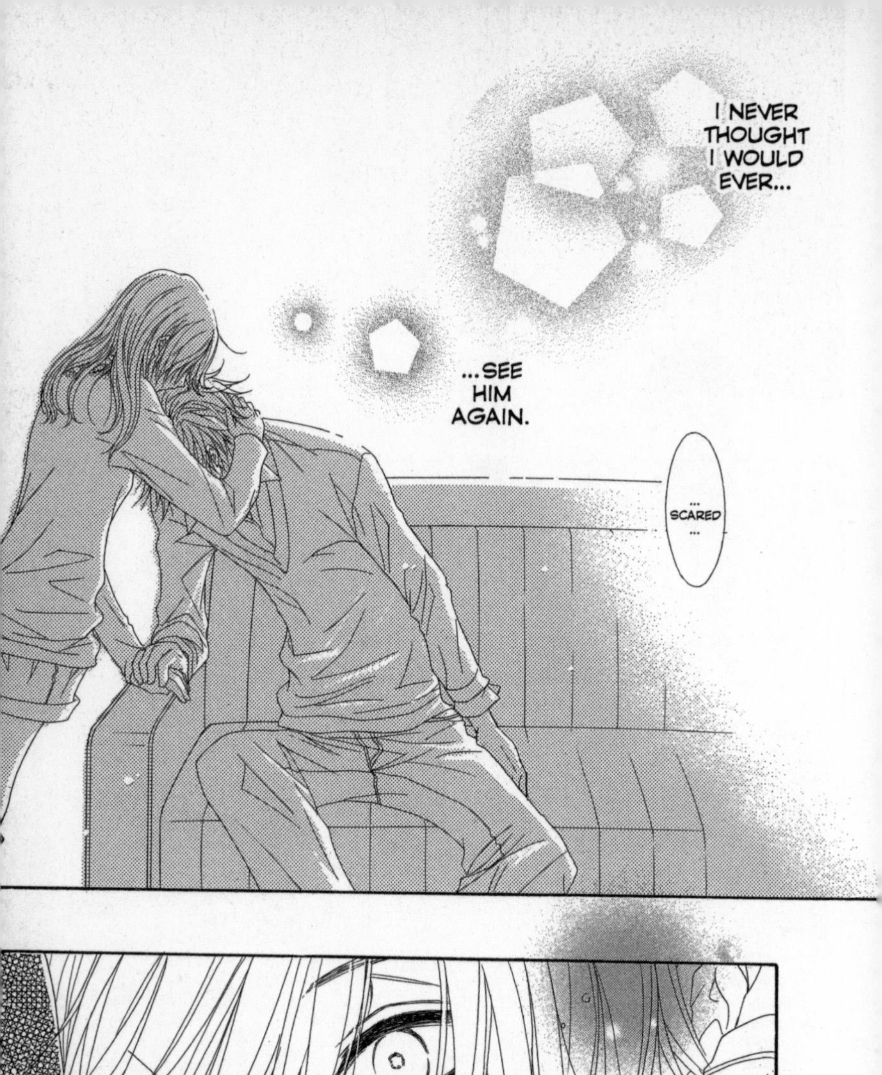
I NEVER THOUGHT I WOULD EVER...
...SEE HIM AGAIN.
...SCARED...
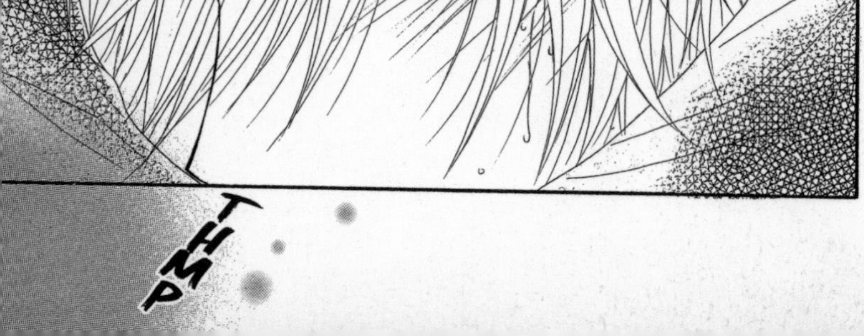
THMP

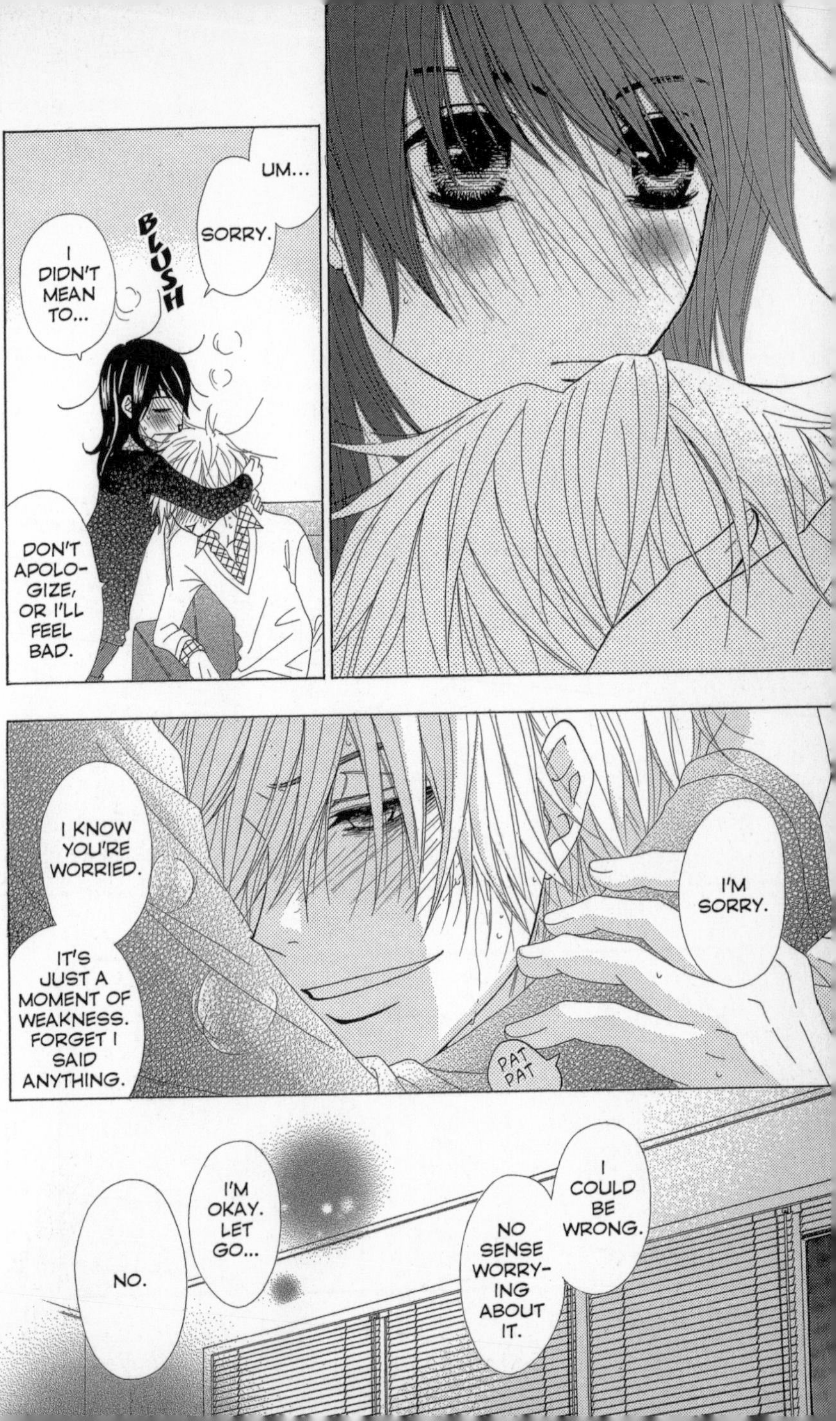
UM...
SORRY.
BLUSH
I DIDN'T MEAN TO...
DON'T APOLOGIZE, OR I'LL FEEL BAD.
I'M SORRY.
PAT PAT
I KNOW YOU'RE WORRIED.
IT'S JUST A MOMENT OF WEAKNESS. FORGET I SAID ANYTHING.
I COULD BE WRONG.
NO SENSE WORRYING ABOUT IT.
I'M OKAY. LET GO...
NO.

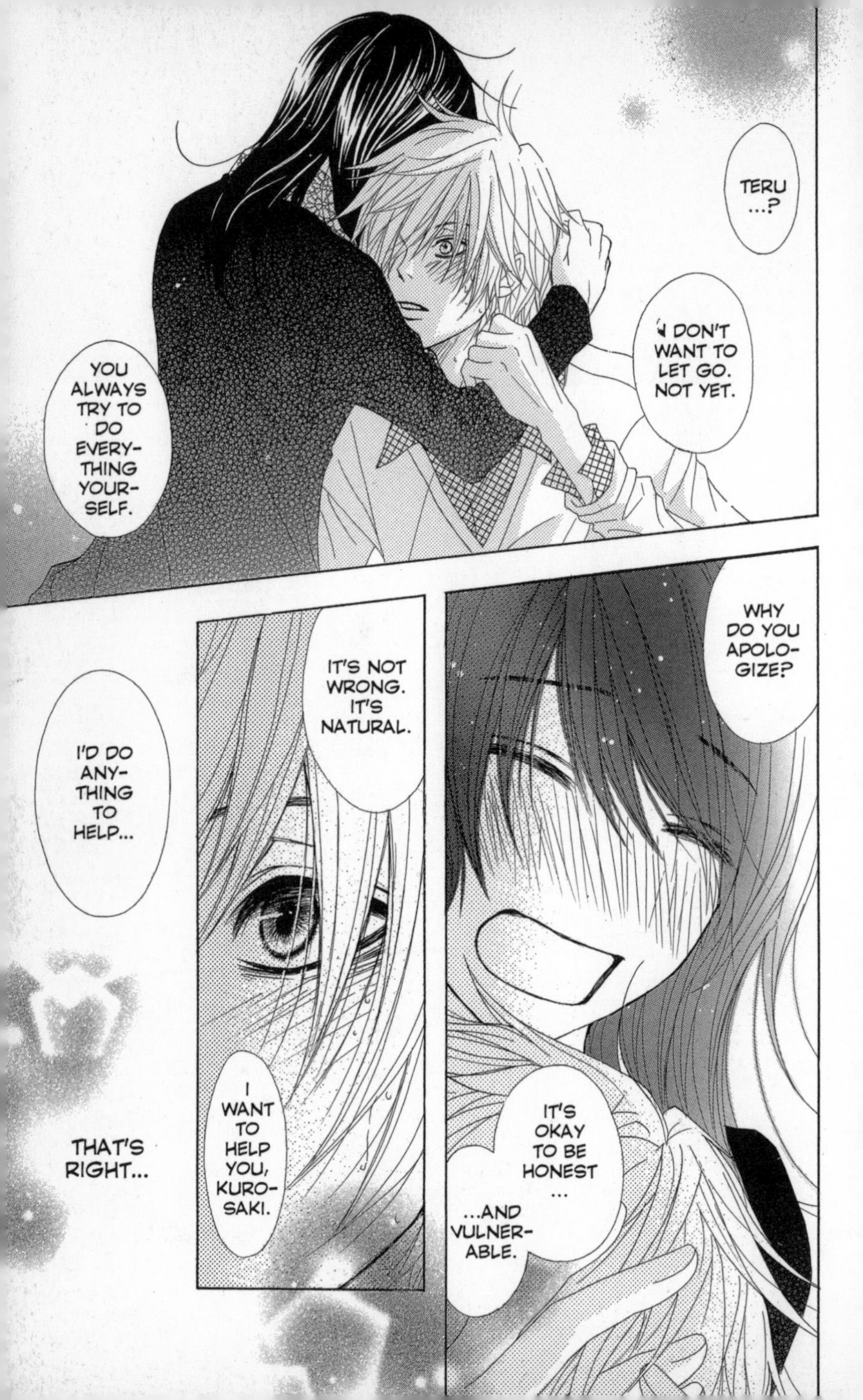
TERU ...?
I DON'T WANT TO LET GO. NOT YET.
YOU ALWAYS TRY TO DO EVERYTHING YOURSELF.
WHY DO YOU APOLOGIZE?
IT'S OKAY TO BE HONEST ...
...AND VULNERABLE.
IT'S NOT WRONG. IT'S NATURAL.
I WANT TO HELP YOU, KUROSAKI.
I'D DO ANYTHING TO HELP...
THAT'S RIGHT...

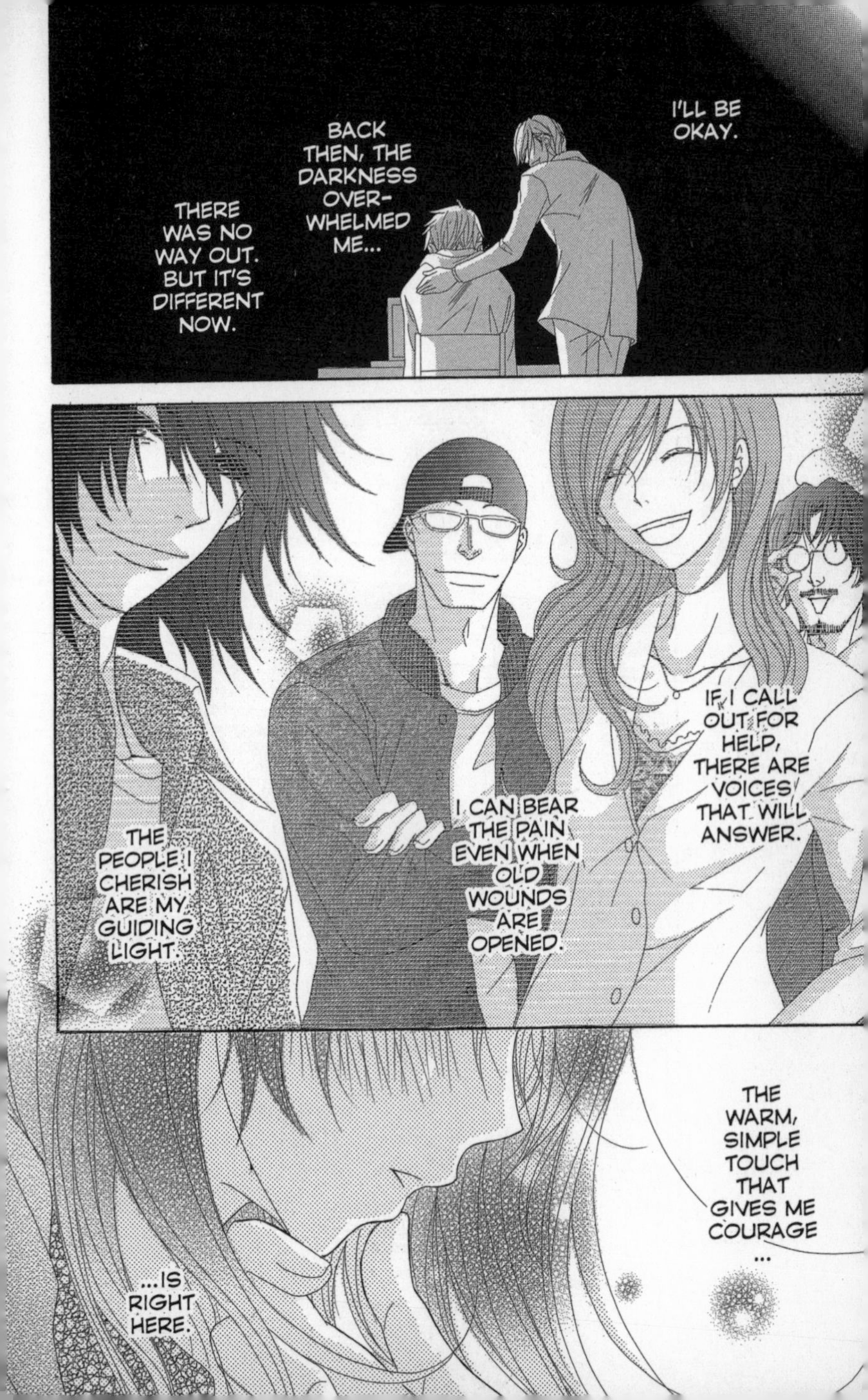
I'LL BE OKAY.
BACK THEN, THE DARKNESS OVER-WHELMED ME...
THERE WAS NO WAY OUT. BUT IT'S DIFFERENT NOW.
IF I CALL OUT FOR HELP, THERE ARE VOICES THAT WILL ANSWER.
I CAN BEAR THE PAIN EVEN WHEN OLD WOUNDS ARE OPENED.
THE PEOPLE I CHERISH ARE MY GUIDING LIGHT.
THE WARM, SIMPLE TOUCH THAT GIVES ME COURAGE...
...IS RIGHT HERE.

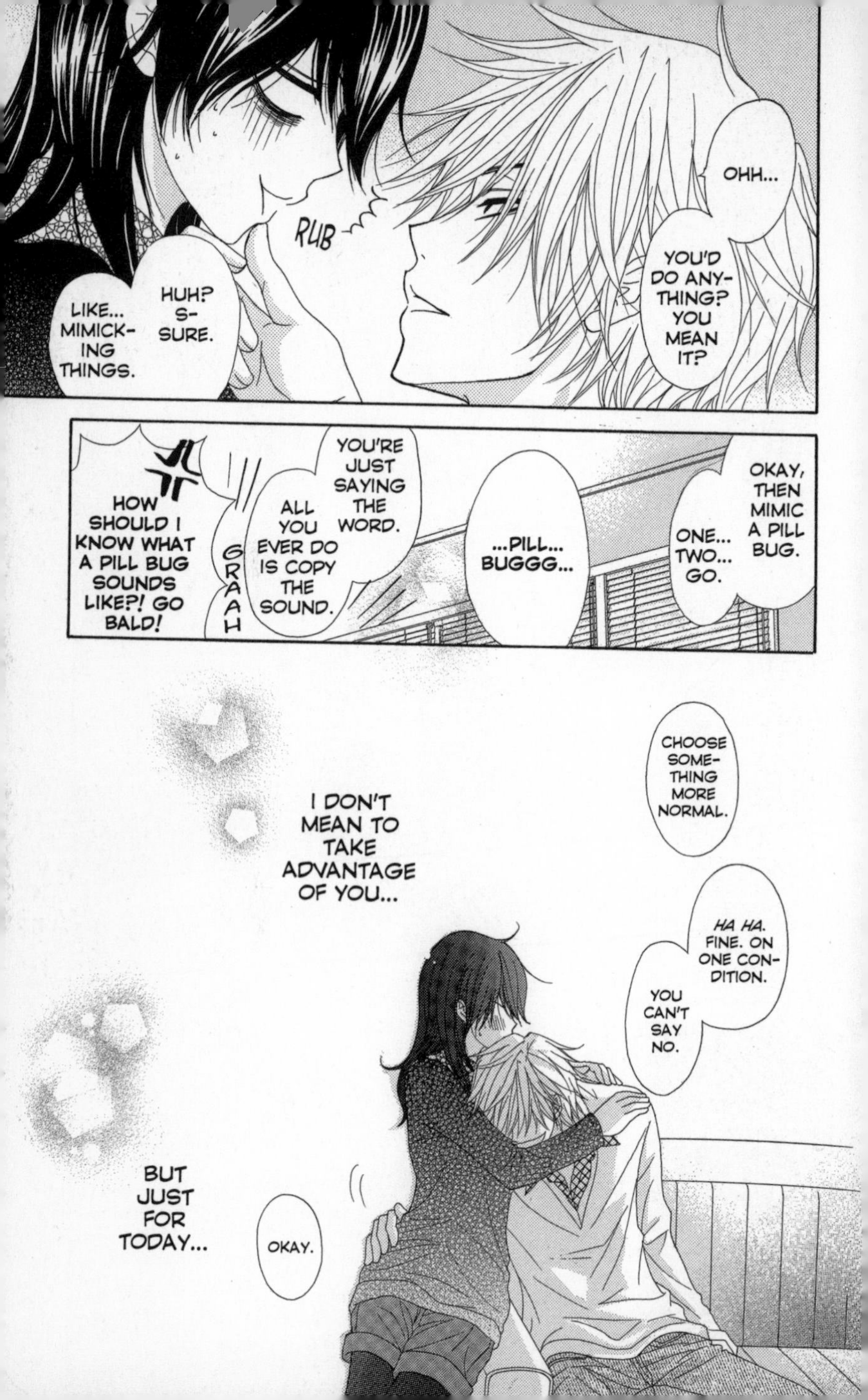
OHH...
YOU'D DO ANYTHING? YOU MEAN IT?
RUB
HUH? S-SURE.
LIKE... MIMICKING THINGS.
OKAY, THEN MIMIC A PILL BUG.
ONE... TWO... GO.
...PILL... BUGGG...
YOU'RE JUST SAYING THE WORD.
ALL YOU EVER DO IS COPY THE SOUND.
GRAAH
HOW SHOULD I KNOW WHAT A PILL BUG SOUNDS LIKE?! GO BALD!
CHOOSE SOMETHING MORE NORMAL.
I DON'T MEAN TO TAKE ADVANTAGE OF YOU...
HA HA. FINE. ON ONE CONDITION.
YOU CAN'T SAY NO.
OKAY.
BUT JUST FOR TODAY...

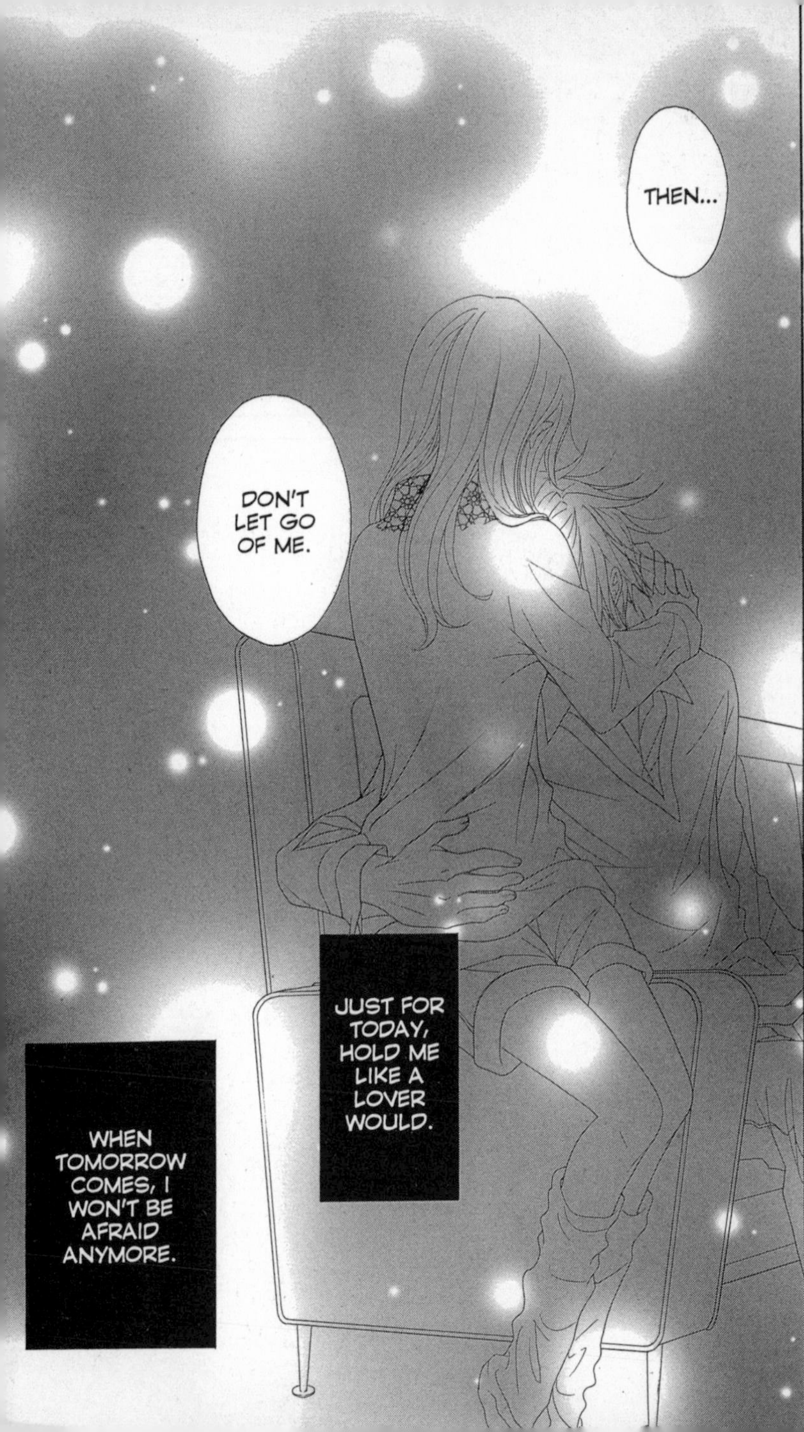
THEN...
DON'T LET GO OF ME.
JUST FOR TODAY, HOLD ME LIKE A LOVER WOULD.
WHEN TOMORROW COMES, I WON'T BE AFRAID ANYMORE.

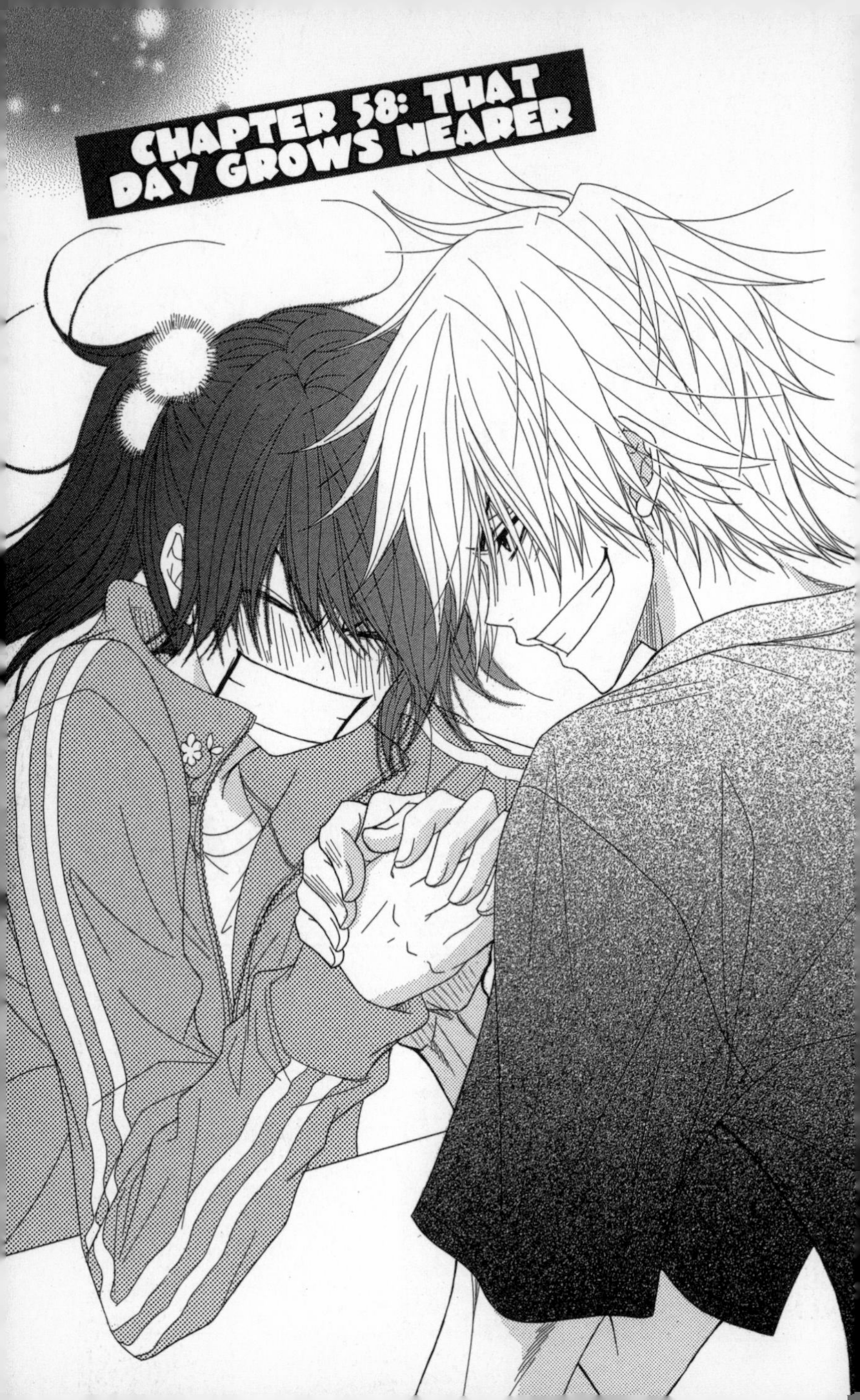
CHAPTER 58: THAT DAY GROWS NEARER

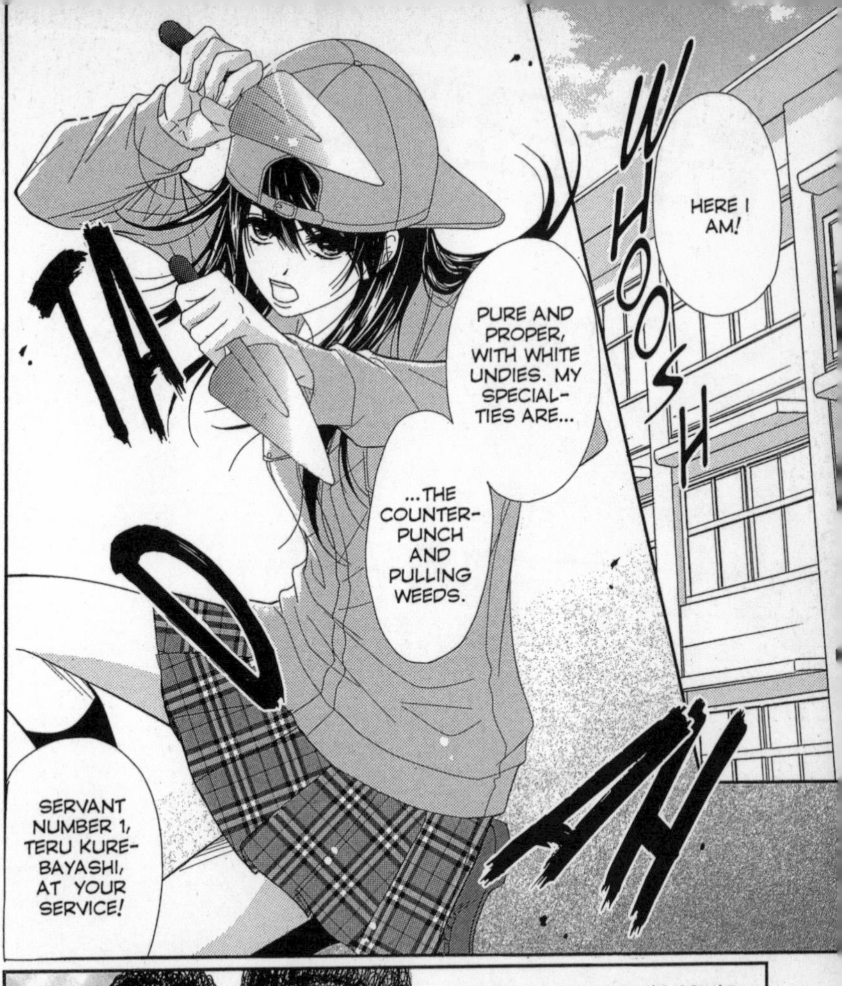
WHOOSH
HERE I AM!
PURE AND PROPER, WITH WHITE UNDIES. MY SPECIAL-TIES ARE...
...THE COUNTER-PUNCH AND PULLING WEEDS.
TADAA
SERVANT NUMBER 1, TERU KURE-BAYASHI, AT YOUR SERVICE!

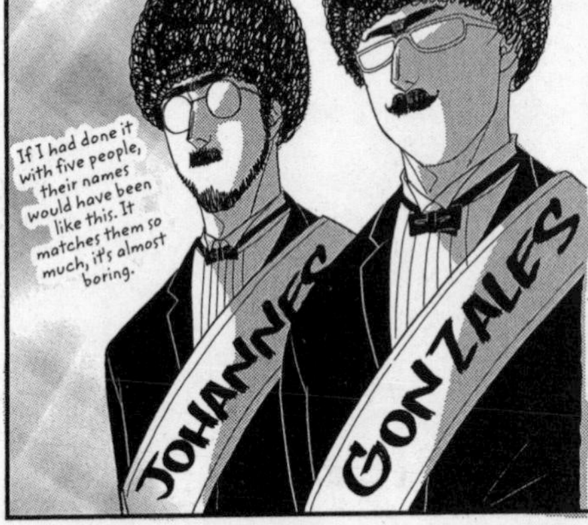
If I had done it with five people, their names would have been like this. It matches them so much, it's almost boring.
JOHANNES
GONZALES

*DENGEKI DAISY* HAS MANY YOUNG READERS, SO I BELIEVE THERE ARE MORE THAN A FEW WHO AREN'T AWARE OF THIS. "IPEIKO" IS THE NAME OF A COMBINATION IN THE GAME OF MAHJONG. IT'S NOT THE NAME OF A PERSON.

FOR SOME REASON, I HAD A DIFFICULT TIME COMING UP WITH NAMES THAT BEGIN WITH THE "I" SOUND FOR THIS VOLUME—EVEN THOUGH THERE ARE A LOT, LIKE "ETHAN" OR "EASTWOOD" OR "ICHIRO." RECENTLY, I'VE BEEN REALLY, REALLY BUSY, SO I THINK MY BRAIN HAS SHRIVELED MORE THAN USUAL.

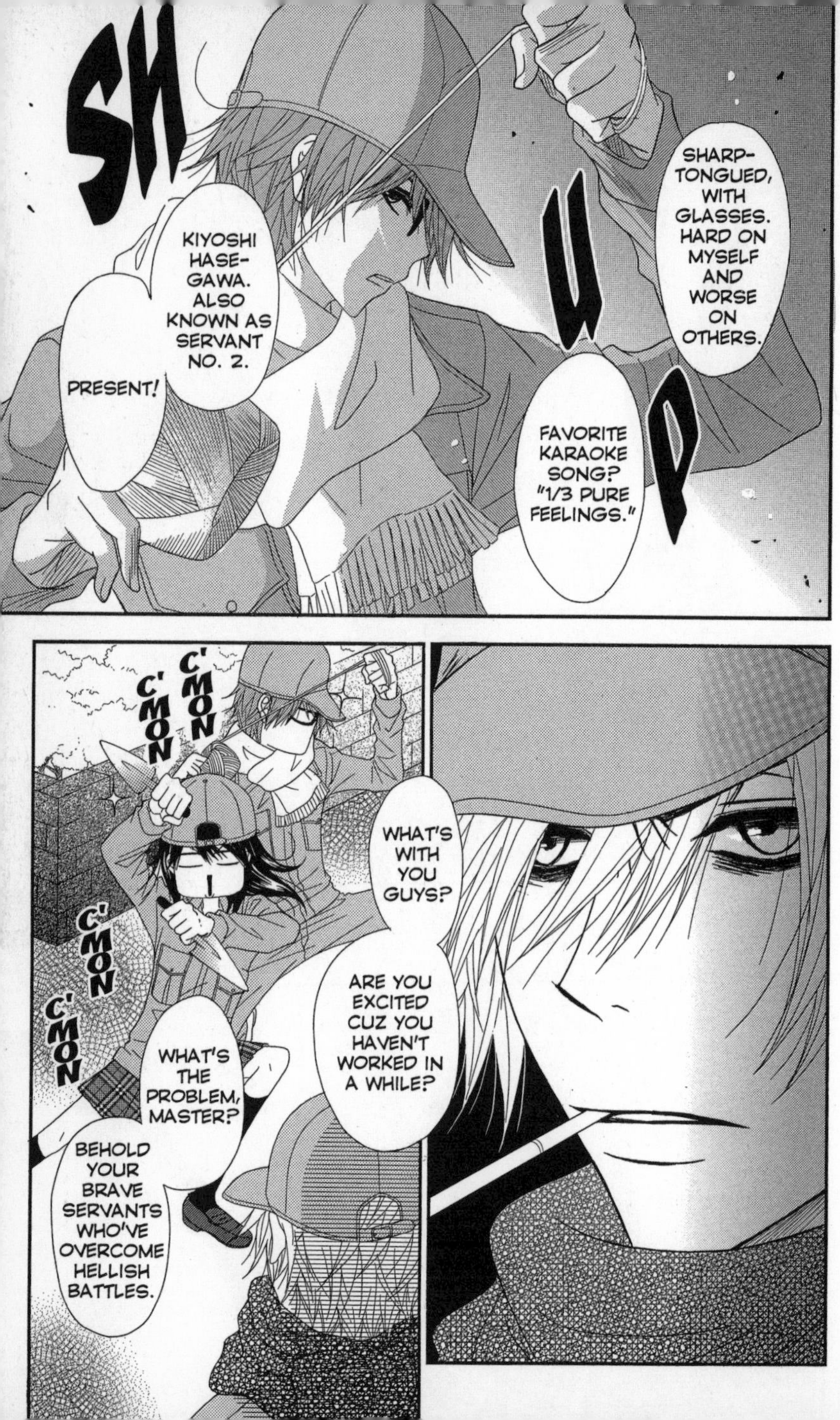
SHARP-TONGUED, WITH GLASSES. HARD ON MYSELF AND WORSE ON OTHERS.
FAVORITE KARAOKE SONG? "1/3 PURE FEELINGS."
SHUP
KIYOSHI HASE-GAWA. ALSO KNOWN AS SERVANT NO. 2.
PRESENT!
WHAT'S WITH YOU GUYS?
ARE YOU EXCITED CUZ YOU HAVEN'T WORKED IN A WHILE?
C'MON C'MON
C'MON C'MON
WHAT'S THE PROBLEM, MASTER?
BEHOLD YOUR BRAVE SERVANTS WHO'VE OVERCOME HELLISH BATTLES.

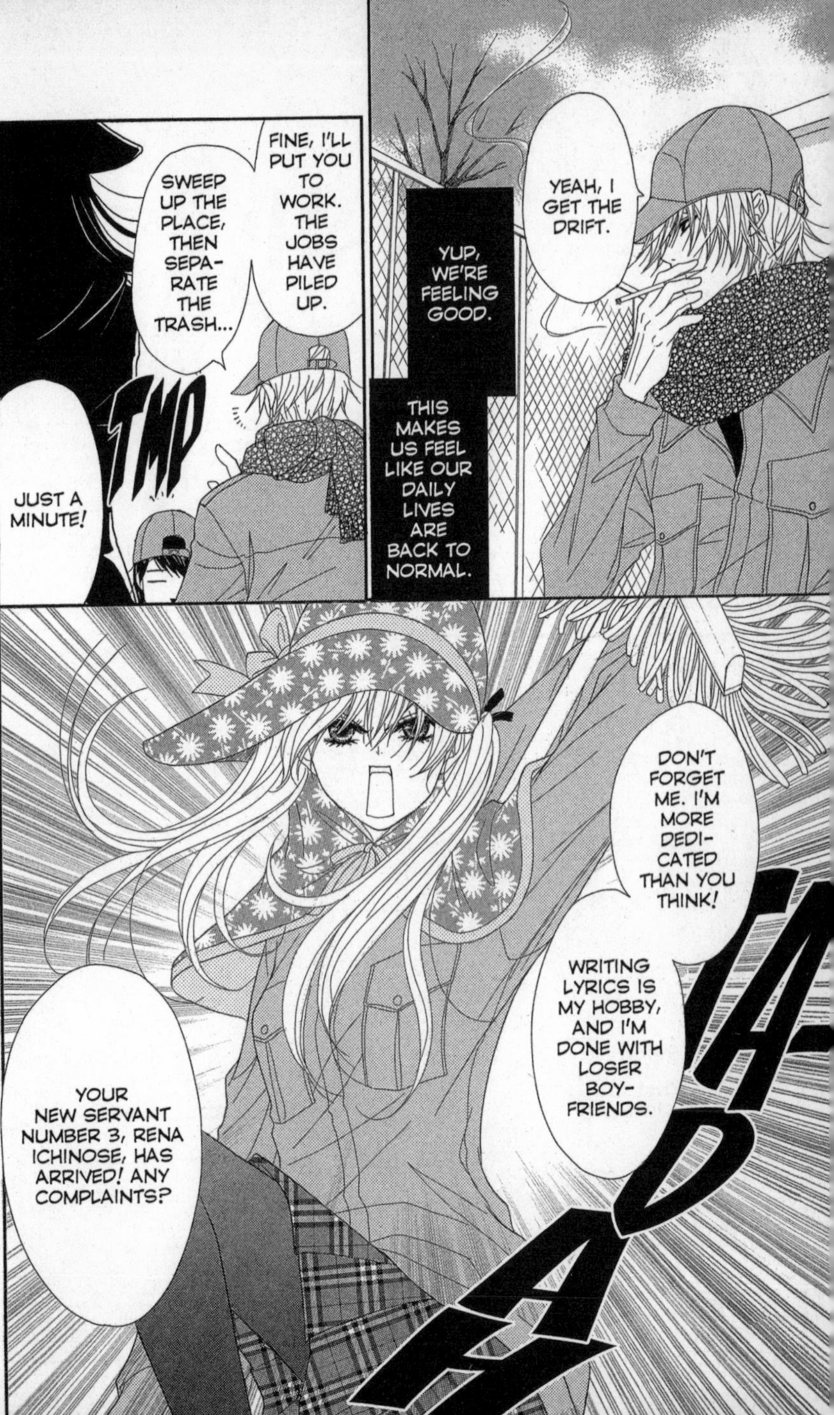
YEAH, I GET THE DRIFT.
YUP, WE'RE FEELING GOOD.
THIS MAKES US FEEL LIKE OUR DAILY LIVES ARE BACK TO NORMAL.
FINE, I'LL PUT YOU TO WORK. THE JOBS HAVE PILED UP.
SWEEP UP THE PLACE, THEN SEPA-RATE THE TRASH...
TMP
JUST A MINUTE!
DON'T FORGET ME. I'M MORE DEDI-CATED THAN YOU THINK!
WRITING LYRICS IS MY HOBBY, AND I'M DONE WITH LOSER BOY-FRIENDS.
YOUR NEW SERVANT NUMBER 3, RENA ICHINOSE, HAS ARRIVED! ANY COMPLAINTS?

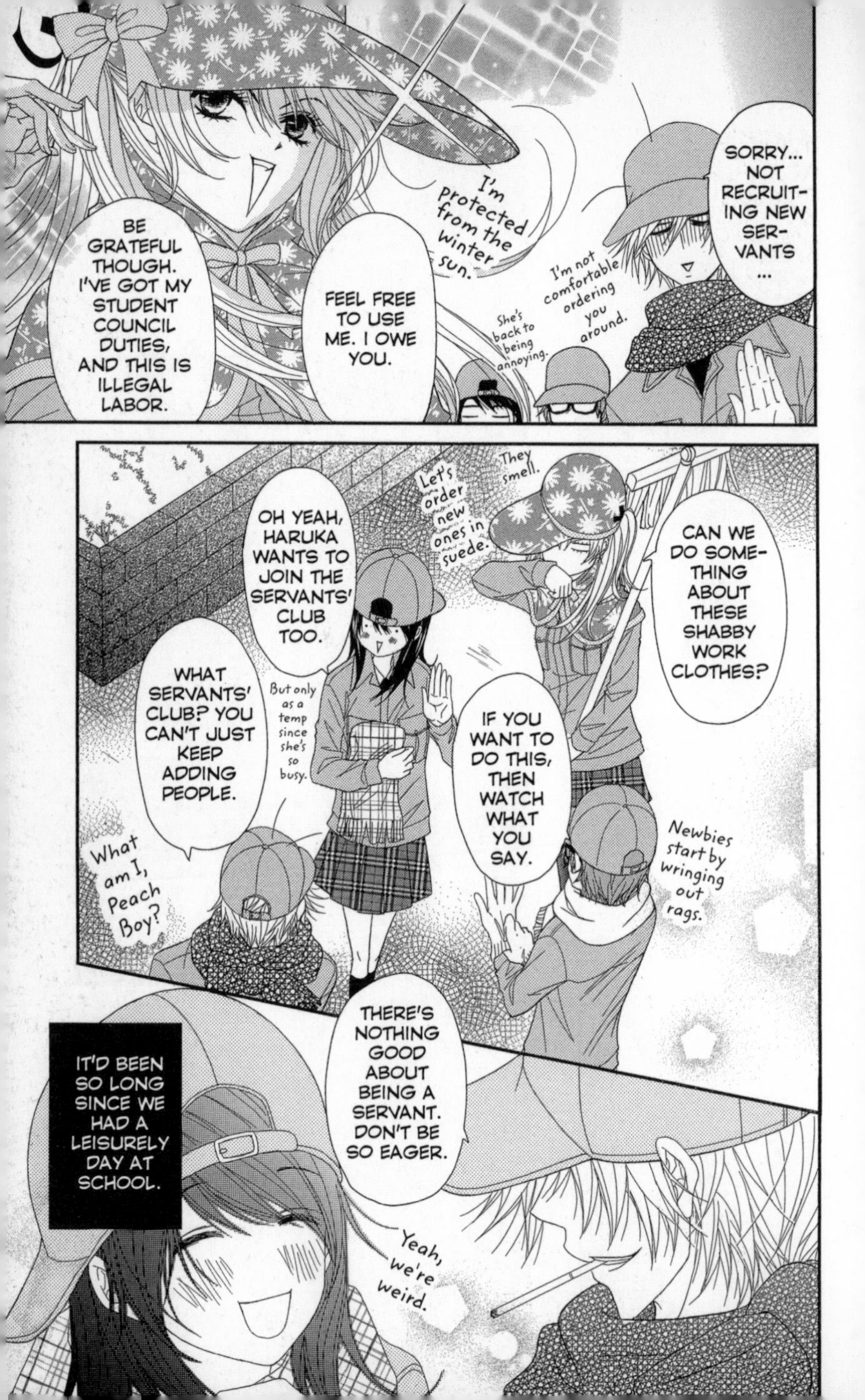
SORRY... NOT RECRUIT-ING NEW SER-VANTS ...
I'm not comfortable ordering you around.
She's back to being annoying.
I'm protected from the winter sun.
FEEL FREE TO USE ME. I OWE YOU.
BE GRATEFUL THOUGH. I'VE GOT MY STUDENT COUNCIL DUTIES, AND THIS IS ILLEGAL LABOR.
CAN WE DO SOME-THING ABOUT THESE SHABBY WORK CLOTHES?
They smell.
Let's order new ones in suede.
OH YEAH, HARUKA WANTS TO JOIN THE SERVANTS' CLUB TOO.
IF YOU WANT TO DO THIS, THEN WATCH WHAT YOU SAY.
But only as a temp since she's so busy.
WHAT SERVANTS' CLUB? YOU CAN'T JUST KEEP ADDING PEOPLE.
Newbies start by wringing out rags.
What am I, Peach Boy?
THERE'S NOTHING GOOD ABOUT BEING A SERVANT. DON'T BE SO EAGER.
IT'D BEEN SO LONG SINCE WE HAD A LEISURELY DAY AT SCHOOL.
Yeah, we're weird.

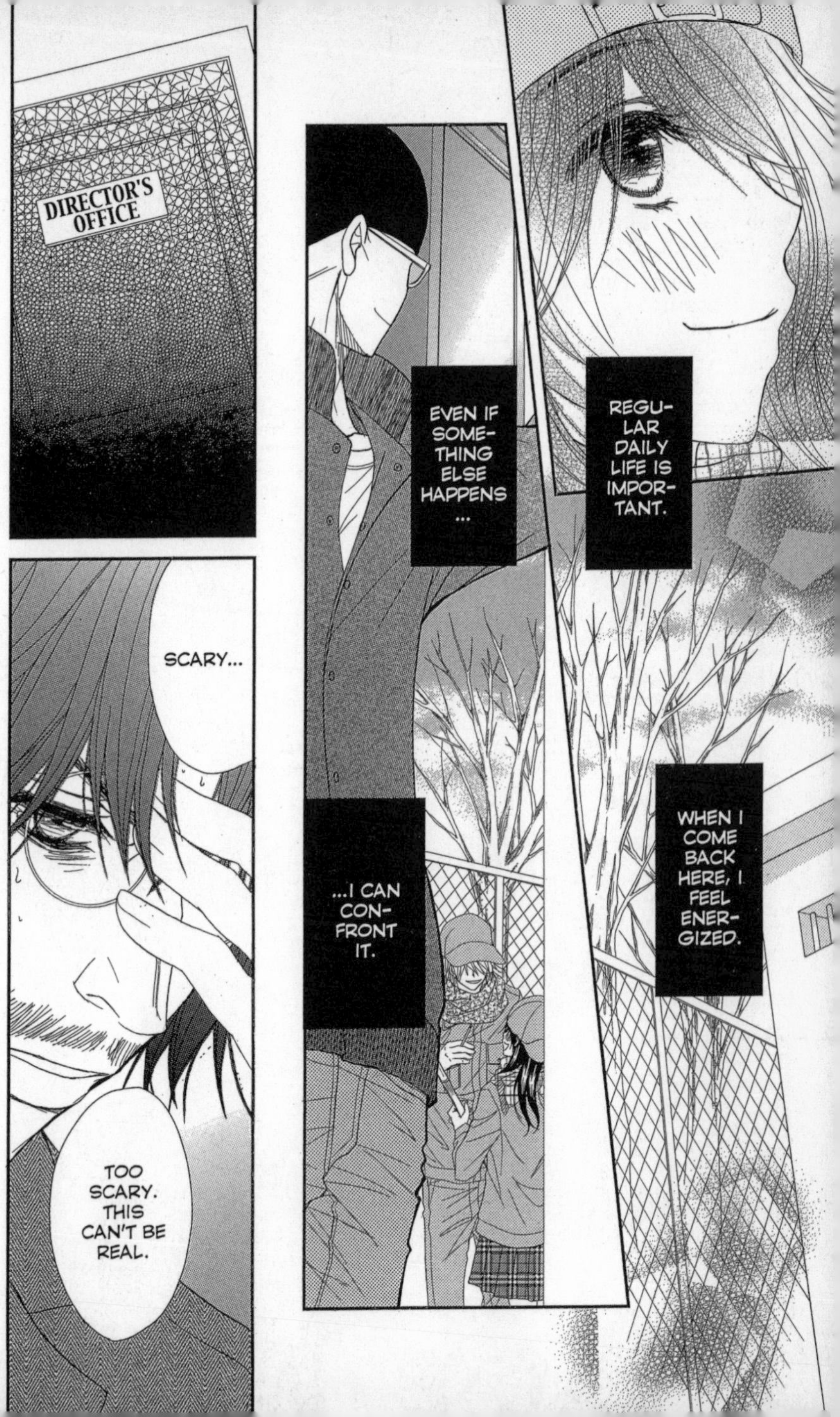
REGULAR DAILY LIFE IS IMPORTANT.
WHEN I COME BACK HERE, I FEEL ENERGIZED.
EVEN IF SOMETHING ELSE HAPPENS...
...I CAN CONFRONT IT.
DIRECTOR'S OFFICE
SCARY...
TOO SCARY. THIS CAN'T BE REAL.

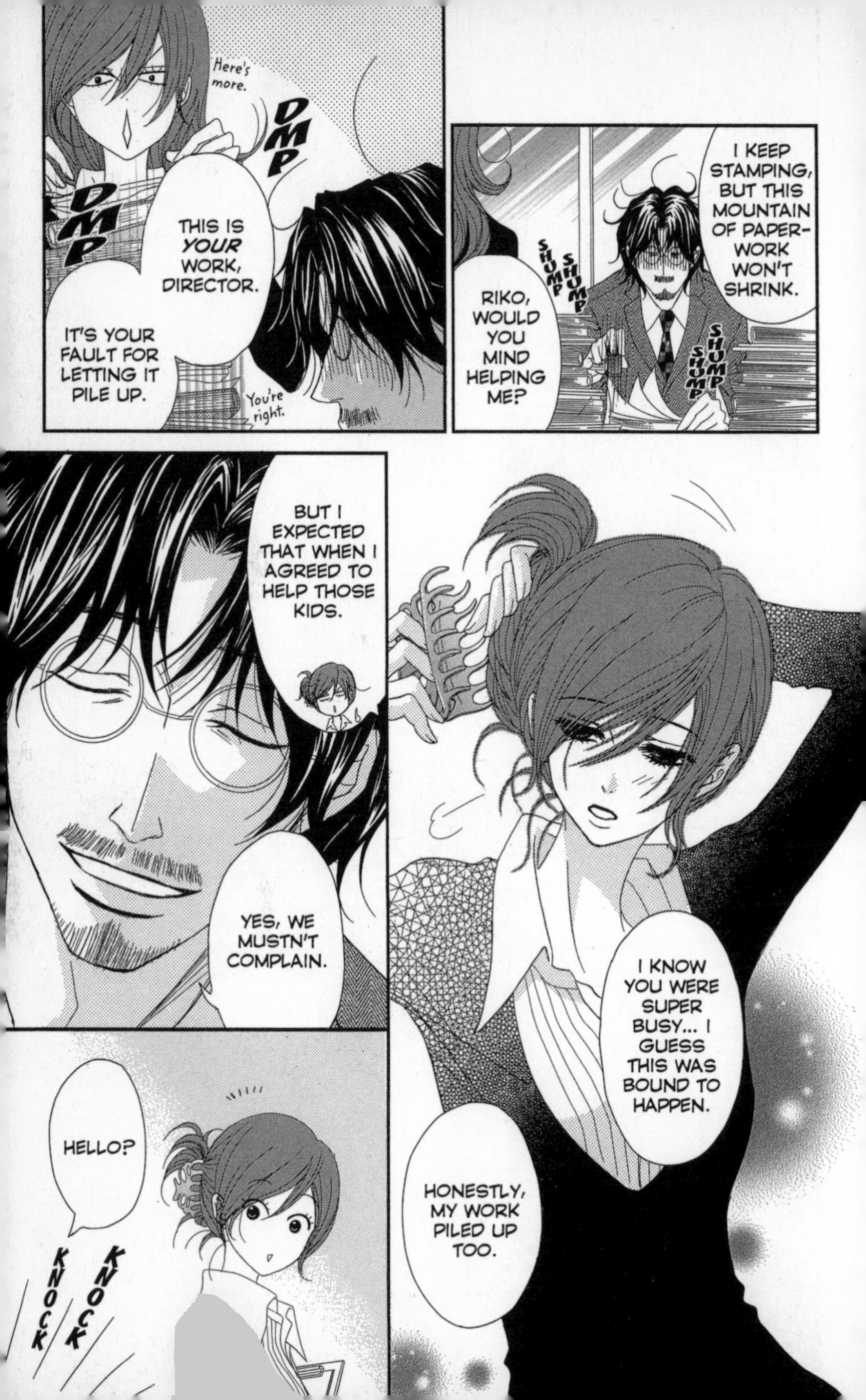
I KEEP STAMPING, BUT THIS MOUNTAIN OF PAPER-WORK WON'T SHRINK.
SHUMP SHUMP
SHUMP SHUMP
RIKO, WOULD YOU MIND HELPING ME?
Here's more.
DMP
DMP
THIS IS YOUR WORK, DIRECTOR.
IT'S YOUR FAULT FOR LETTING IT PILE UP.
You're right.
I KNOW YOU WERE SUPER BUSY... I GUESS THIS WAS BOUND TO HAPPEN.
HONESTLY, MY WORK PILED UP TOO.
BUT I EXPECTED THAT WHEN I AGREED TO HELP THOSE KIDS.
YES, WE MUSTN'T COMPLAIN.
KNOCK KNOCK
HELLO?

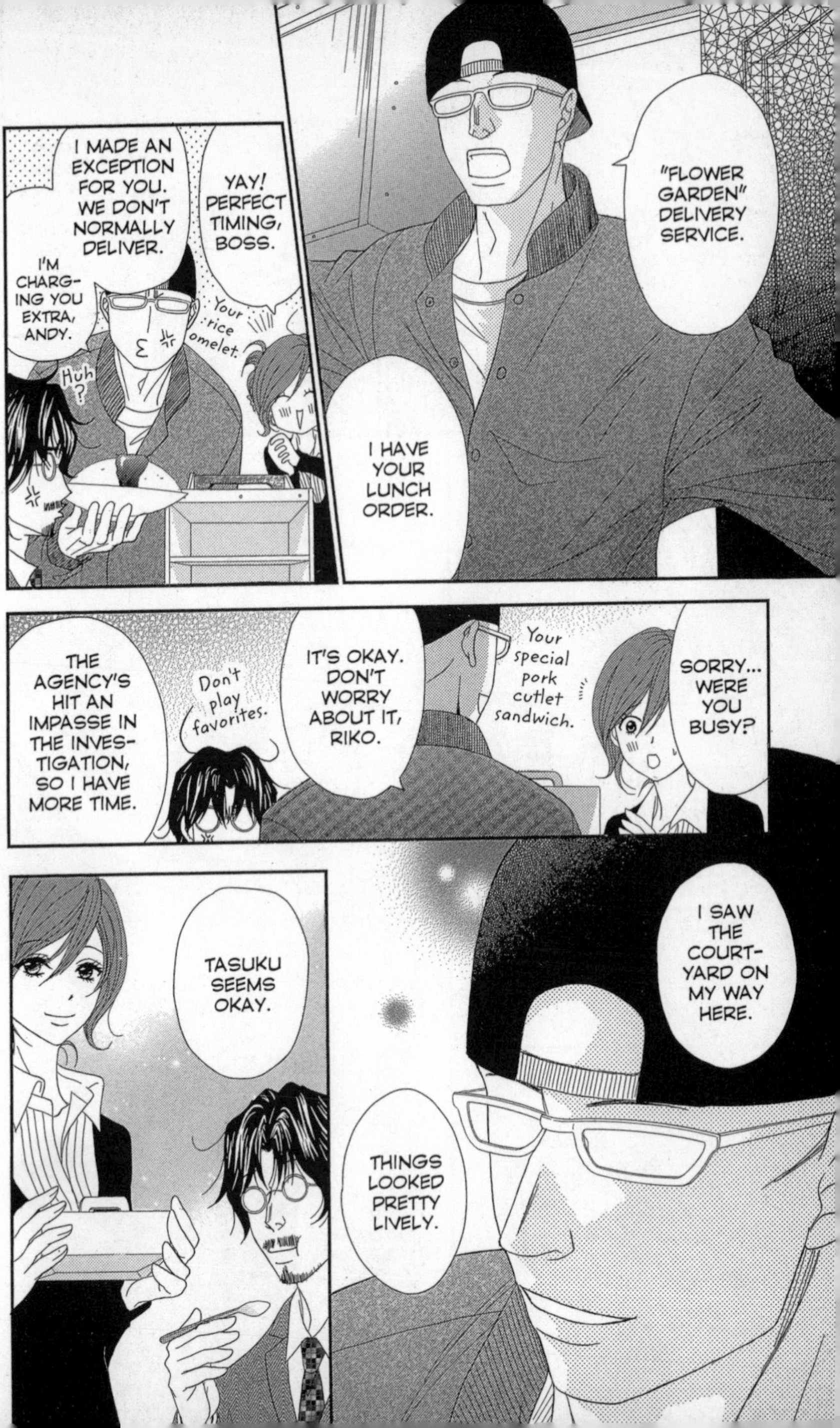
"FLOWER GARDEN" DELIVERY SERVICE.
I HAVE YOUR LUNCH ORDER.
YAY! PERFECT TIMING, BOSS.
Your rice omelet.
I MADE AN EXCEPTION FOR YOU. WE DON'T NORMALLY DELIVER.
I'M CHARGING YOU EXTRA, ANDY.
Huh?
SORRY... WERE YOU BUSY?
Your special pork cutlet sandwich.
IT'S OKAY. DON'T WORRY ABOUT IT, RIKO.
Don't play favorites.
THE AGENCY'S HIT AN IMPASSE IN THE INVESTIGATION, SO I HAVE MORE TIME.
I SAW THE COURTYARD ON MY WAY HERE.
THINGS LOOKED PRETTY LIVELY.
TASUKU SEEMS OKAY.

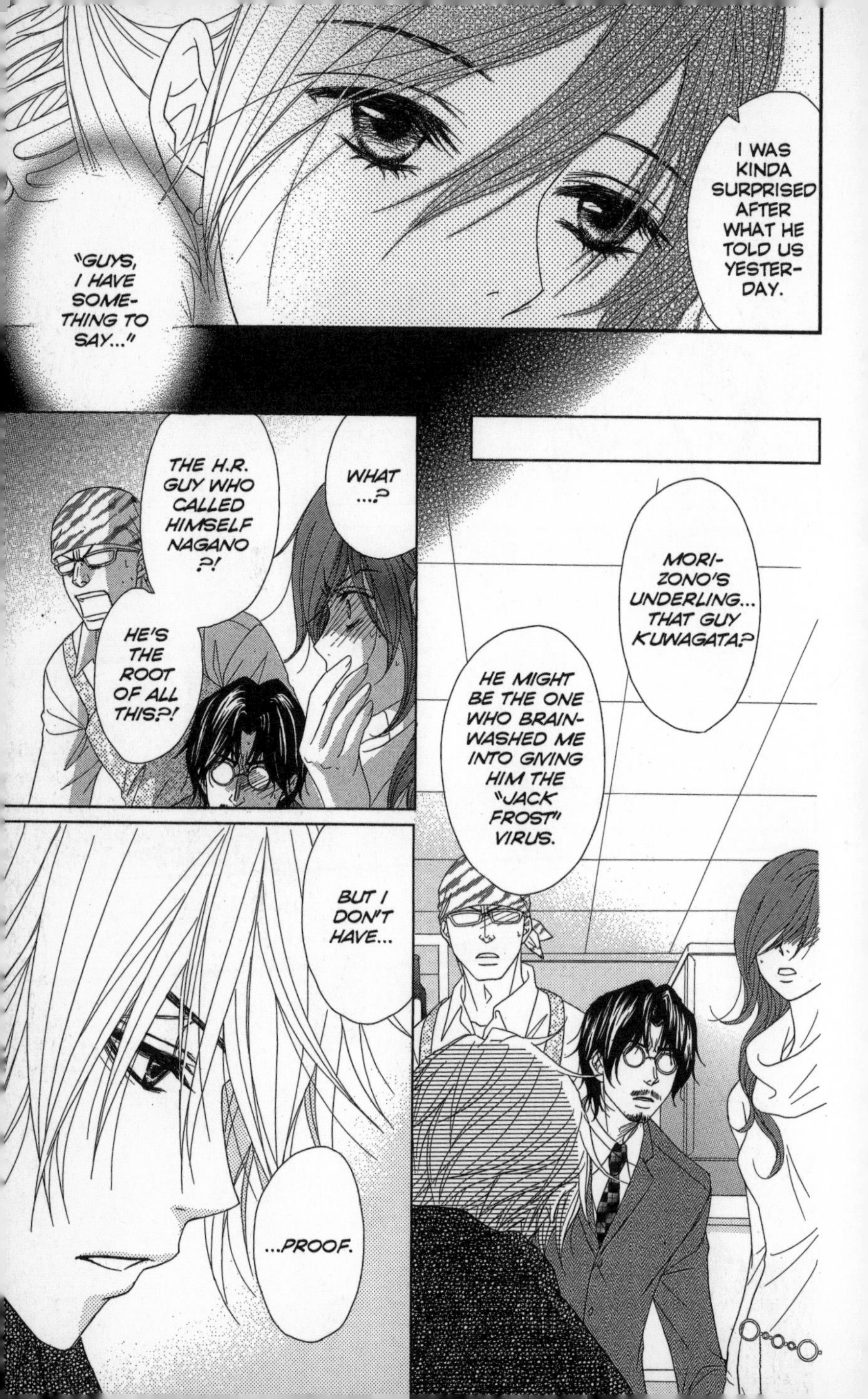
I WAS KINDA SURPRISED AFTER WHAT HE TOLD US YESTER-DAY.
"GUYS, I HAVE SOME-THING TO SAY..."
MORI-ZONO'S UNDERLING... THAT GUY KUWAGATA?
HE MIGHT BE THE ONE WHO BRAIN-WASHED ME INTO GIVING HIM THE "JACK FROST" VIRUS.
WHAT ...?
THE H.R. GUY WHO CALLED HIMSELF NAGANO ?!
HE'S THE ROOT OF ALL THIS?!
BUT I DON'T HAVE...
...PROOF.

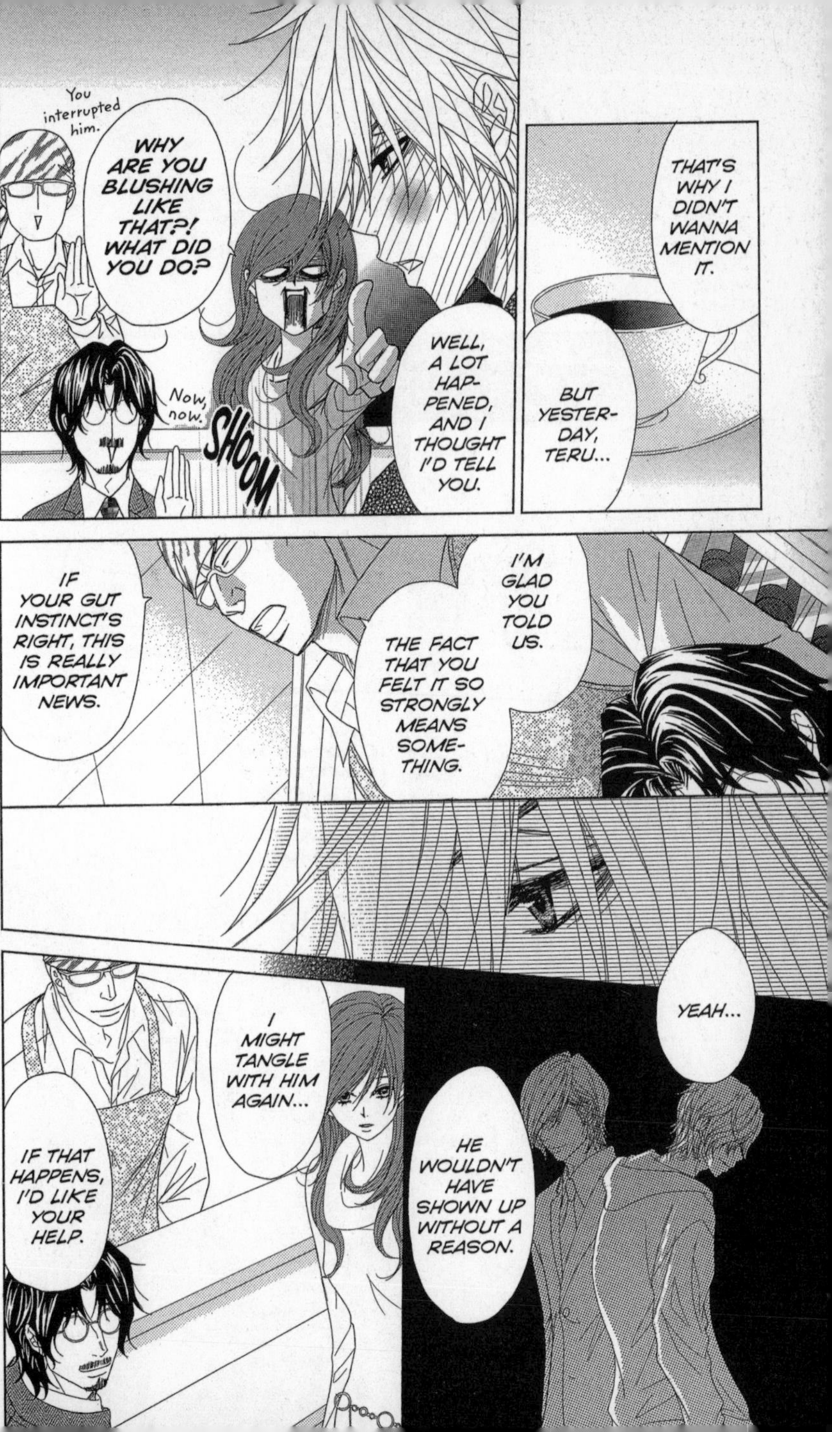
THAT'S WHY I DIDN'T WANNA MENTION IT.
BUT YESTER-DAY, TERU...
WELL, A LOT HAP-PENED, AND I THOUGHT I'D TELL YOU.
WHY ARE YOU BLUSHING LIKE THAT?! WHAT DID YOU DO?
You interrupted him.
Now, now.
SHOOM
I'M GLAD YOU TOLD US.
THE FACT THAT YOU FELT IT SO STRONGLY MEANS SOME-THING.
IF YOUR GUT INSTINCT'S RIGHT, THIS IS REALLY IMPORTANT NEWS.
YEAH...
HE WOULDN'T HAVE SHOWN UP WITHOUT A REASON.
I MIGHT TANGLE WITH HIM AGAIN...
IF THAT HAPPENS, I'D LIKE YOUR HELP.

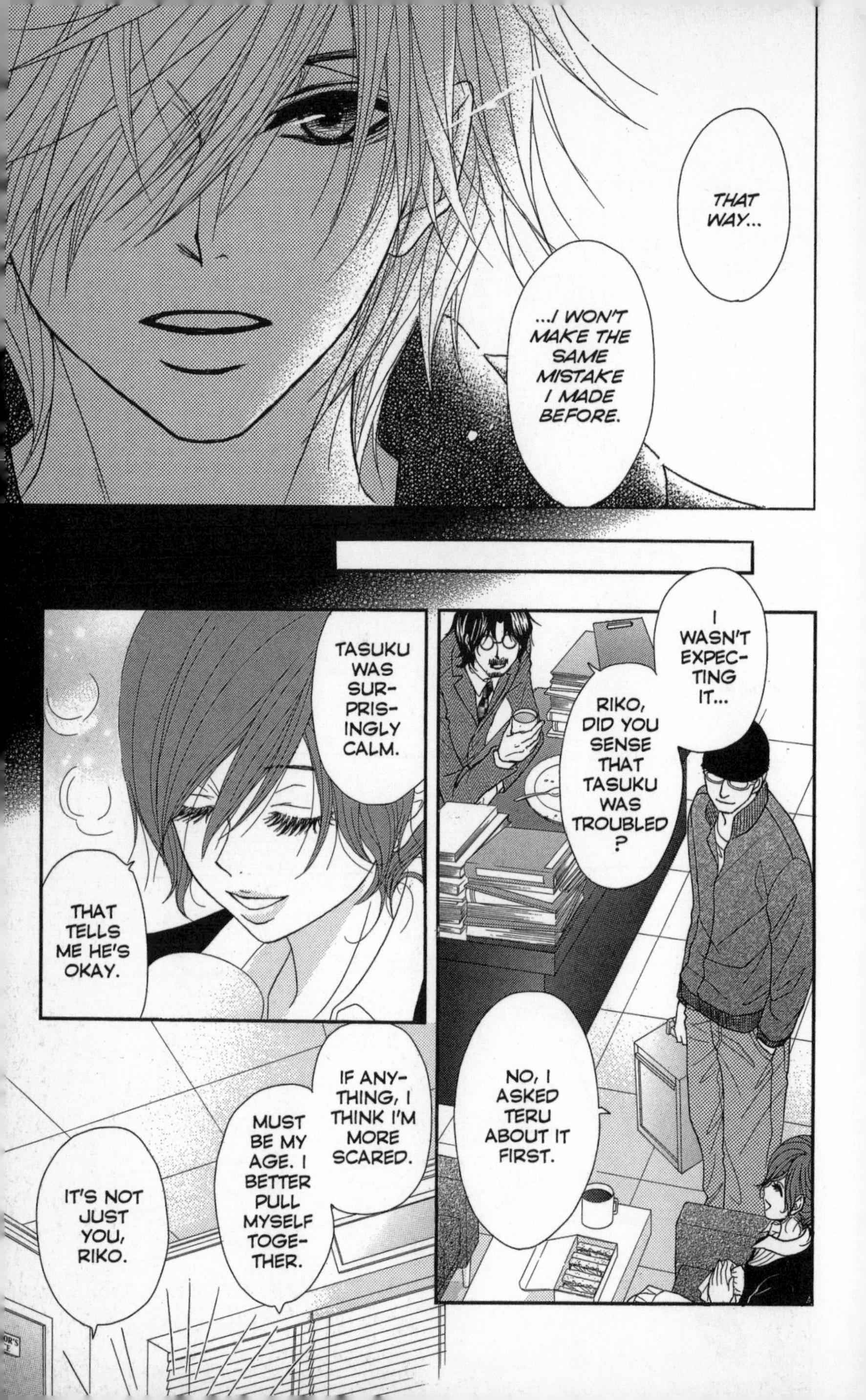
THAT WAY...
...I WON'T MAKE THE SAME MISTAKE I MADE BEFORE.
I WASN'T EXPEC-TING IT...
RIKO, DID YOU SENSE THAT TASUKU WAS TROUBLED?
NO, I ASKED TERU ABOUT IT FIRST.
TASUKU WAS SUR-PRIS-INGLY CALM.
THAT TELLS ME HE'S OKAY.
IF ANY-THING, I THINK I'M MORE SCARED.
MUST BE MY AGE. I BETTER PULL MYSELF TOGE-THER.
IT'S NOT JUST YOU, RIKO.

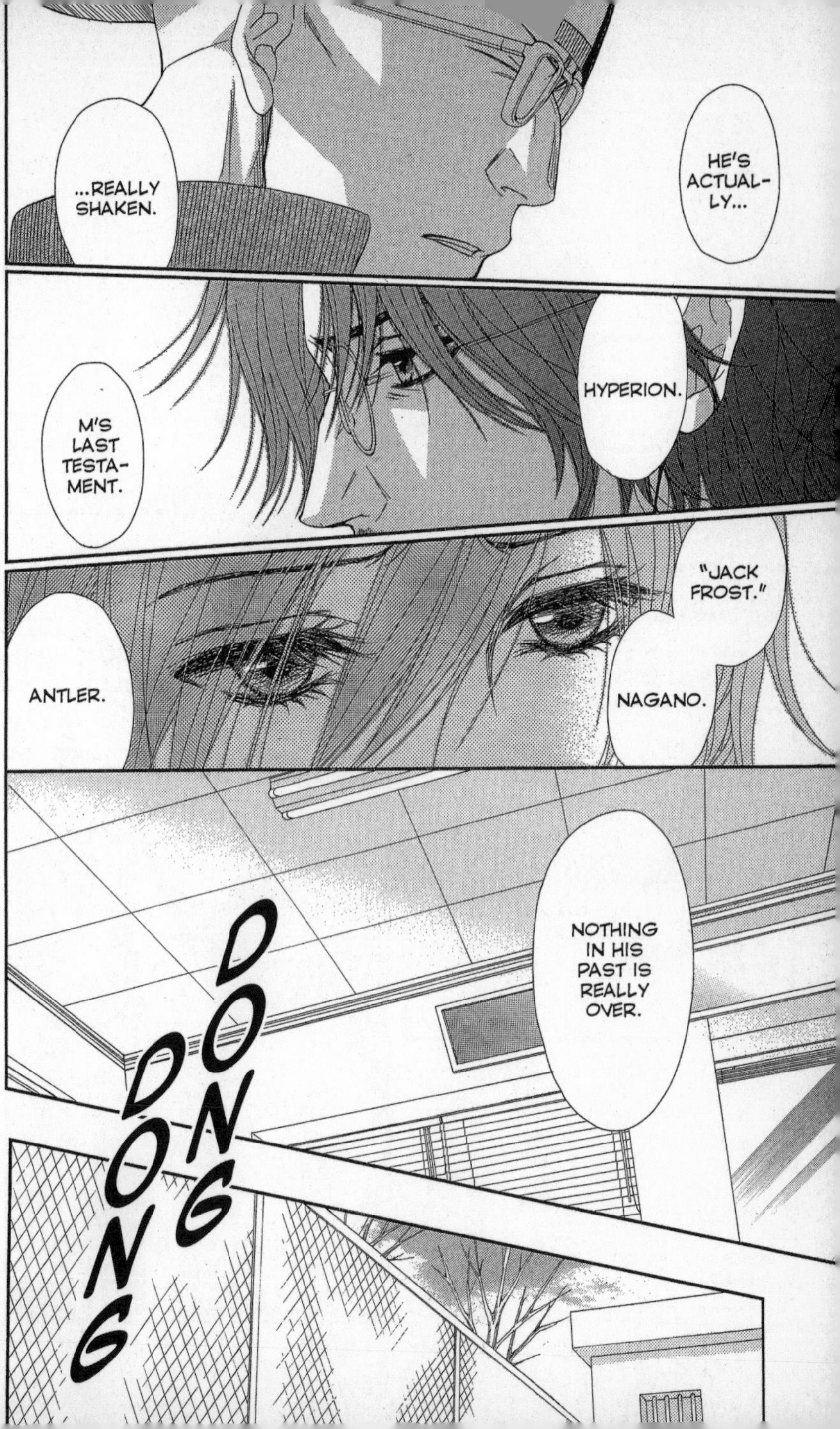
HE'S ACTUAL-LY...
...REALLY SHAKEN.
HYPERION.
M'S LAST TESTA-MENT.
"JACK FROST."
NAGANO.
ANTLER.
NOTHING IN HIS PAST IS REALLY OVER.
DONG
DONG

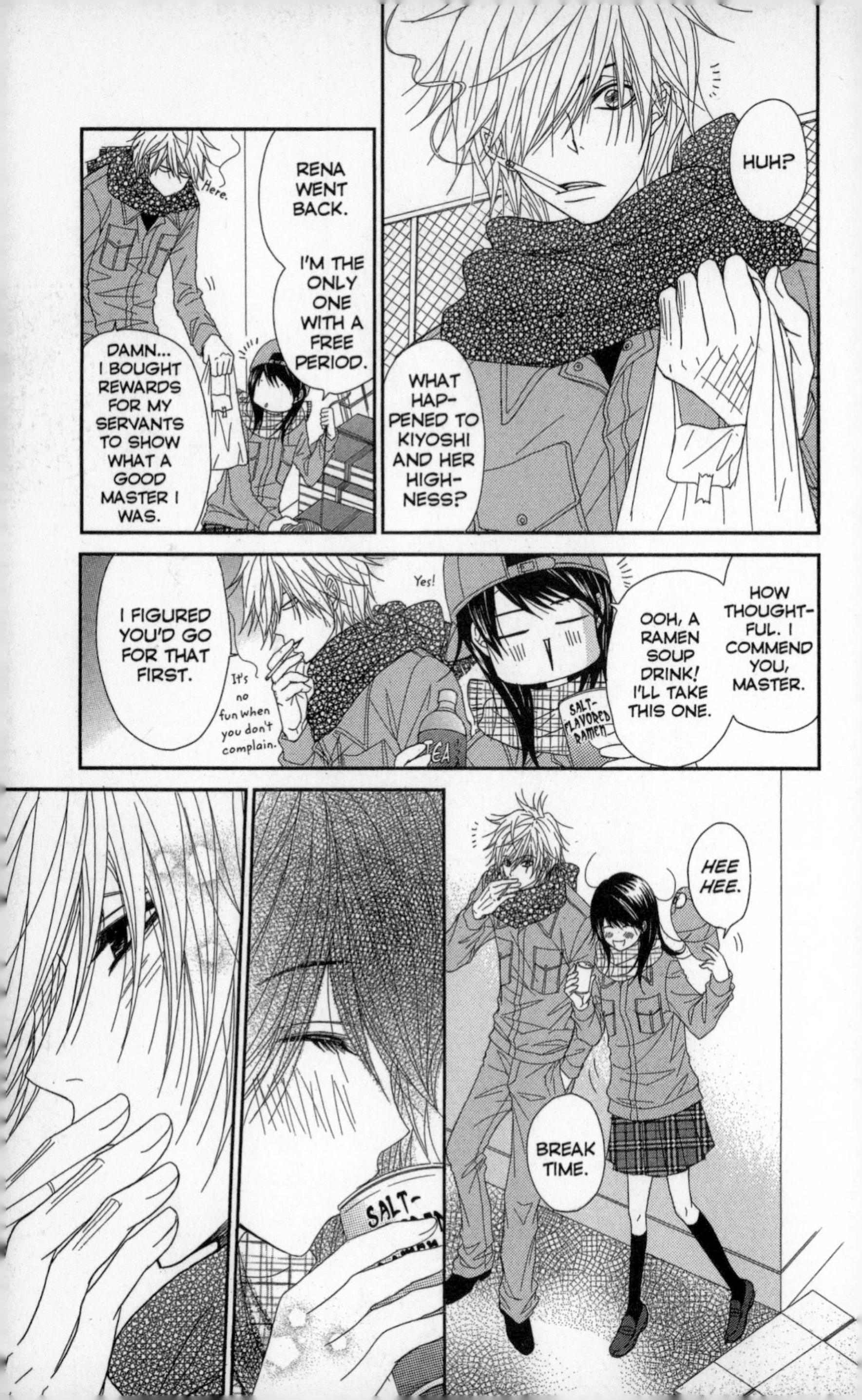
HUH?
WHAT HAP-PENED TO KIYOSHI AND HER HIGH-NESS?
RENA WENT BACK.
I'M THE ONLY ONE WITH A FREE PERIOD.
Here.
DAMN... I BOUGHT REWARDS FOR MY SERVANTS TO SHOW WHAT A GOOD MASTER I WAS.
HOW THOUGHT-FUL. I COMMEND YOU, MASTER.
OOH, A RAMEN SOUP DRINK! I'LL TAKE THIS ONE.
SALT-FLAVORED RAMEN
Yes!
TEA
I FIGURED YOU'D GO FOR THAT FIRST.
It's no fun when you don't complain.
HEE HEE.
BREAK TIME.
SALT-

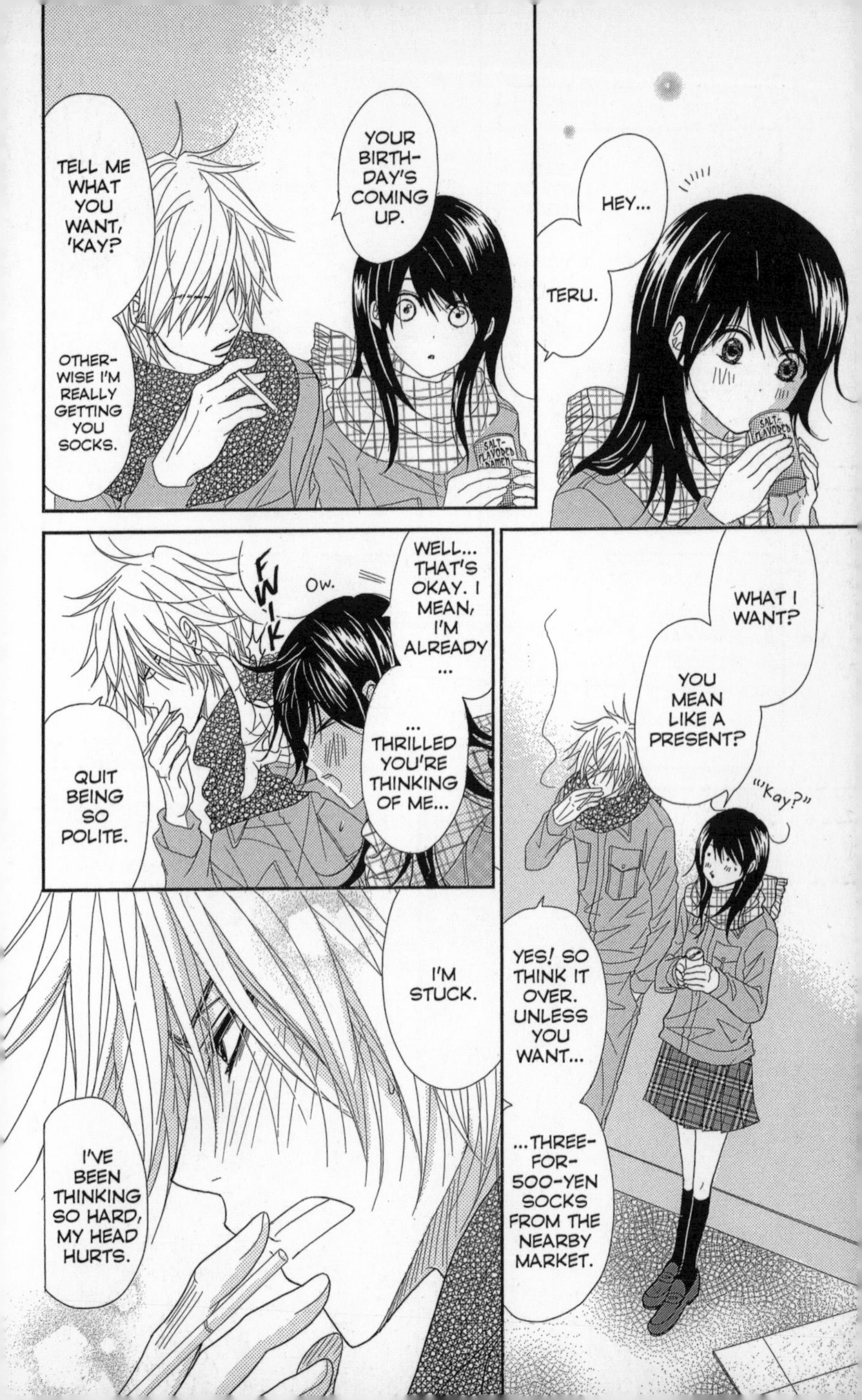
HEY...
TERU.
SALT-FLAVORED RAMEN
YOUR BIRTH-DAY'S COMING UP.
TELL ME WHAT YOU WANT, 'KAY?
OTHER-WISE I'M REALLY GETTING YOU SOCKS.
WHAT I WANT?
YOU MEAN LIKE A PRESENT?
"Kay?"
YES! SO THINK IT OVER. UNLESS YOU WANT...
...THREE-FOR-500-YEN SOCKS FROM THE NEARBY MARKET.
WELL... THAT'S OKAY. I MEAN, I'M ALREADY ...
... THRILLED YOU'RE THINKING OF ME...
FWIK
OW.
QUIT BEING SO POLITE.
I'M STUCK.
I'VE BEEN THINKING SO HARD, MY HEAD HURTS.

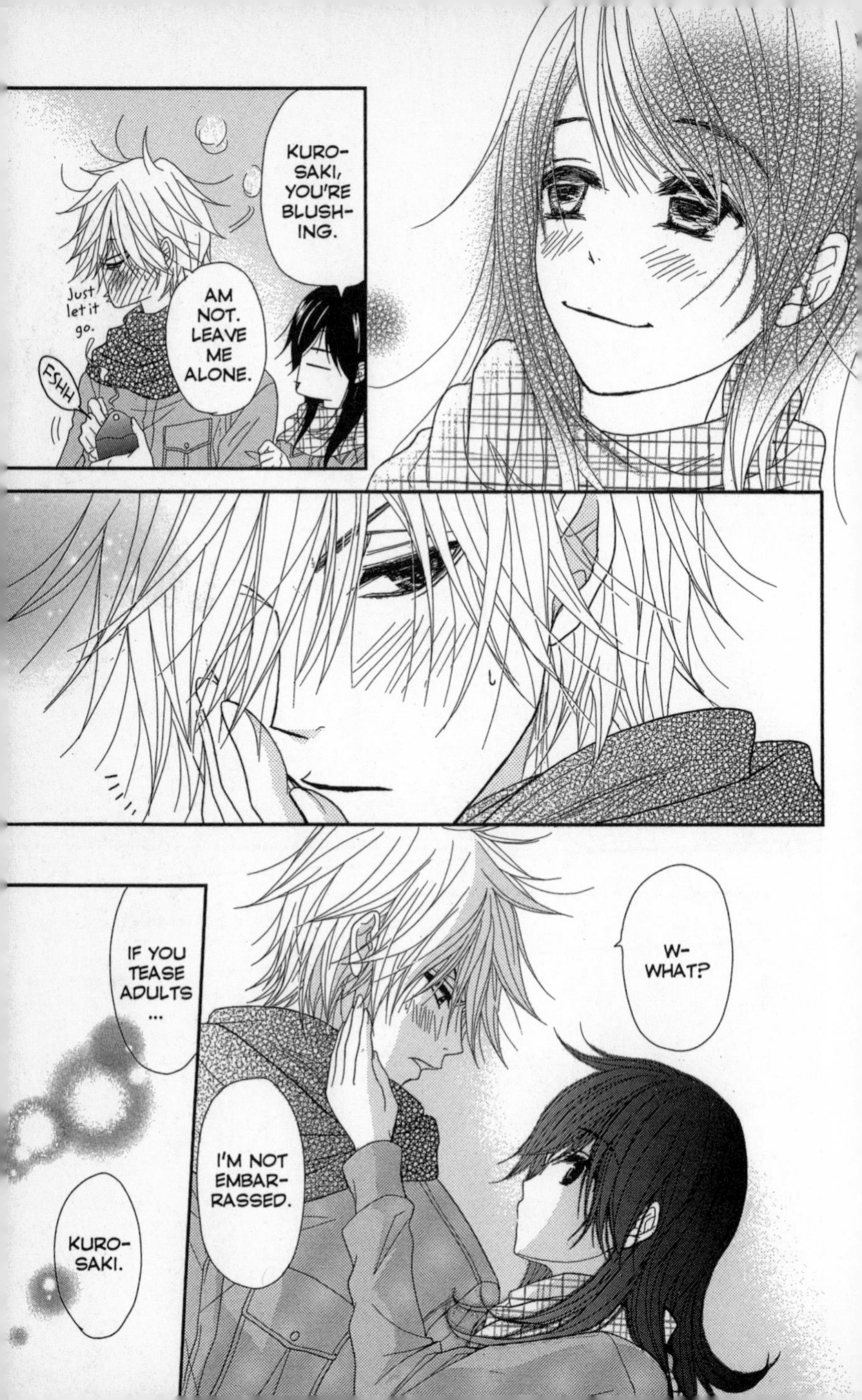
KURO-SAKI, YOU'RE BLUSH-ING.
AM NOT. LEAVE ME ALONE.
Just let it go.
FSHH
W-WHAT?
IF YOU TEASE ADULTS ...
I'M NOT EMBAR-RASSED.
KURO-SAKI.

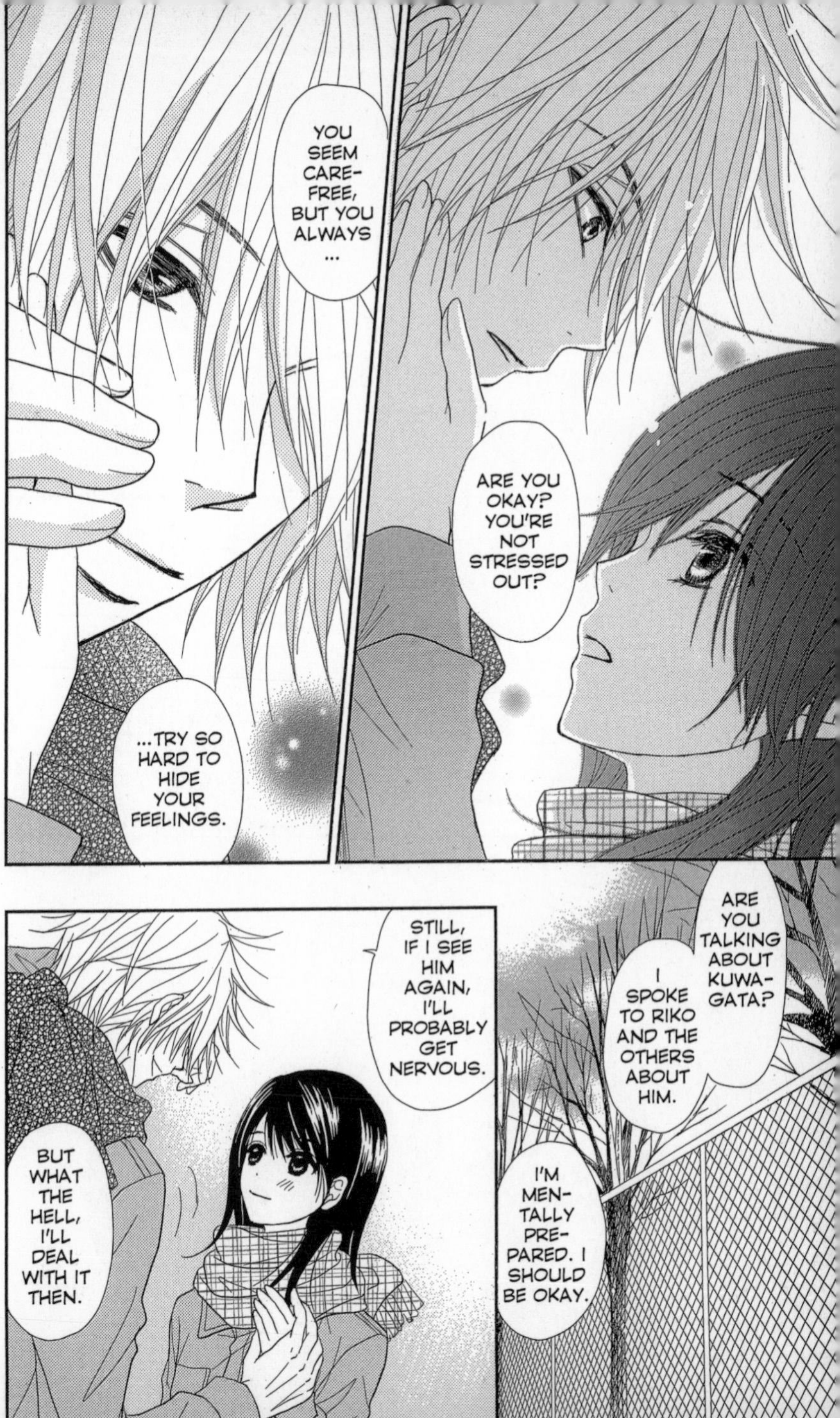
ARE YOU OKAY? YOU'RE NOT STRESSED OUT?
YOU SEEM CARE-FREE, BUT YOU ALWAYS ...
...TRY SO HARD TO HIDE YOUR FEELINGS.
ARE YOU TALKING ABOUT KUWA-GATA?
I SPOKE TO RIKO AND THE OTHERS ABOUT HIM.
I'M MEN-TALLY PRE-PARED. I SHOULD BE OKAY.
STILL, IF I SEE HIM AGAIN, I'LL PROBABLY GET NERVOUS.
BUT WHAT THE HELL, I'LL DEAL WITH IT THEN.

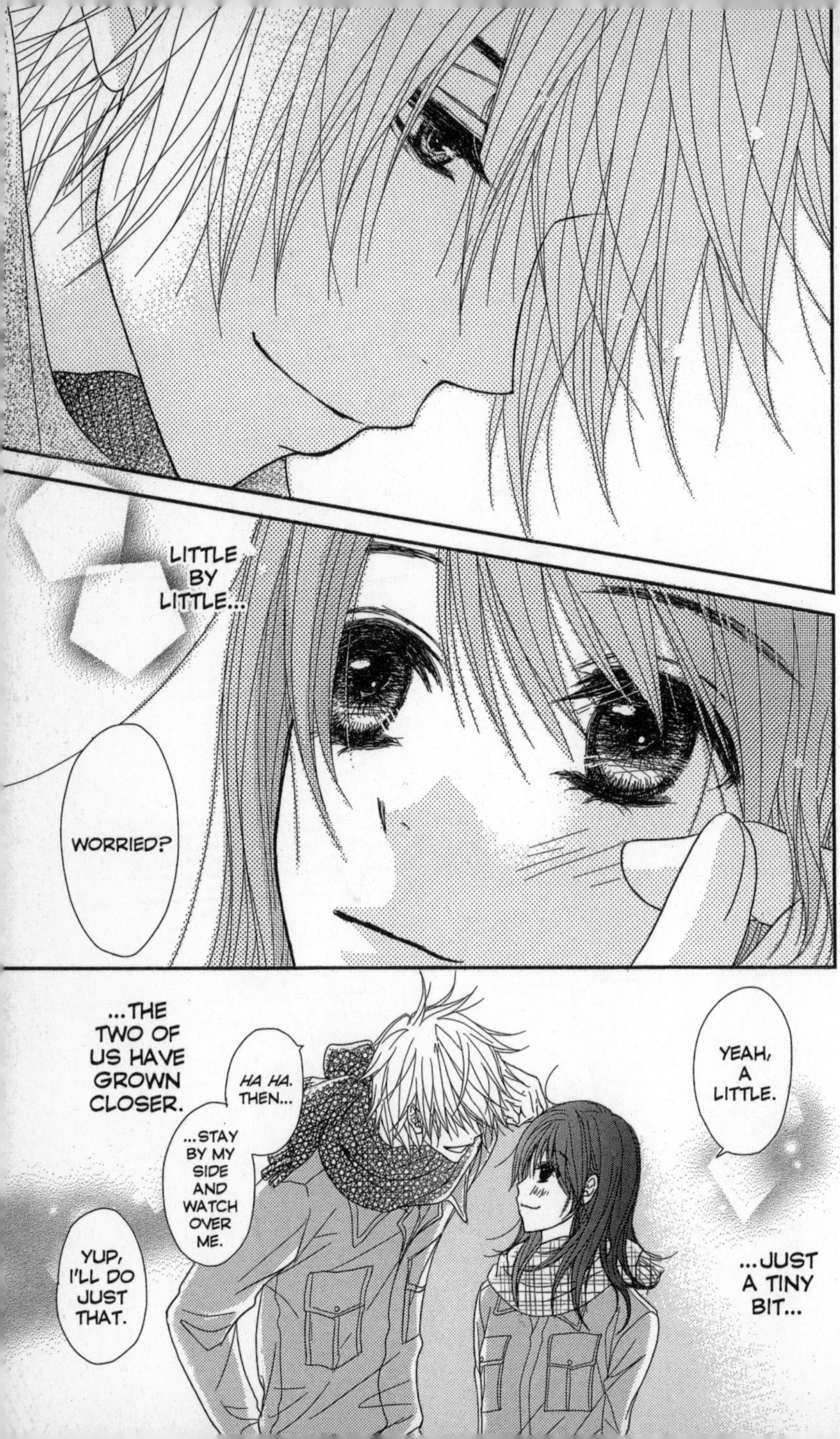
LITTLE BY LITTLE...
WORRIED?
YEAH, A LITTLE.
...JUST A TINY BIT...
...THE TWO OF US HAVE GROWN CLOSER.
HA HA. THEN...
...STAY BY MY SIDE AND WATCH OVER ME.
YUP, I'LL DO JUST THAT.

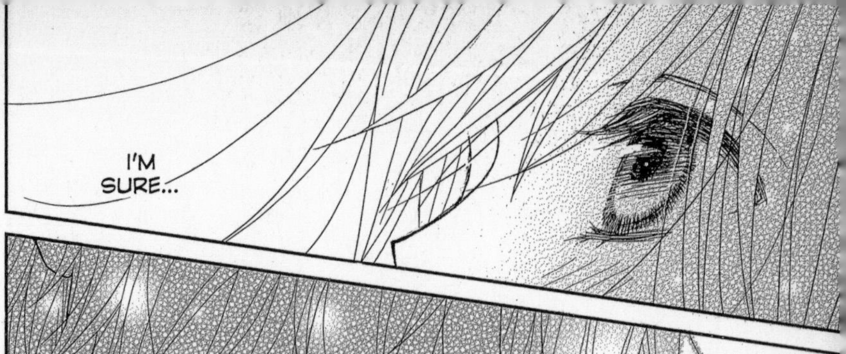
I'M SURE...
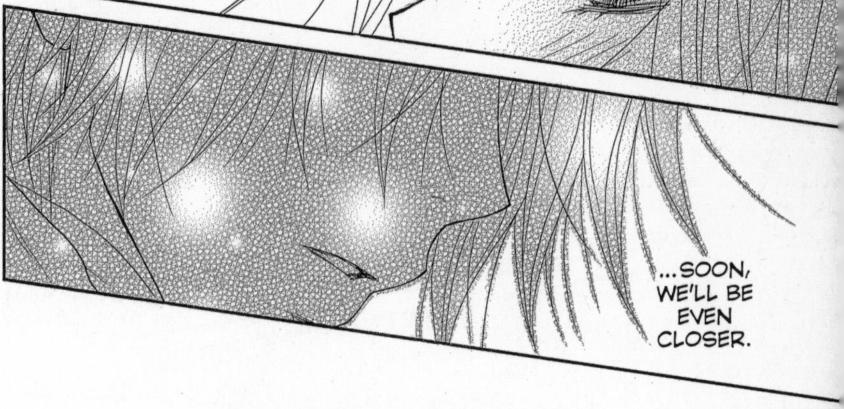
...SOON, WE'LL BE EVEN CLOSER.
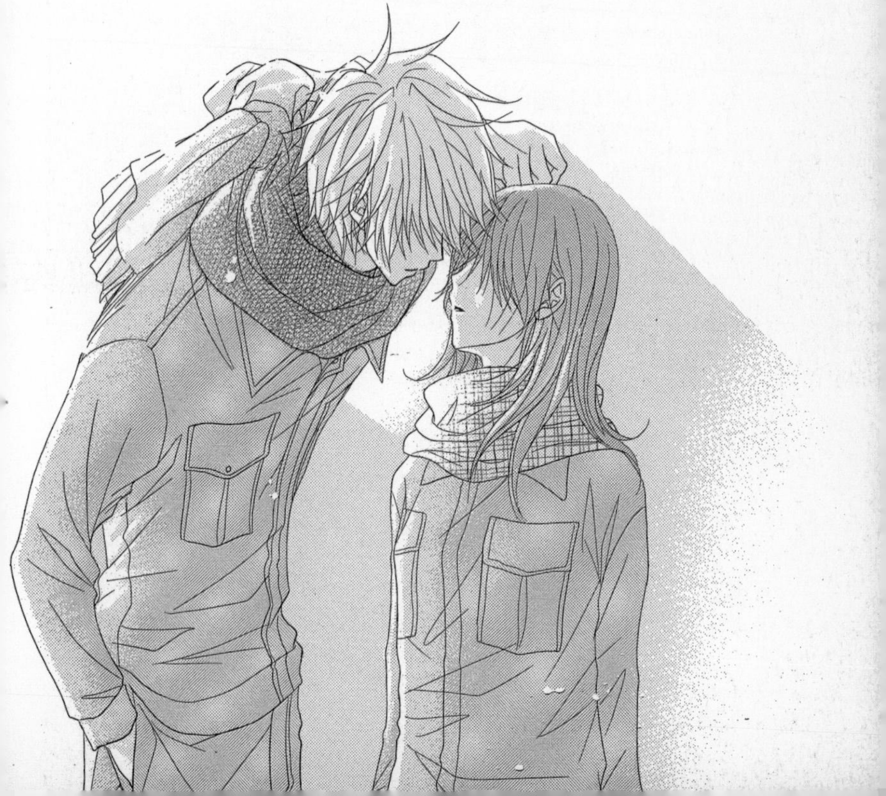

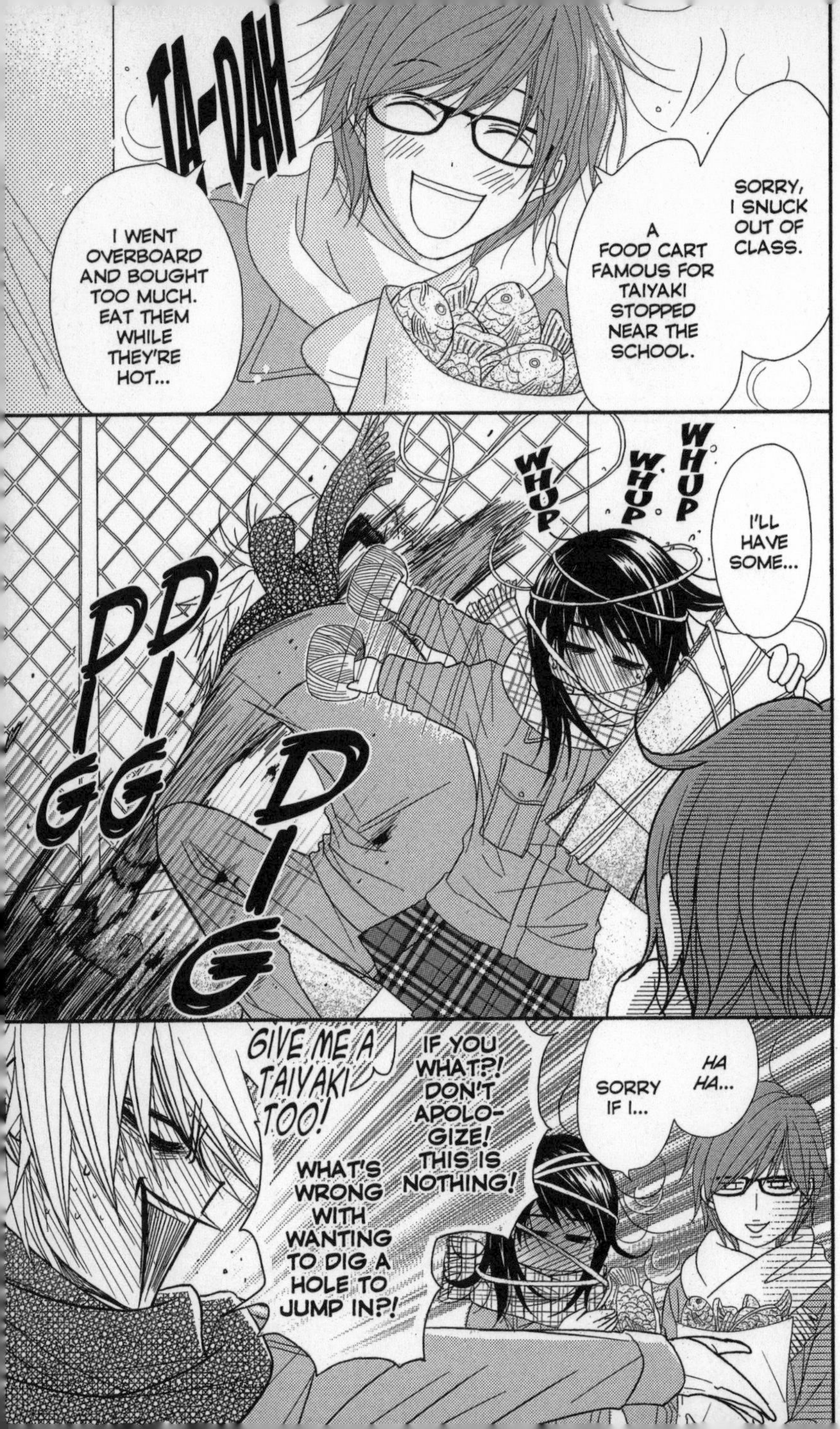
SORRY, I SNUCK OUT OF CLASS.
A FOOD CART FAMOUS FOR TAIYAKI STOPPED NEAR THE SCHOOL.
TA-DAH
I WENT OVERBOARD AND BOUGHT TOO MUCH. EAT THEM WHILE THEY'RE HOT...
I'LL HAVE SOME...
WHUP
WHUP
WHUP
DIG
DIG
DIG
HA HA...
SORRY IF I...
IF YOU WHAT?! DON'T APOLO-GIZE! THIS IS NOTHING!
GIVE ME A TAIYAKI TOO!
WHAT'S WRONG WITH WANTING TO DIG A HOLE TO JUMP IN?!

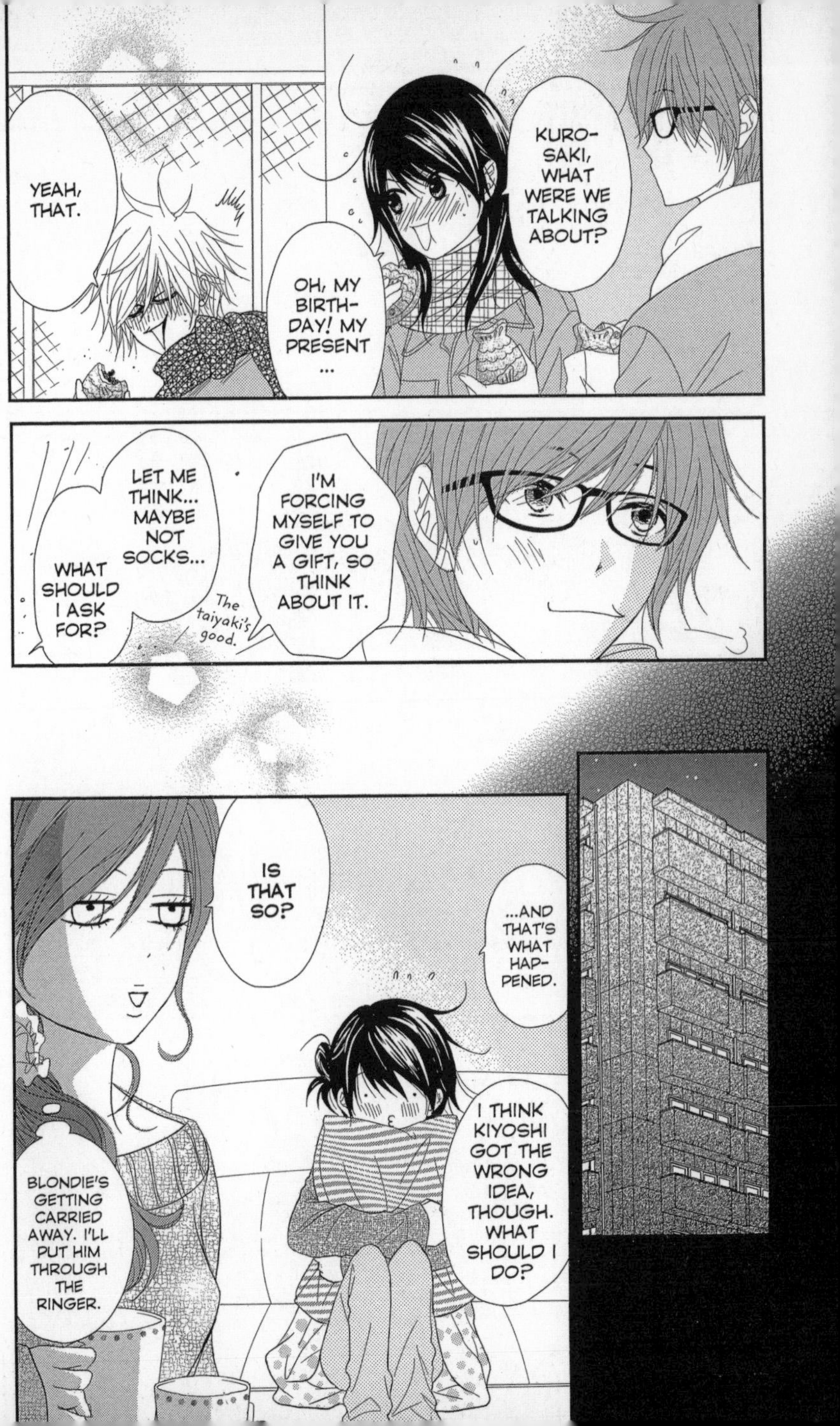
KURO-SAKI, WHAT WERE WE TALKING ABOUT?
OH, MY BIRTH-DAY! MY PRESENT ...
YEAH, THAT.
I'M FORCING MYSELF TO GIVE YOU A GIFT, SO THINK ABOUT IT.
The taiyaki's good.
LET ME THINK... MAYBE NOT SOCKS...
WHAT SHOULD I ASK FOR?
...AND THAT'S WHAT HAP-PENED.
I THINK KIYOSHI GOT THE WRONG IDEA, THOUGH. WHAT SHOULD I DO?
IS THAT SO?
BLONDIE'S GETTING CARRIED AWAY. I'LL PUT HIM THROUGH THE RINGER.

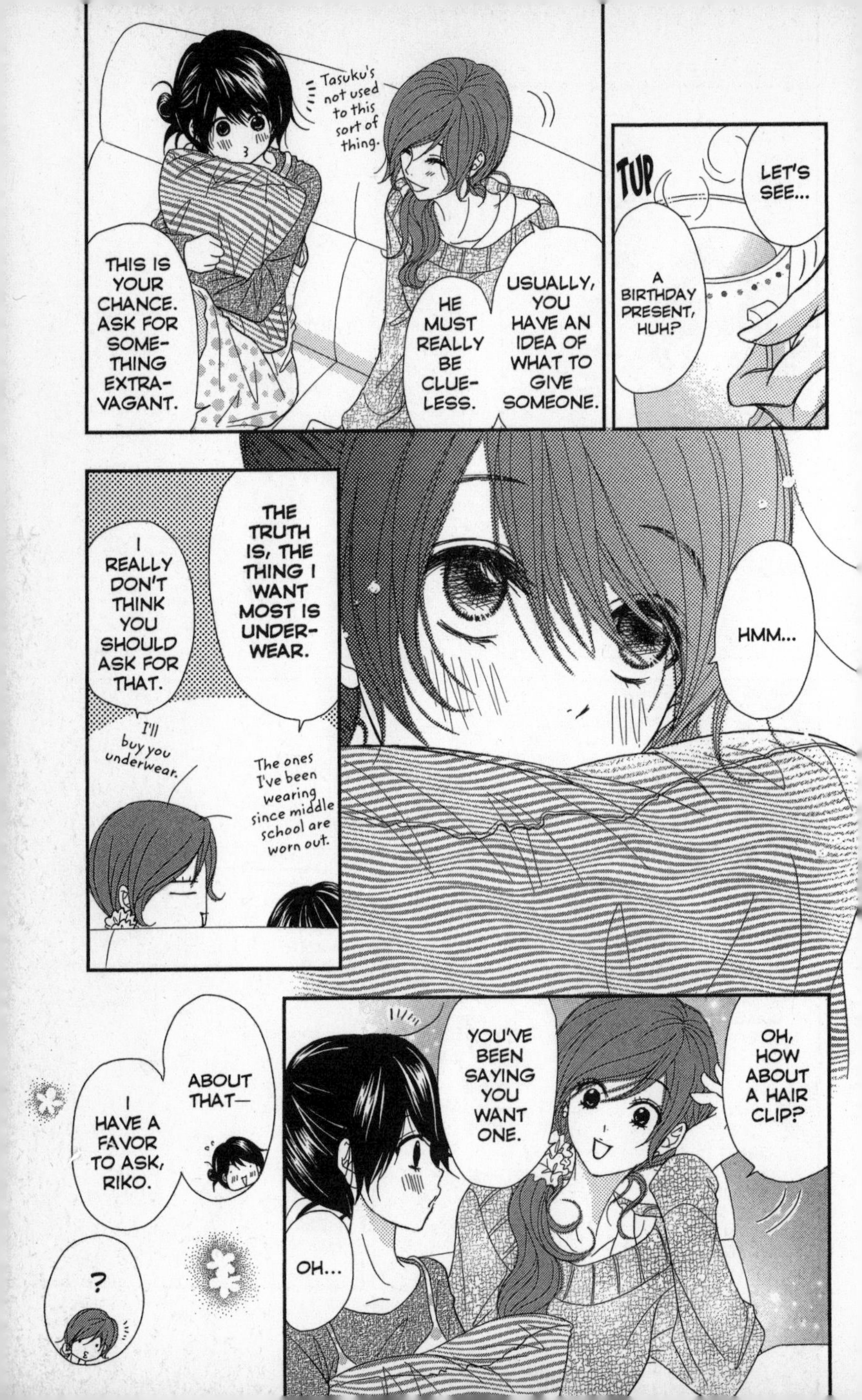
LET'S SEE...
TUP
A BIRTHDAY PRESENT, HUH?
USUALLY, YOU HAVE AN IDEA OF WHAT TO GIVE SOMEONE.
HE MUST REALLY BE CLUE-LESS.
Tasuku's not used to this sort of thing.
THIS IS YOUR CHANCE. ASK FOR SOME-THING EXTRA-VAGANT.
HMM...
THE TRUTH IS, THE THING I WANT MOST IS UNDER-WEAR.
I REALLY DON'T THINK YOU SHOULD ASK FOR THAT.
The ones I've been wearing since middle school are worn out.
I'll buy you underwear.
OH, HOW ABOUT A HAIR CLIP?
YOU'VE BEEN SAYING YOU WANT ONE.
OH...
ABOUT THAT—
I HAVE A FAVOR TO ASK, RIKO.
?

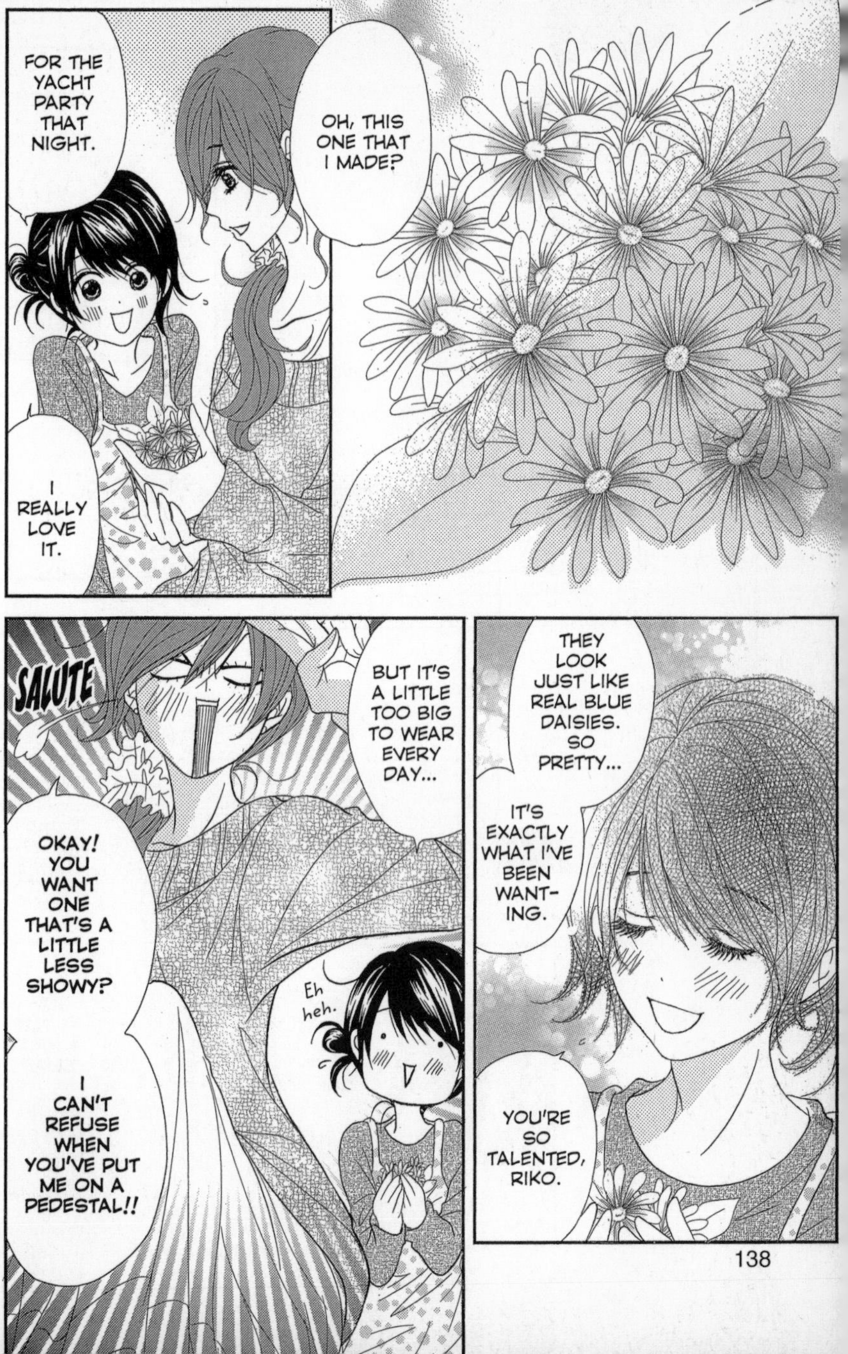
OH, THIS ONE THAT I MADE?
FOR THE YACHT PARTY THAT NIGHT.
I REALLY LOVE IT.
THEY LOOK JUST LIKE REAL BLUE DAISIES. SO PRETTY...
IT'S EXACTLY WHAT I'VE BEEN WANT-ING.
YOU'RE SO TALENTED, RIKO.
BUT IT'S A LITTLE TOO BIG TO WEAR EVERY DAY...
Eh heh.
SALUTE
OKAY! YOU WANT ONE THAT'S A LITTLE LESS SHOWY?
I CAN'T REFUSE WHEN YOU'VE PUT ME ON A PEDESTAL!!

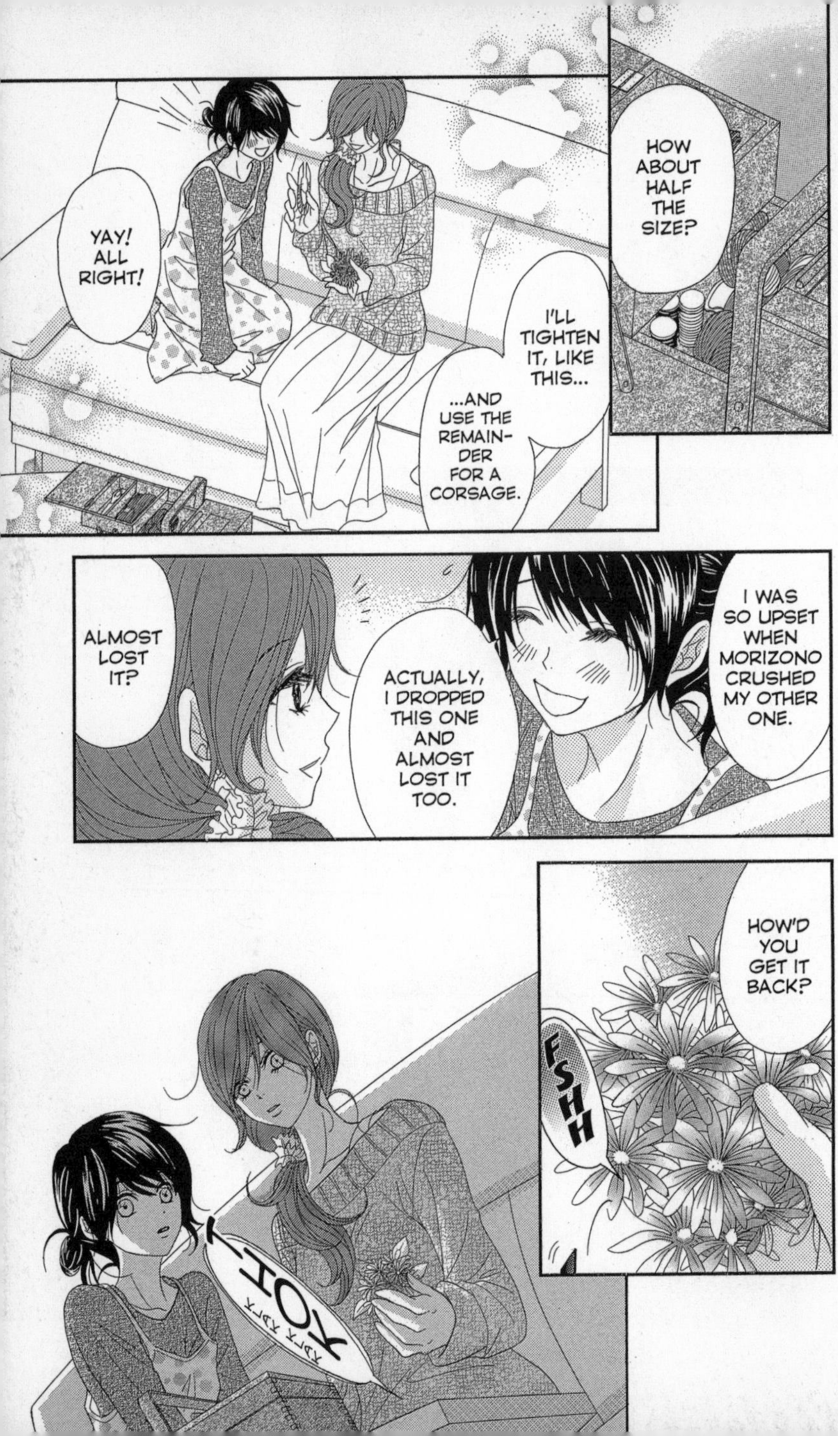
HOW ABOUT HALF THE SIZE?
I'LL TIGHTEN IT, LIKE THIS...
...AND USE THE REMAIN-DER FOR A CORSAGE.
YAY! ALL RIGHT!
I WAS SO UPSET WHEN MORIZONO CRUSHED MY OTHER ONE.
ACTUALLY, I DROPPED THIS ONE AND ALMOST LOST IT TOO.
ALMOST LOST IT?
HOW'D YOU GET IT BACK?
FSHH

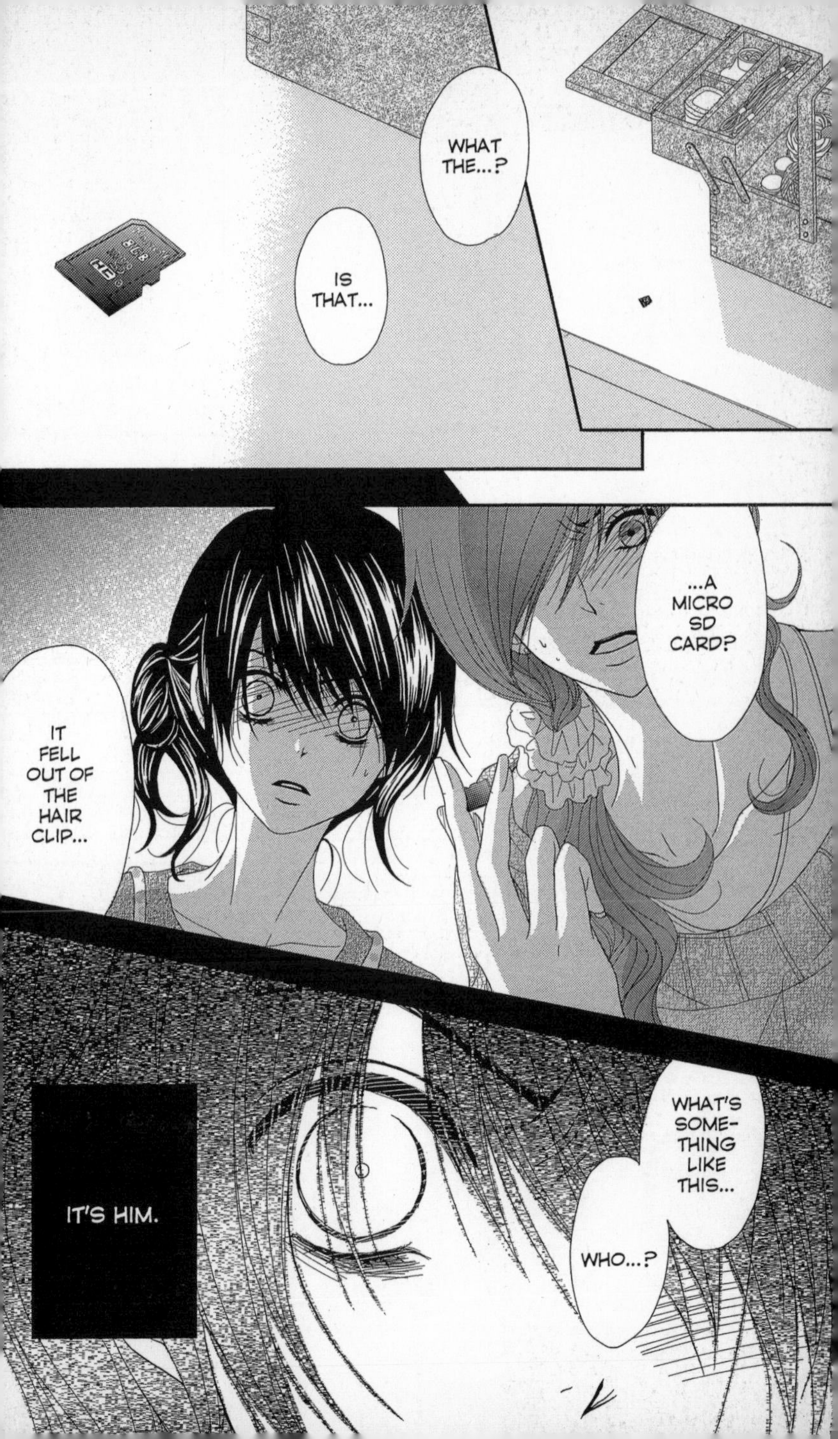
WHAT THE...?
IS THAT...
...A MICRO SD CARD?
IT FELL OUT OF THE HAIR CLIP...
WHAT'S SOMETHING LIKE THIS...
WHO...?
IT'S HIM.

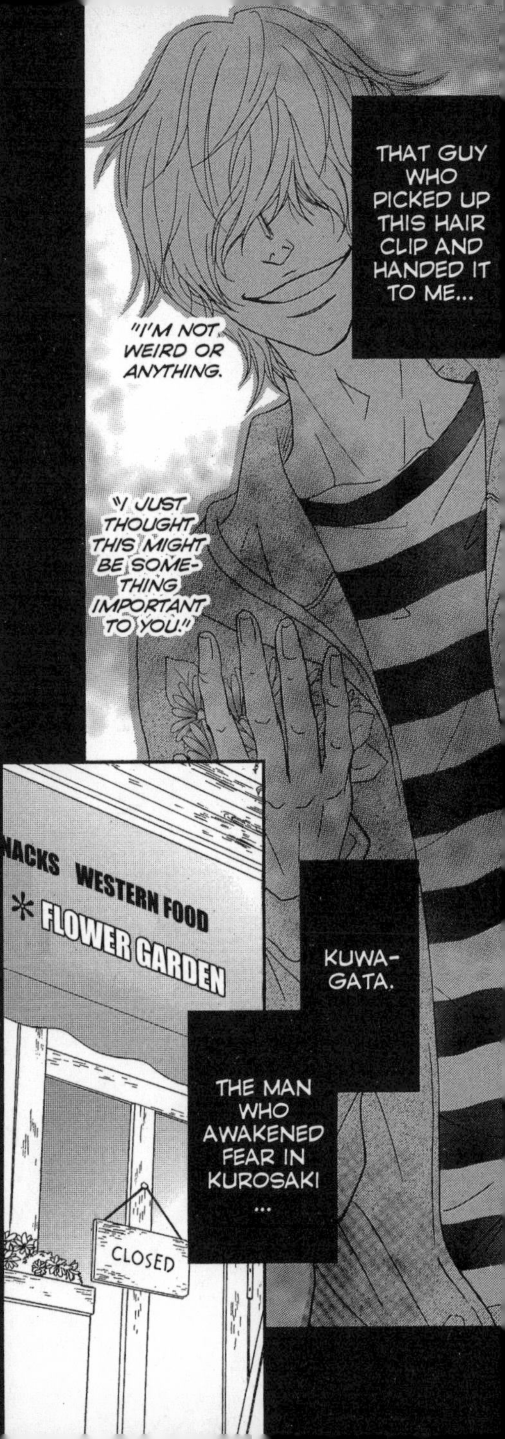
THAT GUY WHO PICKED UP THIS HAIR CLIP AND HANDED IT TO ME...
"I'M NOT WEIRD OR ANYTHING.
"I JUST THOUGHT THIS MIGHT BE SOME-THING IMPORTANT TO YOU."
NACKS WESTERN FOOD
* FLOWER GARDEN
CLOSED
KUWA-GATA.
THE MAN WHO AWAKENED FEAR IN KUROSAKI ...

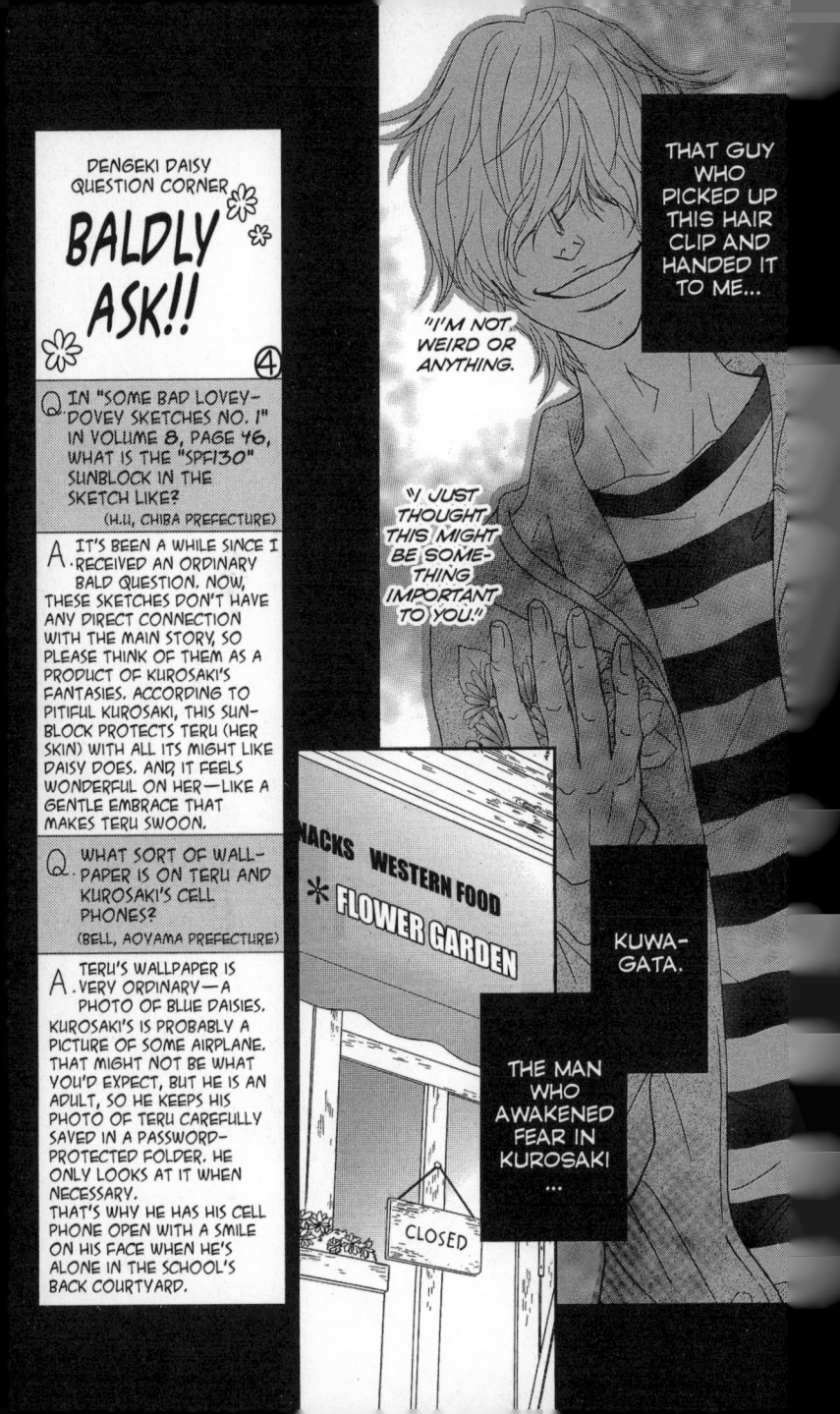

DENGEKI DAISY QUESTION CORNER

# BALDLY ASK!!

④

**Q.** IN "SOME BAD LOVEY-DOVEY SKETCHES NO. 1" IN VOLUME 8, PAGE 46, WHAT IS THE "SPF130" SUNBLOCK IN THE SKETCH LIKE?

(H.U, CHIBA PREFECTURE)

**A.** IT'S BEEN A WHILE SINCE I RECEIVED AN ORDINARY BALD QUESTION. NOW, THESE SKETCHES DON'T HAVE ANY DIRECT CONNECTION WITH THE MAIN STORY, SO PLEASE THINK OF THEM AS A PRODUCT OF KUROSAKI'S FANTASIES. ACCORDING TO PITIFUL KUROSAKI, THIS SUN-BLOCK PROTECTS TERU (HER SKIN) WITH ALL ITS MIGHT LIKE DAISY DOES. AND, IT FEELS WONDERFUL ON HER—LIKE A GENTLE EMBRACE THAT MAKES TERU SWOON.

**Q.** WHAT SORT OF WALL-PAPER IS ON TERU AND KUROSAKI'S CELL PHONES?

(BELL, AOYAMA PREFECTURE)

**A.** TERU'S WALLPAPER IS VERY ORDINARY—A PHOTO OF BLUE DAISIES. KUROSAKI'S IS PROBABLY A PICTURE OF SOME AIRPLANE. THAT MIGHT NOT BE WHAT YOU'D EXPECT, BUT HE IS AN ADULT, SO HE KEEPS HIS PHOTO OF TERU CAREFULLY SAVED IN A PASSWORD-PROTECTED FOLDER. HE ONLY LOOKS AT IT WHEN NECESSARY.
THAT'S WHY HE HAS HIS CELL PHONE OPEN WITH A SMILE ON HIS FACE WHEN HE'S ALONE IN THE SCHOOL'S BACK COURTYARD.

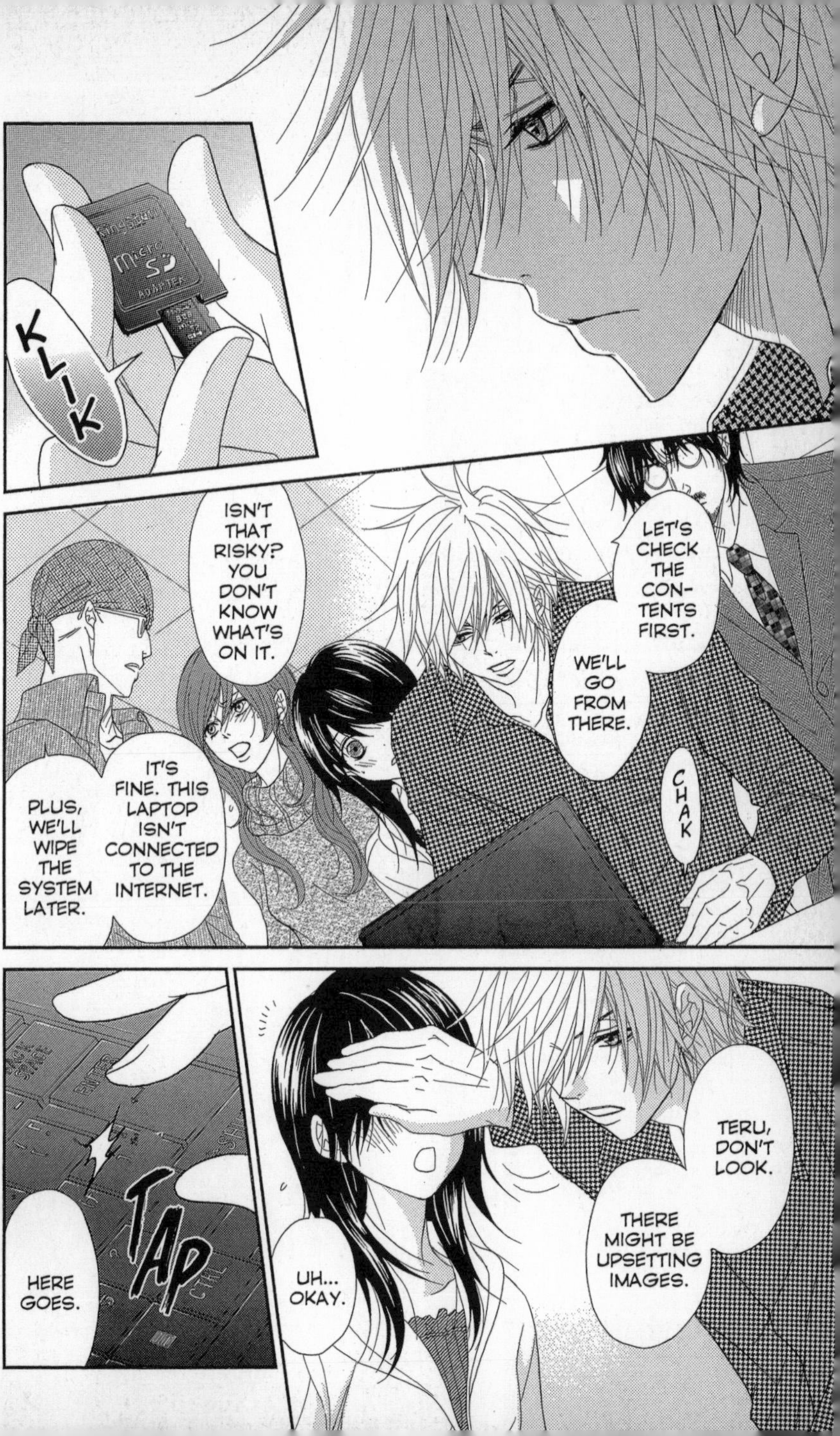
KLIK
LET'S CHECK THE CON-TENTS FIRST.
WE'LL GO FROM THERE.
CHAK
ISN'T THAT RISKY? YOU DON'T KNOW WHAT'S ON IT.
IT'S FINE. THIS LAPTOP ISN'T CONNECTED TO THE INTERNET.
PLUS, WE'LL WIPE THE SYSTEM LATER.
TERU, DON'T LOOK.
THERE MIGHT BE UPSETTING IMAGES.
UH... OKAY.
TAP
HERE GOES.

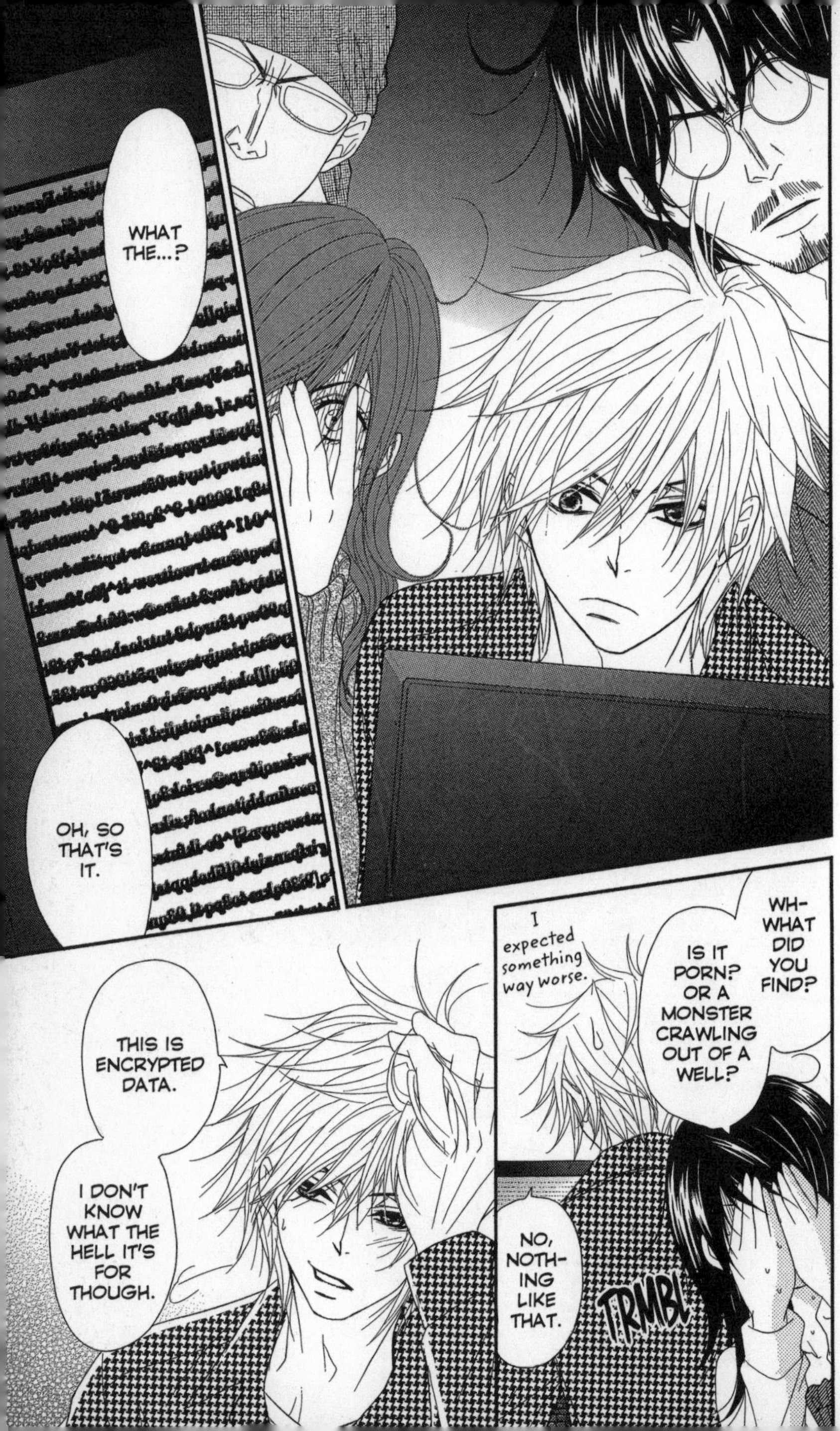
WHAT THE...?
OH, SO THAT'S IT.
WH-WHAT DID YOU FIND?
IS IT PORN? OR A MONSTER CRAWLING OUT OF A WELL?
I expected something way worse.
NO, NOTHING LIKE THAT.
TRMBL
THIS IS ENCRYPTED DATA.
I DON'T KNOW WHAT THE HELL IT'S FOR THOUGH.

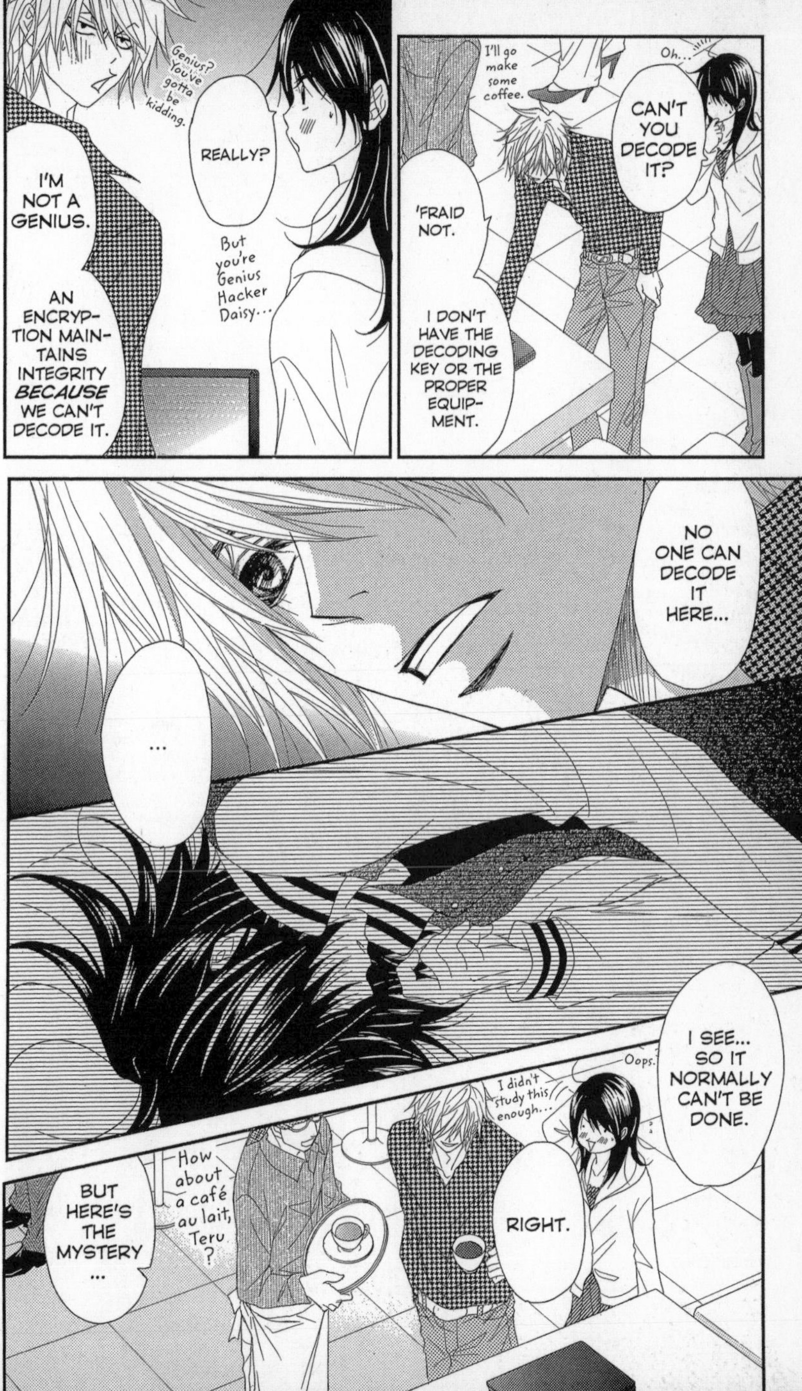
Oh...
CAN'T YOU DECODE IT?
I'll go make some coffee.
'FRAID NOT.
I DON'T HAVE THE DECODING KEY OR THE PROPER EQUIPMENT.
REALLY?
Genius? You've gotta be kidding.
I'M NOT A GENIUS.
But you're Genius Hacker Daisy...
AN ENCRYPTION MAINTAINS INTEGRITY BECAUSE WE CAN'T DECODE IT.
NO ONE CAN DECODE IT HERE...
...
I SEE... SO IT NORMALLY CAN'T BE DONE.
Oops.
I didn't study this enough...
RIGHT.
How about a café au lait, Teru?
BUT HERE'S THE MYSTERY...

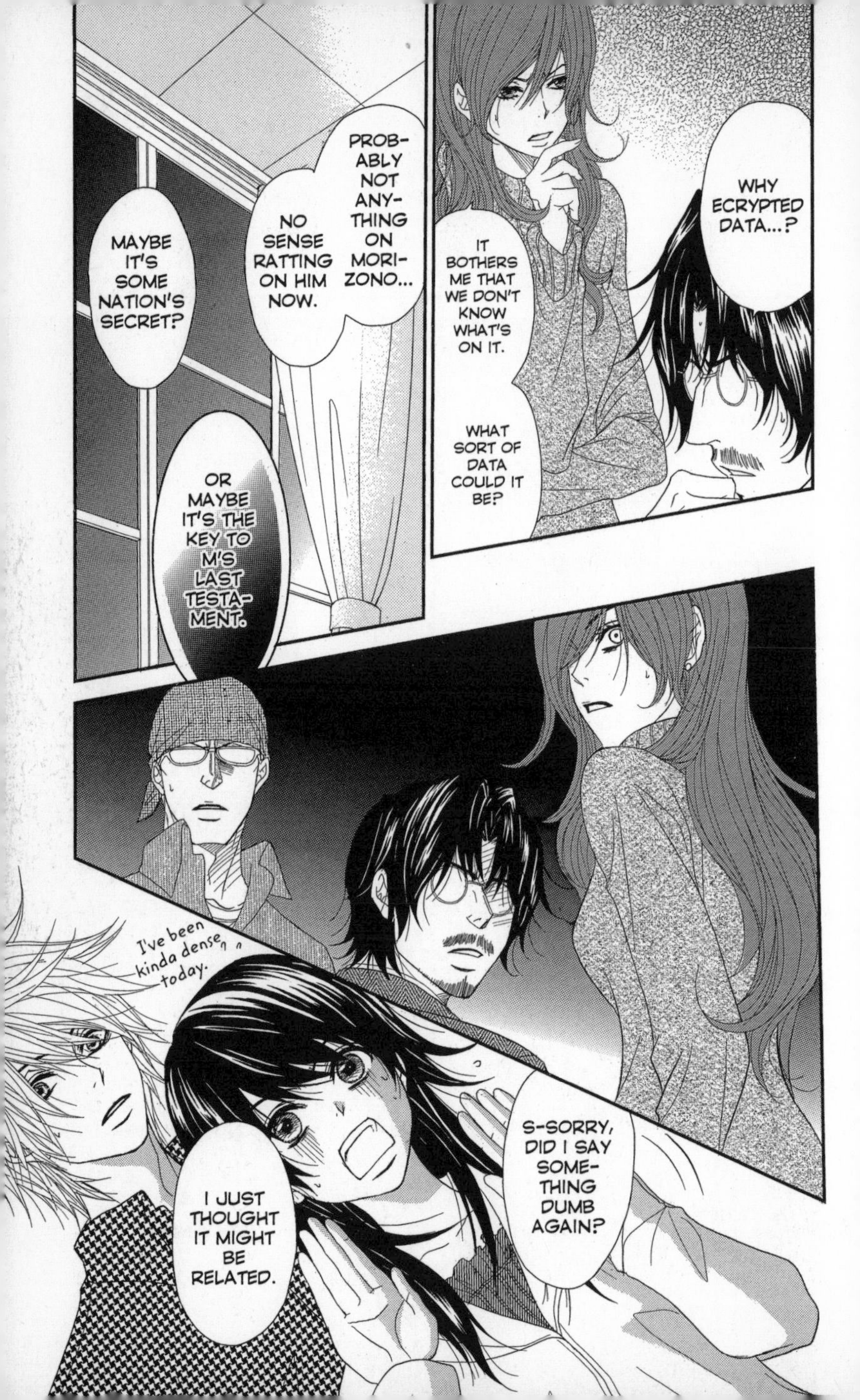
WHY ECRYPTED DATA...?
IT BOTHERS ME THAT WE DON'T KNOW WHAT'S ON IT.
WHAT SORT OF DATA COULD IT BE?
PROBABLY NOT ANYTHING ON MORIZONO...
NO SENSE RATTING ON HIM NOW.
MAYBE IT'S SOME NATION'S SECRET?
OR MAYBE IT'S THE KEY TO M'S LAST TESTAMENT.
S-SORRY, DID I SAY SOMETHING DUMB AGAIN?
I JUST THOUGHT IT MIGHT BE RELATED.
I've been kinda dense today.

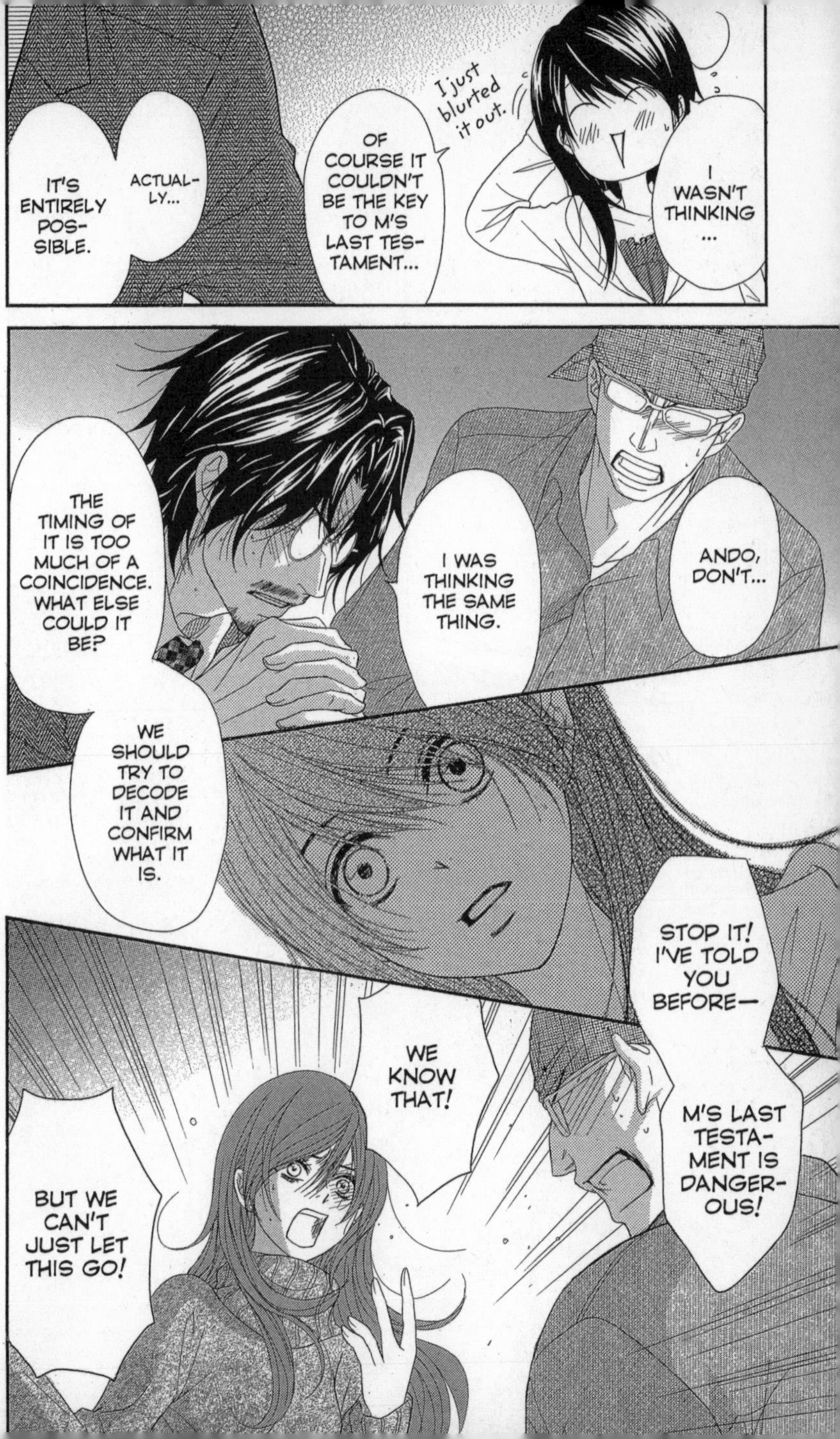
I WASN'T THINKING ...
I just blurted it out.
OF COURSE IT COULDN'T BE THE KEY TO M'S LAST TES-TAMENT...
ACTUAL-LY...
IT'S ENTIRELY POS-SIBLE.
ANDO, DON'T...
I WAS THINKING THE SAME THING.
THE TIMING OF IT IS TOO MUCH OF A COINCIDENCE. WHAT ELSE COULD IT BE?
WE SHOULD TRY TO DECODE IT AND CONFIRM WHAT IT IS.
STOP IT! I'VE TOLD YOU BEFORE—
M'S LAST TESTA-MENT IS DANGER-OUS!
WE KNOW THAT!
BUT WE CAN'T JUST LET THIS GO!

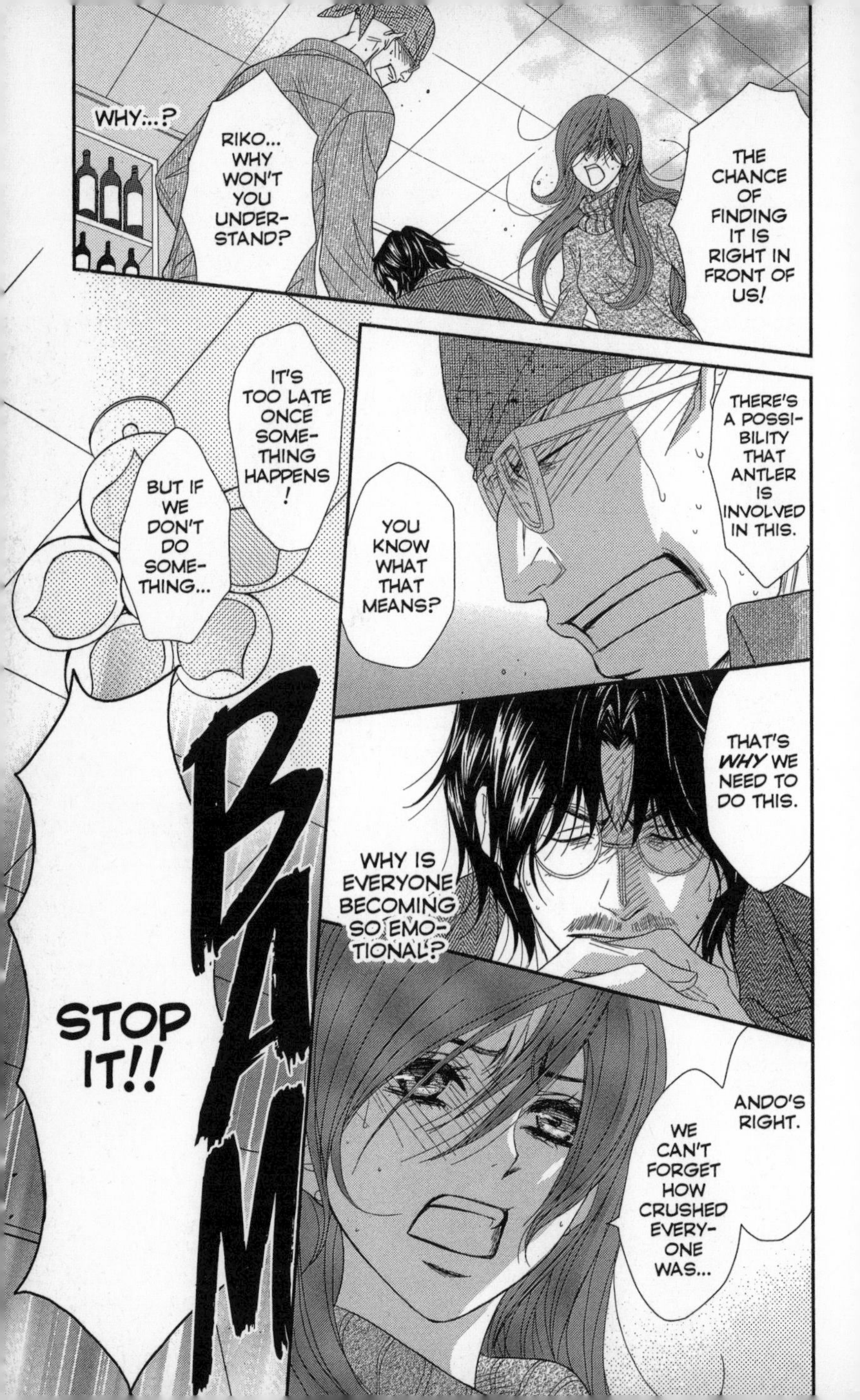
THE CHANCE OF FINDING IT IS RIGHT IN FRONT OF US!
RIKO... WHY WON'T YOU UNDERSTAND?
WHY...?
THERE'S A POSSIBILITY THAT ANTLER IS INVOLVED IN THIS.
YOU KNOW WHAT THAT MEANS?
IT'S TOO LATE ONCE SOMETHING HAPPENS!
BUT IF WE DON'T DO SOMETHING...
THAT'S WHY WE NEED TO DO THIS.
WHY IS EVERYONE BECOMING SO EMOTIONAL?
ANDO'S RIGHT.
WE CAN'T FORGET HOW CRUSHED EVERYONE WAS...
BAM
STOP IT!!

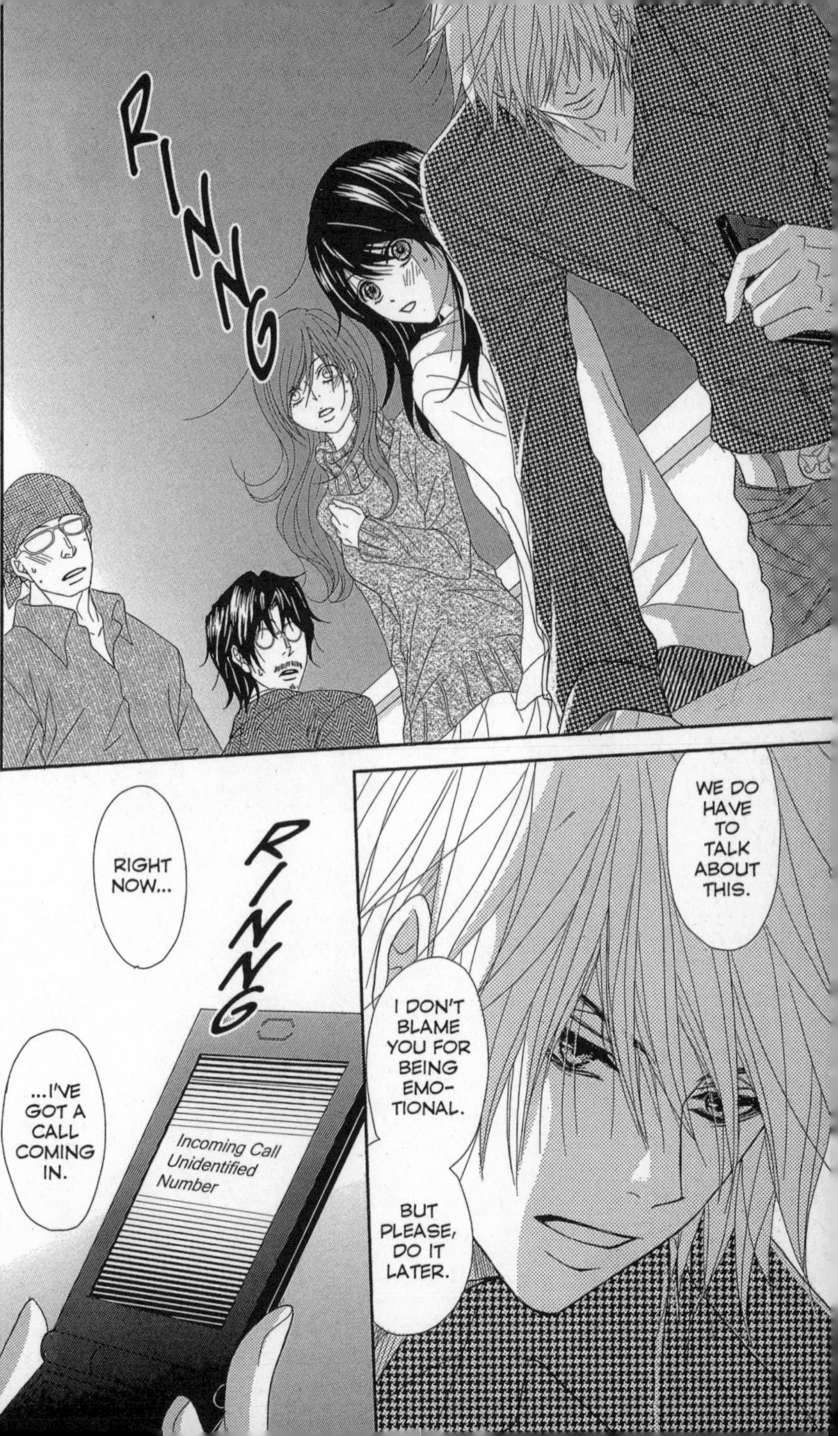
RINNG
WE DO HAVE TO TALK ABOUT THIS.
I DON'T BLAME YOU FOR BEING EMO-TIONAL.
BUT PLEASE, DO IT LATER.
RIGHT NOW...
RINNG
...I'VE GOT A CALL COMING IN.
Incoming Call
Unidentified Number

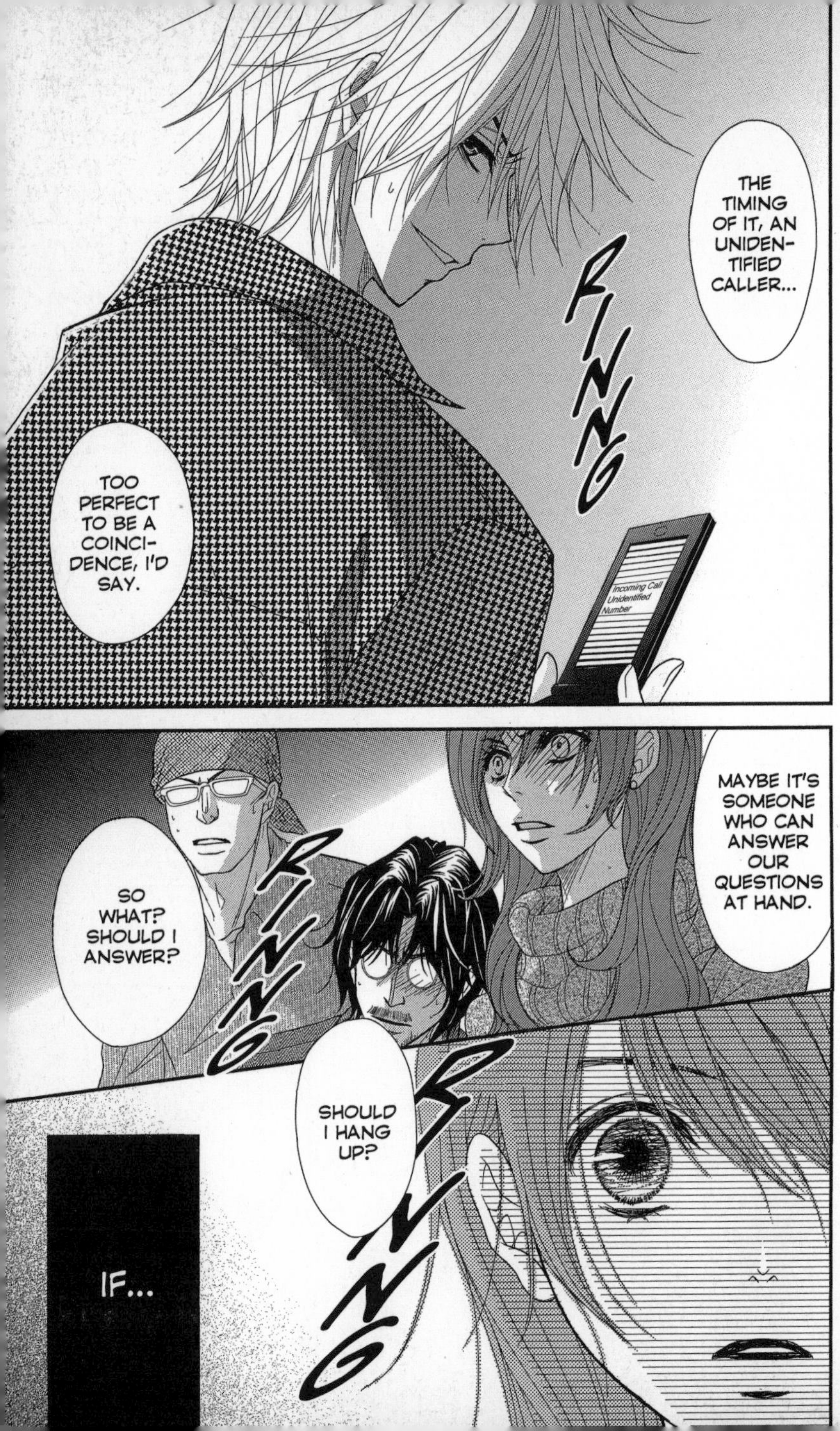
THE TIMING OF IT, AN UNIDEN-TIFIED CALLER...
RINNG
Incoming Call Unidentified Number
TOO PERFECT TO BE A COINCI-DENCE, I'D SAY.
MAYBE IT'S SOMEONE WHO CAN ANSWER OUR QUESTIONS AT HAND.
SO WHAT? SHOULD I ANSWER?
RINNG
SHOULD I HANG UP?
RINNG
IF...

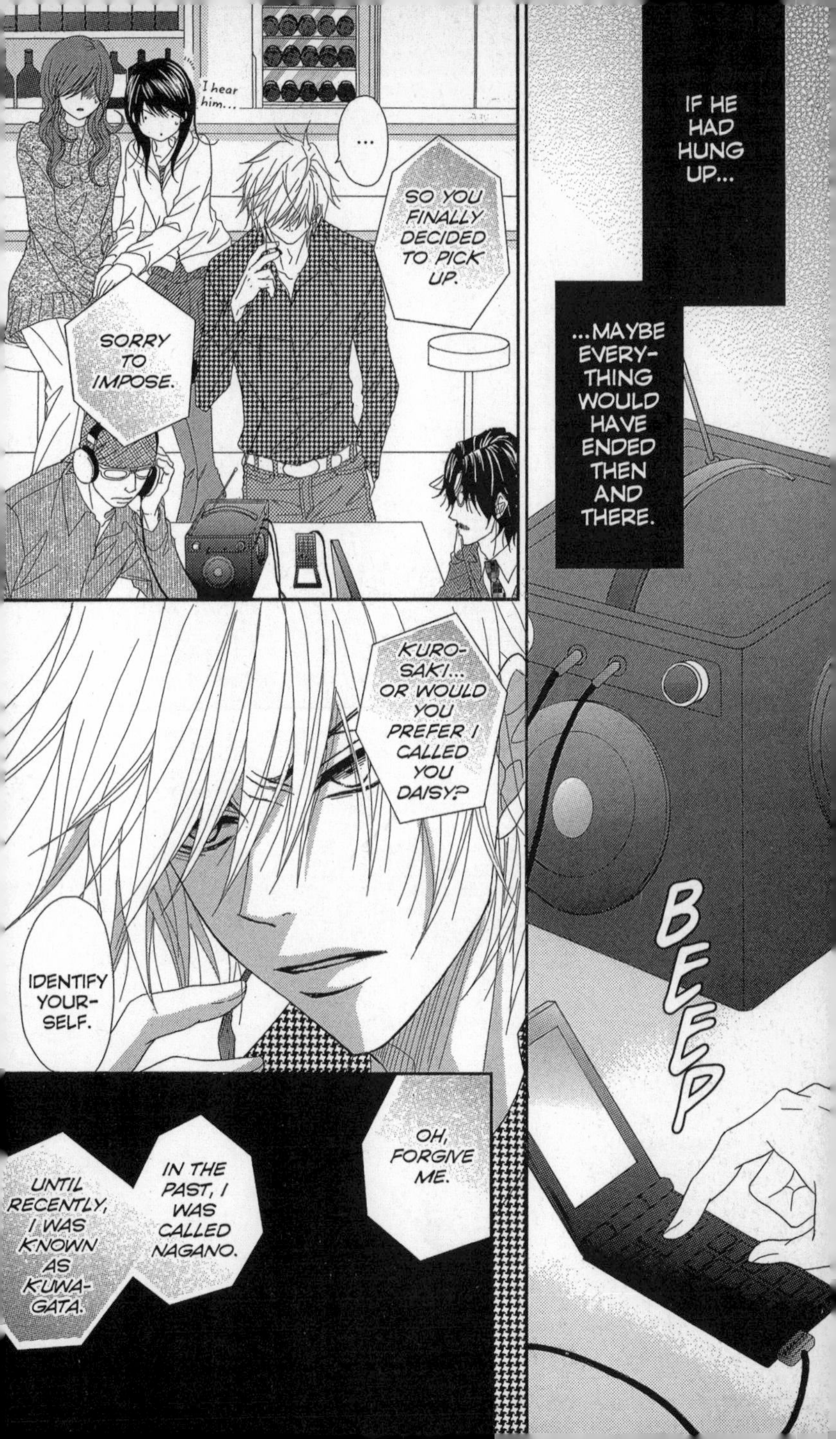
IF HE HAD HUNG UP...
...MAYBE EVERYTHING WOULD HAVE ENDED THEN AND THERE.
BEEP
I hear him...
...
SO YOU FINALLY DECIDED TO PICK UP.
SORRY TO IMPOSE.
KUROSAKI... OR WOULD YOU PREFER I CALLED YOU DAISY?
IDENTIFY YOURSELF.
OH, FORGIVE ME.
IN THE PAST, I WAS CALLED NAGANO.
UNTIL RECENTLY, I WAS KNOWN AS KUWAGATA.

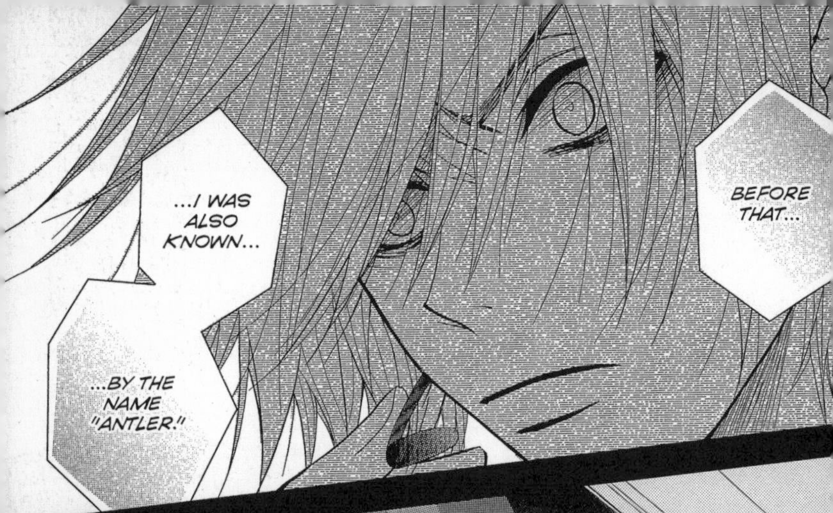
BEFORE THAT...
...I WAS ALSO KNOWN...
...BY THE NAME "ANTLER."
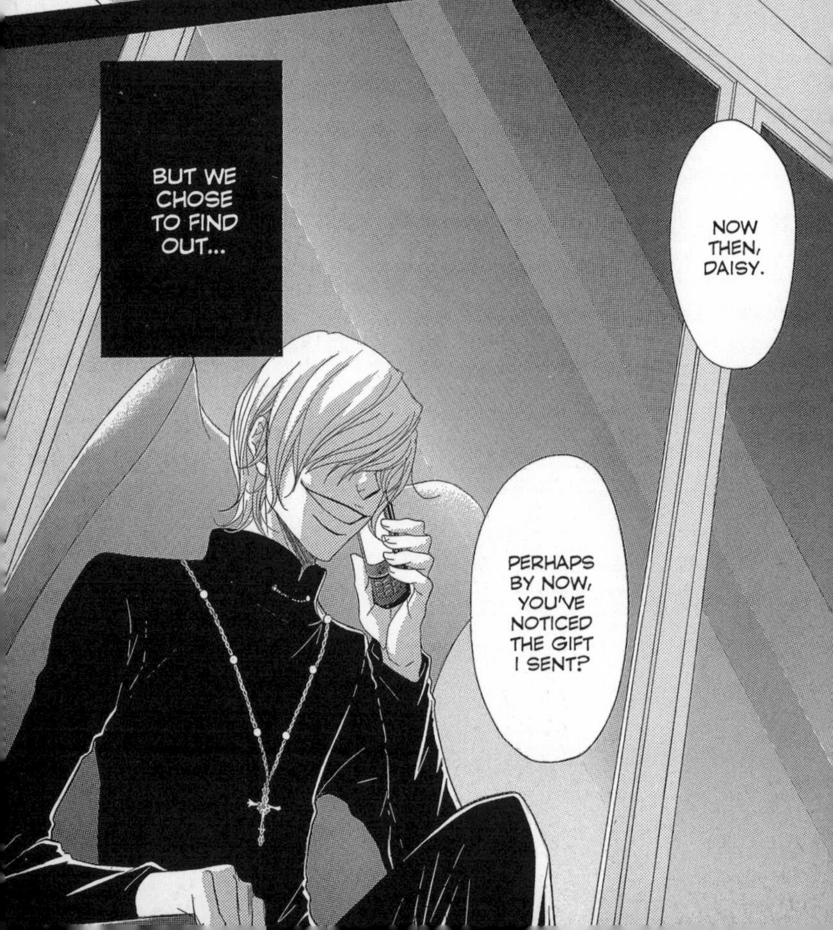
BUT WE CHOSE TO FIND OUT...
NOW THEN, DAISY.
PERHAPS BY NOW, YOU'VE NOTICED THE GIFT I SENT?

# THE BEST ☆ OF ☆ THE SECRET SCHOOL CUSTODIAN OFFICE

THE 7TH ONE OF THIS SUPER POPULAR SECTION ♥

THERE IS A *DENGEKI DAISY* FAN SEGMENT BOLDLY FEATURED IN *BETSUCOMI* THAT IS APTLY TITLED "THE SECRET SCHOOL CUSTODIAN OFFICE♥"! WITH ARBITRARY EYES, WE EXAMINED ALL THE GREAT WORK FEATURED THERE AND PICKED THE "BEST" AMONG THEM THAT WE WANTED TO LEAVE FOR POSTERITY!

**THE "BEST OF" FOR VOLUME 12 IS... ZOOM IN ON ♡ TASUKU KUROSAKI 2!"**

FOR A GUY LIVING ALONE, KUROSAKI LIVES IN A BIG AND WELL-KEPT APARTMENT. THIS TIME, WE FOCUSED ON HIS ROOM!

## ZOOM IN ON♥ TASUKU KUROSAKI 2

WE ZOOM IN ON KUROSAKI'S ROOMS AND INCLUDE ANECDOTES OF SOME THINGS THAT KUROSAKI HAS DONE IN THOSE ROOMS!

### KUROSAKI'S LIVING ROOM

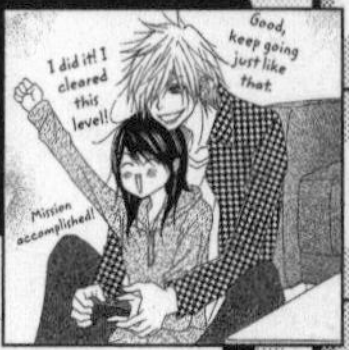
Good, keep going just like that.
I did it! I cleared this level!
Mission accomplished!

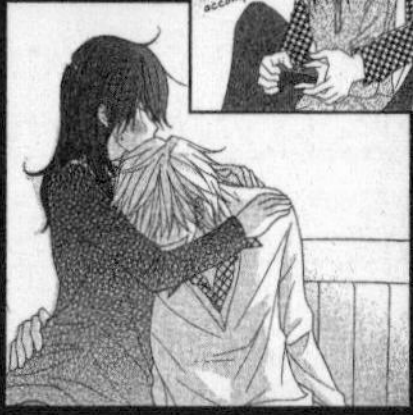

THIS IS THE ROOM WHERE THE LOVEY-DOVEY SOFA SITS—THE ONE THAT BRINGS BIG SMILES TO READERS. IT'S NEAR THIS SOFA WHERE YOU SEE KUROSAKI FAWNING OVER TERU AND INDULGING IN HER KINDNESS. IT'S A WELL-KEPT ROOM NOW, BUT BEFORE TERU'S ARRIVAL, HE HAD NEVER CLEANED THE BLINDS AND THE COVERS, AND CDS AND DVDS ON THE STORAGE RACK WERE MISMATCHED.

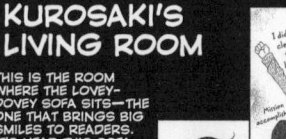

### KUROSAKI'S COMPUTER ROOM

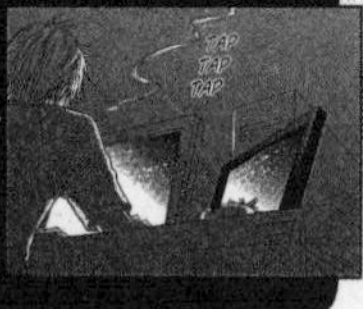
TAP TAP TAP

THIS IS THE ROOM KUROSAKI WOULDN'T ALLOW TERU INTO, CLAIMING HE HAD A LOT OF PERVERTED STUFF INSIDE IT. IN REALITY, THERE ARE MULTIPLE COMPUTERS IN A ROW. IT IS KUROSAKI'S DARK SANCTUARY.

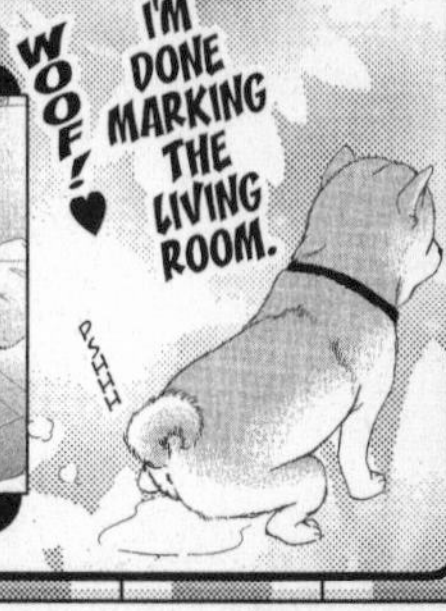
I'M DONE MARKING THE LIVING ROOM.
WOOF!♥

ZOOM IN ON♥ TASUKU KUROSAKI 1 IS IN VOLUME 6. WOOF!♥

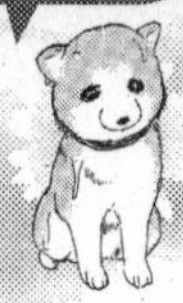

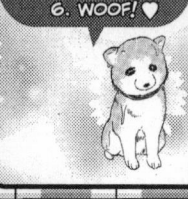

### KUROSAKI'S BEDROOM

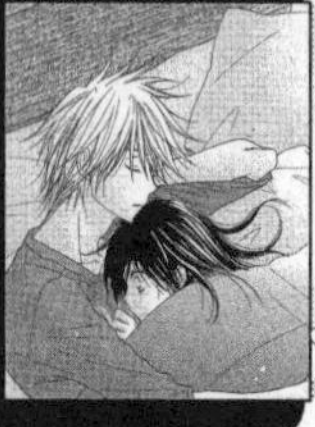

THIS IS THE ROOM WHERE TERU WOKE UP WITH KUROSAKI...THE MORNING AFTER MAKING (FAILED) ADVANCES AT HIM. KUROSAKI'S EXCESSIVE KINDNESS WORKED AGAINST HIM, BUT WE'D HAVE TO SAY THAT THE SECOND HE GOT INTO BED WITH HER, IT IMPLIED A DELIBERATE ATTEMPT ON HIS PART. THEREFORE, KUROSAKI IS GUILTY.

**JUDGES' COMMENTS**

■ HE WAS IN THE BEDROOM WITH HER IN "I WILL PROTECT HIM" (CHAPTER 7), AND "CLOSE FRIEND" (CHAPTER 8). KUROSAKI IS GUILTY. (HEAD JUDGE: KYOUSUKE MOTOMI)

■ THE LIVING ROOM WILL GET MUCH MORE ATTENTION FROM HERE ON OUT! KUROSAKI'S APPEARANCES IN THAT ROOM ARE RAPIDLY ON THE RISE!! (JUDGE: *DAISY* EDITOR)

*BETSUCOMI*, THE MAGAZINE THAT SERIALIZES *DAISY*, GOES ON SALE EVERY MONTH AROUND THE 13TH!

PLEASE LOOK FOR IT IF YOU WANT TO READ "THE SECRET SCHOOL CUSTODIAN OFFICE"!♥

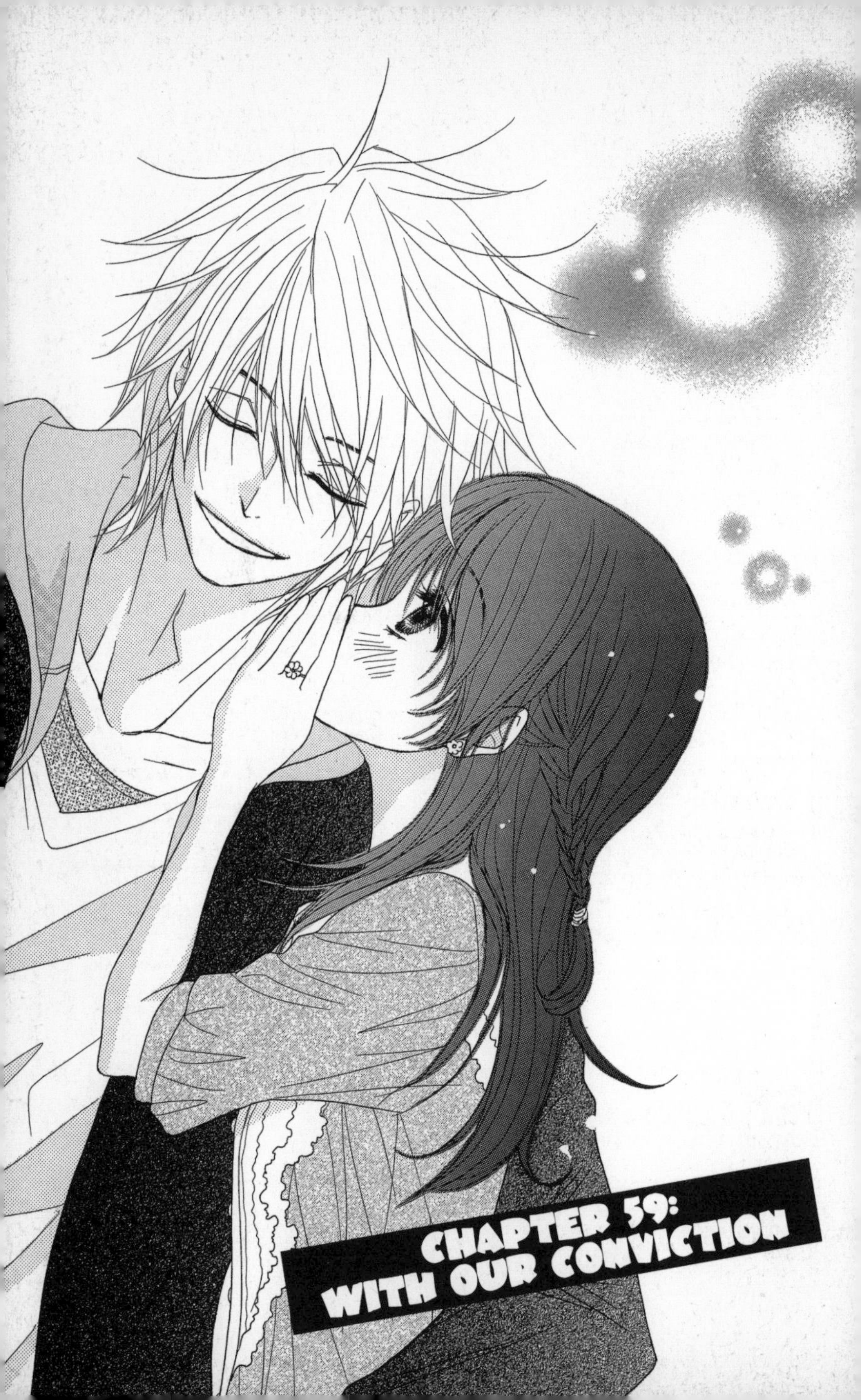
CHAPTER 59:
WITH OUR CONVICTION

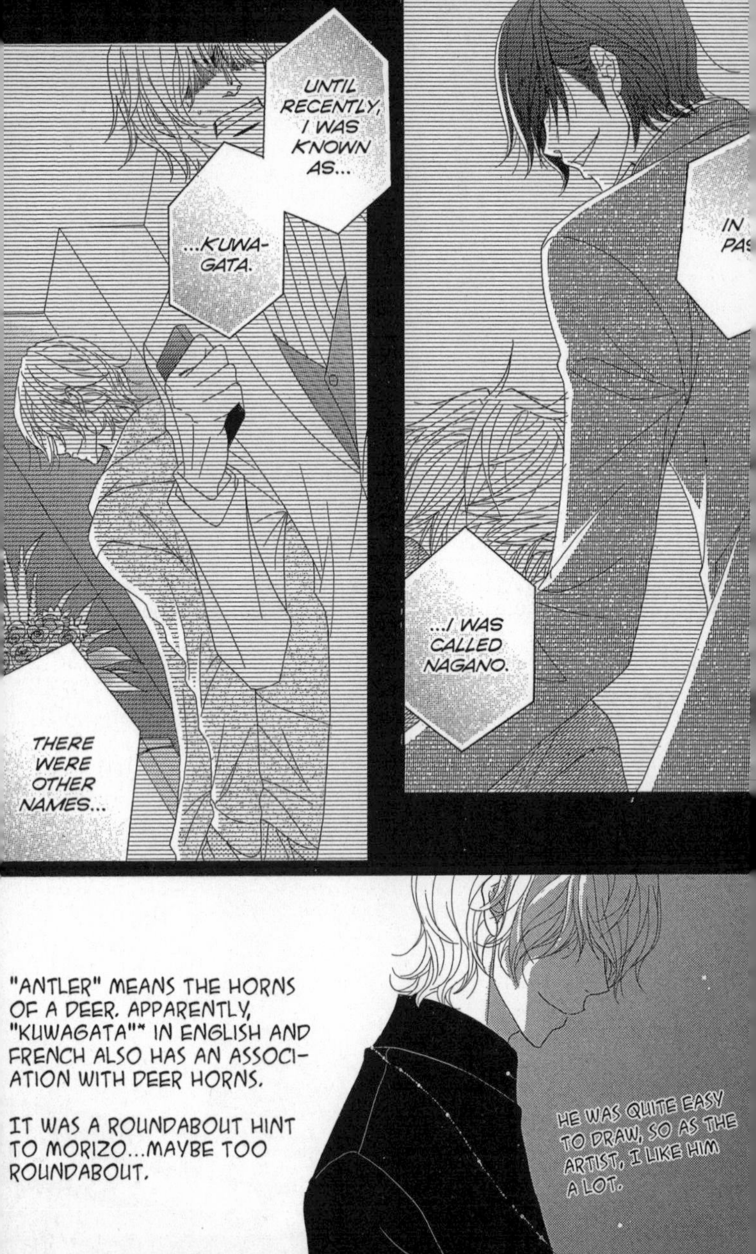
IN PAS
...I WAS CALLED NAGANO.
UNTIL RECENTLY, I WAS KNOWN AS...
...KUWA-GATA.
THERE WERE OTHER NAMES...
"ANTLER" MEANS THE HORNS OF A DEER. APPARENTLY, "KUWAGATA"* IN ENGLISH AND FRENCH ALSO HAS AN ASSOCI-ATION WITH DEER HORNS.
IT WAS A ROUNDABOUT HINT TO MORIZO...MAYBE TOO ROUNDABOUT.
HE WAS QUITE EASY TO DRAW, SO AS THE ARTIST, I LIKE HIM A LOT.

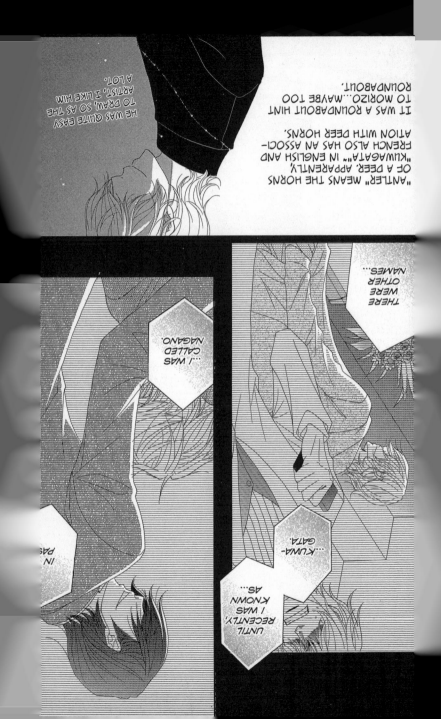

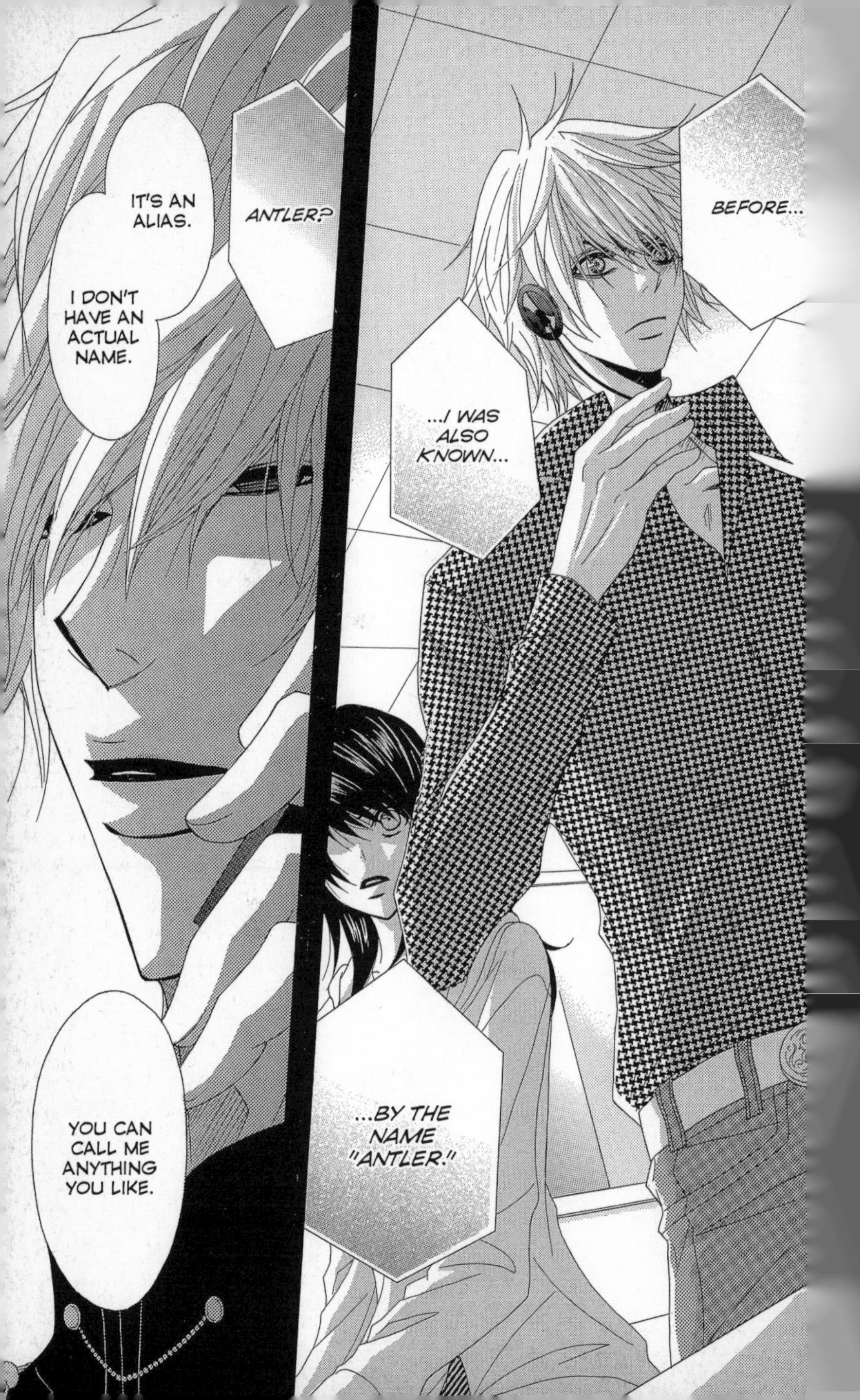
BEFORE...
...I WAS ALSO KNOWN...
...BY THE NAME "ANTLER."
ANTLER?
IT'S AN ALIAS.
I DON'T HAVE AN ACTUAL NAME.
YOU CAN CALL ME ANYTHING YOU LIKE.

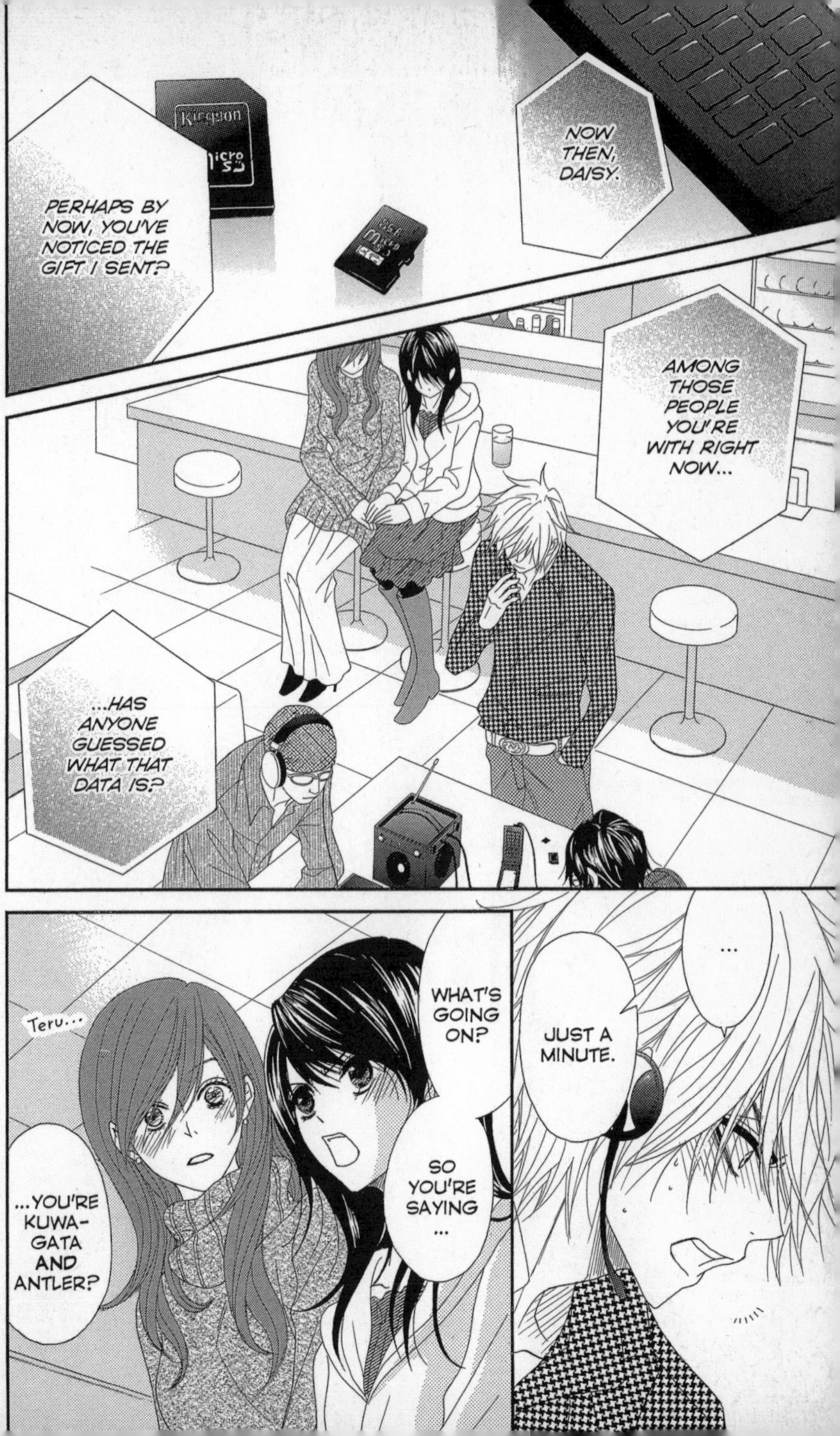
NOW THEN, DAISY.
PERHAPS BY NOW, YOU'VE NOTICED THE GIFT I SENT?
AMONG THOSE PEOPLE YOU'RE WITH RIGHT NOW...
...HAS ANYONE GUESSED WHAT THAT DATA IS?
...
JUST A MINUTE.
WHAT'S GOING ON?
SO YOU'RE SAYING ...
Teru...
...YOU'RE KUWA-GATA AND ANTLER?

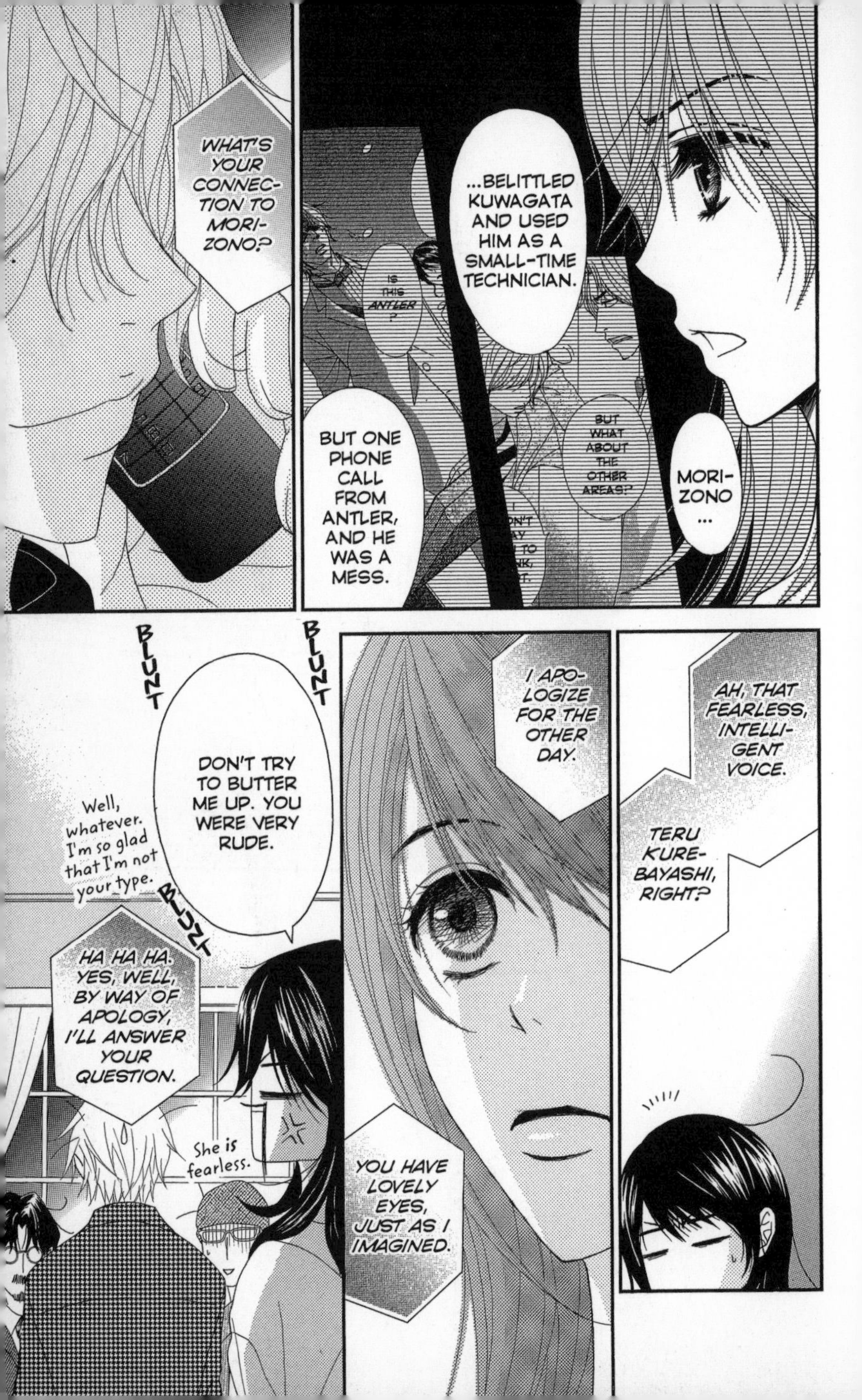
MORI-ZONO...
...BELITTLED KUWAGATA AND USED HIM AS A SMALL-TIME TECHNICIAN.
BUT WHAT ABOUT THE OTHER AREAS?
IS THIS ANTLER?
BUT ONE PHONE CALL FROM ANTLER, AND HE WAS A MESS.
WHAT'S YOUR CONNECTION TO MORI-ZONO?
AH, THAT FEARLESS, INTELLIGENT VOICE.
TERU KURE-BAYASHI, RIGHT?
I APOLOGIZE FOR THE OTHER DAY.
YOU HAVE LOVELY EYES, JUST AS I IMAGINED.
BLUNT
DON'T TRY TO BUTTER ME UP. YOU WERE VERY RUDE.
BLUNT
BLUNT
Well, whatever. I'm so glad that I'm not your type.
HA HA HA. YES, WELL, BY WAY OF APOLOGY, I'LL ANSWER YOUR QUESTION.
She is fearless.

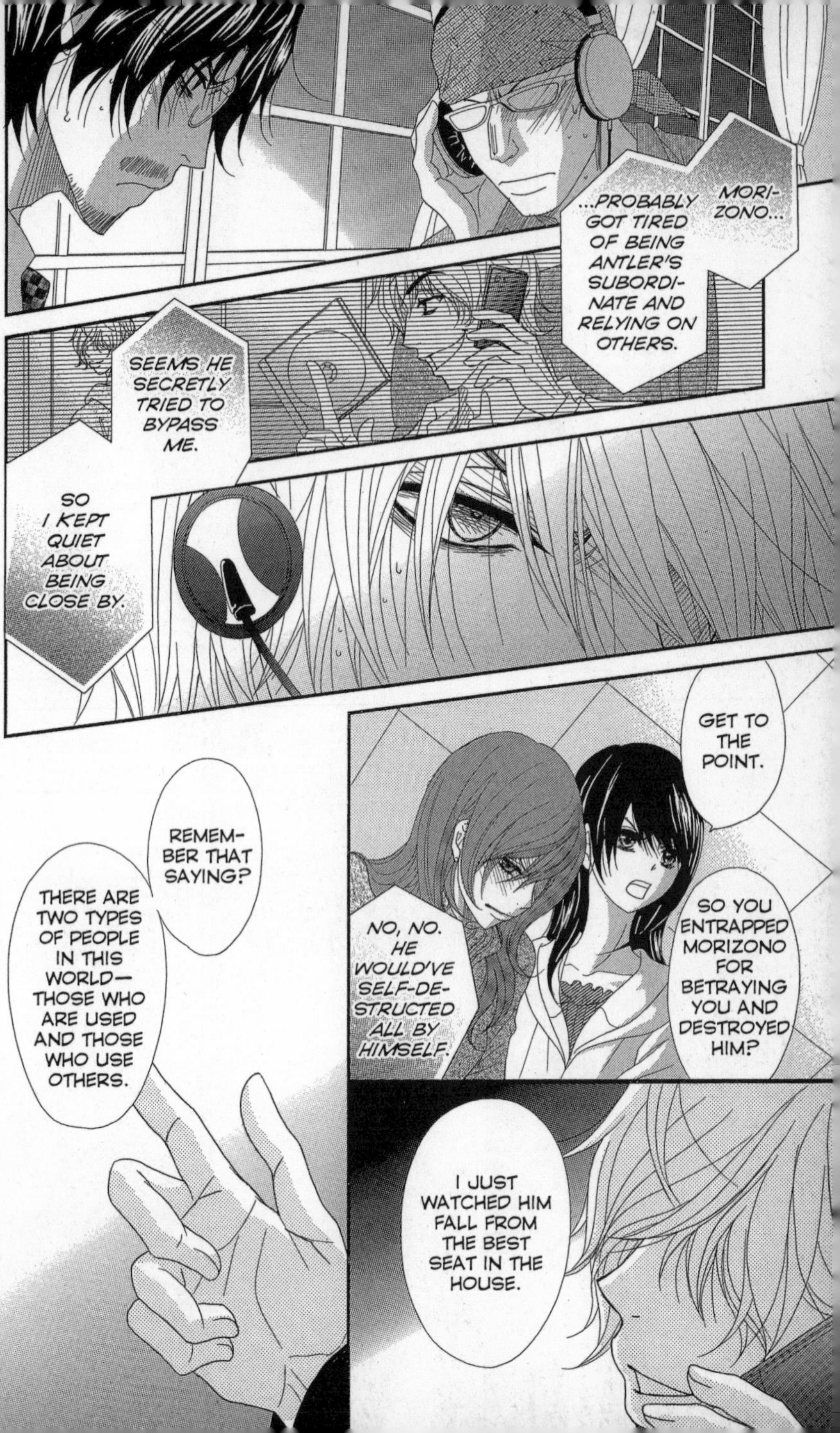
MORI-ZONO...
...PROBABLY GOT TIRED OF BEING ANTLER'S SUBORDINATE AND RELYING ON OTHERS.
SEEMS HE SECRETLY TRIED TO BYPASS ME.
SO I KEPT QUIET ABOUT BEING CLOSE BY.
GET TO THE POINT.
SO YOU ENTRAPPED MORIZONO FOR BETRAYING YOU AND DESTROYED HIM?
NO, NO. HE WOULD'VE SELF-DESTRUCTED ALL BY HIMSELF.
I JUST WATCHED HIM FALL FROM THE BEST SEAT IN THE HOUSE.
REMEMBER THAT SAYING?
THERE ARE TWO TYPES OF PEOPLE IN THIS WORLD—THOSE WHO ARE USED AND THOSE WHO USE OTHERS.

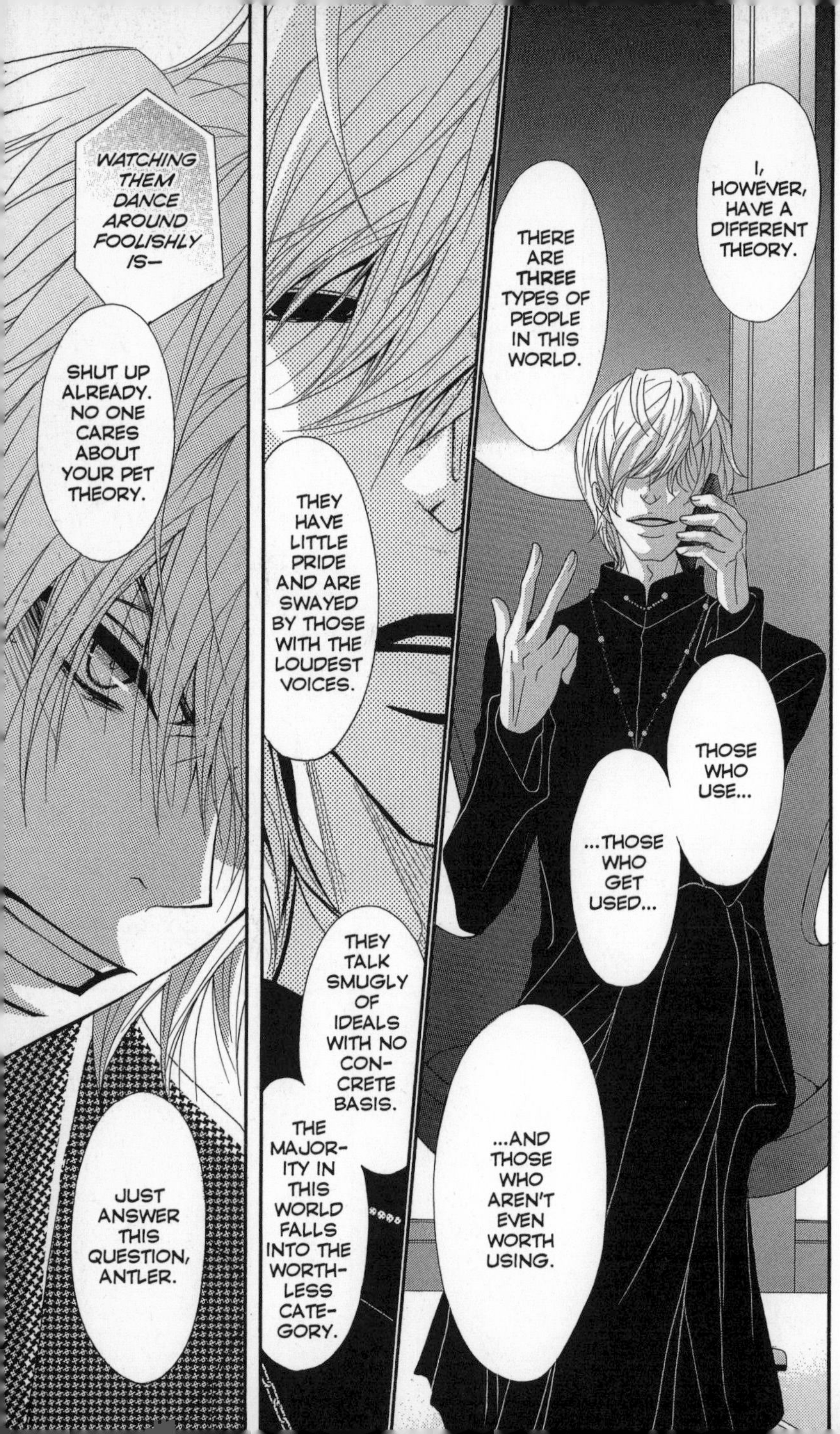
I, HOWEVER, HAVE A DIFFERENT THEORY.
THERE ARE THREE TYPES OF PEOPLE IN THIS WORLD.
THOSE WHO USE...
...THOSE WHO GET USED...
...AND THOSE WHO AREN'T EVEN WORTH USING.
THEY HAVE LITTLE PRIDE AND ARE SWAYED BY THOSE WITH THE LOUDEST VOICES.
THEY TALK SMUGLY OF IDEALS WITH NO CON-CRETE BASIS.
THE MAJOR-ITY IN THIS WORLD FALLS INTO THE WORTH-LESS CATE-GORY.
WATCHING THEM DANCE AROUND FOOLISHLY IS—
SHUT UP ALREADY. NO ONE CARES ABOUT YOUR PET THEORY.
JUST ANSWER THIS QUESTION, ANTLER.

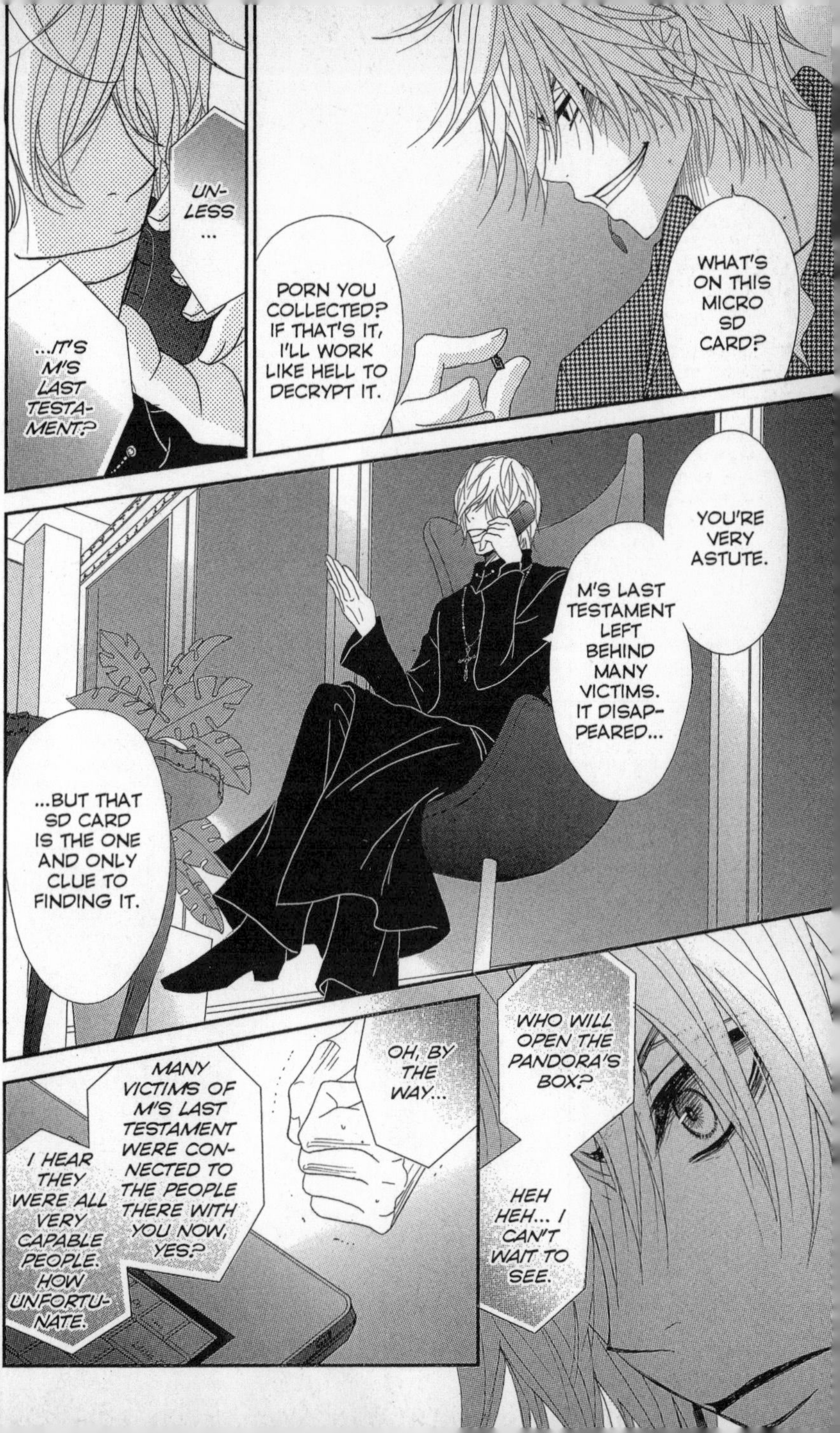
WHAT'S ON THIS MICRO SD CARD?
PORN YOU COLLECTED? IF THAT'S IT, I'LL WORK LIKE HELL TO DECRYPT IT.
UN-LESS...
...IT'S M'S LAST TESTA-MENT?
YOU'RE VERY ASTUTE.
M'S LAST TESTAMENT LEFT BEHIND MANY VICTIMS. IT DISAP-PEARED...
...BUT THAT SD CARD IS THE ONE AND ONLY CLUE TO FINDING IT.
WHO WILL OPEN THE PANDORA'S BOX?
HEH HEH... I CAN'T WAIT TO SEE.
OH, BY THE WAY...
MANY VICTIMS OF M'S LAST TESTAMENT WERE CON-NECTED TO THE PEOPLE THERE WITH YOU NOW, YES?
I HEAR THEY WERE ALL VERY CAPABLE PEOPLE. HOW UNFORTU-NATE.

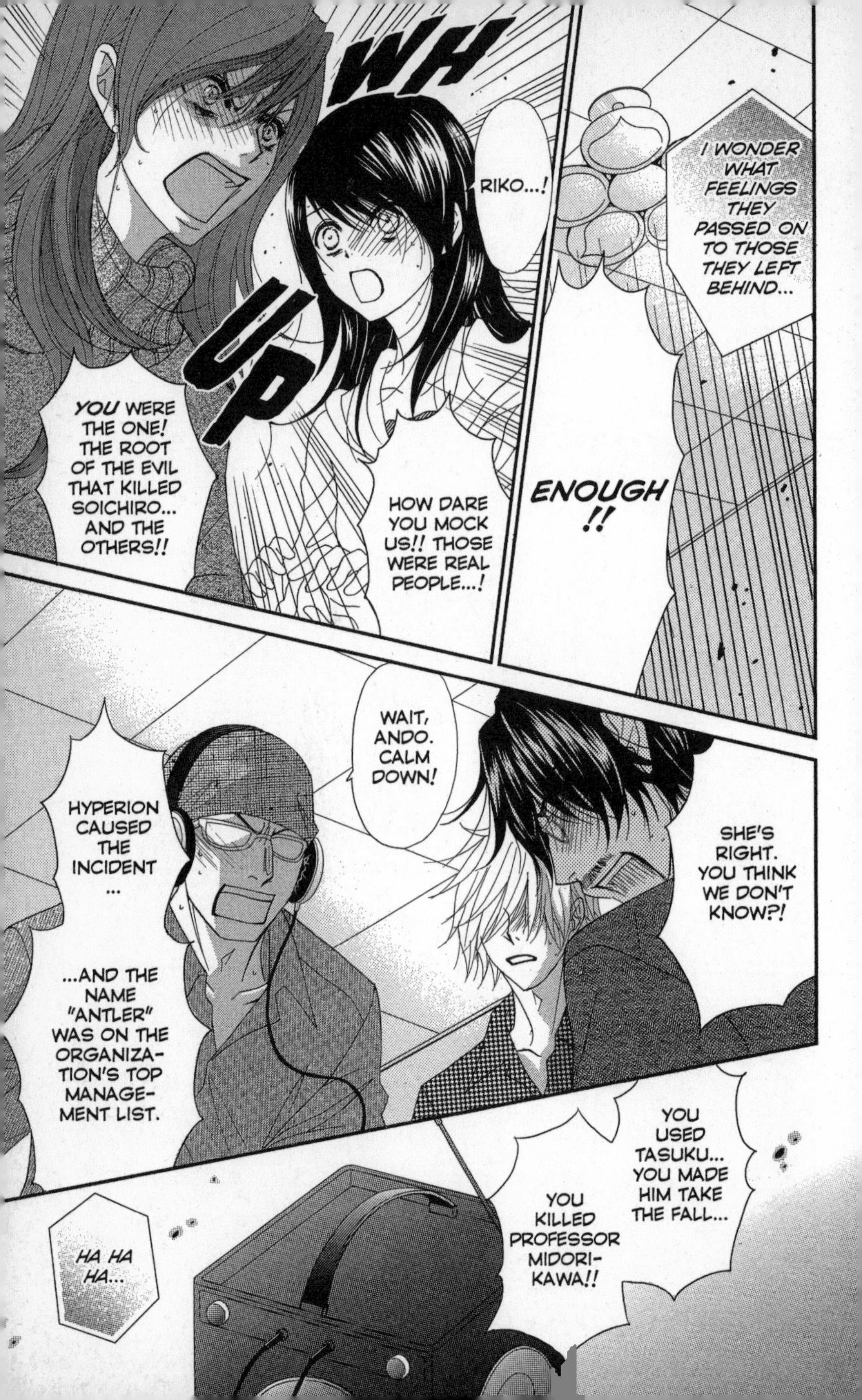
I WONDER WHAT FEELINGS THEY PASSED ON TO THOSE THEY LEFT BEHIND...
ENOUGH!!
RIKO...!
WHUP
YOU WERE THE ONE! THE ROOT OF THE EVIL THAT KILLED SOICHIRO... AND THE OTHERS!!
HOW DARE YOU MOCK US!! THOSE WERE REAL PEOPLE...!
SHE'S RIGHT. YOU THINK WE DON'T KNOW?!
WAIT, ANDO. CALM DOWN!
HYPERION CAUSED THE INCIDENT ...
...AND THE NAME "ANTLER" WAS ON THE ORGANIZATION'S TOP MANAGEMENT LIST.
YOU USED TASUKU... YOU MADE HIM TAKE THE FALL...
YOU KILLED PROFESSOR MIDORIKAWA!!
HA HA HA...

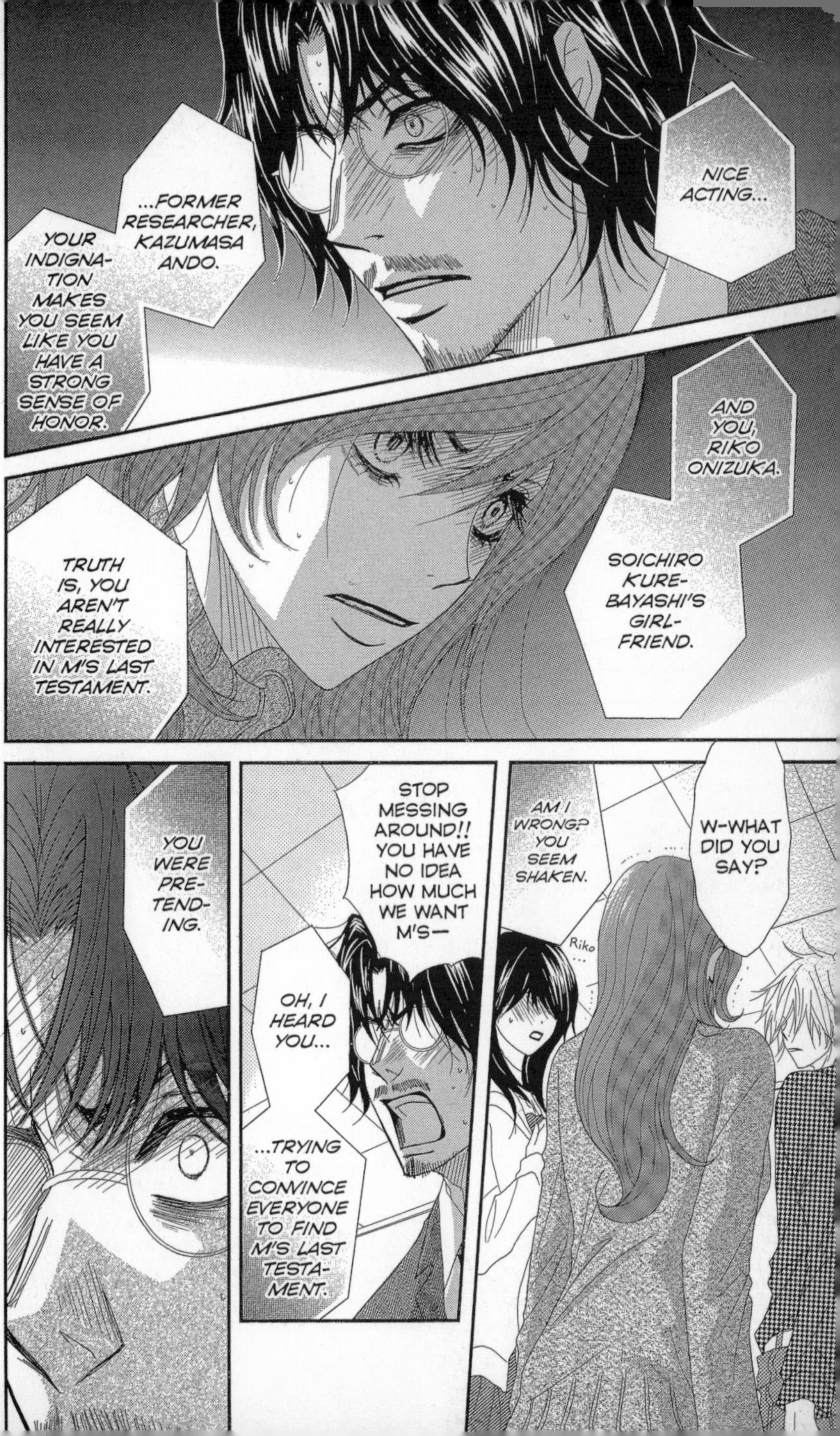
NICE ACTING...
...FORMER RESEARCHER, KAZUMASA ANDO.
YOUR INDIGNATION MAKES YOU SEEM LIKE YOU HAVE A STRONG SENSE OF HONOR.
AND YOU, RIKO ONIZUKA.
SOICHIRO KURE-BAYASHI'S GIRL-FRIEND.
TRUTH IS, YOU AREN'T REALLY INTERESTED IN M'S LAST TESTAMENT.
W-WHAT DID YOU SAY?
AM I WRONG? YOU SEEM SHAKEN.
Riko...
STOP MESSING AROUND!! YOU HAVE NO IDEA HOW MUCH WE WANT M'S—
OH, I HEARD YOU...
...TRYING TO CONVINCE EVERYONE TO FIND M'S LAST TESTA-MENT.
YOU WERE PRE-TEND-ING.

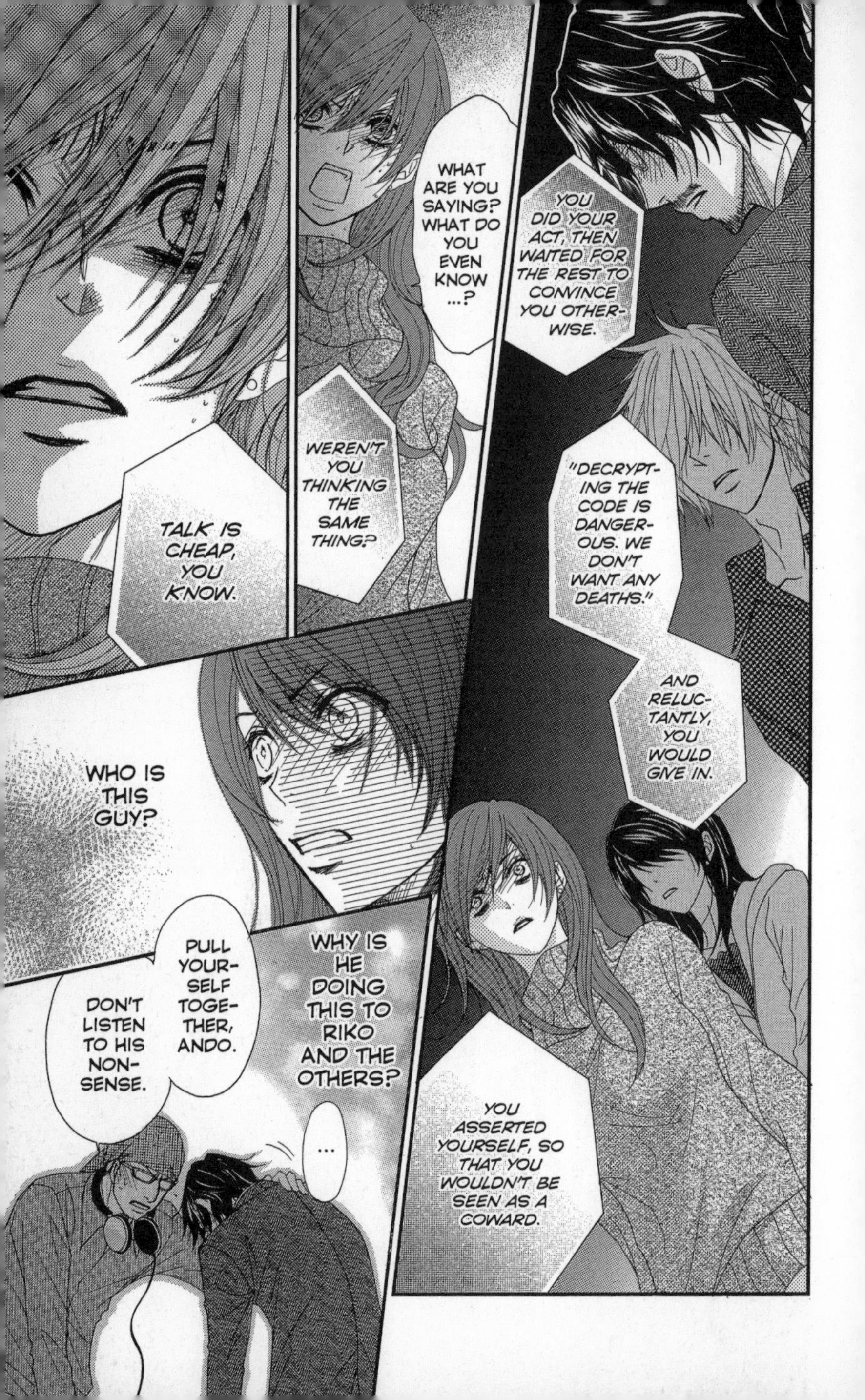
YOU DID YOUR ACT, THEN WAITED FOR THE REST TO CONVINCE YOU OTHERWISE.
"DECRYPTING THE CODE IS DANGEROUS. WE DON'T WANT ANY DEATHS."
AND RELUCTANTLY, YOU WOULD GIVE IN.
YOU ASSERTED YOURSELF, SO THAT YOU WOULDN'T BE SEEN AS A COWARD.
WHAT ARE YOU SAYING? WHAT DO YOU EVEN KNOW ...?
WEREN'T YOU THINKING THE SAME THING?
TALK IS CHEAP, YOU KNOW.
WHO IS THIS GUY?
WHY IS HE DOING THIS TO RIKO AND THE OTHERS?
PULL YOURSELF TOGETHER, ANDO.
DON'T LISTEN TO HIS NONSENSE.
...

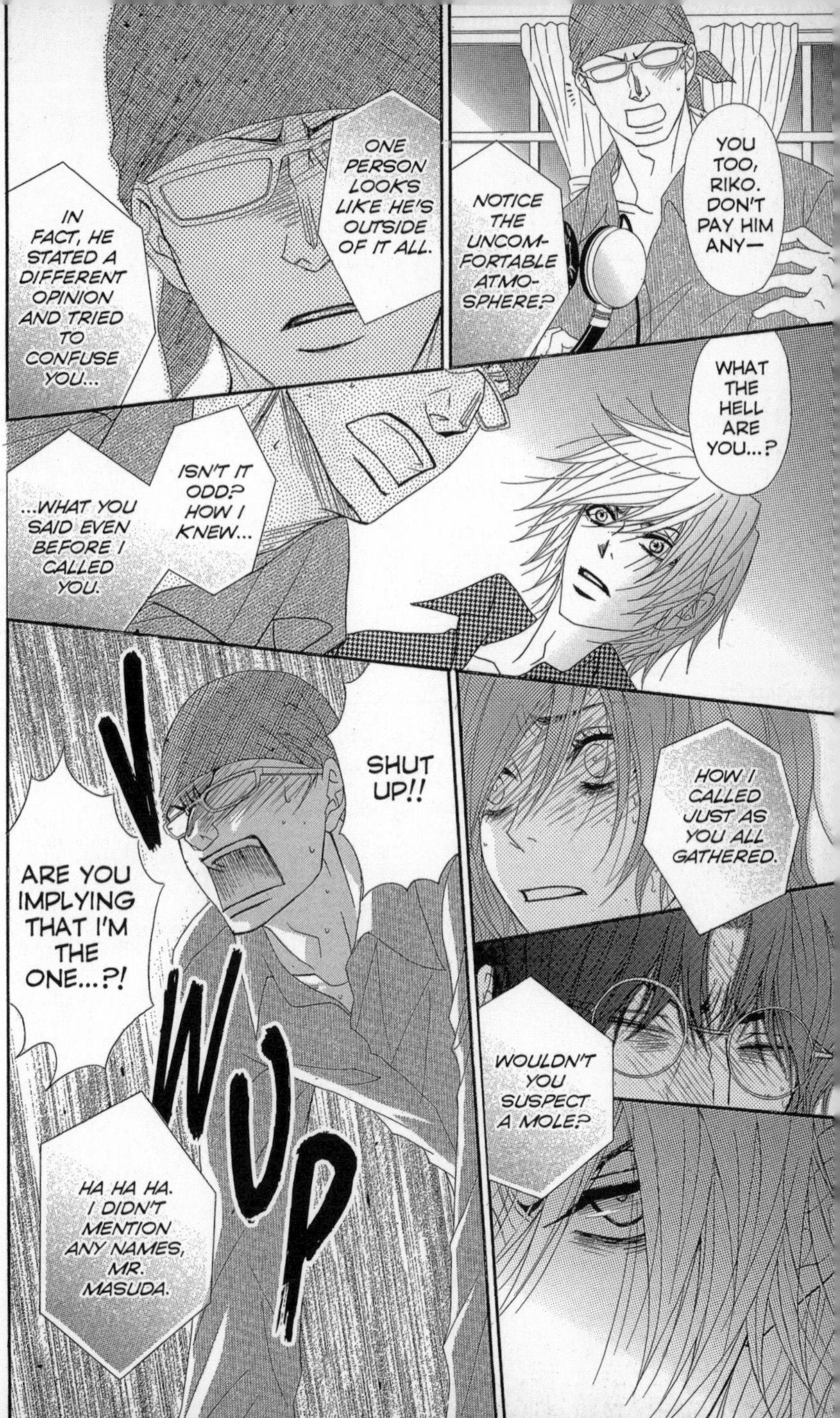
YOU TOO, RIKO. DON'T PAY HIM ANY—
NOTICE THE UNCOMFORTABLE ATMOSPHERE?
ONE PERSON LOOKS LIKE HE'S OUTSIDE OF IT ALL.
IN FACT, HE STATED A DIFFERENT OPINION AND TRIED TO CONFUSE YOU...
WHAT THE HELL ARE YOU...?
ISN'T IT ODD? HOW I KNEW...
...WHAT YOU SAID EVEN BEFORE I CALLED YOU.
HOW I CALLED JUST AS YOU ALL GATHERED.
WOULDN'T YOU SUSPECT A MOLE?
SHUT UP!!
ARE YOU IMPLYING THAT I'M THE ONE...?!
VWUP
HA HA HA. I DIDN'T MENTION ANY NAMES, MR. MASUDA.

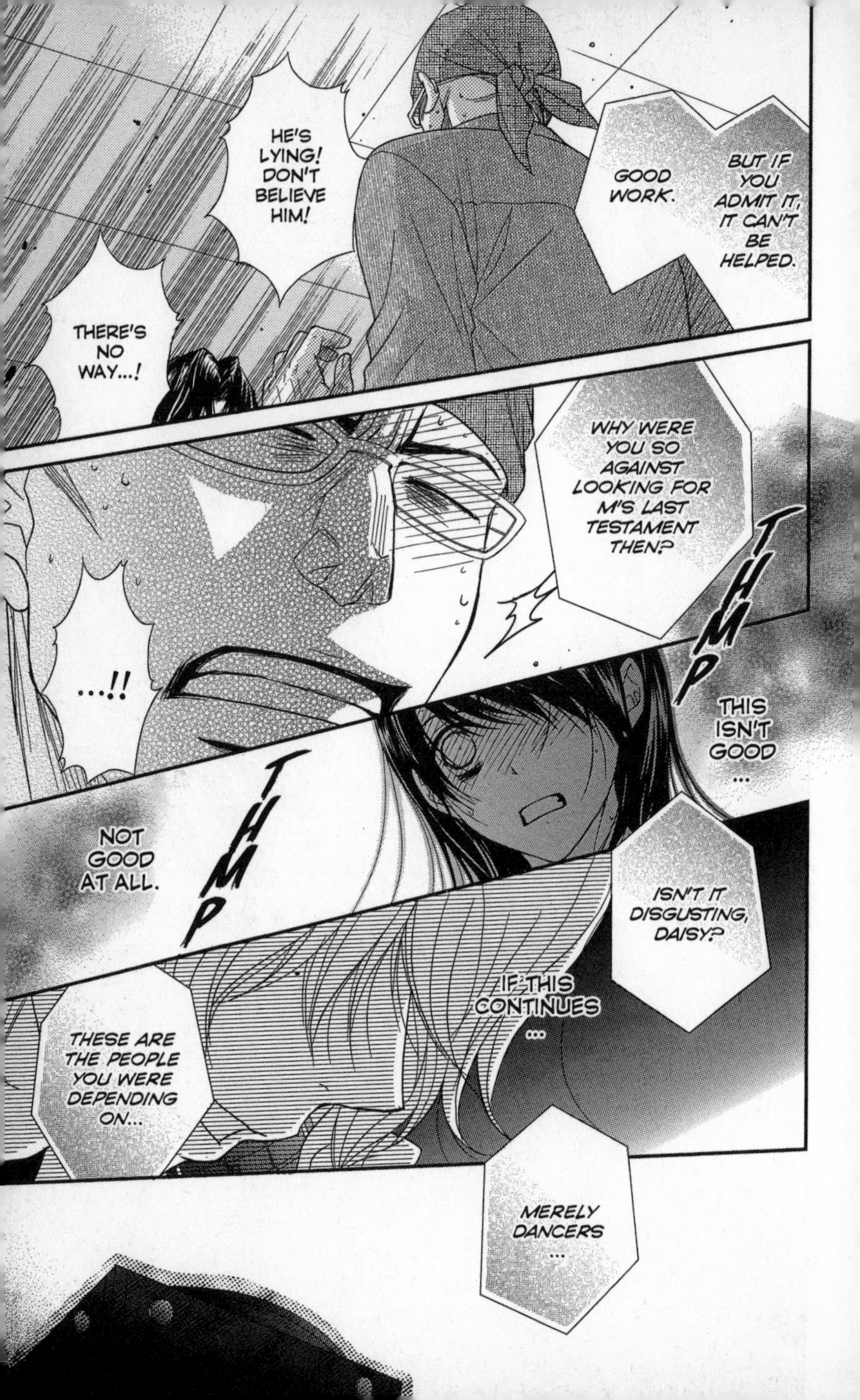
BUT IF YOU ADMIT IT, IT CAN'T BE HELPED.
GOOD WORK.
HE'S LYING! DON'T BELIEVE HIM!
THERE'S NO WAY...!
WHY WERE YOU SO AGAINST LOOKING FOR M'S LAST TESTAMENT THEN?
...!!
THUMP
THIS ISN'T GOOD ...
THUMP
NOT GOOD AT ALL.
ISN'T IT DISGUSTING, DAISY?
IF THIS CONTINUES ...
THESE ARE THE PEOPLE YOU WERE DEPENDING ON...
MERELY DANCERS ...

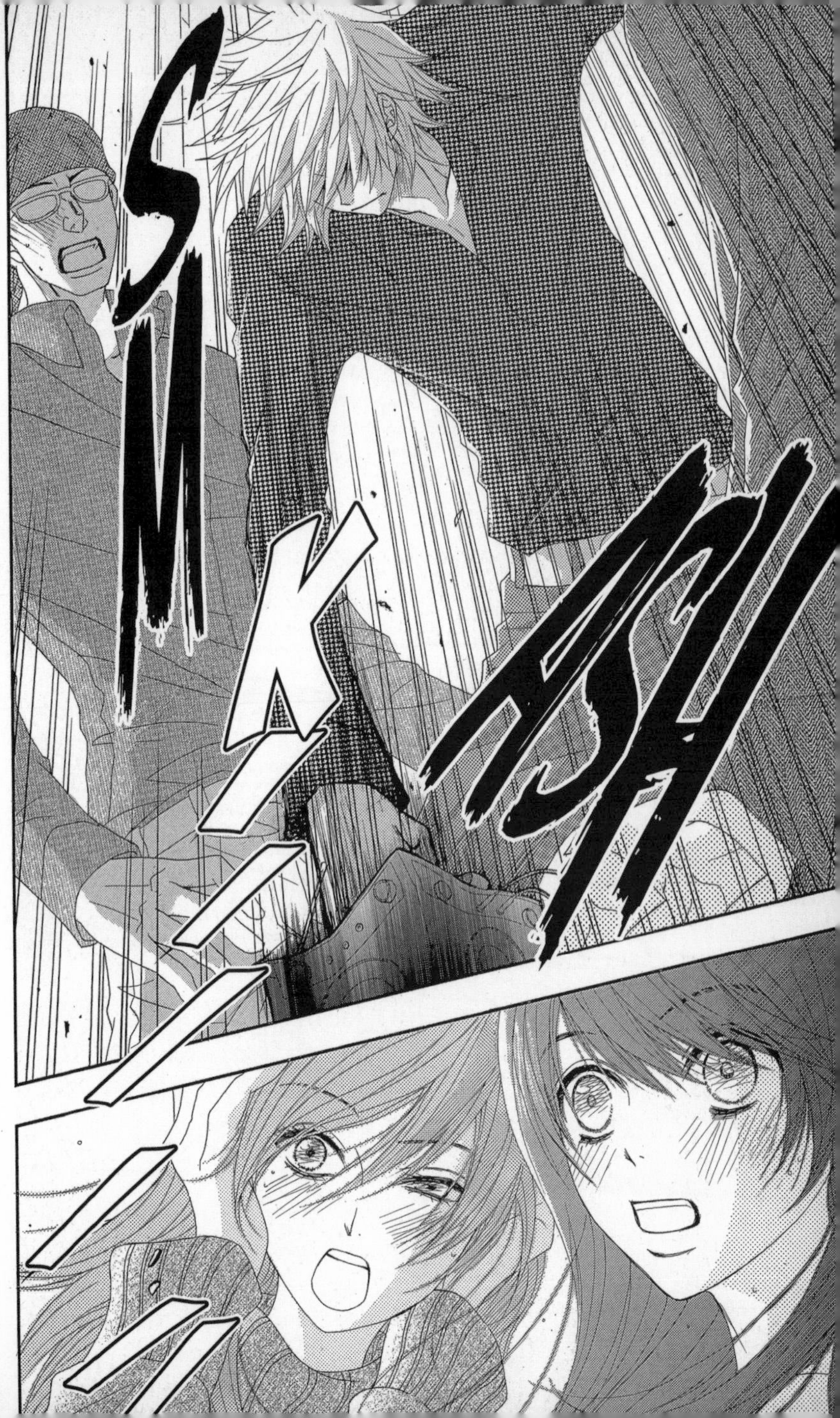
SMASH
K

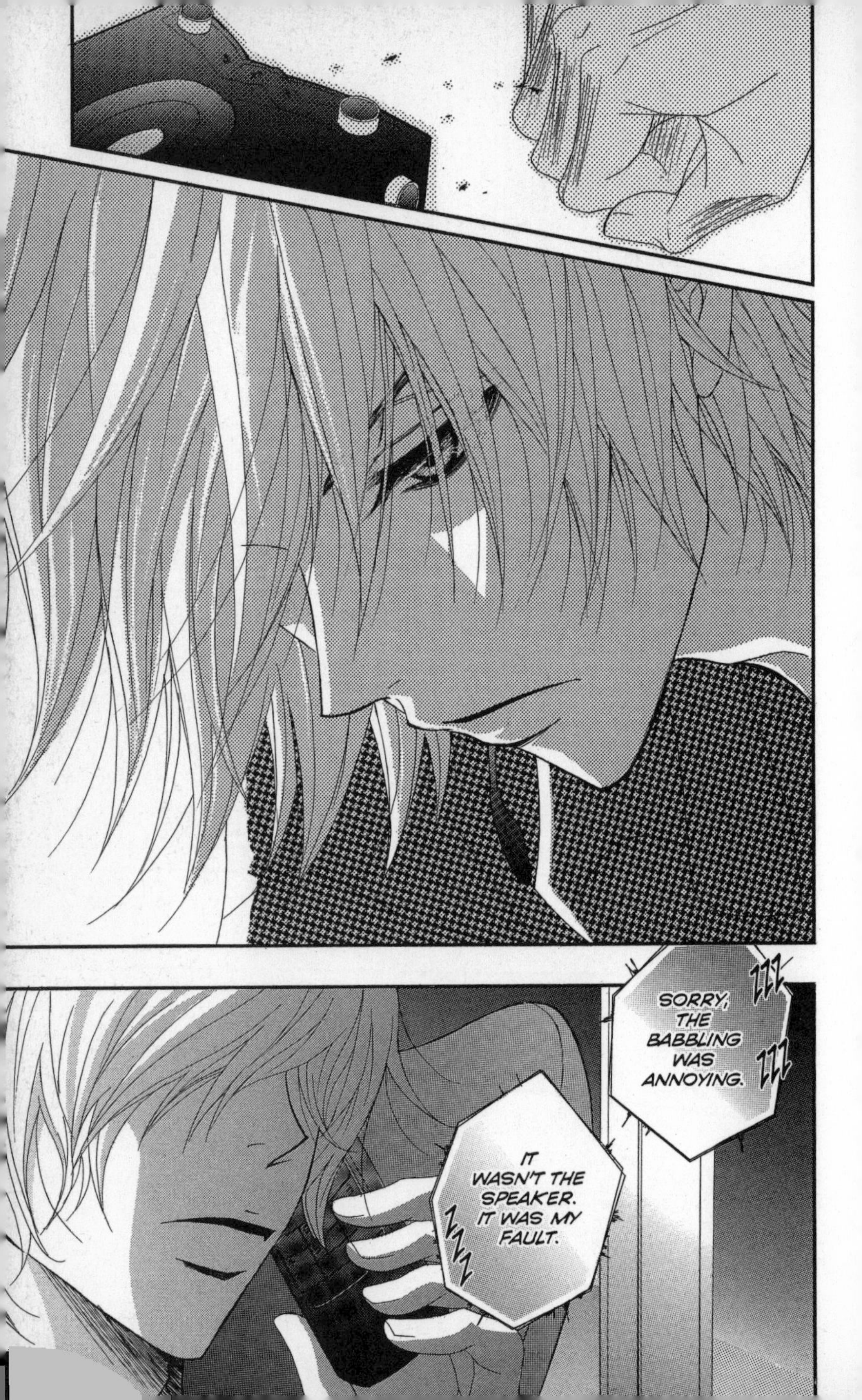
SORRY, THE BABBLING WAS ANNOYING.
IT WASN'T THE SPEAKER. IT WAS MY FAULT.

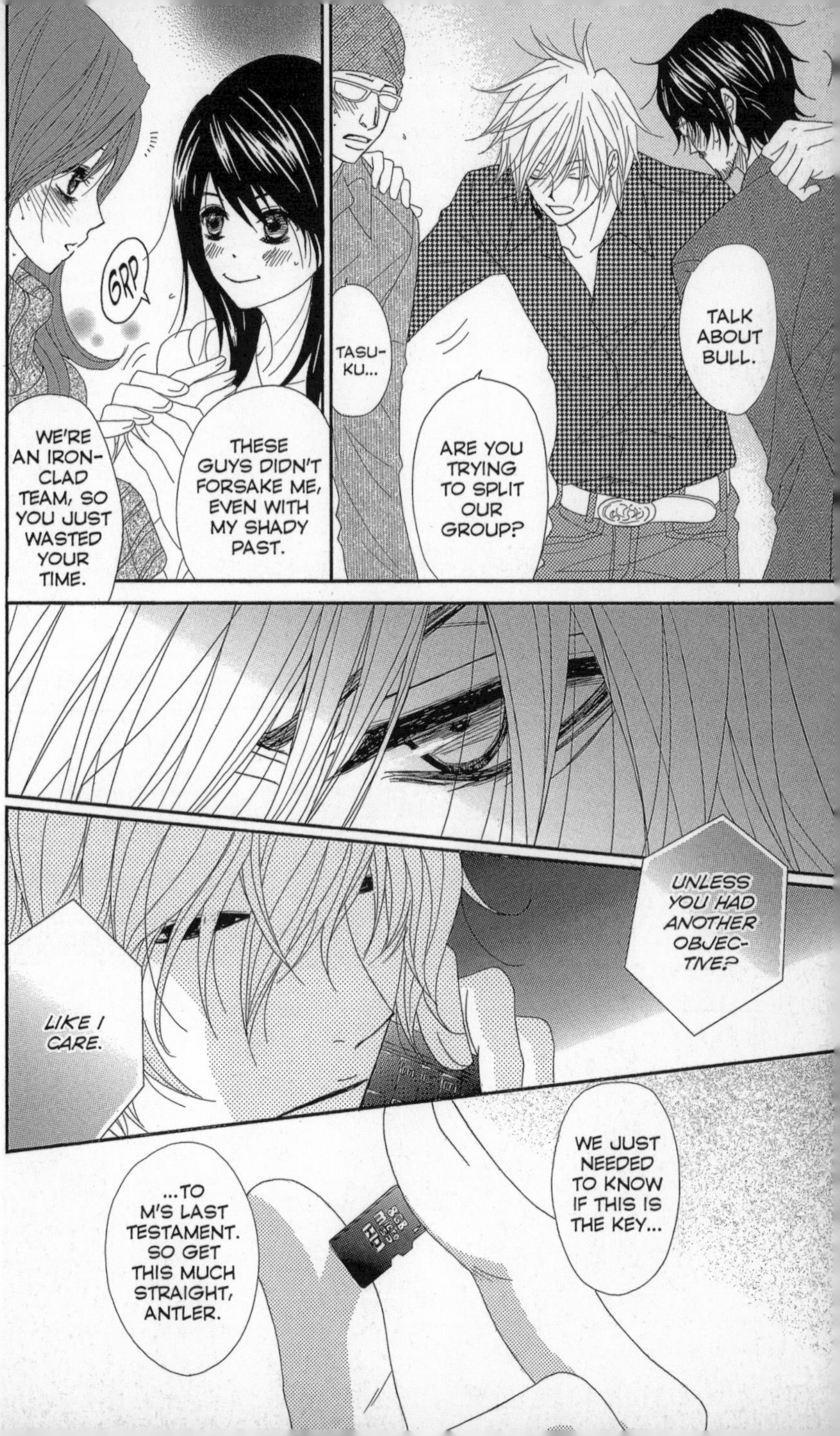
TALK ABOUT BULL.
ARE YOU TRYING TO SPLIT OUR GROUP?
TASU-KU...
GRP
THESE GUYS DIDN'T FORSAKE ME, EVEN WITH MY SHADY PAST.
WE'RE AN IRON-CLAD TEAM, SO YOU JUST WASTED YOUR TIME.
UNLESS YOU HAD ANOTHER OBJEC-TIVE?
LIKE I CARE.
WE JUST NEEDED TO KNOW IF THIS IS THE KEY...
...TO M'S LAST TESTAMENT. SO GET THIS MUCH STRAIGHT, ANTLER.

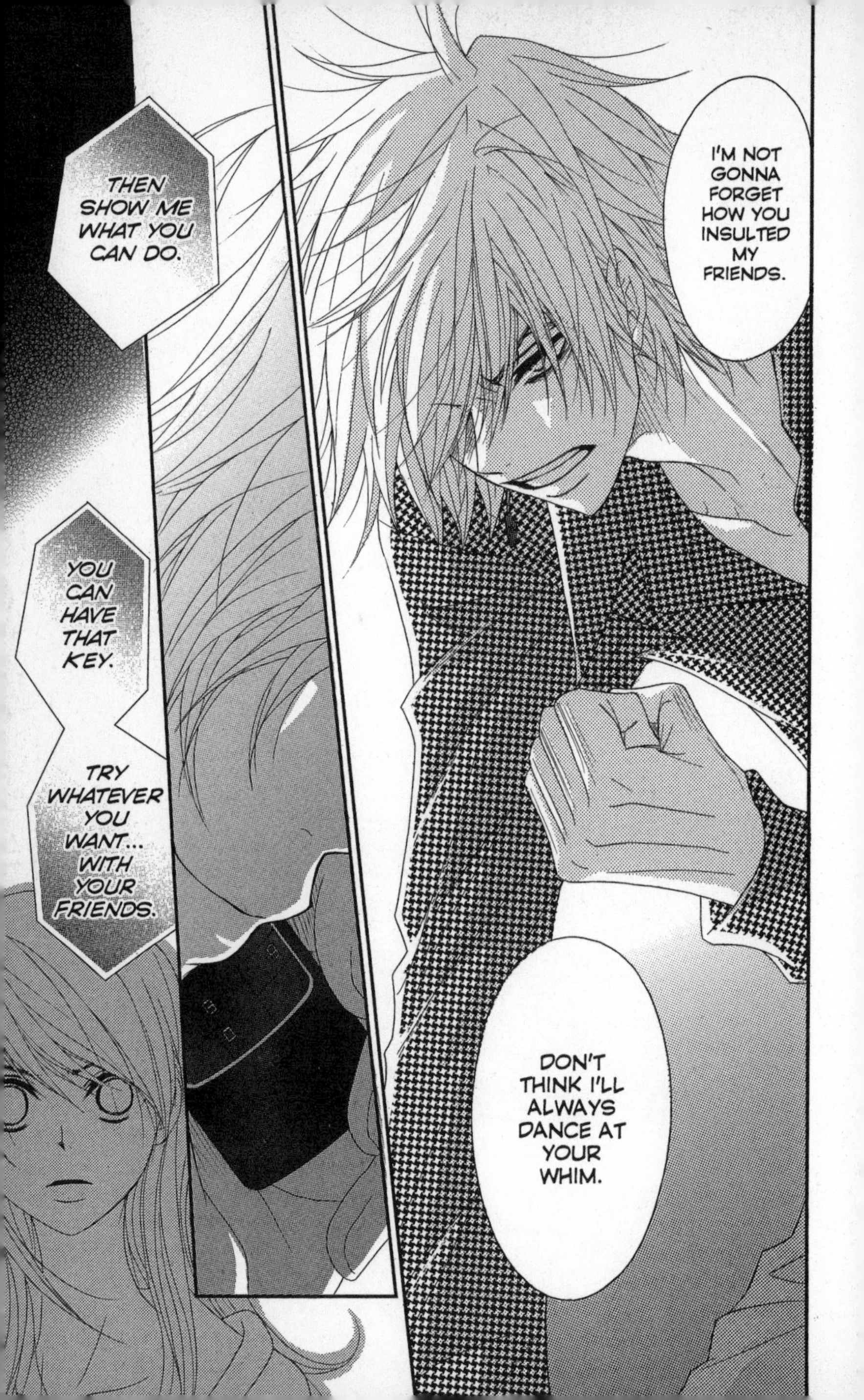
I'M NOT GONNA FORGET HOW YOU INSULTED MY FRIENDS.
DON'T THINK I'LL ALWAYS DANCE AT YOUR WHIM.
THEN SHOW ME WHAT YOU CAN DO.
YOU CAN HAVE THAT KEY.
TRY WHATEVER YOU WANT... WITH YOUR FRIENDS.

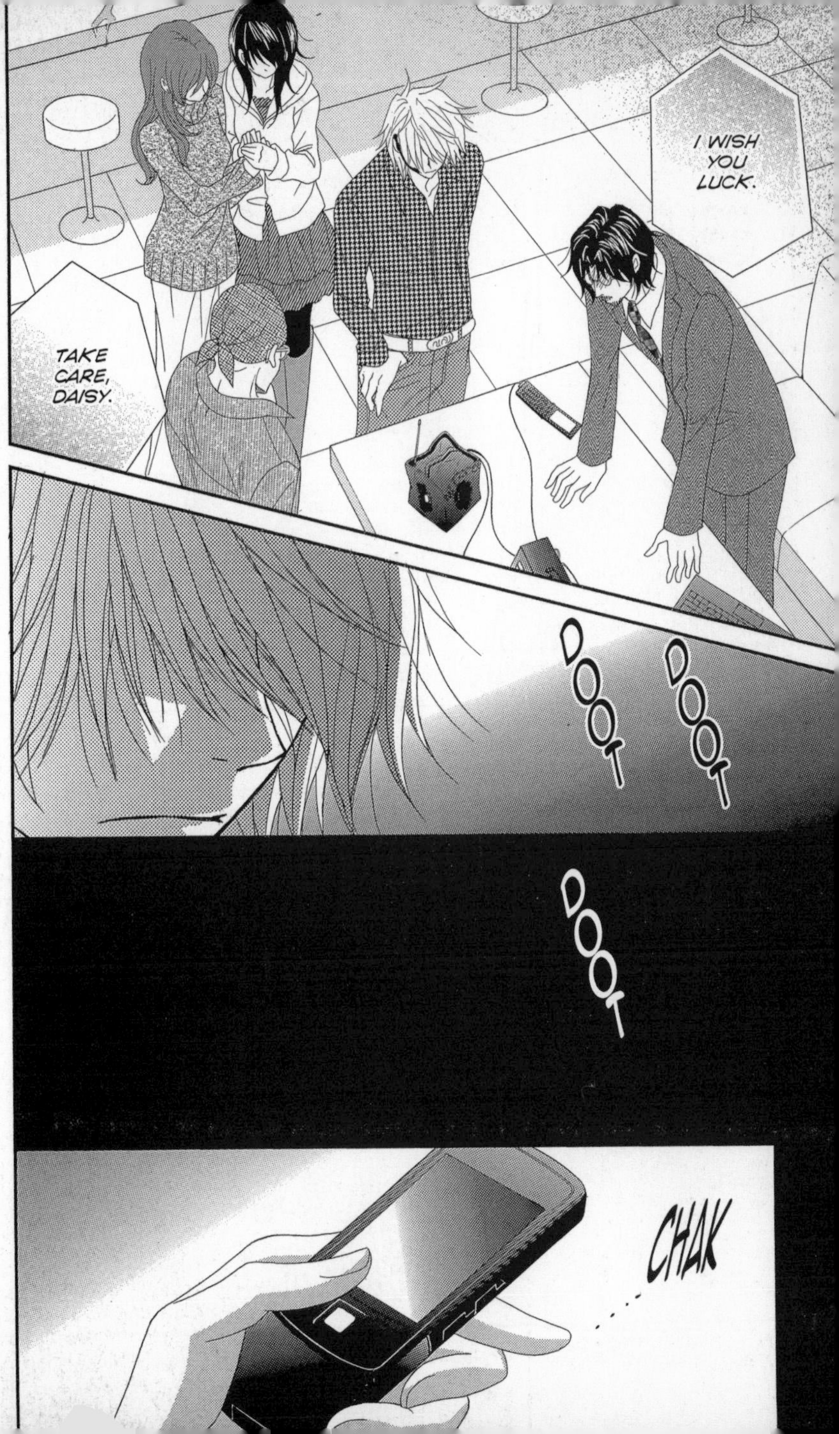
I WISH YOU LUCK.
TAKE CARE, DAISY.
DOOT
DOOT
DOOT
CHAK

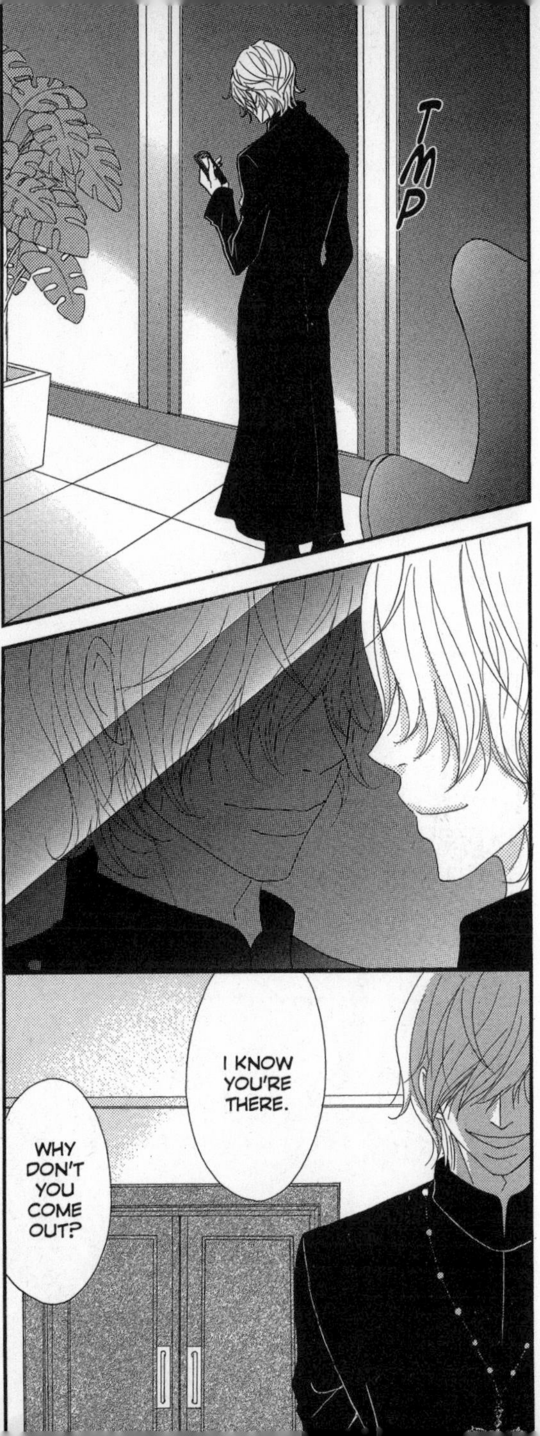
TMP
I KNOW YOU'RE THERE.
WHY DON'T YOU COME OUT?

DENGEKI DAISY QUESTION CORNER

# BALDLY ASK!!

⑤

Q. BESIDES THE HAIR ON HIS HEAD, WHAT OTHER HAIR IS KUROSAKI CONCERNED ABOUT?

(M.F., TOCHIGI PREFECTURE)

A. EVER SINCE KIYOSHI TOLD HIM THAT TERU SAID TO A FRIEND, "IT MUST BE PAINFUL TO PLUCK HAIR AROUND THE NIPPLES," KUROSAKI HAS BEEN A BIT CONCERNED ABOUT THE HAIR AROUND HIS NIPPLES. KUROSAKI DOESN'T SEEM TO HAVE GROWN ANY NIPPLE HAIRS AT THIS TIME.

Q. IN VOLUME 10, CHAPTER 45, TERU IS WEARING WOOL PANTIES. IS TERU THE TYPE WHO WILL WEAR WOOL PANTIES NO MATTER HOW OLD SHE IS AND NOT WORRY ABOUT IT AT ALL? FYI, I DO TOO.

(NOSEHAIRS, TOKYO)

A. I THINK SO. I THINK WOOL PANTIES ARE A VERY ADORABLE ITEM. I THINK KUROSAKI LIKES THEM A LOT TOO. YOU DON'T GET COLD IN THEM.

Q. IN VOLUME 3, CHAPTER 13, HARUKA ASKS, "IS KUROSAKI GOOD? IS HE FAST? [EDITED]" WHAT IS THE TRUTH OF THE MATTER?

(Y.H, NAGANO PREFECTURE)

A. THIS IS A WHOLESOME LOVE COMEDY, SO I CAN'T TELL YOU THE DETAILS, BUT KUROSAKI TRAINS DAILY. A TOP-CLASS ATHLETE NEVER LEAVES OUT IMAGE TRAINING. KUROSAKI DOES DAILY IMAGE TRAINING AS WELL. ACTUALLY, ALL HE DOES IS IMAGE TRAINING. NOTHING BUT IMAGE TRAINING. TODAY, TOO. GO KUROSAKI!!!!!

THAT'S ALL FOR THIS TIME!! WE'LL PROBABLY CONTINUE NEXT VOLUME!!

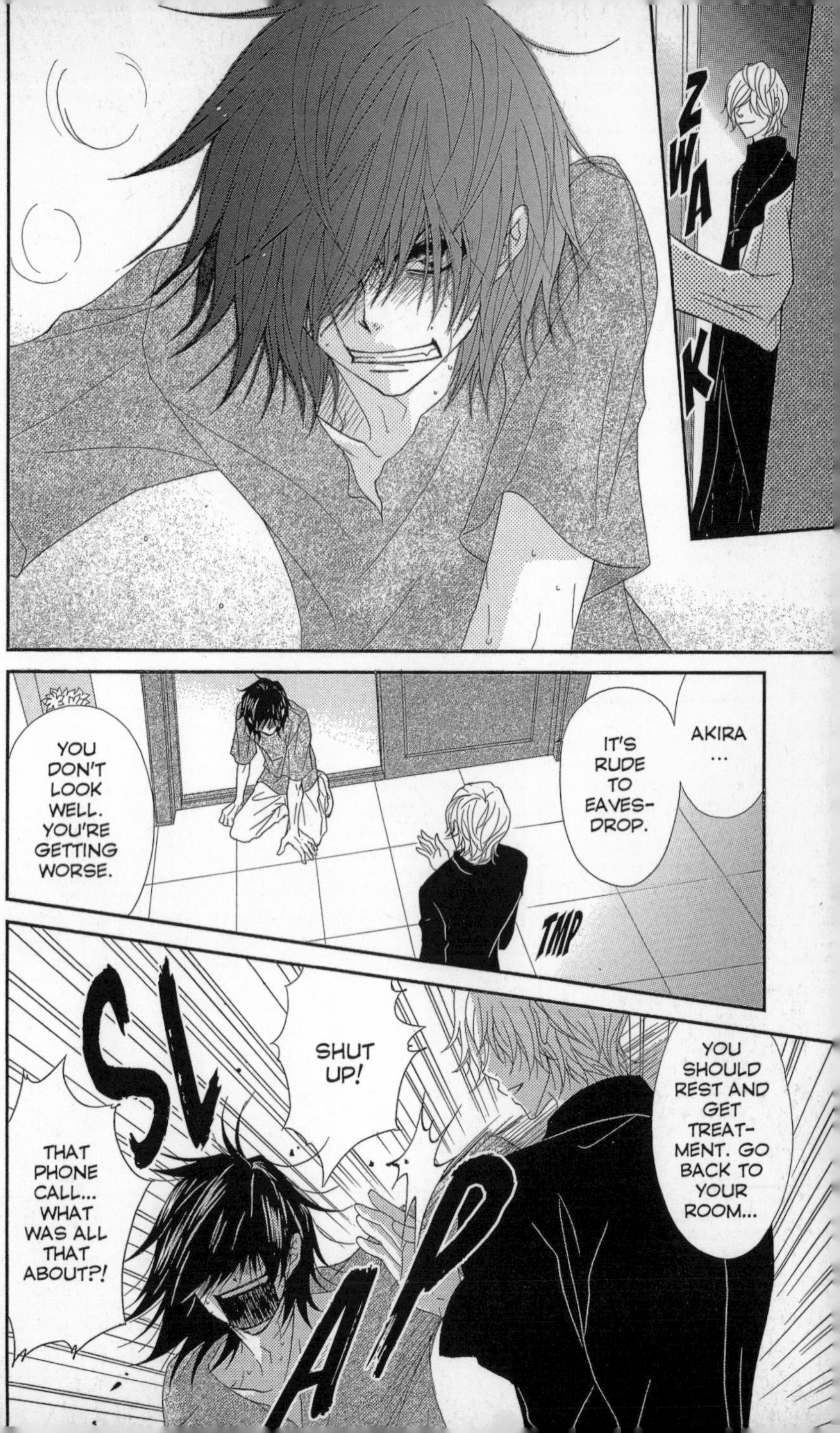
ZWAK
AKIRA ...
IT'S RUDE TO EAVES-DROP.
YOU DON'T LOOK WELL. YOU'RE GETTING WORSE.
TMP
YOU SHOULD REST AND GET TREAT-MENT. GO BACK TO YOUR ROOM...
SHUT UP!
THAT PHONE CALL... WHAT WAS ALL THAT ABOUT?!
SLAP

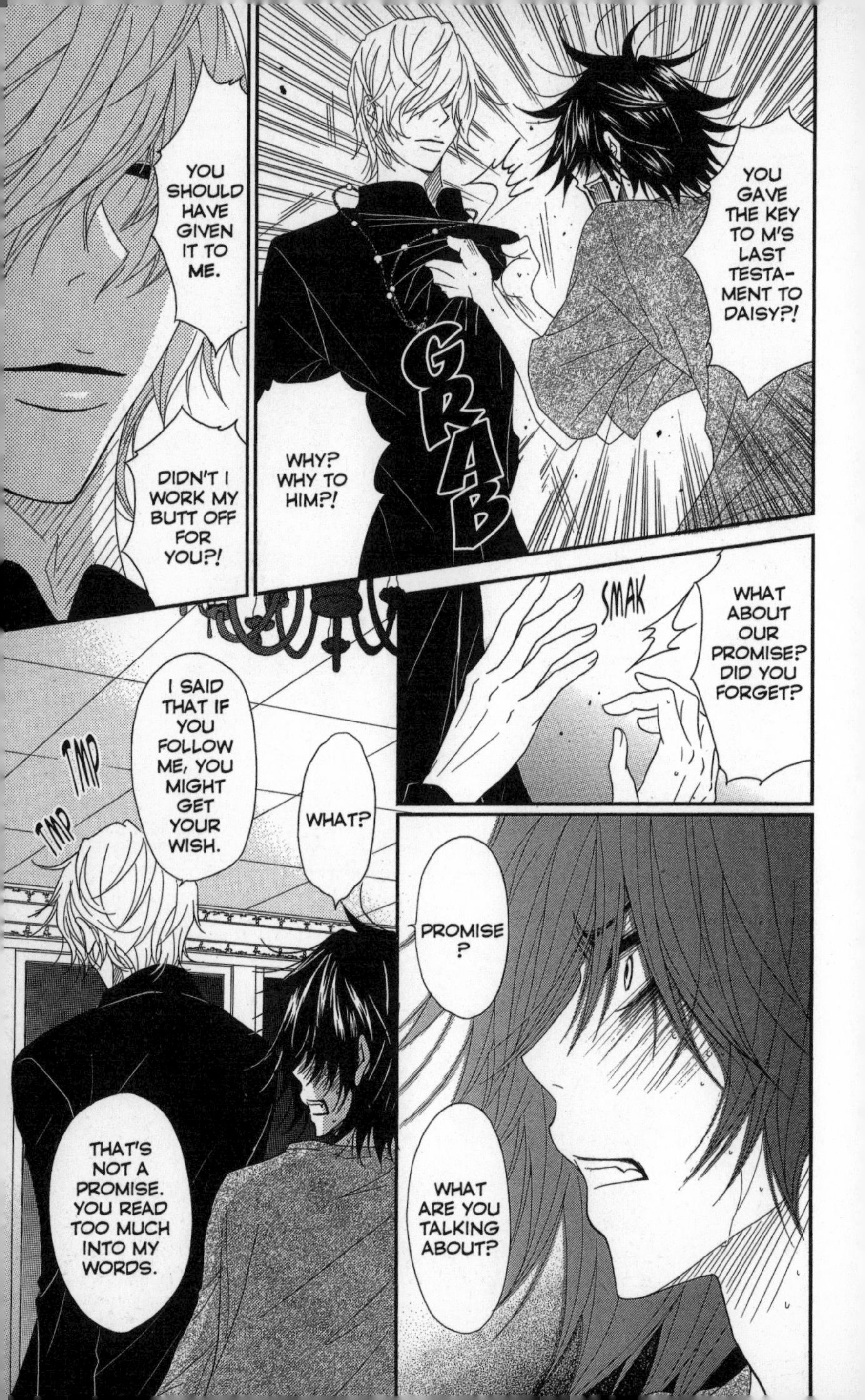
YOU GAVE THE KEY TO M'S LAST TESTA-MENT TO DAISY?!
GRAB
WHY? WHY TO HIM?!
YOU SHOULD HAVE GIVEN IT TO ME.
DIDN'T I WORK MY BUTT OFF FOR YOU?!
WHAT ABOUT OUR PROMISE? DID YOU FORGET?
SMAK
WHAT?
I SAID THAT IF YOU FOLLOW ME, YOU MIGHT GET YOUR WISH.
TMP
TMP
PROMISE?
WHAT ARE YOU TALKING ABOUT?
THAT'S NOT A PROMISE. YOU READ TOO MUCH INTO MY WORDS.

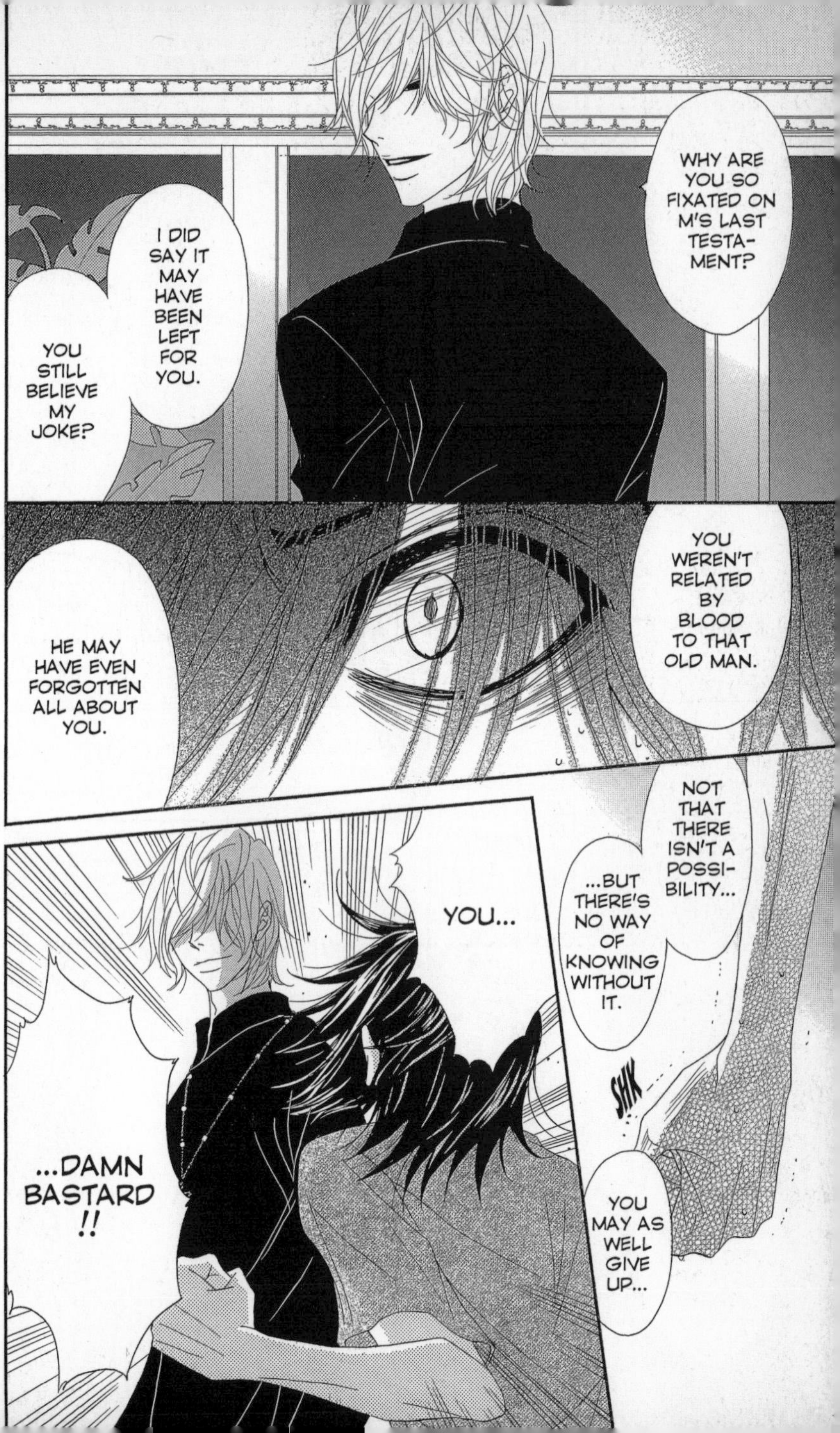
WHY ARE YOU SO FIXATED ON M'S LAST TESTA-MENT?
I DID SAY IT MAY HAVE BEEN LEFT FOR YOU.
YOU STILL BELIEVE MY JOKE?
YOU WEREN'T RELATED BY BLOOD TO THAT OLD MAN.
HE MAY HAVE EVEN FORGOTTEN ALL ABOUT YOU.
NOT THAT THERE ISN'T A POSSI-BILITY...
...BUT THERE'S NO WAY OF KNOWING WITHOUT IT.
YOU...
SHK
YOU MAY AS WELL GIVE UP...
...DAMN BASTARD !!

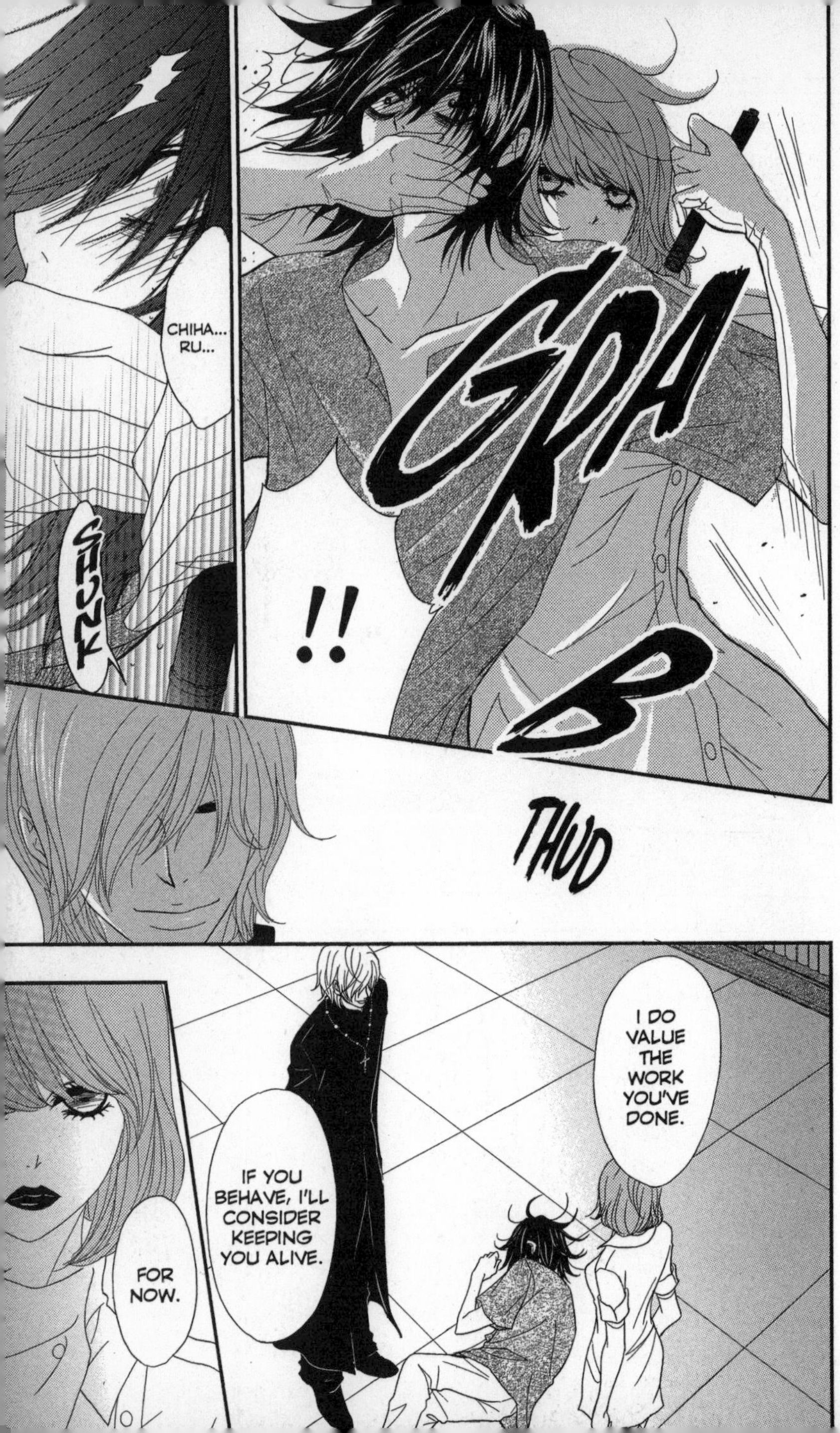
GRAB
!!
CHIHA... RU...
SHUNK
THUD
I DO VALUE THE WORK YOU'VE DONE.
IF YOU BEHAVE, I'LL CONSIDER KEEPING YOU ALIVE.
FOR NOW.

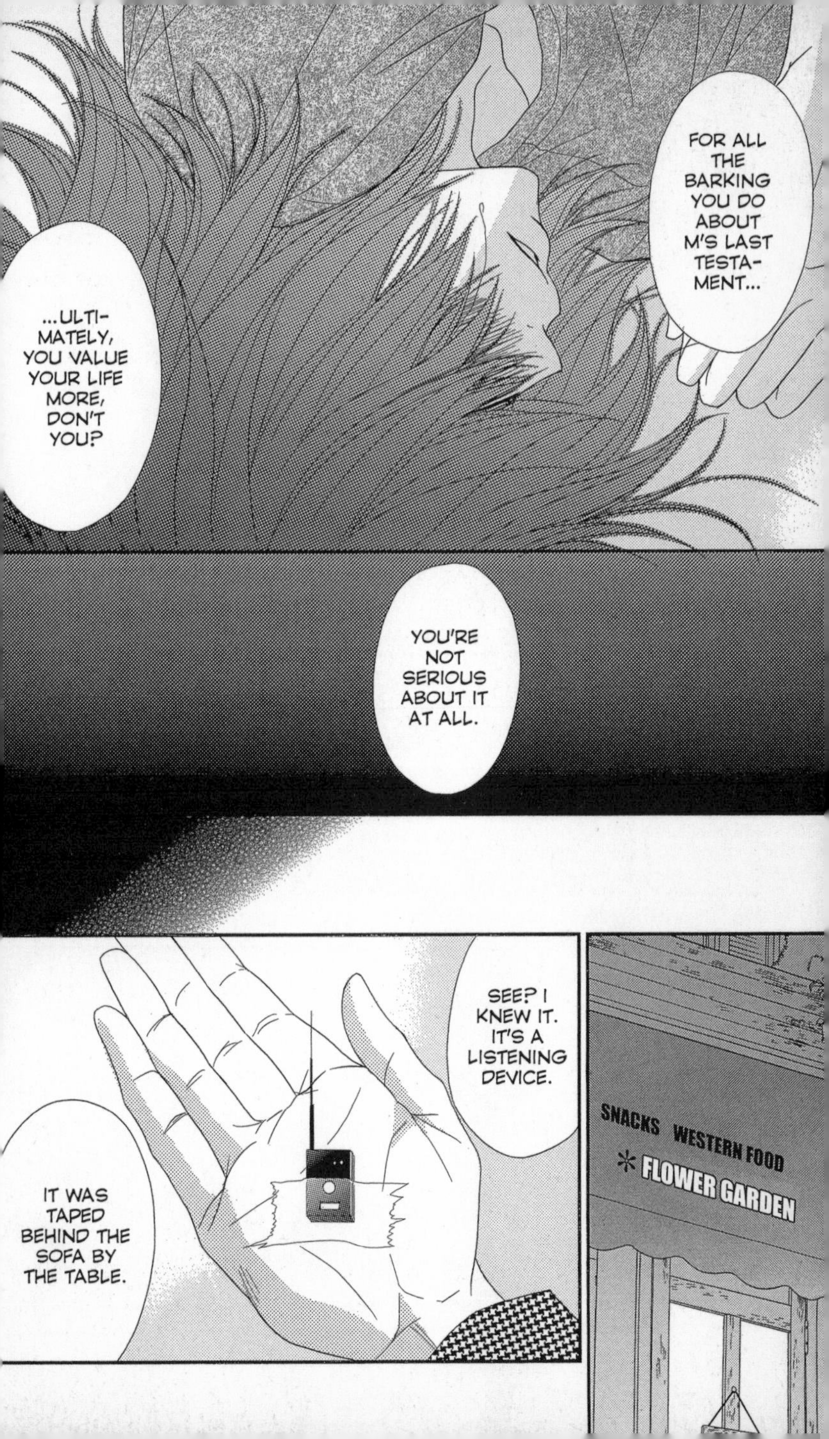
FOR ALL THE BARKING YOU DO ABOUT M'S LAST TESTA-MENT...
...ULTI-MATELY, YOU VALUE YOUR LIFE MORE, DON'T YOU?
YOU'RE NOT SERIOUS ABOUT IT AT ALL.
SNACKS WESTERN FOOD
FLOWER GARDEN
SEE? I KNEW IT. IT'S A LISTENING DEVICE.
IT WAS TAPED BEHIND THE SOFA BY THE TABLE.

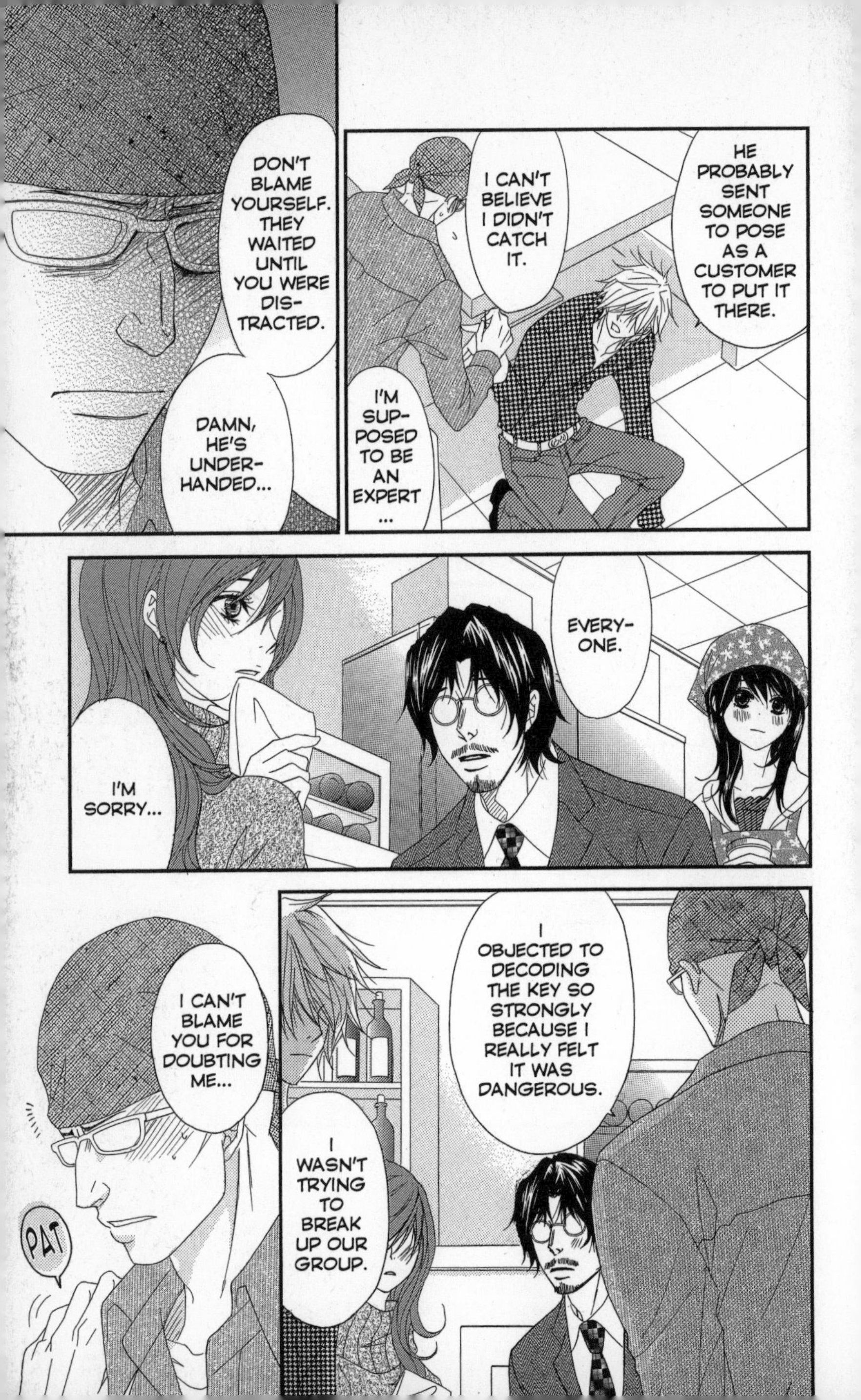
HE PROBABLY SENT SOMEONE TO POSE AS A CUSTOMER TO PUT IT THERE.
I CAN'T BELIEVE I DIDN'T CATCH IT.
I'M SUP-POSED TO BE AN EXPERT ...
DON'T BLAME YOURSELF. THEY WAITED UNTIL YOU WERE DIS-TRACTED.
DAMN, HE'S UNDER-HANDED...
EVERY-ONE.
I'M SORRY...
I OBJECTED TO DECODING THE KEY SO STRONGLY BECAUSE I REALLY FELT IT WAS DANGEROUS.
I WASN'T TRYING TO BREAK UP OUR GROUP.
I CAN'T BLAME YOU FOR DOUBTING ME...
PAT

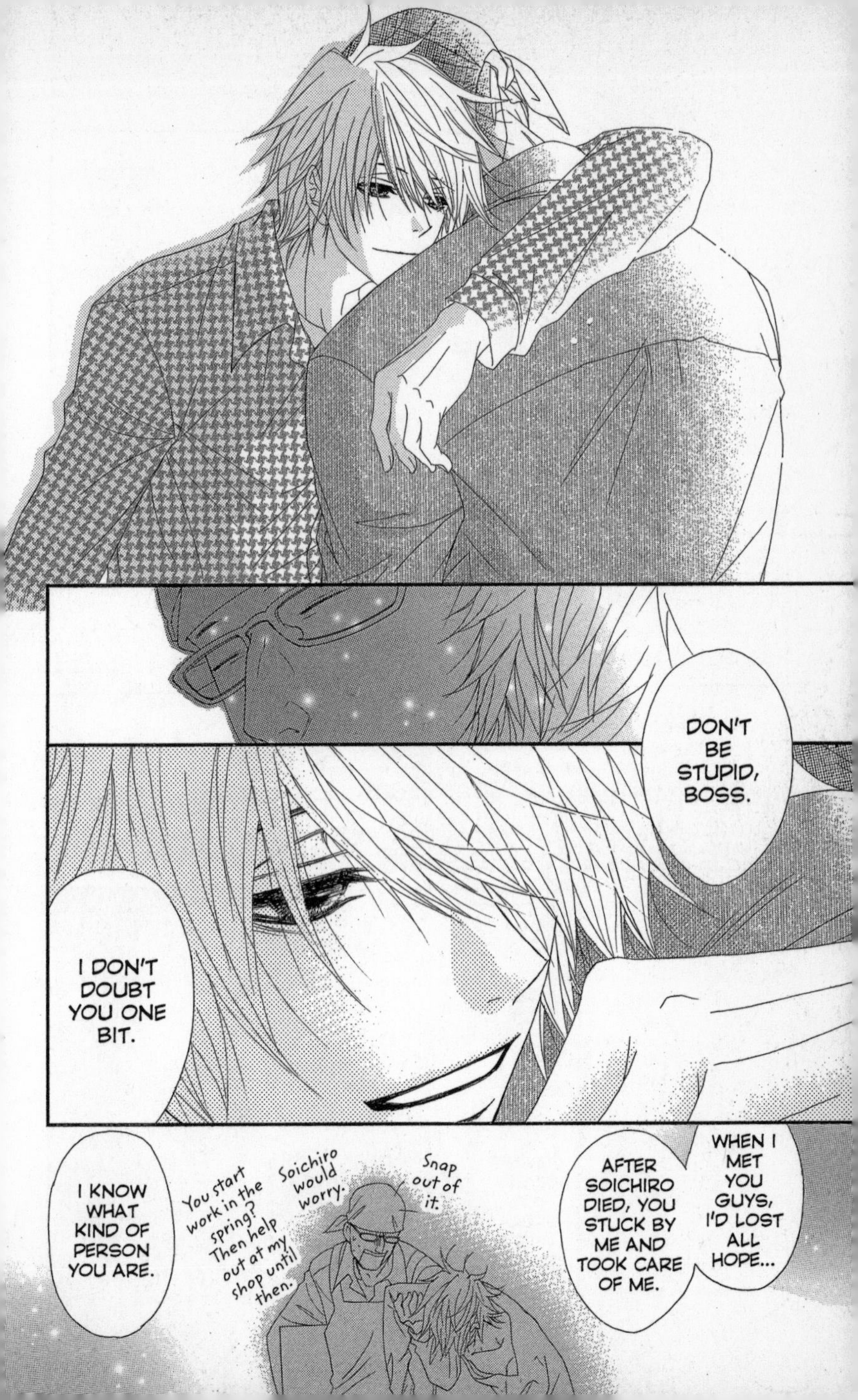
DON'T BE STUPID, BOSS.
I DON'T DOUBT YOU ONE BIT.
WHEN I MET YOU GUYS, I'D LOST ALL HOPE...
AFTER SOICHIRO DIED, YOU STUCK BY ME AND TOOK CARE OF ME.
Snap out of it.
Soichiro would worry.
You start work in the spring? Then help out at my shop until then.
I KNOW WHAT KIND OF PERSON YOU ARE.

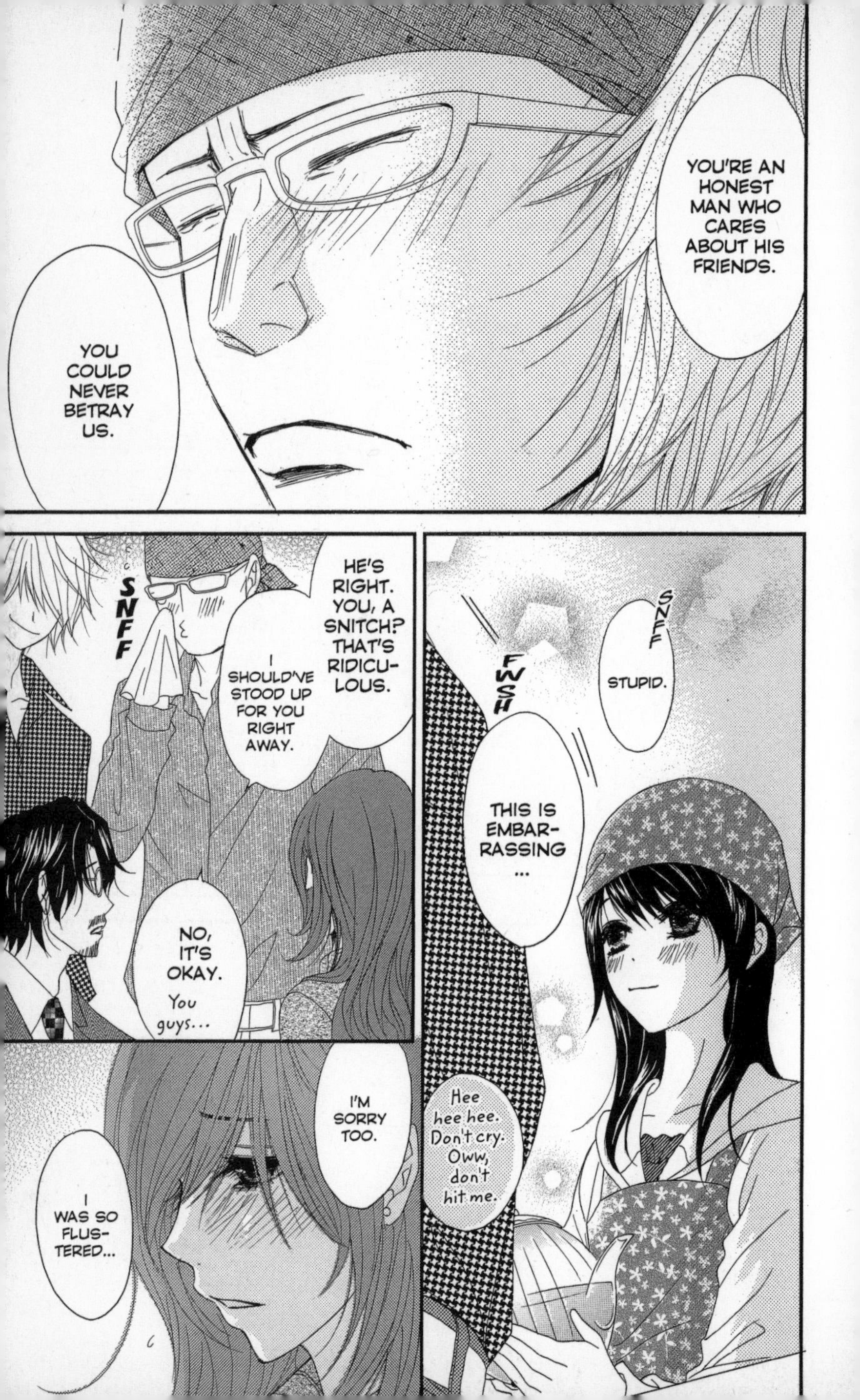
YOU'RE AN HONEST MAN WHO CARES ABOUT HIS FRIENDS.
YOU COULD NEVER BETRAY US.
SNFF
STUPID.
FWSH
THIS IS EMBARRASSING...
Hee hee hee. Don't cry. Oww, don't hit me.
HE'S RIGHT. YOU, A SNITCH? THAT'S RIDICULOUS.
SNFF
I SHOULD'VE STOOD UP FOR YOU RIGHT AWAY.
NO, IT'S OKAY.
You guys...
I'M SORRY TOO.
I WAS SO FLUSTERED...

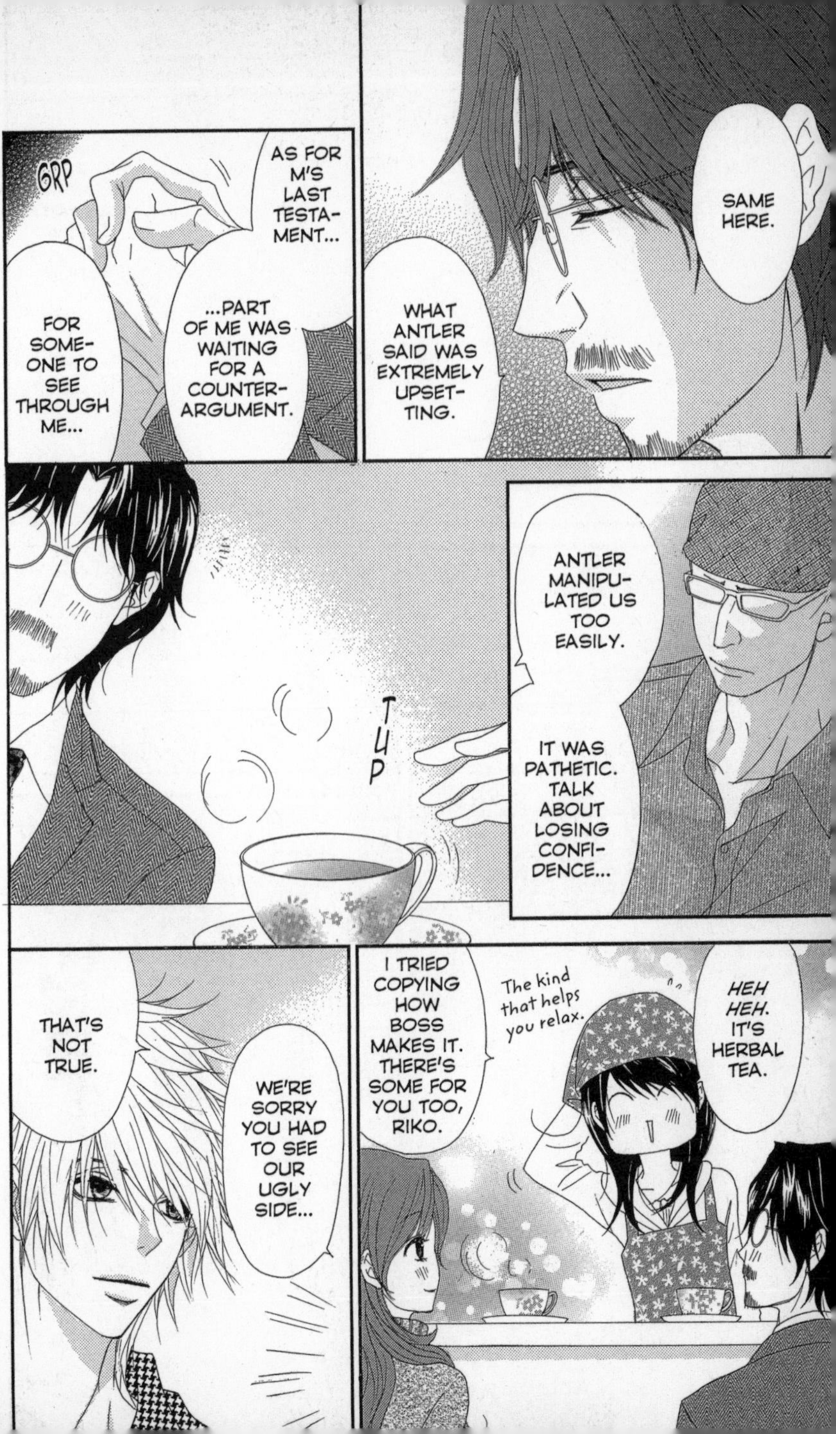
SAME HERE.
WHAT ANTLER SAID WAS EXTREMELY UPSET-TING.
AS FOR M'S LAST TESTA-MENT...
...PART OF ME WAS WAITING FOR A COUNTER-ARGUMENT.
FOR SOME-ONE TO SEE THROUGH ME...
GRP
ANTLER MANIPU-LATED US TOO EASILY.
IT WAS PATHETIC. TALK ABOUT LOSING CONFI-DENCE...
TUP
HEH HEH. IT'S HERBAL TEA.
The kind that helps you relax.
I TRIED COPYING HOW BOSS MAKES IT. THERE'S SOME FOR YOU TOO, RIKO.
THAT'S NOT TRUE.
WE'RE SORRY YOU HAD TO SEE OUR UGLY SIDE...

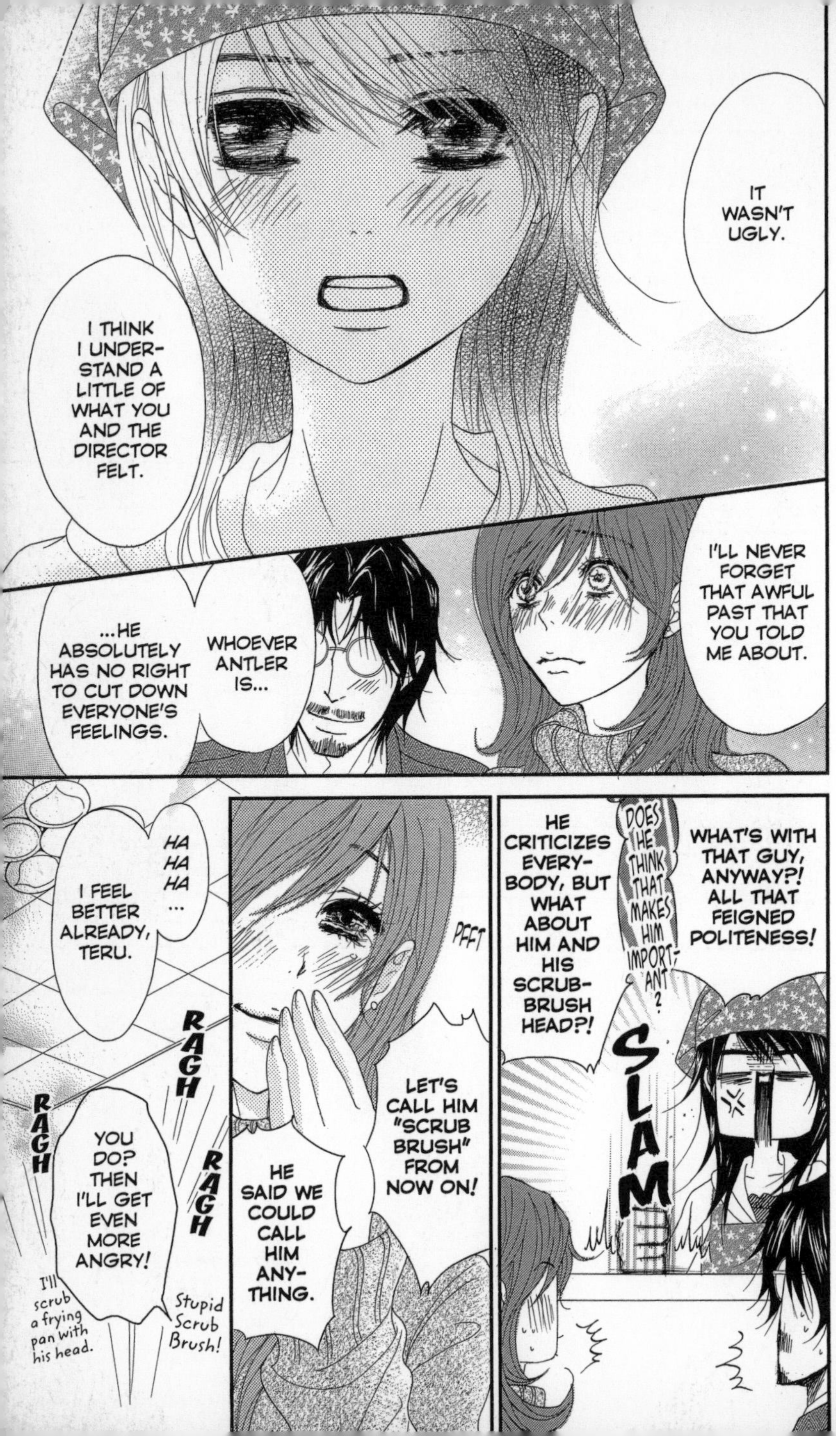
IT WASN'T UGLY.
I THINK I UNDERSTAND A LITTLE OF WHAT YOU AND THE DIRECTOR FELT.
I'LL NEVER FORGET THAT AWFUL PAST THAT YOU TOLD ME ABOUT.
WHOEVER ANTLER IS...
...HE ABSOLUTELY HAS NO RIGHT TO CUT DOWN EVERYONE'S FEELINGS.
WHAT'S WITH THAT GUY, ANYWAY?! ALL THAT FEIGNED POLITENESS!
DOES HE THINK THAT MAKES HIM IMPORTANT?
HE CRITICIZES EVERYBODY, BUT WHAT ABOUT HIM AND HIS SCRUB-BRUSH HEAD?!
SLAM
PFFT
LET'S CALL HIM "SCRUB BRUSH" FROM NOW ON!
HE SAID WE COULD CALL HIM ANYTHING.
HA HA HA ...
I FEEL BETTER ALREADY, TERU.
RAGH
RAGH
RAGH
YOU DO? THEN I'LL GET EVEN MORE ANGRY!
Stupid Scrub Brush!
I'll scrub a frying pan with his head.

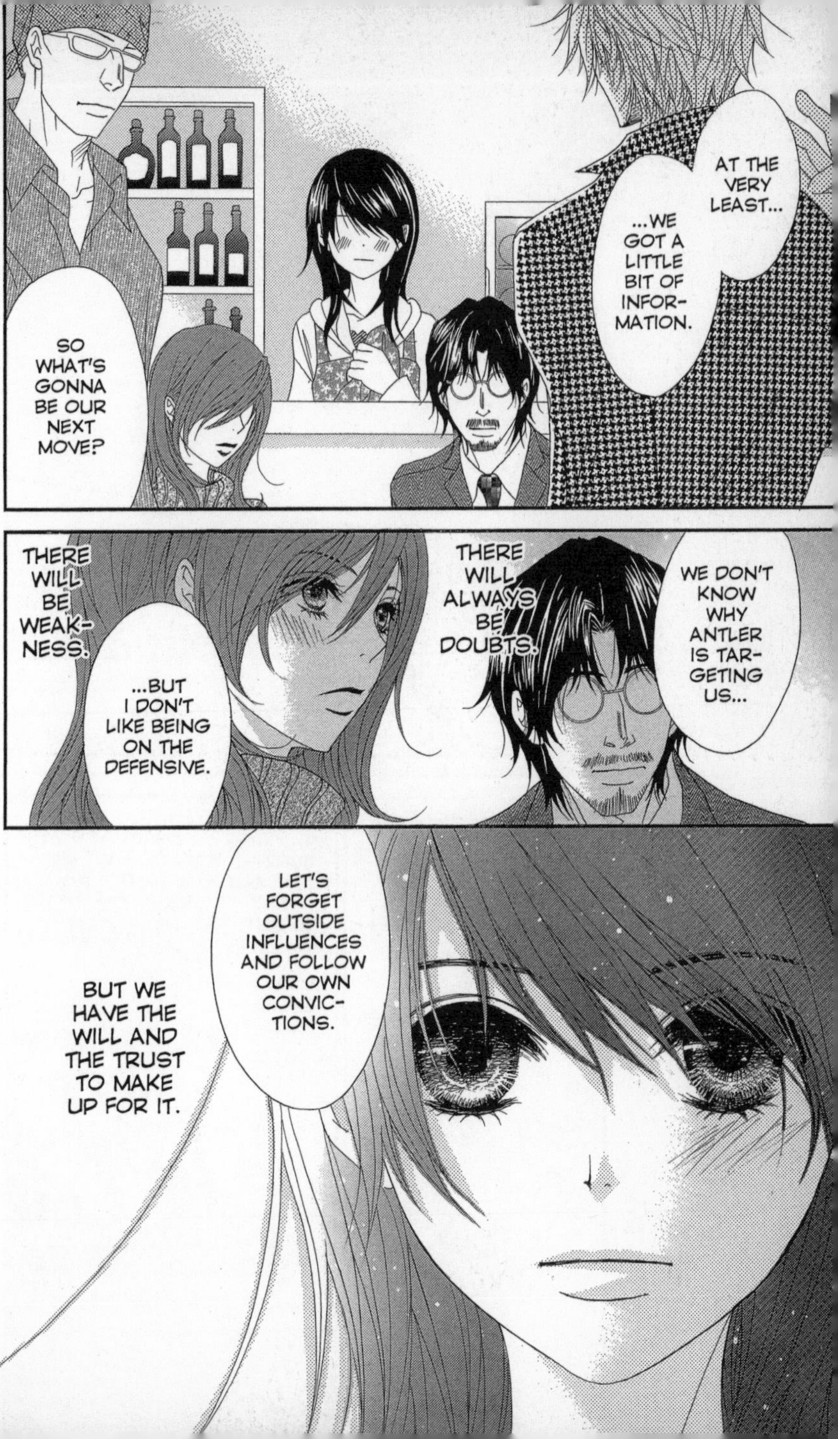
AT THE VERY LEAST...
...WE GOT A LITTLE BIT OF INFOR-MATION.
SO WHAT'S GONNA BE OUR NEXT MOVE?
WE DON'T KNOW WHY ANTLER IS TAR-GETING US...
THERE WILL ALWAYS BE DOUBTS.
THERE WILL BE WEAK-NESS.
...BUT I DON'T LIKE BEING ON THE DEFENSIVE.
LET'S FORGET OUTSIDE INFLUENCES AND FOLLOW OUR OWN CONVIC-TIONS.
BUT WE HAVE THE WILL AND THE TRUST TO MAKE UP FOR IT.

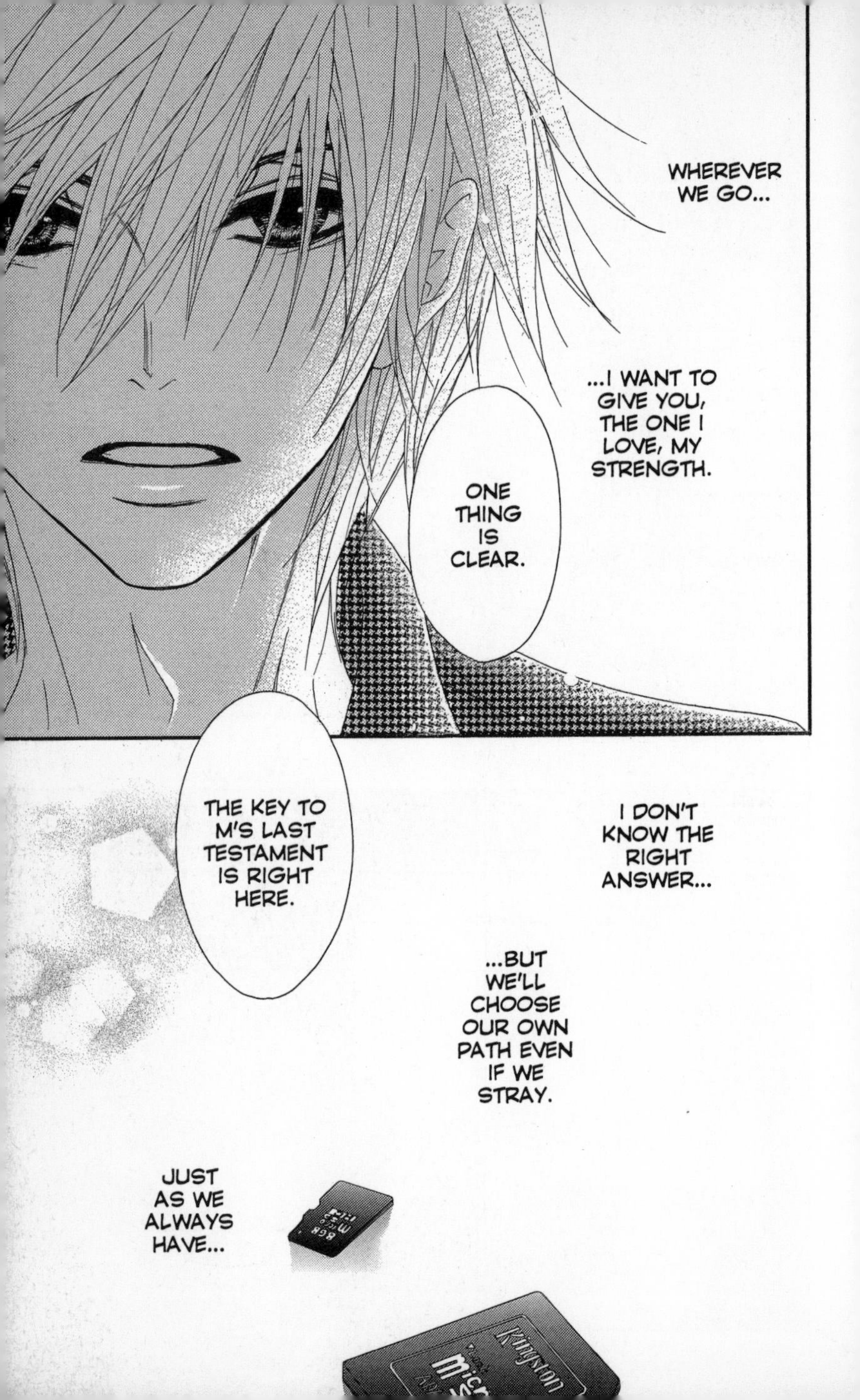
WHEREVER WE GO...
...I WANT TO GIVE YOU, THE ONE I LOVE, MY STRENGTH.
ONE THING IS CLEAR.
I DON'T KNOW THE RIGHT ANSWER...
THE KEY TO M'S LAST TESTAMENT IS RIGHT HERE.
...BUT WE'LL CHOOSE OUR OWN PATH EVEN IF WE STRAY.
JUST AS WE ALWAYS HAVE...

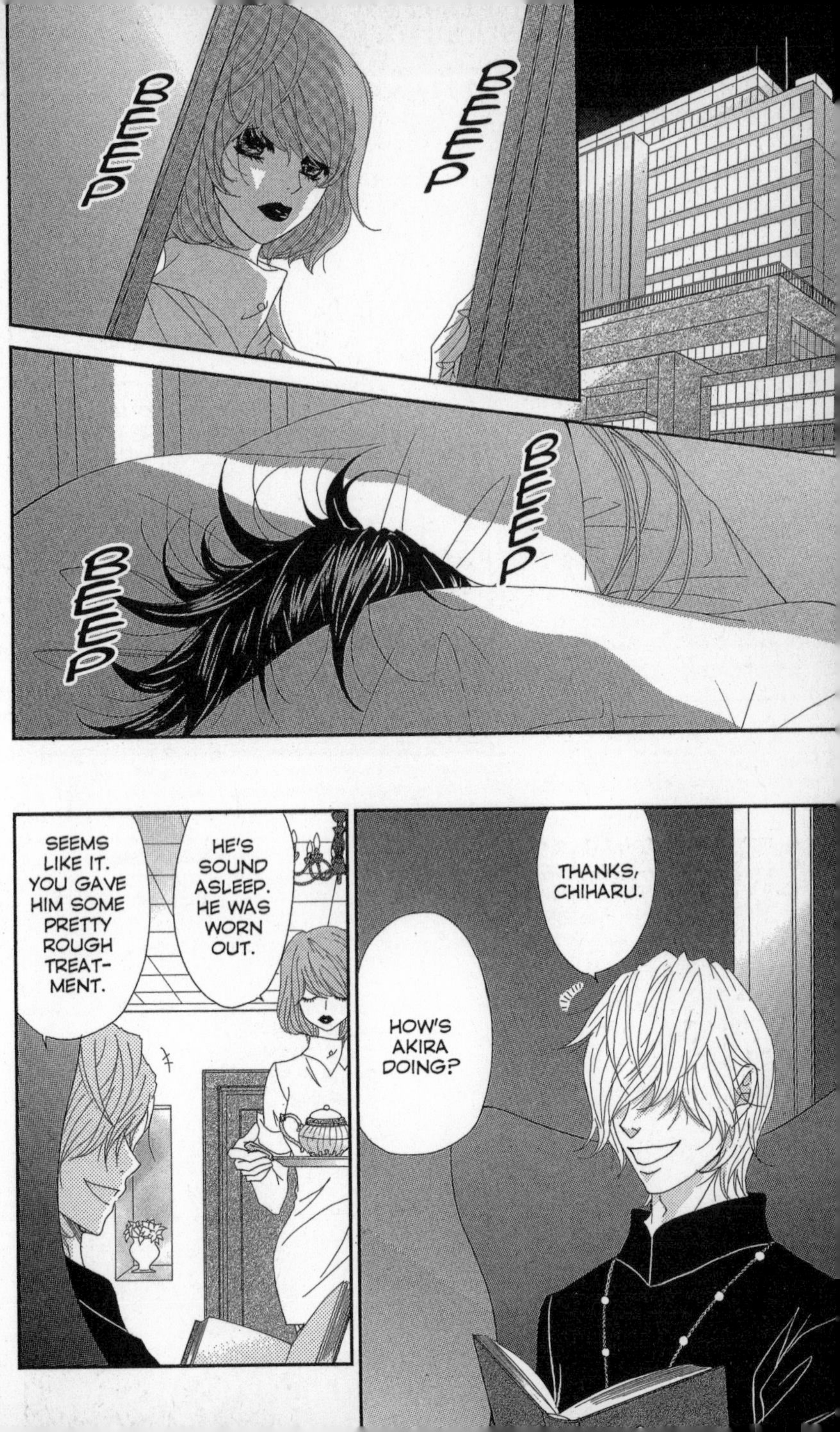
BEEP
BEEP
BEEP
BEEP
THANKS, CHIHARU.
HOW'S AKIRA DOING?
HE'S SOUND ASLEEP. HE WAS WORN OUT.
SEEMS LIKE IT. YOU GAVE HIM SOME PRETTY ROUGH TREAT-MENT.

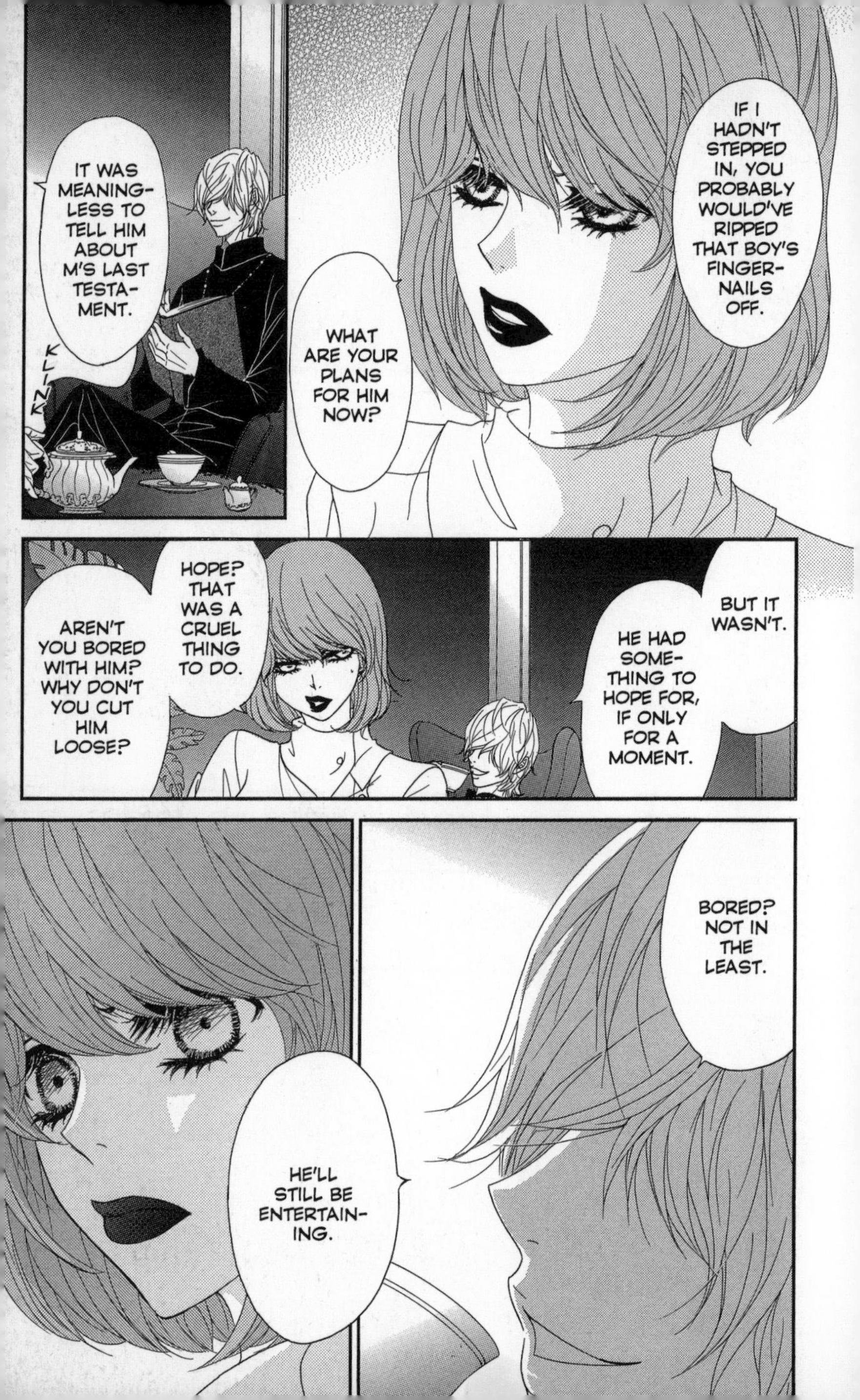
IF I HADN'T STEPPED IN, YOU PROBABLY WOULD'VE RIPPED THAT BOY'S FINGER-NAILS OFF.
WHAT ARE YOUR PLANS FOR HIM NOW?
IT WAS MEANING-LESS TO TELL HIM ABOUT M'S LAST TESTA-MENT.
KLINK
BUT IT WASN'T.
HE HAD SOME-THING TO HOPE FOR, IF ONLY FOR A MOMENT.
HOPE? THAT WAS A CRUEL THING TO DO.
AREN'T YOU BORED WITH HIM? WHY DON'T YOU CUT HIM LOOSE?
BORED? NOT IN THE LEAST.
HE'LL STILL BE ENTERTAIN-ING.

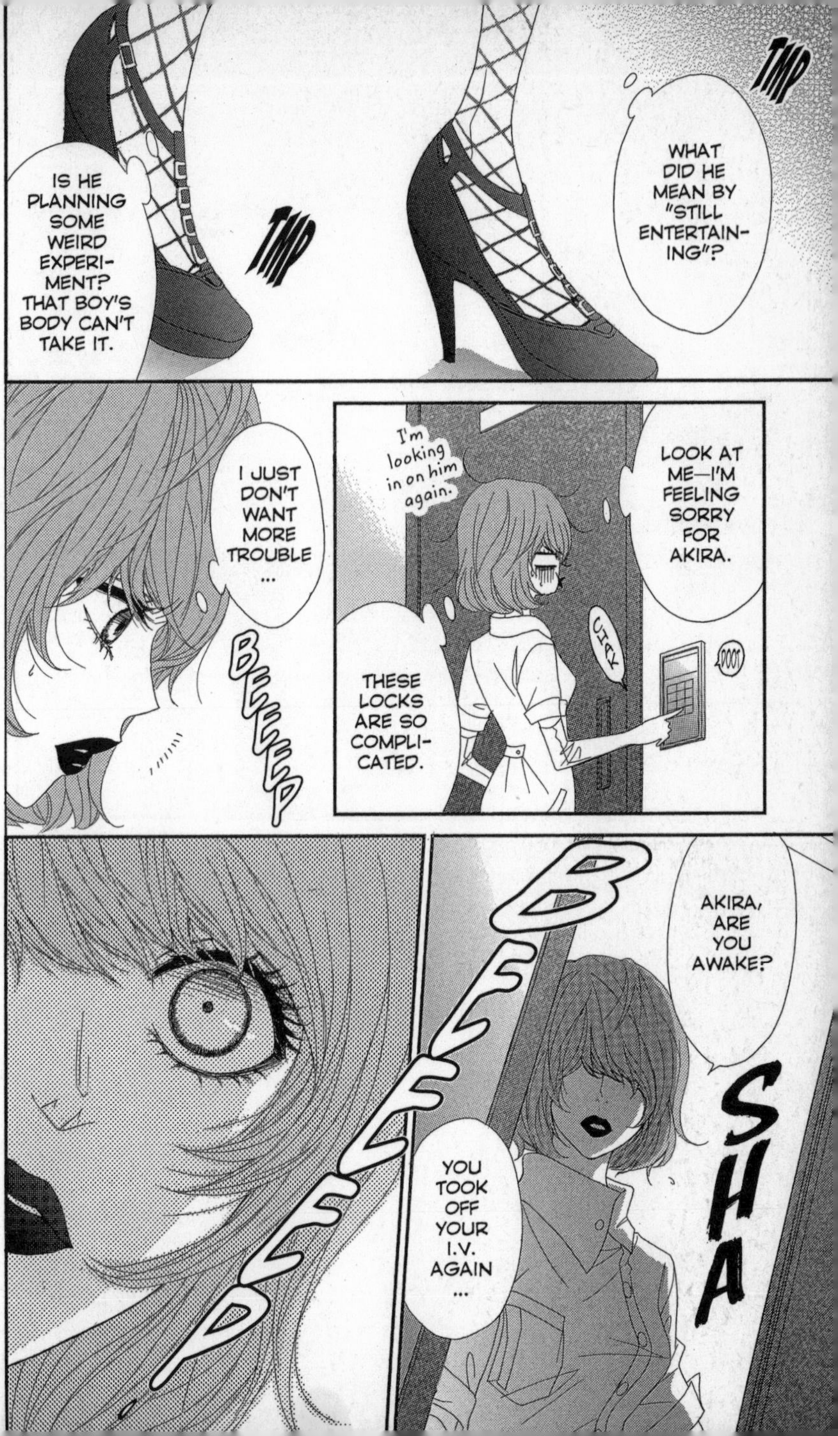
TMP
WHAT DID HE MEAN BY "STILL ENTERTAINING"?
TMP
IS HE PLANNING SOME WEIRD EXPERIMENT? THAT BOY'S BODY CAN'T TAKE IT.
LOOK AT ME—I'M FEELING SORRY FOR AKIRA.
I'm looking in on him again.
DOOT
CLICK
THESE LOCKS ARE SO COMPLICATED.
I JUST DON'T WANT MORE TROUBLE...
BEEEP
SHA
AKIRA, ARE YOU AWAKE?
YOU TOOK OFF YOUR I.V. AGAIN...
BEEEEEP

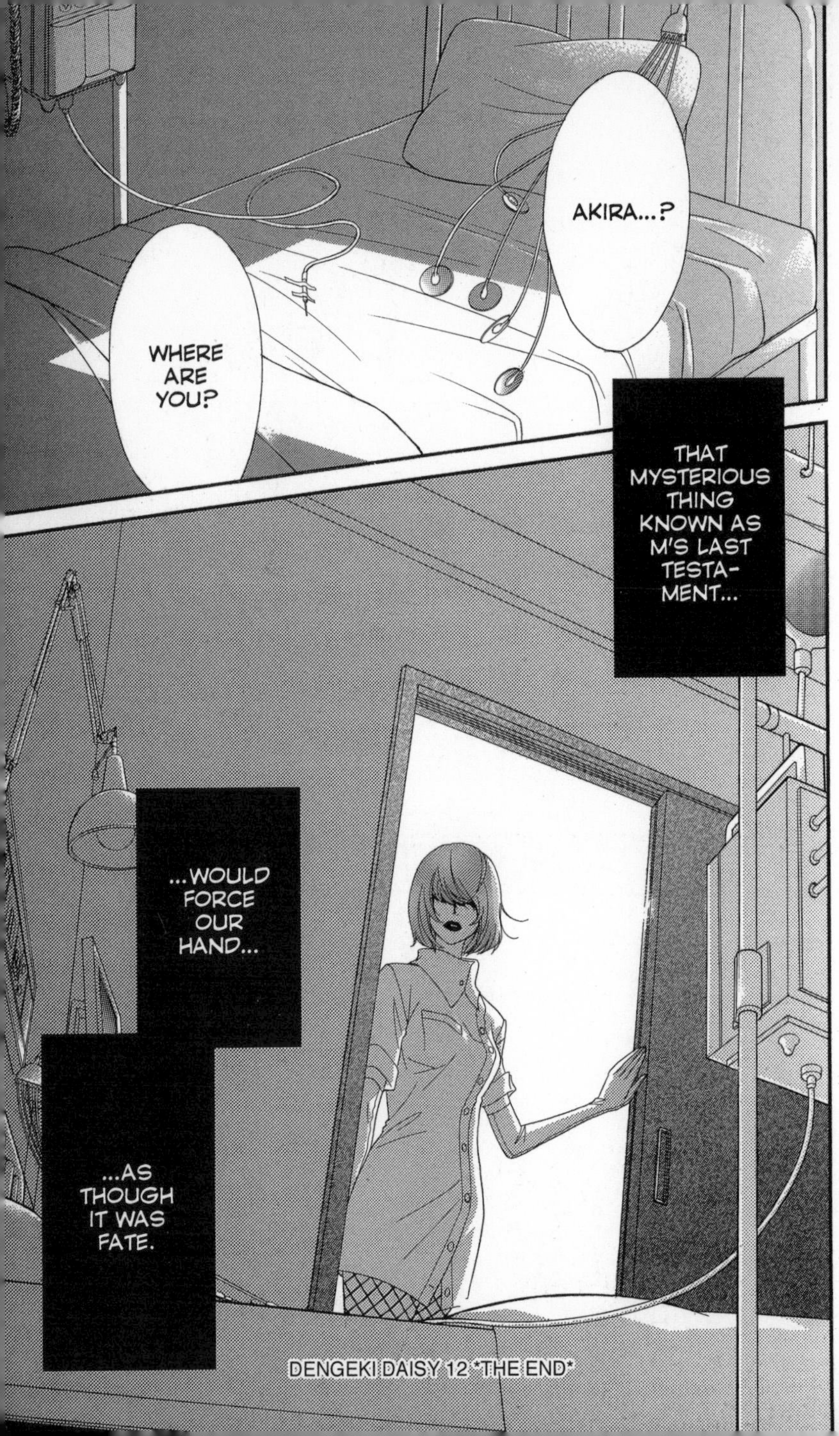
AKIRA...?
WHERE ARE YOU?
THAT MYSTERIOUS THING KNOWN AS M'S LAST TESTA-MENT...
...WOULD FORCE OUR HAND...
...AS THOUGH IT WAS FATE.
DENGEKI DAISY 12 *THE END*